THE MARGARET FULTON
COOKBOOK

MARGARET FULTON
SUZANNE GIBBS

photography Geoff Lung

first published 1968

Acknowledgements

A big 'thank you' to my daughter Louise and her husband John Keats for inviting our team to work on photography at their beautiful farm in Kangaroo Valley in New South Wales. Louise is photographed on p. 51 preparing freshly cooked prawns. Her sister Kate is photographed with an Isa Brown chicken at the farm on p. 70. We would also like to thank Louise Lister for the use of her portrait of the three generations of women in the Fulton clan. Thank you also to Daniel Mercer who gave up many weekends to scan the original book into a form with which we could work. We would also like to thank Anders Ousback for the loan of his ceramics, glassware and linen, much of it his own design, used in many of the photographs. The terrine mould on p. 118 is from The Art of Food and Wine, Queen Street, Woollahra. The ceramic pâté dish on p. 13 is available at Margaret Fulton's Kitchen (www.margaretfultonskitchen.com.au).

Suzanne Gibbs

For more information go to www.margaretfulton.com.au

THE MARGARET FULTON COOKBOOK

First published in 1968.
First revised and updated edition published in 2004 by
Jannie Brown and Suzanne Gibbs. Distributed by Hardie Grant Books.

This edition published in 2006 by
Hardie Grant Books
85 High Street
Prahran, Victoria 3181, Australia
www.hardiegrant.com.au

Text © Margaret Fulton 2004
Photographs © Geoff Lung 2004

All rights reserved. No part of this publication may be reproduced, stored in a retrieval system, or transmitted, in any form or by any means, electronic, mechanical, photocopying, recording or otherwise, without the prior permission of the publisher in writing.

Cataloguing-in-Publication data
is available from the National Library of Australia.

ISBN 1 74066 452 3

Original Words and Recipes Margaret Fulton
Food and Editing Suzanne Gibbs
Project Director Jannie Brown
Art Direction and Design Yolande Gray Design
Photography Geoff Lung
Photographic Assistant Emma Reilly
Styling Amber Keller
Illustrations John Coye
Sub Editing Kate Gibbs
Food Assistant Chris Sheppard
Project Assistant and Guardian Angel Eddie Ho
Proofing Victoria Carey

Set in Granjon 12.5 pt.
Colour separations by Splitting Image, Melbourne
Printed in China by SNP Leefung
10 9 8 7 6 5 4 3 2 1

Front cover: Cheese Soufflé, see page 42.

*I would like to dedicate this book to my daughter Suzanne,
who has inherited my joy and love of cooking, and my two grand-daughters
Kate and Louise with whom my life is magically entwined.
They are my present and my future.*

2	the first course
14	soups
32	eggs & cheese
50	fish
68	poultry
88	meat
122	vegetables
142	salads
158	pasta, rice, other grains & pulses
180	desserts
206	cakes & biscuits
244	good things for the pantry
256	great dishes from my travels
280	entertaining
298	some of the basics
309	index
315	weights & measures

introduction

I have always believed that good food and good cooking are part of all that is best in life, all that is warm, friendly and rewarding; and that love is as essential an ingredient to a good meal as it is to a good marriage.

The most vivid memories of my youth are linked with my mother's kitchen – coming home to the warmth of a log fire and good food, lovingly prepared. The highlight of each day was the evening meal, when the family gathered to share not only the food, but the day's happenings. A trying day never seemed so bad at the end of that meal and a good day turned into a celebration.

Cookery is now accepted as one of the creative arts and one by which a person can express their own individuality. Never look on this book as a set of rigid rules, but rather as a starting point. Once a dish has been mastered, be adventurous – give it the stamp of your personality by adding your favourite flavours or your choice of garnish.

As a guide for beginner cooks I have used a system to indicate the simplicity of each recipe:
- A simple and quick recipe that a beginner could accomplish with ease.
- • Dishes for the average cook with a knowledge of basic techniques, but requiring a little more time.
- • • A special dish, requiring more skill and probably taking some time to prepare.

Beginners should not be discouraged from trying out 3-star recipes – just be prepared to give them more time and concentration.

Happy cooking.

It was while my mother was writing *The Margaret Fulton Cookbook* that I too began to cook seriously. Still a teenager, I cooked simple grills and salads at first, but learned that the griller must be heated first, the salad greens must be carefully prepared and that the oil and vinegar dressing should be added last. Then I experimented by testing her recipe for Indian ghee rice and was thrilled at how successful it was. Her communication of that recipe gave me the sort of incentive I needed to take off to London and do the Diploma course at the Cordon Bleu School of Cookery.

Thirty years later I was chatting with my close friend, Jannie Brown, with whom I had flatted all those years ago. We both agreed that the new generation of cooks interested in the quality, freshness and goodness of food would also respond with confidence to the very essence of *The Margaret Fulton Cookbook*. Margaret's unique approach and ability to communicate to the home cook, makes her recipes accessible and achievable.

So, with Margaret's blessing, Jannie and I set to work to create this update of Margaret's original book.

Margaret has inspired generations of Australian cooks. We hope this book will introduce future generations to her simple philosophy of eating well, in a loving environment. With my daughters Kate and Louise representing the younger generation, we have continued the work my mother started.

Margaret Fulton   *Suzanne Gibbs*

CHEESE BISCUITS AND OLIVES

the first course

The first course is the curtain-raiser to any meal and often sets the mood for what is to follow. The choice is vast and may range from simple crisp vegetables as munched by the ancient Greeks and Romans to the more elaborate foods eaten by later civilisations.

The Russians introduced caviar, while the Spanish enjoy a glass of wine or sherry with tapas, a selection of dishes such as grilled fresh sardines, garlic prawns and fried spiced almonds. In Italy they serve an antipasto tray of olives, small vegetable dishes, salami and hams. The French have their pâtés and terrines and the Scandinavians know the value of pickled and smoked fish as a pre-dinner appetiser. Many of these delicacies are available at any good delicatessen and, along with fresh fruit and vegetables, combine to make simple but delicious appetisers.

DRINKS BEFORE DINNER — WHAT TO SERVE?

You can serve a variety of small dishes if you are having friends in for drinks. Perhaps a tray of raw vegetables with olives, salami and nuts and another of hot savoury tartlets and a few well-made canapés.

If you intend to serve a first course, a few olives and nuts with a pre-dinner drink is sufficient. Smoked salmon, pâté and melon or figs with prosciutto are among the best known first-course dishes. In other chapters I have included recipes that may be served as a first course, many of which are also suitable for a light lunch. Hors d'oeuvres and canapés are served with drinks before dinner to whet the appetite. They should be light, piquant and never larger than bite-size.

SIMPLE HORS D'OEUVRE

Olives are just about the best and simplest offerings with a drink. When preparing olives, wash first to remove any brine and dry well with a paper towel. If the olives have not been cracked, slash with a knife to allow the flavours to permeate the flesh. The pit can also be removed, if desired.

herbed olives: Put 1 small red chilli, 1 lightly crushed clove garlic, a sprig of fresh thyme and a broken bay leaf with black olives in a jar. Cover with olive oil and top with a lid. Keep in a cool place for at least a week. Drain and serve.

preserved lemon olives: Put 1–2 teaspoons slivered peel of preserved Moroccan lemon (available at good delicatessens) in a jar of black or green olives. If preserved lemons are hard to find use the thin rind from 1 lemon. Cover with olive oil, top with a lid and keep in a cool place for at least a week. Drain and serve.

greek-style olives: Pack olives in layers in a jar, arranging alternately with slices of lemon and celery. Cover with olive oil, top with a lid and keep in a cool place for at least a week. Drain and serve.

devilled nuts: Melt 1 tablespoon butter in pan, sauté 1 cup shelled walnuts, almonds or pecans until they take on colour, 3–5 minutes. Drain on paper towels and sprinkle with salt and a little curry powder or chilli powder.

ANTIPASTO

Arrange crisp fresh vegetables such as celery sticks or tender stalks and fennel pieces on a platter. Olives, small artichokes in olive oil, cooked capsicum or pimientos in oil, cheese, anchovies, salami, prosciutto and any cold meats may also be added. Serve a small bowl of oil and vinegar dressing alongside for dipping.

A more elaborate antipasto selection might include stuffed mushrooms or mussels, or grilled sardines. Garnish the platter with lemon wedges and serve with mayonnaise or virgin olive oil in small bowls. Crusty bread slices may also be offered.

some good antipasto dishes

EGGPLANT PARMIGIANA *(p. 134)*
ARTICHOKES IN WINE *(p. 125)*
SWEET AND SOUR ONIONS *(p. 137)*
FRIED CAPSICUM *(p. 131)*
EGGPLANT CAVIAR *(p. 132)*
LEEKS À LA GRECQUE *(p. 10)*
FRIED ZUCCHINI SALAD WITH MINT *(p. 147)*

CHEESE PASTRY •

Pastry savouries are popular and this easily prepared pastry is successful every time. Use to make pastry cases or almond cheese rounds.

2 cups plain flour
125 g butter
2 tablespoons grated Parmesan cheese
2 eggs
½ teaspoon salt

Sift the flour with a pinch of salt into a bowl and rub in the butter until mixture resembles fine breadcrumbs. Stir in the Parmesan. Beat eggs and salt. Take out 1 tablespoon of the beaten egg, mix with 1 teaspoon water and set aside for glazing. Make well in centre of the flour mixture and pour in the remaining egg. Lightly mix to a smooth dough. Knead lightly, wrap in cling wrap and chill for at least 2 hours.

ALMOND CHEESE ROUNDS •

These savoury biscuits keep well if stored in an airtight container, so they may be made days before required.

1 quantity cheese pastry *(see above)*
beaten egg, for glazing
slivered blanched almonds
sea salt crystals

Preheat the oven to 190°C. On a lightly floured board, roll out the dough to about 3 mm thick. Using a fluted, round cutter cut out circles arranging them on an ungreased baking tray. Brush with egg glaze, sprinkle with almonds and a pinch of salt crystals. Bake for 15 minutes, or until golden. Makes about 80.

CHEESE BISCUITS •

90 g butter
¾ cup finely grated cheddar cheese
1 tablespoon grated Parmesan cheese
¾ cup plain flour
½ teaspoon paprika
a pinch of cayenne pepper
½ teaspoon salt
beaten egg, for glazing
1 tablespoon sesame or cumin seeds

Preheat the oven to 180°C. Cream butter and cheeses. Sift the flour, paprika, cayenne and salt into creamed mixture. Mix well to form a dough, wrap in cling film and chill at least 1 hour. Roll out on lightly floured board or between sheets of plastic, to 6 mm thickness. Cut into rounds with a biscuit cutter or straws by cutting into 6 mm x 10 cm strips. Put on baking trays, brush with egg glaze and sprinkle with sesame or cumin seeds if liked. Bake for 8–10 minutes. Cool on wire racks and store in an airtight container. Makes about 40.

GOUGÈRES ••

The perfect accompaniment for a glass of red wine, gougères are ideal for making ahead of time. Simply shape them on a baking tray and freeze. When they are frozen, transfer into freezer bags ready for baking any time.

1 quantity choux pastry
(made with milk in place of the water, see p. 301)
100 g Gruyère cheese, grated
beaten egg, for glazing

Preheat the oven to 220°C. Fold the cheese into the choux pastry with a wooden spoon then spoon small balls of the mixture on a buttered baking tray. Brush with a little beaten egg and bake for 20 minutes until puffed and golden. Serve piping hot. Makes 30.

FIRST-COURSE DISHES

When a first course is called for, it is hard to improve on a savoury tart served warm. Onion and olive tart is equally at home at a cocktail party, a lunch or at the dinner table. Some of the best first-course dishes are usually the simplest.

oysters au naturel: The flavour of oysters is so delicate that they are best served with just a squeeze of lemon juice, a grinding of black pepper, and a little salt and buttered brown bread. Serve well chilled. They may also be served with a cocktail sauce.

cocktail sauce: Mix 1 tablespoon tomato ketchup, a dash of Tabasco, a squeeze of lemon juice and 4 tablespoons thick mayonnaise or cream. Season with salt and pepper and a dash of Worcestershire sauce. I use Lea & Perrins. Grated horseradish or onion may be added.

seafood cocktail: For each serving allow 2 chilled oysters and ⅓ cup cooked prawns, crabmeat or lobster. Place in cocktail glasses on shredded lettuce and drizzle with cocktail sauce.

smoked salmon: Allow 60 g per person and serve on a chilled plate with quarters of lemon and brown bread and butter. Capers, chopped egg and chopped onion are sometimes arranged in little mounds at the side of the plate. Freshly ground black pepper, straight from the mill, is essential.

pâté: Allow 60 g per person, serve with toast or melba toast. Some people like cornichons or something crisp to nibble added to the plate.

melon and ham: Thinly sliced prosciutto or braesola or any of the specialty hams go very well with melon. Set 1 or 2 peeled melon wedges on a plate and arrange wafer-thin slices of ham over the melon or at the side.

avocado with seafood: Halve a chilled avocado. Combine shellfish such as prawns, diced crayfish or flaked crabmeat with a little mayonnaise or oil and vinegar dressing. Fill avocado with chilled seafood. *Serves 2.*

ONION AND OLIVE TART ••

The French call this pissaladière, an onion and olive tart with a yeast dough or pastry base. Look at pizza crust (see p. 294) if you want a yeast base.

1½ cups plain flour
a pinch of salt
125 g butter
¼ cup water
1 kg onions, sliced
⅓ cup olive oil
4 medium tomatoes, sliced
12 anchovy fillets
20 pitted black olives

Sift the flour and salt into a bowl. Rub in the butter until mixture resembles breadcrumbs, then stir in the water and mix to form a dough. Wrap in cling wrap and chill for 30 minutes.

Meanwhile, cook the onions in the olive oil over a very low heat for at least 30 minutes. When the onions are cooked but not brown, remove from heat and drain, reserving the oil. Allow to cool. Preheat the oven to 200°C. Roll out the pastry and line a 29 cm x 21 cm rectangular flan ring. Spread the cooled onions over the pastry, garnish with tomatoes, anchovy fillets and olives. Drizzle the reserved oil over the tart. Bake for 40–45 minutes. *Serves 6–8.*

ONION AND OLIVE TART

SCALLOPS PROVENÇALE •

500–750 g scallops
salt and freshly ground pepper
plain flour
60 g butter
2 tablespoons olive oil
2 tablespoons chopped parsley
1 clove garlic, finely chopped
lemon juice

Remove the tough membrane from the scallops and rinse well, retaining only scallop and coral. Dry, season with salt and pepper then roll in flour, shaking off any surplus. Melt half the butter with the oil in a heavy-based frying pan. When the butter begins to froth, add scallops. Sear over a high heat for 30 seconds only on each side. Put scallops in scallop shells or ramekins. Sprinkle with parsley and garlic and a few drops of lemon juice. Melt the remaining butter and pour a few drops on each scallop. Serve hot. Serves 4–6.

SEARED SCALLOP SALAD •

Prepare the scallops as for scallops Provençale *(see recipe above)*. Pile a small mound of baby green leaves in the centre of each dinner plate. Sear scallops in a hot frying pan. Transfer to the plates, piling on to the greens. Heat remaining butter and a tablespoon of olive oil in the pan, add 2 teaspoons good balsamic vinegar and stir to combine. Drizzle over the scallops and greens. Serves 4.

INDONESIAN SATAYS •

500 g pork fillet
juice of 1 lemon
1 clove garlic, crushed
2 tablespoons light soy sauce

peanut sauce:
3 tablespoons peanut butter
30 g butter
½ teaspoon sugar
½ teaspoon Tabasco
¼ cup coconut cream or fresh cream

Cut pork into 2 cm cubes. Combine lemon juice, garlic and soy sauce. Marinate pork cubes in this mixture, turning occasionally, for 2–4 hours. Drain and reserve the marinade. Thread cubes on skewers, 3–4 cubes to each, and grill for 6–8 minutes. Serve hot with sauce. Makes about 12.

peanut sauce: In a saucepan, blend the reserved marinade with the sauce ingredients, except coconut milk or cream. Cook over a low heat, stirring constantly until it is thick. Remove from the heat and gradually stir in the coconut cream. Pour the sauce over the satays or serve as a dip. Serves 4 as a first course or 8–10 as part of an hors d'oeuvres tray.

SEARED SCALLOP SALAD

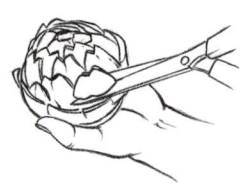

Remove any tough, discoloured leaves then snip the sharp points of the outer leaves with scissors.

Cut one-third off the top of the artichoke and trim the stalk.

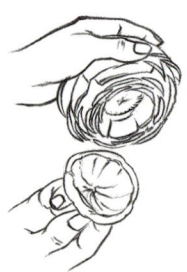

Use a sharp pointed knife to cut the centre leaves out to reveal the choke. This can be done when the artichoke is raw or cooked. Sauce or dressing may then be put into the cavity.

VEGETABLES À LA GRECQUE ••

Almost any vegetable can be cooked Greek style (in sauce à la Grecque). An earthenware flameproof casserole or a flat stainless steel pan is best for cooking vegetables in this manner. They should poach gently in the sauce until just tender. Serve chilled as a first-course appetiser or with crusty French bread as a light lunch dish. Good, too, with grilled meat and poultry.

vegetable of choice (see below)
1 tablespoon fresh tarragon or 1 teaspoon dried tarragon
1 tablespoon lemon juice
1 clove garlic, crushed
1 tablespoon finely chopped parsley
1 tomato, peeled, seeded and diced
a few sprigs of fresh thyme
salt and freshly ground black pepper
1 bay leaf
¼ cup olive oil
1 cup water

Place the ingredients in a heavy-based saucepan or fireproof casserole with the prepared vegetables *(see below)*. Cover and bring to the boil. Reduce the heat and simmer gently until the vegetable is tender but firm. Let the mixture cool, then chill.

The following vegetables may be prepared à la Grecque.

mushrooms: Carefully wash 500 g button mushrooms, trim stems and proceed as for above recipe.

leeks: Select 6 leeks (the smaller the better). Trim the leeks to 4 cm above the forking. Make a slit down the length of one side, not right through, stopping before the roots. Hold the leeks under cold running water, flicking back the leaves to remove all traces of grit or sand. If the leeks are large, say 4 cm across, cut them in halves, lengthwise. Proceed as for above recipe. The leeks are ready when a skewer easily pierces the root end.

onions: Select 500 g small white salad onions, peel and blanch for 2 minutes. Proceed as for above recipe.

artichokes: Trim tough outer leaves and stems of artichokes. Cook in boiling, salted water for 15 minutes, drain, add to sauce à la Grecque and cook gently for 30 minutes. Allow to cool. Pull off a leaf at a time and eat the tender base of each leaf. Avoid the 'choke' or fuzzy centre. This is usually cut or spooned out *(see illustration)*.

zucchini: Cut 8–10 zucchini into slices 6 mm thick. Place in pan with sauce à la Grecque and simmer gently until zucchini is tender but firm, about 4 minutes. Serves 4–6.

TUNA AND AVOCADO TARTARE •

½ red bird's eye chilli,
  seeded and finely chopped
375 g sashimi tuna
1 small red salad onion, finely diced
2 teaspoons sesame oil
1 tablespoon chopped parsley
  or fresh coriander
1 tablespoon tiny capers, drained
juice of 1 lime
freshly ground black pepper
1 avocado
watercress sprigs or other
  small salad greens, to garnish
extra virgin olive oil
thin toast (optional)

When preparing chilli, work under cold running water and wash your hands immediately afterwards, or simply wear rubber gloves. Cut the tuna into tiny dice and place in bowl with the chilli, onion, sesame oil, parsley or coriander, capers and half the lime juice. Season with a good grinding of pepper and spoon into 4 small ramekins or deep 7 cm-diameter biscuit cutters set over a tray.

Peel the avocado, halve and cut thin slices crosswise from around the stone. Arrange in layers over the tuna, to fit snugly in the ramekin. Turn each ramekin out on to a serving plate and top with watercress sprigs. Drizzle with a little extra virgin olive oil and the remaining lime juice and serve, if liked, with thin toast or melba toast (see p. 31). Serves 4.

SMOKED SALMON STACK ••

3 round pita breads
olive oil
baby rocket leaves or watercress
12 slices smoked salmon
2 Lebanese cucumbers, cut into
  thin matchstick strips
slices of pickled pink ginger

dressing:
1 tablespoon rice wine vinegar
2 teaspoons light soy sauce
1 teaspoon grated fresh ginger or wasabi
  (Japanese horseradish)
2 tablespoons peanut oil
1 tablespoon sesame oil

Brush the pita bread rounds with olive oil and cut into 15 mm strips. Grill until pale golden. Turn and brush the other side with the oil, grilling until the second side is just golden. Cool and store airtight until ready to serve. Arrange 4 or 5 toasted pita strips on each of 6 dinner plates in a stack to form a base for the salad. On top of each, arrange first the baby rocket leaves, then 2 salmon slices, curled attractively and halved first if large, the strips of cucumber and a few slices of pickled ginger. Lastly, drizzle the dressing over each. Serve immediately.

dressing: Combine the vinegar, soy sauce and ginger in a bowl. Gradually whisk in the oils. Let the ingredients sit and infuse until ready to serve. Serves 6.

CHICKEN LIVER PÂTÉ ••

500 g chicken livers
1 medium onion, finely chopped
500 g butter, melted
1 teaspoon fresh thyme leaves
1 bay leaf
1 teaspoon fresh rosemary leaves
3 cloves garlic
⅓ cup brandy
⅓ cup port
⅓ cup red wine
4 eggs
1 teaspoon salt
1 teaspoon freshly ground black pepper
bay leaves, to garnish

Using kitchen scissors, trim the chicken livers of all sinew and cut in half. Cook the onion in a frying pan with 2 tablespoons of the melted butter until softened. Add herbs, garlic, brandy, port and red wine and bring to the boil. Simmer over a moderate heat until reduced to a thick syrupy glaze. Cool and remove the bay leaf.

Preheat the oven to 180°C. Fit a food processor with a metal blade and add the chicken livers, cooled glaze, eggs and melted butter, reserving a little butter to spoon over the top later. Season well with salt and pepper. Process until very smooth and then turn the mixture into individual ovenproof ramekins. Place the dishes in a baking pan and half fill them with boiling water. Cover with a sheet of baking paper and bake for 45–50 minutes. Remove from the oven, top with bay leaves, cool and pour the reserved melted butter into each to seal the pâté from the air. Serve with crackers, toast, crusty bread or melba toast (see p. 31).

Serves 6–8.

EASY CHICKEN LIVER PÂTÉ •

500 g chicken livers
155 g butter
2 tablespoons finely chopped shallots
1 clove garlic, finely chopped
1 bay leaf
a sprig of fresh thyme
salt and freshly ground black pepper
2 tablespoons brandy
2 tablespoons butter

Examine the chicken livers and remove any dark spots and sinews. Heat 30 g butter in a frying pan. Add the shallots and garlic and fry gently until softened. Add the chicken livers to the pan with the bay leaf and thyme. Season with salt and pepper and fry for 3–5 minutes until the livers are stiffened and lightly browned but still pink inside.

Remove the bay leaf and thyme and blend the livers in a blender or food processor in 3 lots. Cream the remaining butter and gradually beat into the liver paste. Add the brandy to the pan in which the livers were cooked and reduce over a high heat until reduced to 1 tablespoon. Fold into the liver mixture, check for seasoning and spoon into a terrine dish or individual ovenproof ramekins. Melt the butter and pour over the pâté to prevent oxidising. Refrigerate for several hours at least before eating.
Will keep for 1 week. Serve with melba toast (see p. 31) or toast triangles. Serves 6.

CHICKEN LIVER PÂTÉ

soups

What wonderful memories I have of soup and my Scottish mother's kitchen.
We had soup every day and each one had its own character
and charm. When I grew older and studied French cooking,
I knew why my mother's soups were so good.

She did not belong to the school of everything thrown
in together and boiled for hours. Barley was used to thicken
mutton broth, but rice was used for chicken.
When tender vegetables were used, the stock was light and
the soup was cooked for only 20 minutes.
She would rather use cream to enrich fish or
tomato soup than pour it over peaches.
Indeed, just a little cream can lift many soups, just as a dash
of dry sherry greatly enhances the flavour of others.

STOCKS

Not all soups are made from stock, but carefully made stock is so essential to good cooking that it is well worth making. Cooled quickly and stored airtight, stock will keep in the refrigerator for a week and will freeze for up to two months. The ingredients are cheap and easily obtainable.

Some specialty food shops sell good stock. Also, canned consommé and stock cubes are an accessible standby for the busy person, but be discriminating in their use.

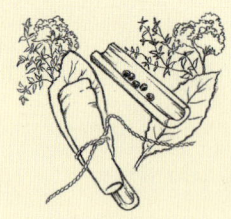

A bouquet garni is a bunch of herbs consisting of a bay leaf, a sprig of thyme, a few peppercorns and 3 or 4 parsley stalks placed between half a carrot and a piece of celery. Tied firmly together with string, this aromatic bouquet is easier to remove from the finished dish than stray leaves.

BEEF STOCK •

1.5 kg soup bones (shank, marrow bone, rib bones or a combination)
250 g diced shin of beef
1 carrot, thickly sliced
2 stalks celery or top leaves
small piece turnip and parsnip *(if available)*
1 onion, halved but not peeled, stuck with 2 whole cloves
6 black peppercorns
bouquet garni
3 litres (12 cups) water

Ask the butcher to crack the bones. Remove any large pieces of meat and chop finely. Wash the bones and place in a large saucepan or stockpot with meat, vegetables, peppercorns and bouquet garni. Cover with cold water and bring to boil. Skim the surface. Lower the heat and simmer gently for 2–3 hours. Strain the liquid into a large bowl and discard the solids. Cool and refrigerate. Next day, remove the fat. Never leave stock in a pot all night.

beef bouillon or brown stock: You will need this for consommé, onion soup and to enrich sauces and casseroles. Use the beef stock recipe but thoroughly brown the bones and vegetables in a baking dish in a 220°C oven or in a heavy-based frying pan over a moderate heat. If the bones are very lean, it may be necessary to add about a tablespoon of butter. Proceed as for the beef stock.

To help keep bouillon clear, crush a few eggshells saved from other cooking and add to the stock, after skimming. Strain through a fine sieve or cheesecloth.

CHICKEN STOCK •

1 boiling fowl or 1 kg chicken bones (feet, neck, wings or backs or a carcass and giblets of chicken)
1 teaspoon salt
1 small onion
1 small carrot
bouquet garni
8 cups water

Place the boiling fowl or bones in a large saucepan or stockpot then add the remaining ingredients. Bring to the boil, carefully skimming the surface. Continue to simmer gently for 1–2 hours. Strain through a fine sieve and discard the solids. Cool as quickly as possible. As soon as stock has cooled, refrigerate or freeze until needed.

FISH STOCK •

Fish stock must be simmered, never boiled. Do not throw away crab, crayfish or prawn heads. Put them in the freezer in plastic freezer bags; they will keep and be ready to add to the stockpot when you need some fish stock. This stock is used in many fish sauces and soups. It can be frozen or will keep well in the refrigerator for a week.

2 kg bones, heads (without gills) or trimmings of any white, non-oily fish
5 cups cold water
1 cup white wine or the juice of 1 lemon plus water to make up a cup
1 teaspoon white peppercorns
bouquet garni

Place all the ingredients and the bouquet garni in a saucepan and bring to the boil. Skim the surface and simmer very gently for 20 minutes. Strain through a fine sieve or cheesecloth.

VEGETABLE STOCK •

Use in place of beef or chicken stock in soups, sauces and casseroles.

1 onion, chopped
1 leek, white part only, chopped
3 stalks celery, chopped
1 parsnip or turnip
1 piece ginger (walnut-size), finely chopped
bouquet garni
12 peppercorns
2 teaspoons coarse salt
8 cups water

Put all the ingredients in a large saucepan or stockpot. Bring to the boil, lower heat and simmer, partially covered for about 1 hour. Pour the liquid through a colander set over another container, pressing the vegetables against the sides of the colander to extract the juices; discard the solids. Pour through a strainer, cool and refrigerate.

CHICKEN AND VEGETABLE BROTH •

30 g butter
2 cups diced vegetables in season (carrots, parsnips, celery, leeks, corn kernels etc)
5 cups chicken stock
¼ cup short-grain rice
salt and freshly ground black pepper
1 tablespoon chopped parsley

In a large saucepan, melt the butter and sauté the vegetables, but do not allow to colour. Add the stock and rice. Cover the pan and simmer for 20 minutes. Add the salt and pepper, to taste, and sprinkle with parsley just before serving. Serves 6.

TOMATO SOUP •

30 g butter
1 medium onion, sliced
1 carrot, sliced
1 tablespoon plain flour
3–4 medium ripe tomatoes, sliced
2½ cups vegetable or chicken stock or water
1 small bay leaf
1 teaspoon sugar (optional)
a pinch of ground nutmeg
salt and freshly ground black pepper
3–4 tablespoons cream (optional)

Melt the butter in a saucepan then add the onion and carrot. Cover and allow to soften for 5–6 minutes. Remove from the heat, stir in the flour, add the tomatoes, stock or water, bay leaf, sugar, spice and seasoning. Stir until boiling and then simmer for 15–20 minutes. Rub through a sieve, pour back into rinsed pan and reheat. Adjust the seasoning and add cream, if liked. A teaspoon of tomato paste may be added with the tomatoes for extra colour and flavour. Serves 4.

PUMPKIN SOUP •

Pumpkin soup may be varied by use of different pumpkin varieties. Golden nugget, jap and butternut each has its own taste. Try varying the flavour by adding a touch of curry powder, ground coriander or cumin to a pumpkin soup. Use the following recipe as a base and add a ¼ to ½ teaspoon of your favourite spice a minute before adding the pumpkin. Enrich if you like with a little cream at the end.

30 g unsalted butter
1 onion, finely chopped
2 cloves garlic
750 g peeled pumpkin, seeded
2 cups chicken stock
2 cups water
salt and freshly ground black pepper
cream (optional)
snipped chives, to garnish

Melt the butter in a large saucepan and sauté the onion and garlic, until soft, without colouring. If adding spice, add now and fry very gently for a minute or so. Add the pumpkin, chicken stock and water. Bring slowly to the boil and simmer, covered for about 15 minutes, until the pumpkin is tender. Cool slightly and purée the mixture in several lots, using a food processor or blender, or by rubbing through a sieve. Season with the salt and pepper, to tase. Add a little more chicken stock or water if necessary to make a good consistency, depending on the pumpkin. Swirl in a little cream, if liked. Reheat gently and ladle the soup into bowls. Garnish with chives. You may also strew over chopped parsley or torn coriander leaves, if liked. Serves 4–6.

PUMPKIN SOUP

CREAM OF CARROT SOUP •

30 g butter
4 medium carrots, sliced
1 onion, sliced
1 potato, peeled and cut into small chunks
4–5 cups chicken or vegetable stock
1 teaspoon salt
freshly ground pepper
cream (optional)
snipped chives or chopped parsley, to garnish

Melt the butter in a saucepan, add the carrots and onion and cook gently until the butter is absorbed. Add the potato and 3 cups of the stock and bring to the boil. Reduce the heat, cover and simmer for 15 minutes. Rub through a sieve or transfer, in batches, to a blender or food processor and purée until smooth. Add the salt and pepper, to taste. Return to the saucepan and heat gently with enough of the remaining stock to achieve the desired consistency. Swirl in a little cream, if liked, then garnish with chives or parsley. Serves 6.

SOUP CHIFFONADE •

1 lettuce
4 spring onions, finely chopped
2 sprigs fresh mint
6 leaves fresh or a pinch of dried tarragon
1 tablespoon chopped parsley or chervil
1 cup fresh or frozen peas
5 cups chicken stock
salt and freshly ground pepper

Shred the lettuce finely and place in a saucepan with the spring onions, finely chopped herbs and peas. Add the chicken stock and season with salt and pepper, to taste. Cover and simmer gently for 15 minutes. Serves 4–6.

note: finely sliced beans may substitute for the peas.

CREAM OF MUSHROOM SOUP ••

30 g butter
1 small onion, finely chopped
250 g flat or button mushrooms, chopped
1 tablespoon plain flour
1 cup milk
salt and freshly ground pepper
2½ cups chicken stock
½ teaspoon dried tarragon (optional)
¼ cup cream (optional)
4 button mushrooms, thinly sliced, to garnish (optional)
2 tablespoons freshly chopped parsley, to garnish

Melt the butter in a large saucepan, add the onion and cook gently for 5 minutes or until softened. Stir in the mushrooms, cover and cook for 5 minutes, tossing the pan occasionally. Sprinkle in the flour and cook for 2 minutes, then gradually pour in the milk, stirring until well blended. Season with the salt and pepper, to taste. Cook, stirring over a gentle heat for a few minutes. Add the stock and tarragon, if using, and simmer for 10 minutes, stirring occasionally. Set aside and cool for 5 minutes.

Place half in a blender or food processor and purée until smooth. Return to the pan and repeat with the remaining soup. Reheat the soup gently for a few minutes, then stir in the cream, if using, and check for seasoning. Serve garnished with mushroom slices, if using, and the parsley. Serves 4–6.

SOUP CHIFFONADE

CREAM OF ASPARAGUS SOUP •

This simple soup is perfectly delicious and, when asparagus is at a reasonable price, well worth making.

2 bunches asparagus
6 cups chicken stock
45 g butter
2 tablespoons plain flour
salt and freshly ground pepper
cream (optional)

Cut away the tougher sections of the asparagus stalks. Cut off 4–5 cm of the tips and reserve. Peel the rest and cut into short pieces. Put the chicken stock on to boil and add the asparagus chunks. Reduce the heat and cook for a further 15 minutes or until tender. Remove the chunks with a slotted spoon to a blender with some of the liquid and purée until smooth. Add the tips to the simmering cooking liquid still in the saucepan and cook for about 6 minutes. Remove with a slotted spoon and set aside.

In another saucepan, melt the butter and blend in the flour. Cook for a minute or so, until a pale 'straw' colour, and then remove from the heat. Cool for a few minutes then gradually stir in the remaining cooking liquid from the saucepan. Stir until smooth and then add the asparagus purée. Season with the salt and pepper, to taste, and enrich with a little cream if desired. Serve with the asparagus tips added to the individual servings. Serves 4–6.

ROASTED TOMATO AND BASIL SOUP ••

Buy fully ripe tomatoes and roast in the oven.

500 g tomatoes, halved and seeded
1 tablespoon olive oil
1 garlic clove, finely chopped
2 tablespoons chopped basil
a pinch of sugar
2 cups chicken stock
freshly ground black pepper
a few basil leaves, shredded, to garnish

Preheat the oven to 180°C. Place the tomato halves, cut-side down, on a lightly greased baking tray. Roast for 20 minutes, then remove from the oven. Slip off the skins and chop the flesh finely, saving all the juices.

Heat the oil and add the tomatoes, garlic and basil. Add the sugar and simmer gently in a saucepan for about 5 minutes. Add the chicken stock and reserved juices and cook for a further 5 minutes. Serve with pepper and basil to garnish. Serves 2–4.

GREEK LEMON SOUP •

3 tablespoons rice
6 cups chicken stock
2 eggs
juice of 1 large lemon
grated rind of 1 lemon
salt and freshly ground pepper

Wash the rice in water and drain. Bring the stock to the boil, gradually add the rice and cook over low heat for about 30 minutes. Beat the eggs with the lemon juice and the rind. Slowly stir 1 cup hot chicken stock into the egg and lemon mixture. Pour back slowly into the hot stock, remove from the heat and stir rapidly to prevent the soup from curdling. Taste for seasoning, adding salt and pepper if needed, and serve. Serves 4–6.

CHICKEN AND SWEET CORN SOUP •

This has to be one of the favourite orders at Chinese restaurants. It's simply made at home, using canned creamed corn.

1 small chicken breast, skinned and boned
½ teaspoon salt
1 x 250 g can creamed corn
5 cups chicken stock
1½ tablespoons cornflour
2 tablespoons Chinese rice wine (shao-hsing)
sesame oil
2 spring onions, shredded finely

Remove any fat from the chicken and chop very finely. Add the salt and 2 tablespoons water to the chicken, mixing well. Mix the creamed corn and chicken together.

Heat the stock in a saucepan and stir in the corn and chicken mixture. Heat very gently, stirring. When it reaches the boil, add the cornflour which has been mixed with a little cold water. Return to the boil, stirring until thickened, for about 1 minute. Lastly, stir in the rice wine. Ladle into bowls and finish each one with a tiny drizzle of sesame oil and a scattering of spring onions. Serves 4.

FRESH NOODLE SOUP WITH CHICKEN ••

You can use different noodles in this dish. Fresh rice noodles and egg noodles are convenient and easy and are available in most supermarkets. You will find a wider variety in Asian food stores.

5 cups chicken stock
2 chicken breast halves
1 onion, finely sliced
2 star anise
3 cm piece ginger, sliced
1 clove garlic, finely chopped
salt and freshly ground pepper
250 g instant rice noodles
2 spring onions, cut into 4 cm lengths
¼ cup fresh coriander leaves
1 cup bean sprouts, trimmed
½ red bird's eye chilli, seeded and sliced
fresh coriander or Thai basil sprigs, to garnish

Heat the chicken stock in a saucepan over a moderate heat. Add the chicken breast, onion, star anise, ginger and garlic. Season with salt and pepper. Reduce the heat and simmer very gently for 8 minutes. Remove the chicken and set aside. Strain the stock, discarding the solids. Slice the chicken thinly.

Place the noodles in a bowl and pour over boiling water, to cover. Leave to stand for a few minutes to heat through and separate, then drain and set aside. In a bowl, mix the spring onions, coriander, bean sprouts and chilli.

To serve, put the noodles in 4 deep bowls and pile the spring onion mixture on top. Ladle over the hot stock with the chicken slices and serve. Garnish with the coriander or Thai basil sprigs. Serves 4.

HEARTY SOUPS

Some of these soups are so filling they really are a meal in themselves and only need to be followed by fruit and cheese, if at all.

FRENCH ONION SOUP ••

45 g butter
1 tablespoon oil
4–5 onions, thinly sliced
2 tablespoons plain flour
8 cups boiling beef stock
½ cup dry white wine
salt and freshly ground black pepper
2 tablespoons brandy (optional)
1 baguette, thickly sliced
1 cup grated Gruyère cheese
   or ½ cup Parmesan cheese

Melt the butter in a large, heavy-based saucepan. Add the oil and onions and cook slowly for 20–30 minutes, stirring occasionally. Be careful not to brown the onions. Blend in the flour and stir over a moderate heat for 3 minutes. Remove from the heat and blend in the boiling stock. Add the wine. Season with salt and pepper, to taste. Simmer covered for 20–30 minutes, skimming occasionally. Preheat the oven to 160°C.

Meanwhile, put the bread in one layer on a baking tray. Bake for 15–20 minutes, until crisp and lightly coloured. If desired, the bread can be brushed with a little olive oil halfway through cooking and rubbed lightly with a cut clove of garlic when baked. Taste the soup and correct if necessary for seasoning, adding salt and pepper. Just before serving, stir in the brandy, if using. Pour into a soup tureen or soup cups over the rounds of bread. Serve the cheese separately. Serves 6.

FRENCH ONION SOUP GRATINÉE ••

Prepare the soup as for French onion soup (*see recipe left*). Meanwhile, cut a baguette into thick slices and toast or bake. Bring the soup to the boil. Divide the bread between individual ovenproof bowls. Pour boiling soup over. Cover with fine slivers of Gruyère cheese and put under a hot griller until the cheese melts and browns lightly. Serve immediately. Serves 6.

MINESTRONE ••

1 cup dried cannellini beans
250 g pancetta or thickly cut bacon, diced
2 cloves garlic, chopped
1 onion, finely chopped
2 large carrots, diced
1 cup sliced celery
2 cups finely shredded cabbage
2 peeled tomatoes, diced
3 litres (12 cups) beef stock
1 cup broken spaghetti
1 cup fresh peas
½ cup chopped parsley
salt and freshly ground pepper
grated Parmesan cheese

Cover the beans with cold water and soak overnight. Drain and put in a saucepan, cover with water and simmer for 30 minutes to 1 hour or until almost tender. Sauté the pancetta, garlic and onion in a large saucepan, until the onion is tender. Add the carrot, celery, cabbage, tomatoes, drained beans and stock. Simmer, covered for 1 hour. Add the spaghetti and peas and cook, covered, for a further 15 minutes. Stir in the parsley and season with salt and pepper, to taste. Serve with the cheese. Serves 8–10.

FRENCH ONION SOUP GRATINÉE

PEA AND HAM SOUP ••

500 g split peas
2 rashers bacon, diced
2 onions, sliced
2.5 litres (10 cups) water
½ teaspoon freshly ground black pepper
1 sprig of fresh thyme
1 bay leaf
1 ham bone
2 carrots, diced
1 cup sliced celery
2 teaspoons salt or to taste
2 tablespoons lemon juice
croutons *(optional)*

Cover the peas with cold water and soak overnight. In a large saucepan, sauté the bacon, then add the onions and sauté until they are golden. Add the drained peas, water, pepper, thyme and bay leaf. Add the ham bone. Bring slowly to the boil, reduce the heat and simmer, half-covered, for 1 hour. Add the carrot and celery and continue to cook for another hour.

Remove the thyme and bay leaf and discard. Take out the ham bone, cut all meat from the bone, removing excess fat and any skin, dice and return the meat to the soup. Add the salt and lemon juice just before serving. Serve with croutons, if liked *(see p. 31)*. Serves 6–8.

note: sliced frankfurts or spicy smoked sausage may be heated in the pea and ham soup. It is then suitable as a main course for lunch.

SCOTCH BROTH •

Traditionally a scrag neck of mutton (about 750g) is used for Scotch broth, lamb shanks make an excellent and accessible substitute.

⅓ cup pearl barley
4 lamb shanks, halved
10 cups water
1 teaspoon salt
½ cup sliced celery
1 carrot, diced
1 leek, diced
1 turnip, diced
1 onion, diced
freshly ground black pepper
chopped parsley

Cover the barley with cold water and soak several hours. Place the lamb shanks in a large saucepan with the cold water and bring slowly to the boil. Skim the surface, add the drained barley and salt and simmer for 20–30 minutes. Add the vegetables and season with the pepper. Continue cooking gently, half-covered, for about 1½ hours. Take out the shanks, remove the meat from the bones, cut into small pieces and return to the broth. Skim any fat, adjust seasoning and add the parsley. Serves 6.

PEA AND HAM SOUP

FISH SOUPS

A SUPERB FISH SOUP CAN BE A MEAL IN ITSELF. MEDITERRANEAN FISH SOUP IS ONE, MADE SIMPLY WITH FRESH BLUE-EYE, SNAPPER, JOHN DORY OR OTHER FIRM WHITE FISH. A MIXTURE OF FISH AND SHELLFISH CAN BE USED AS WELL.

CREAM OF OYSTER SOUP •
An excellent way to use bottled oysters.

30 g butter
2 tablespoons plain flour
3 cups fish stock
1–2 dozen oysters
½ cup cream
salt and freshly ground pepper

Melt the butter in a saucepan, add the flour and cook without browning for a minute or two. Add the stock and bring to the boil, stirring constantly. Simmer for 10 minutes. Place the oysters and cream in a tureen or soup bowls and pour the boiling soup over. Adjust the seasoning. If the soup cannot be served immediately, place the saucepan in a larger saucepan of hot water. Do not allow the soup to come to the boil, as the oysters will toughen. Serves 4.

THAI SOUR SPICY PRAWN SOUP •
Tom yam goong is a favourite soup in Thailand. It is very hot and spicy with a delicious touch of sour.

8 large or 16 small prawns
2 stalks lemongrass
4 kaffir lime leaves or a strip of lime rind
4–5 white button mushrooms or canned straw mushrooms
2–3 tiny bird's eye chillies, split and seeded
4 cups chicken stock
4 tablespoons lime juice
2 tablespoons Thai fish sauce (nam pla)
1 cup fresh coriander leaves

Wash the prawns, shell and devein, leaving the tails on. Crush the tender white ends of the lemongrass, then cut diagonally into fine slices. Halve the lime leaves or finely shred the lime rind if using, slice the mushrooms finely, leaving straw mushrooms whole. Slice chillies (use only 1 chilli if your taste doesn't run to very hot).

Heat the stock in a large saucepan. Add the lemongrass, lime leaves, mushrooms, chilli and lime juice and fish sauce. Bring to the boil, reduce the heat and simmer for 2 minutes. Add the prawns and cook only until they turn pink. Add the coriander leaves and serve in bowls. Serves 4.

FISH CHOWDER •

30 g butter
2 thick rashers streaky bacon, diced
1 medium onion, chopped
2 cups fish stock or water
1 cup sweet corn kernels
2 potatoes, peeled and diced
500 g fresh or smoked fish,
   cut into 2 cm pieces
1 ½ cups milk
salt and freshly ground pepper
2 tablespoons chopped parsley

Melt the butter in a saucepan and add the bacon and onion. Sauté gently until the onion is softened then add the stock or water, corn and potatoes. Bring to a simmer and cook until the potatoes are tender. Meanwhile, cut the fish into small pieces and add to the saucepan. Continue to cook for a further 5 minutes or until the fish is cooked. Heat the milk, add to the soup and reheat gently without boiling. Season with salt and pepper and stir in the parsley. Americans often serve a soup like this with plain crackers. *Serves 4–6*.

MEDITERRANEAN FISH SOUP ••

3 tablespoons olive oil
1 onion, chopped
2 stalks celery, chopped
2 tablespoons chopped celery leaves
1–2 cloves garlic, crushed
a good pinch of saffron threads
2 tomatoes, peeled and diced
4–5 cups fish stock or water
¾ cup dry white wine
salt and freshly ground pepper
a pinch of cayenne pepper
1.5 kg mixed fish, such as blue-eye,
   snapper or John Dory
lemon juice (optional)
8 slices crusty bread, dried in slow oven
chopped parsley, to garnish

Heat the oil in a heavy-based saucepan, add the onion and celery and cook very slowly until transparent, but not coloured. Add the celery leaves, garlic and saffron, then the tomatoes. Cook, stirring occasionally, until reduced to a pulp. Add the stock or water and the wine. Season with the salt, pepper and cayenne pepper. Simmer for 5 minutes. Add the fish and cook gently. Fish steaks take only 5–8 minutes. Taste and, if necessary, add more seasoning. Lemon juice can be added to taste. Place a piece of bread in each bowl and ladle over the soup. Garnish with the parsley. Serve, if liked, with rouille (*see following*). *Serves 4–6*.

rouille: Place 4 cloves garlic in a mortar or blender with 3 slices bread, crusts removed, 1 chilli, seeded, and a pinch of saffron threads. Process to a paste and add ½ cup olive oil, in a thin stream, blending as for mayonnaise, until the sauce is thick and smooth. Add a little of the fish soup liquid to thin if necessary and 1 tablespoon of tomato paste. Serve the rouille separately for everyone to add a dollop to their soup bowl.

ICED SOUPS

Iced soups are delicious when appetites flag in hot weather and they make an elegant first course for a dinner party served on a bed of crushed ice. If the weather should suddenly change, simply serve them hot and add any cream just before serving.

Cut off most of the green top and trim the roots.

Holding the root end, make a slit down the leek not quite through to the centre. This enables the leaves to be opened out and flushed with cold running water to remove sand and grit.

VICHYSSOISE •

3 small leeks
45 g butter
1 onion, finely chopped
salt and freshly ground pepper
7 cups chicken stock
2 potatoes, peeled and thinly sliced
¼–½ cup cream
snipped chives, to garnish

Wash the leeks well and cut into very thin slices. Use the white part only or include only about 2.5 cm of the green for a little colour. Heat the butter and add the leeks, onion, salt and pepper. Cover and cook over a low heat, without browning. Add the stock and potatoes, cook until vegetables are tender, then put through a sieve or cool slightly and blend, until smooth, in a blender or food processor. Adjust seasonings and leave to cool before chilling in the refrigerator. When ready to serve, stir in half the cream. Ladle into bowls and swirl some of the remaining cream into each, then sprinkle with the chives. Serve well chilled or hot, depending on the weather and tastes. *Serves 6-8.*

AVOCADO SOUP •

2 medium avocados, peeled,
  stoned and sliced
1 cup cream
4 cups chicken stock
salt and freshly ground pepper
a pinch of ground nutmeg
1 tablespoon lemon juice
extra cream, to finish

Purée avocados with the cream in the blender or food processor, or mash together and rub through a sieve. For a cold soup, add purée to cold stock, season with salt, pepper, nutmeg and lemon juice, then chill. For a hot soup, add purée to hot stock and heat to just below boiling point. Season and serve immediately. Finish soup with a swirl of cream on each serving. *Serves 6–8.*

BEETROOT AND CUCUMBER SOUP •

3 beetroot
½ onion, finely chopped
5 cups chicken, beef or vegetable stock
1 Lebanese cucumber
2 teaspoons wine vinegar
salt and freshly ground black pepper
¼ cup light sour cream
1 diced Lebanese cucumber and 1 diced cooked beetroot, to garnish

Peel the beetroot and shred coarsely. Place in a saucepan with the onion and 2 cups of the stock, cover and cook gently until the beetroot is tender. Meanwhile, peel, seed and roughly chop the cucumber, add it to the beetroot and cool slightly. Purée in a blender or food processor adding some of the remaining stock to help make a smooth purée.

Add the remaining stock and, when ready to serve, reheat gently. Season with vinegar and salt and pepper. Add a little sour cream and garnish each serving with the cucumber and beetroot. Serves 4.

ACCOMPANIMENTS FOR SOUP

Among the garnishes for soups are macaroni, spaghetti, noodles, all broken into pieces, tender vegetables cut into shapes, finely chopped parsley or snipped chives along with other herbs. The following titbits glamourise soup and, except for cheese croûtes, may be made ahead and reheated, if needed.

melba toast: Toast sliced white bread on each side. While still warm remove crusts, and slice through the centre to make two slices. Cut each slice diagonally into triangles and arrange on a baking tray. Dry in a 150°C oven, until crisp and very lightly coloured. Serve these in a small basket.

croutons: Cut crusts off 1.25 cm-thick slices of bread, then cut into 1.25 cm cubes. Fry in butter or oil until golden. Drain on paper towel. Serve with puréed vegetable and meat soups, such as pea and ham.

cheese biscuits: See recipe for almond cheese rounds and cheese biscuits *(see p. 5)*

tiny puffs (profiteroles): When making choux pastry *(see p. 301)*, save 2 tablespoons of the paste. Make a cone of greaseproof paper and fill with paste. Snip off the tip of the cone and pipe small portions about the size of a pea onto a lightly greased baking tray. Bake in a 190°C oven for 10 minutes. They are delicious with consommé.

cheese croûtes: Cut small rounds of stale bread. Toast on one side and spread the untoasted side with equal quantities of butter and finely grated cheese mixed together. Brown under griller and serve immediately.

eggs & cheese

EGGS

We can take a lesson from the French when it comes to cooking eggs. In France the egg comes into its own, not only as a simple and delicious breakfast food, but also as gourmet fare.

Eggs can be prepared in countless ways. With fresh eggs on hand you have an important ingredient for many classic dishes and delicacies. Eggs enrich soups and sauces, glaze pastries, bind meat stuffings, coat fried foods and are essential in most batters, cakes and pastries.

For best results, eggs should be cooked on a low heat. Even boiled eggs should not be cooked at a rapid boil. The exception is the omelette, which should be cooked quickly and served immediately.

SIMPLE WAYS TO COOK EGGS

to boil eggs: A boiled egg has been a popular breakfast for hundreds of years. It is light, simple, supremely quick and very nourishing; but its cooking is a matter of split second finesse. If the egg is farm fresh, a grinding of black pepper and a little salt puts this simple food into the gourmet class.

Soft-boiled eggs have soft whites and liquid yolks. The whites of medium-boiled eggs are firm, but the yolks are still soft. Hard-boiled eggs have firm whites and yolks. To boil eggs, place in a saucepan of tepid water and bring them up to the boil. This helps to prevent cracking. Start timing when the water begins to simmer.

If the eggs you are using are cold, put a teaspoon of vinegar in the water to help set any leaking white and to stop it spreading in the pot. Often, very fresh eggs that are hard-boiled are difficult to shell. Counter this with a teaspoon of salt added to the water. Once hard-boiled, cool eggs quickly in plenty of cold water.

to poach eggs: Poached eggs are delicious on hot buttered toast and are excellent with spinach or smoked salmon. Only fresh eggs will hold a good shape.

Take a shallow saucepan with a lid, half fill it with water and bring to the boil. If you are uncertain about the freshness of the eggs, add 1 teaspoon white vinegar to the water. Break the egg into a cup and slip it gently into the simmering water. As soon as the last egg is in, cover and remove the saucepan from the heat. In 3½ minutes they should be done, or 4 minutes if you prefer firmer eggs. Lift out with an egg slice, drain on a tea towel or paper towel and then slide the egg onto buttered toast.

Egg size	Soft	Medium	Hard
Small (42–49 g)	2 min. 40 sec.	3 min. 20 sec.	7 min.
Medium (50–58 g)	3 min.	3 min. 50 sec.	8 min.
Large (59–66 g)	3 min. 20 sec.	4 min. 15 sec.	10 min.

to scramble eggs: Scrambled eggs are akin to omelettes, in that all sorts of delicious things can be mixed in with them.

Allow at least 2 eggs per person. Break them into a bowl. Add some salt and freshly ground pepper. Some add a little milk or cream (a tablespoon per egg). Beat with a fork, until the whites and yolks are thoroughly mixed. Melt a little butter in a small saucepan, preferably non-stick. Don't let the butter get too hot, just foaming should do. Now add the beaten eggs and stir gently at first over a moderate heat, until eggs begin to set. Now stir more rapidly, using a scraping motion, until almost set, but still creamy. Take the eggs off the heat before they are fully cooked. The eggs continue cooking while in the hot pan. At this stage, a little more butter or cream can be added to stop further cooking and to enrich the eggs. Serve immediately on hot buttered toast.

variations: 1 tablespoon grated cheese, 1 or 2 slices smoked salmon, cut into wide strips, or chopped herbs such as chives, parsley, tarragon and chervil may be added to eggs as you take them from the heat.

to fry eggs: Melt some bacon fat, butter, or olive oil, 1 teaspoon to each egg, in a frying pan. Break the egg into a cup and slide it in to the pan. If the egg sizzles and splutters violently, the pan is too hot, so turn the heat down quickly. If the eggs cook too quickly, the whites toughen and are unappetising. If there is no reaction at all, the pan is not hot enough. It should be hot enough to set the whites. When done, reduce the heat. As the egg gently fries, baste with a little fat until the thin coating of white over the yolk sets. When set and still wobbly, it is done, sunny-side up. Some people like it a little firmer or turned over.

bacon and eggs: Remove the rind from the bacon. Melt a little bacon fat or butter, about 1 teaspoon. Add the bacon and cook slowly for 4–6 minutes. If crisp bacon is liked, keep pouring off the fat. This may be kept for frying the eggs. Do not fry the bacon too quickly or it will 'frizzle' and become hard. Push the bacon to the side of pan, or remove to a plate and keep hot. Slide in eggs and cook.

storing eggs: Never wash eggs before storing. Store with pointed end downwards and away from strong-flavoured foods. Keep eggs in a refrigerator or the coolest possible place in the house, preferably in an egg rack or in the carton they were purchased, away from the sun.

ASPARAGUS SOLDIERS •

Try dipping freshly cooked hot asparagus into the soft yolk, just the way kids love to do with toast.

1 bunch asparagus
4 eggs
salt and freshly ground pepper

Take care to wash the asparagus thoroughly and trim any tough ends. The true test is to break off the tougher ends. Take a piece of crumpled foil and make a pillow of it. Place in a saucepan of hot salted water and lay the asparagus with the tips resting on the foil and the stalks in the water. Cover with a lid, bring to the boil and cook for 5 minutes, or until tender. Lift out the asparagus with an egg slice and put on a clean folded tea towel or paper towel and keep warm. Meanwhile, soft-boil the eggs *(see opposite)*. Serve the asparagus alongside the soft-boiled eggs. Have salt and freshly ground pepper to hand.

BAKED EGGS IN RAMEKINS •

These eggs are cooked very gently 'au bain-marie', using a baking dish of hot water. The result should be soft and creamy without any crust. The seasonings can vary, depending on what is at hand. A little diced ham, spring onions and fresh herbs make a good base. Ovenproof ramekins are ideal.

1 or 2 slices of ham, finely diced
1 tablespoon finely chopped fresh herbs such as parsley, chervil or chives
1–2 tablespoons finely chopped spring onions
4 eggs
½ cup cream
freshly ground white pepper
butter

Preheat the oven to 180°C. Spoon a little ham, herbs and spring onions into each of 4 buttered small ramekins. Place in a baking dish quarter-filled with boiling water. Drop an egg into each ramekin and then pour cream over each. Season with pepper and top each with a nut of butter. Cover the dish with a sheet of baking paper and bake for about 8 minutes or until just set. Alternatively cook on top of the stove, covered with a lid or piece of foil until the eggs have just set. Serve immediately, sprinkled with a little salt if liked. Serves 4.

EGGS WITH SPINACH AND HOLLANDAISE • • •

1 quantity hollandaise sauce (see p. 303)
2 cups baby English spinach leaves
4 eggs
4 slices thick toast
1 ripe tomato, seeded and diced

First make the hollandaise sauce. Cover and set aside in a warm place. Stir-fry the spinach in a heavy-based frying pan, with a little water clinging to the leaves, lightly until just wilted. Set aside and keep warm. Poach the eggs over a gentle heat, until the whites are set, for 3–5 minutes (see p. 34). While the eggs are poaching, toast the bread. Gently remove the poached eggs with a slotted spoon. Place some spinach on each piece of toast, top with a poached egg and spoon hollandaise sauce over. Spoon over the tomato. Serves 4.

CRABMEAT SCRAMBLED EGGS •

½ cup crabmeat
4 eggs
½ teaspoon salt
a pinch of cayenne pepper
¼ teaspoon freshly ground black pepper
1 tablespoon chopped spring onions
60 g butter

Carefully flake the crabmeat and remove any membranes or cartilage. Beat the eggs with the salt, cayenne, black pepper and spring onions. In a small pan, melt half the butter and pour in the eggs. Raise the heat and scramble the eggs, stirring with a scraping movement until almost set. Add the crabmeat and remaining butter then fold through gently over the heat, until the crabmeat has heated through. Serve with hot buttered toast. Serves 2.

EGGS BENEDICT •••

The dish made famous at Brennan's restaurant in New Orleans.

1 quantity hollandaise sauce (see p. 303)
6 eggs
3 English muffins, halved
6 slices ham
chopped parsley, to garnish

Prepare the hollandaise sauce, cover and set aside in a warm place. Butter a frying pan and fill with enough water to cover the eggs. Bring to the boil, lower the heat to simmering and add a little salt. Break the eggs, one at a time, into a cup and gently slide into the water. Cook until the whites are firm, for 3–5 minutes. While the eggs are poaching, toast the muffins. Gently move the poached eggs with slotted spoon. Place the ham on each of the muffins, top with the poached eggs and spoon the hollandaise sauce over. Garnish with parsley, if desired. Serves 6.

HUEVOS RANCHEROS ••

Ranch-style eggs, a famous Latin American dish that makes a great weekend lunch or brunch dish. Serve 1 or 2 eggs per person.

3 tablespoons olive oil
1 small onion, chopped
1 clove garlic, crushed
1 small red capsicum, halved, seeded and shredded
2 ripe tomatoes, peeled, seeded and diced
salt and freshly ground pepper
a dash of Tabasco sauce
1 tablespoon chopped fresh coriander
4 eggs
4–8 tortillas
fresh coriander sprigs, to garnish

Heat half the oil in a frying pan and cook the onion, garlic and capsicum gently until soft. Add the tomatoes and simmer until thick. Season with the salt, pepper, Tabasco and coriander. Make 4 depressions in the sauce and break an egg first into a cup and then transfer gently into each depression. Cover the pan and cook 3–4 minutes, or until the eggs are set. Meanwhile, heat the remaining oil and fry the tortillas 30 seconds on each side, or until crisp. Place 1 or 2 tortillas on each plate. Use an egg slice to lift 1 or 2 eggs and surrounding sauce onto each tortilla, and then scatter with coriander sprigs. Serves 2–4.

EGGS TAPENADE •

A platter of delicious eggs, stuffed with robust flavours, is a favourite in France. Serve them on their own with plenty of crusty bread, followed by a green salad, or offer as an appetiser before a main meal.

125 g pitted black olives
6 anchovy fillets, drained and rinsed
3 tablespoons capers, drained
100 g tuna in oil, drained
1 lemon
⅓ cup olive oil
8 hard-boiled eggs

Crush the olives in a mortar or chop in a food processor. Add the anchovy fillets, capers, tuna and the juice of half a lemon. Pound or process until the mixture has formed a fairly smooth paste. Still pounding, or with the motor still running, add the oil in a slow, steady stream. Taste and add more lemon juice if liked. Set aside (can be made a few days ahead and stored airtight in the refrigerator).

Halve the eggs lengthwise. Mash or sieve the yolks and mix with the tapenade. Pipe or spoon into the egg whites and arrange on a serving platter. Serves 4–6.

OMELETTES

Many a good cook's reputation has been built on the ability to make an omelette. The perfect omelette must be beaten quickly, cooked in seconds and served immediately. Some claim that the traditional French omelette of 2–3 eggs should be beaten, cooked and served in 90 seconds. It can be done if the stage is set, with the eggs broken in the bowl, the filling, if any, heated and at hand and the fortunate omelette eater already sitting at the table.

BASIC OMELETTE •

Anyone who can make the basic French omelette and goes on to discover the other great omelettes, will always be able to serve a delicious meal at a moment's notice.

3 eggs
salt and freshly ground pepper
1–2 teaspoons butter
extra butter

Beat the eggs with a fork only enough to blend the yolks and whites thoroughly. Add salt and pepper, to taste. Melt the butter in an omelette pan over a moderate heat. As the butter melts and foams, tilt the pan to film the base and sides. When the foam has almost subsided and the butter starts to colour, pour in the eggs. With a fork, pull the edges of the egg mass towards the centre as it thickens. The liquid part will run into vacant spaces. Repeat until there is no more liquid, but the eggs are still very soft. Spoon on the prepared filling *(see following page)*. Lift the handle of the pan so that the omelette rolls over on to the warmed plate. Smear the top with a little extra butter to give it that professional sheen and serve immediately.

variations:
Lightly mix one of the following into the beaten eggs:

cheese: Sprinkle in ⅓ cup shredded cheese.
parsley: Mix in lightly 1 tablespoon chopped parsley.
herbs: Add 1 tablespoon chopped fresh oregano, thyme, basil, tarragon, chives, parsley or dill, in any combination.
ham: Add less salt to the eggs and mix in 2 tablespoons diced ham.

Using a fork, pull the edges of the egg mass towards the centre as it thickens. The liquid part will run into vacant spaces.

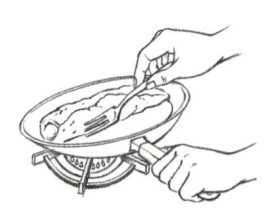

Spoon on the prepared filling and fold the omelette gently first one side towards centre then the other,

Lift the handle of the pan so that the omelette rolls over on to the warmed plate.

BASIC OMELETTE WITH HERBS

FILLINGS •

cheese: Mix ½ cup grated cheese with 1 tablespoon finely chopped parsley. Sprinkle half the mixture over the omelette before folding and the rest over the top.

crab or salmon: Slice 1 firm tomato, fry in melted butter and add a pinch of salt, pepper and sugar. Add 2 tablespoons flaked crabmeat or salmon and heat gently.

tomato and mushroom: Slice 1 tomato and 4 small mushrooms and fry in 2 teaspoons butter for 5 minutes. Add a pinch of sugar, salt, pepper and rosemary or basil if liked. Enough for 1–3 omelettes.

asparagus: Use only the tips of freshly cooked asparagus. Season lightly and heat in a little melted butter.

FLUFFY OMELETTE •

3 eggs, separated
salt and freshly ground pepper
2 teaspoons plain flour
½ cup milk or cream
30 g butter

Separate the eggs and beat the yolks with salt, pepper and flour before adding the milk or cream. Beat the egg whites stiffly and fold lightly into the yolk mixture. Heat the butter in an omelette pan, pour in the mixture and put over a low heat, until set and golden brown underneath. Brown the top under the griller, fill and fold as desired. Serves 1–2.

cheese variation: Make fluffy omelette. When top is beginning to turn golden, sprinkle with 2–3 tablespoons grated cheese. Put back under griller, until the cheese melts and browns. Fold and serve.

GOAT CHEESE, SPINACH AND TOMATO OMELETTE •

1 tomato, diced
1 handful baby English spinach leaves
15 g butter
2–3 eggs
salt and freshly ground pepper
1 tablespoon water
45 g fresh goat cheese, cubed

Cook the tomato for a minute or two in a small frying pan with the spinach leaves, in a tiny piece of the measured butter. Remove and set aside on a plate. Break the eggs into a bowl and beat lightly with a fork, just to combine the whites with the yolks. Add the seasonings and water. Melt the remaining butter in a frying pan and, when the foam has subsided, pour in the beaten eggs. Using a fork, pull the egg mixture from the edge towards the centre, allowing the uncooked mixture to run to the outside. Do this until the eggs have begun to set and the omelette is still quite soft. Scatter with the tomato and spinach and goat cheese then flip over one half of the omelette to the centre. Flip over again, if liked, to fold the omelette into a triangle. Shake the omelette on to a heated plate. Serve immediately with crusty bread or toast. Serves 1–2.

ZUCCHINI AND PEPPER FRITTATA ••

The Italian version of the Spanish tortilla (potato omelette). Serve warm or at room temperature in wedges with crusty bread.

½ cup finely chopped onion
1½ cups thinly sliced zucchini
1 red capsicum, cut into thin strips
1 green capsicum, cut into thin strips
2 tablespoons olive oil
8 large eggs
¼ cup freshly grated Parmesan cheese
2 tablespoons chopped parsley
salt and freshly ground black pepper

In a 23 cm frying pan, cook the onion, zucchini and capsicum in 1 tablespoon of the oil over a moderate heat. Stir for 8–10 minutes, or until the vegetables are tender.

In a bowl, whisk together the eggs, Parmesan and parsley. Add the vegetable mixture, season with salt and pepper and stir until combined. Clean the pan thoroughly and use to heat the remaining oil over a moderate heat, until hot but not smoking. Pour in the egg mixture, distributing the vegetables evenly, and cook the frittata, without stirring, for 6–8 minutes, or until the edge is set but the centre is still soft. Use a metal spatula to help lift underneath, check that the omelette has not caught anywhere, then invert carefully or lift onto a large warmed plate. Slide the omelette back and cook other side, adding more oil to the pan if necessary. Slide the frittata onto a serving plate and cut it into wedges to serve. Serves 6.

CHEESE OMELETTE SOUFFLÉ ••

3 eggs, separated
1 tablespoon finely grated cheese
2 teaspoons snipped chives
1 tablespoon cream
30 g butter
extra grated cheese

Preheat the oven to 190°C. Combine the egg yolks with the cheese, chives and cream in a bowl. Whip the egg whites until stiff peaks form. Pour in the yolk mixture and fold gently with a large metal spoon.

Heat the butter in an ovenproof omelette pan and pour in the mixture. Bake for 12–15 minutes, or until golden and risen. Slide out on to a heated serving dish. Fold and sprinkle with the extra cheese. Serves 1–2.

SPANISH POTATO OMELETTE •

1 onion, chopped
about 4 tablespoons olive oil for frying
2–3 potatoes, peeled and diced
6 eggs
salt and freshly ground pepper

Fry the onion gently in 1 tablespoon oil, until golden. Remove from the frying pan and set aside. Add a little more oil and fry the potatoes slowly, until tender. Add to the onion in a bowl and wipe out the pan. Beat the eggs with a few drops of water and season with salt and pepper, to taste. Stir in the cooled onion and potatoes. Heat a little more oil in the pan and pour in the egg mixture. Cook over a gentle heat until set and golden underneath. Use a metal spatula to check that the omelette has not caught. Invert carefully or lift onto a large warmed plate. Put a little more oil in the pan and slide the omelette back to cook other side. Cut into wedges to serve. Serves 3–4.

HOT SAVOURY SOUFFLÉS

There is usually the makings of a soufflé if you have fresh eggs and small leftovers of some fine flavoured dish in the refrigerator. Once you are familiar with the basic recipe, it's a simple matter to make a variety of soufflés with the addition of other flavours.

For a high soufflé, cut a double fold of baking paper to fit around the dish.

Tie with string to make secure.

The soufflé mixture is then turned into the prepared dish.

CHEESE SOUFFLÉ ••

a little soft or melted butter
2 tablespoons dried toasted breadcrumbs
1 cup milk
1 bay leaf
60 g butter
3 tablespoons plain flour
3 eggs, separated
½ cup grated Parmesan or Gruyère cheese
1–2 tablespoons cream
a pinch of grated nutmeg
1 tablespoon grated cheddar cheese

Brush a 15 cm or 5–6 cup soufflé dish with soft or melted butter and dust inside thoroughly with half the breadcrumbs. Put the milk and bay leaf in a small saucepan over a very low heat, cover and infuse for about 7 minutes.

Preheat the oven to 190°C. Melt the butter in a heavy-based saucepan, remove from the heat and blend in the flour. Cook the mixture for a minute or two, stirring well with a wooden spoon. Remove the bay leaf from the milk, cool slightly and then pour all at once onto the flour mixture. Blend thoroughly and stir constantly over a moderate heat, until boiling. Simmer 2–3 minutes and season with salt and pepper. Add the egg yolks and Parmesan or Gruyère cheese, beating after each addition. Add the cream and nutmeg, taste and adjust seasoning.

Whisk the egg whites until they stand in stiff peaks and fold gently but quickly into the mixture. Turn into the prepared soufflé dish and sprinkle with grated cheddar cheese mixed with remaining breadcrumbs. Bake for 30 minutes. A soufflé waits for no one so make sure it is served immediately. Serves 4.

note: a soufflé made with about 1½ cups sauce and 3–4 eggs in a 5–6 cup dish, will take 30 minutes to cook in the preheated oven. It will rise well above the rim of the dish. At this stage the centre will be creamy, as some people prefer. For a well-cooked soufflé, leave for a further 5 minutes in the oven. A soufflé made with 5–6 eggs requires a 7–8 cup dish and will take 40–45 minutes to cook.

CHEESE SOUFFLÉ

VARIATIONS OF CHEESE SOUFFLÉ

herb: Prepare the cheese soufflé mixture, fold in 1 tablespoon finely chopped herbs such as chives, parsley, marjoram and oregano, in any combination. Fill a prepared soufflé dish with mixture, top with cheese and breadcrumbs and bake.

mushroom: Prepare the cheese soufflé mixture then sauté 6–8 sliced mushrooms in a little butter. Half fill a prepared soufflé dish with the cheese mixture, scatter over the mushrooms, fill with the remaining mixture, top with cheese and breadcrumbs and bake.

seafood: Prepare the cheese soufflé mixture, add to a prepared soufflé dish in alternate layers with 1 cup diced prawns, crabmeat or lobster which has been tossed in 1 tablespoon butter over a high heat and flamed with 1 tablespoon warm brandy or whisky. Top with cheese and breadcrumbs and bake.

spinach and ham: Prepare the cheese soufflé mixture. Stir-fry 2 handfuls of baby English spinach leaves until just softened. Fold through the cheese soufflé mixture with ½ cup diced ham.

MACARONI CHEESE •

Great for Sunday suppers or those times that call for comfort food, this lovely cheesy macaroni is livened up with ham and crunchy golden breadcrumbs.

375 g macaroni
30 g butter
2 tablespoons plain flour
a pinch of cayenne pepper
1 teaspoon dry mustard powder
salt and freshly ground pepper
2 cups milk
100 g ham, cut into large dice (*optional*)
90 g Gruyère or tasty cheese, cubed
freshly grated Parmesan cheese
buttered breadcrumbs (*see below*)

Drop the macaroni into a large saucepan of boiling, salted water and cook for 8–10 minutes, or until tender but still with a bite. Meanwhile, melt the butter in a saucepan over a low heat. Add the flour and seasonings and cook for 1 minute. Add the milk gradually, stirring over a low heat until the sauce thickens and is creamy. Gently mix in the ham, cheese and drained macaroni and put into a buttered ovenproof dish. Scatter with the Parmesan cheese and buttered breadcrumbs and bake in a preheated 190°C oven for 15–20 minutes until golden. Serve piping hot. Serves 4.

to make buttered breadcrumbs: Make 1 cup soft breadcrumbs in a food processor, toss in 1 tablespoon melted butter or olive oil in a dry frying pan over a low heat until pale golden.

MACARONI CHEESE

QUICHE LORRAINE AND OTHER SAVOURY TARTS

A quiche is an open-faced tart with a savoury custard filling. Most widely known is quiche Lorraine, which traditionally contains only eggs, cream or milk, and bacon or ham. Other fillings may include cheese, tomatoes, onions, crabmeat, smoked salmon, mushrooms or other vegetables. Combine your chosen filling with a savoury custard, pour into the pastry shell and bake until puffed and brown.

Use a metal flan ring with fluted edges which can stand on a baking sheet. The tart will then easily slide onto a plate for serving. There should be a lot of creamy filling encased in very little pastry.

Quiches lend themselves to advance preparation. The flan ring lined with pastry may be made well ahead of time and chilled while the filling can also be prepared and stored in the refrigerator.

QUICHE LORRAINE ••

The classic quiche lorraine contains no cheese, but a few tablespoons of grated cheese can be added to the egg mixture, if desired.

3–4 rashers bacon
1 shortcrust flan case, baked blind (*see p. 300*)
2 eggs
1 teaspoon plain flour
a pinch of ground nutmeg
½ teaspoon salt
a pinch of cayenne pepper
½ cup each cream and milk

Trim the rind off the bacon and grill or fry until crisp. Cut into bite-sized pieces. Place in pastry case. Preheat the oven to 190°C.

Beat together the eggs, flour, nutmeg, salt, cayenne, cream and milk, only until combined (over-beating causes bubbles on top). Strain over the bacon and bake for 10 minutes. Reduce heat to moderate 180°C and bake a further 20 minutes, or until a knife inserted in the custard comes out clean. Serve warm. Serves 4–6.

variations:
crab: Substitute the bacon for 1 cup of flaked crabmeat and add a tablespoon of dry sherry to the custard.

spinach: Add ½ cup of chopped, well-drained cooked English spinach, omitting the bacon and adding a little grated nutmeg.

QUICHE LORRAINE

LEEK QUICHE ••

30 g butter
¼ cup water
½ teaspoon salt
1½ cups sliced leeks
2 eggs
¼–½ cup cream
½ cup milk
a pinch of ground nutmeg
a pinch of freshly ground pepper
½ cup grated Gruyère cheese
1 shortcrust flan case, baked blind
 (see p. 300)
2 teaspoons extra butter

Preheat the oven to 190°C. In a heavy-based saucepan, heat the butter and water with the salt. Add the leeks, cover and cook for 6–8 minutes, or until liquid in the pan has almost evaporated. Lower the heat and cook gently until the leeks are very soft. Cool.

Beat the eggs, cream and milk, nutmeg and pepper until just combined. Add leeks and grated cheese. Pour into the prepared flan case and dot with small pieces of the extra butter. Bake for 10 minutes. Lower the heat to 180°C and bake a further 20 minutes or until custard is set. Serves 6.

MUSHROOM QUICHE ••

1 tablespoon chopped spring onions
30 g butter
250 g button mushrooms, finely sliced
½ teaspoon salt
a squeeze of lemon juice
2 eggs
a pinch of cayenne pepper
½ cup cream and ¼–½ cup milk
1 teaspoon plain flour
1 shortcrust flan case, baked blind
 (see p. 300)
2 tablespoons grated Gruyère cheese

Preheat the oven to 190°C. Cook the onions in the butter, but do not allow to brown. Stir in the mushrooms, salt and lemon juice. Cover and cook over a gentle heat for about 8 minutes. Uncover, raise the heat and boil until the liquid evaporates. Cool. Beat the eggs, cayenne, cream, milk and flour until mixed. Gently stir in the mushroom mixture.

Pour into the prepared flan case, sprinkle with the cheese and bake for 10 minutes. Reduce the heat to 180°C and bake 20 minutes longer or until set. Serves 6.

CHEESE SNACKS

We often look to cheese when wanting a snack in a hurry. Certain types of cheese are more suited to cooking than others. The most useful varieties in the kitchen are the sharp-tasting Parmesan, the nutty Gruyère or Emmenthal and the soft melting mozzarella. Cheddar is also good as it grates easily and melts well.

WINEMAKER'S RAREBIT •
A time-honoured snack that is at its best served with a glass of chilled white wine.

1½ cups grated Gruyère cheese
¼ cup milk or cream
½ teaspoon dry mustard
salt and cayenne pepper
15 g butter
¼ cup light dry white wine
1 egg, well beaten
4 slices buttered toast

Put cheese and milk or cream into saucepan and heat gently, stirring until cheese begins to melt. Lower heat, add mustard, salt, cayenne, butter then wine and egg. Stir until mixture thickens a little but do not allow to boil. Pour over toast and serve at once. Serves 4.

CROQUE MONSIEUR •
These are fried cheese and ham sandwiches, often bought in Paris as we might buy a hamburger for a quick snack.

Allow 2 slices of bread per sandwich. Cut slices of ham and Gruyère cheese the same size. Butter one side of the bread only, lay a slice of cheese on top and spread with a little Dijon mustard, lay a slice of ham on this and top with a slice of bread. Press down well and fry in a frying pan of sizzling butter until golden on both sides. Cut into triangles to serve.

CHEESE CHARLOTTE •
Easy to make, this cheese pudding is lovely with a salad for a light meal.

90 g butter
12 x 1 cm-thick slices white bread, crusts removed
1 cup grated mature cheddar cheese
1½ cups milk
2 eggs, beaten
salt and freshly ground pepper
a pinch of dry mustard
2 tablespoons chopped fresh chives

Preheat oven to 180°C. Butter all the bread slices, cut 4 or 5 slices into 2.5 cm-wide fingers and use to line a deep, straight-sided casserole, buttered side against the casserole. Cut the remaining slices into cubes.

Make alternate layers of bread cubes and grated cheese in the casserole. Mix together the milk, eggs, mustard and chives. Add salt and pepper, to taste. Pour into the casserole and cook for 30 minutes. Serves 4.

fish

Five of the happiest years of my life were spent
in a little fishing village on the Hawkesbury River,
on the eastern coast of Australia.

It was there I got a 'nose' for fish and learnt the joys of eating
very fresh fish. It started with a local fisherman bringing me
part of his catch in exchange for the bountiful citrus fruits
that grew in my garden. I learnt to recognise quality and
freshness in fish. It is fresh when the eyes are bright, the flesh
is firm, the gills red and the scales do not come off easily.
Fish should smell of the sea!

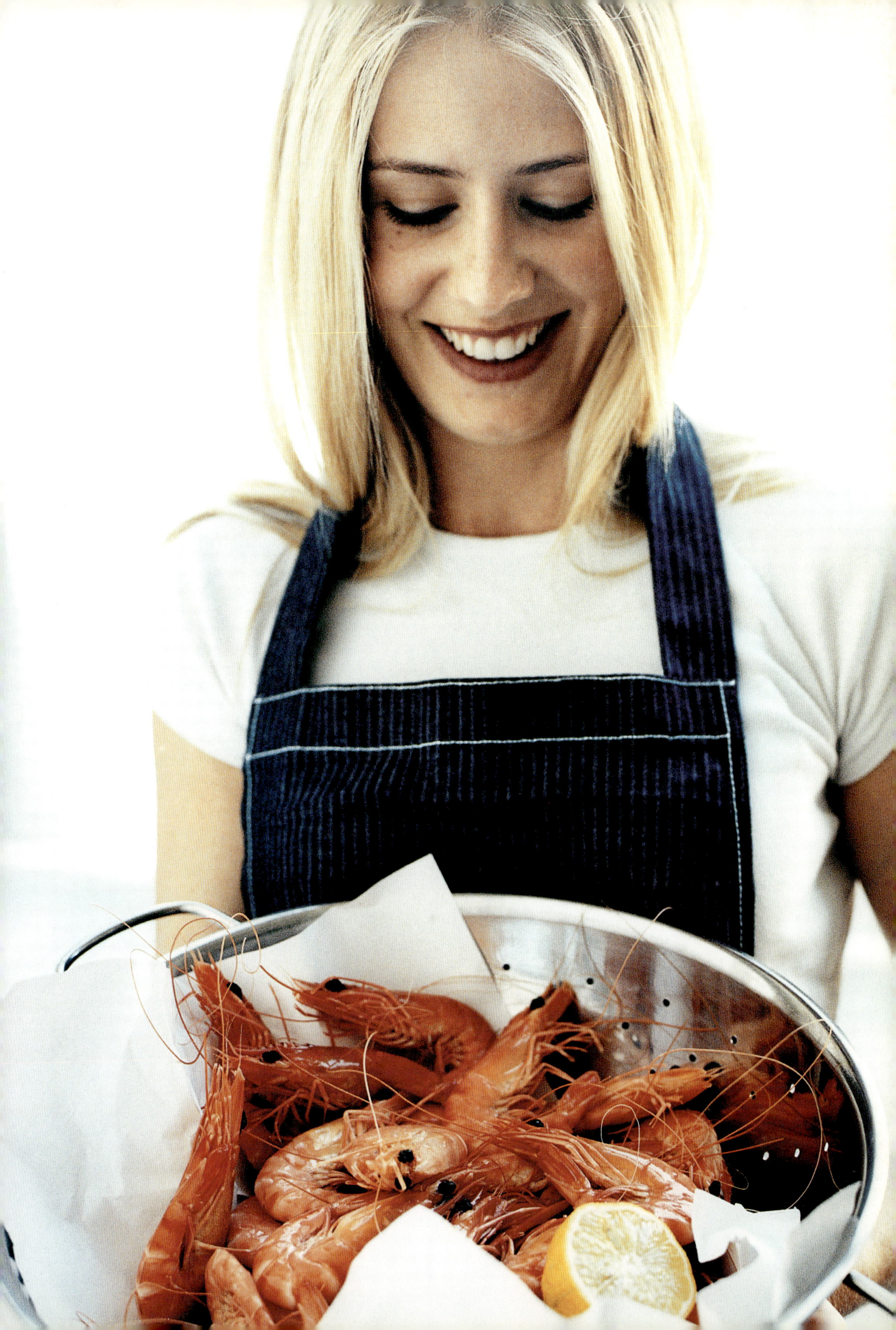

FISH

FISH IS A DELICATE MEAT AND MUST BE COOKED CAREFULLY TO PRESERVE ITS MOISTURE AND FINE FLAVOUR. TO OVERCOOK IT SEEMS A CRIME.

SOME ENJOY THEIR FISH (ESPECIALLY WHEN IT IS THE CATCH OF THE DAY) SIMPLY WITH LEMON OR SOME MELTED BUTTER, BUT THERE ARE MANY OTHER WAYS OF SERVING IT. HOLLANDAISE SAUCE IS GREAT WITH POACHED FISH, SAUCE TARTARE PARTNERS CRISP FRIED FISH AND WHAT COULD BE NICER THAN A THICK GRILLED FISH STEAK TOPPED WITH MELTING PARSLEY BUTTER?

When preparing mussels, remove the beard (actually the byssal threads with which they use to attach themselves to a solid surface) from the mussel with a sharp tug downwards towards the point. Wash the mussels in several changes of cold water and they're now ready for cooking. (For mussel recipes, see p. 62).

TO PREPARE FISH

filleting: For round fish such as flathead, use a sharp, flexible knife to make a clean cut along the backbone from the back of the head to the tail. Carefully ease away the flesh from the bones and detach the fillet on one side. Turn over and cut away the second fillet. For flat fish such as flounder, lay the fish on a board with the tail towards you. Make a cut down the backbone from the head to the tail. Starting from the head on the left fillet and using a sharp, flexible knife, cut between the bones and the flesh and remove the fillet. Turn the fish over and remove the second fillet working from tail to head. Repeat in the same way for the other two fillets.

skinning: To skin, place fillets skin-side down, tail towards you, and cut the flesh from the skin at the tail tip. Dip your fingers in salt and hold skin firmly. Slide knife along skin under fish until fillet and skin are separated. Trim fillets, wash and dry on a paper towel. Drying is most important for a perfect result.

TO DEEP-FRY FISH

As a world-wide favourite, it would be hard to find any meal more popular than fish and chips. Frying is suitable for fish fillets, and small whole fish such as whitebait.

coatings:
- **milk and seasoned flour.**
- **a preliminary dusting with flour, a dip in beaten egg and then dry white breadcrumbs.**
- **fritter batter.**

The temperature of cooking oil or fat is most important. It must be hot enough to seal the coating in order to preserve the flavour and natural moisture of the fish. >

FISH AND CHIPS

To test for correct heat put a small piece of white bread into the heated oil and wait for bubbles to sizzle around it. The bread should brown in 1 minute. The oil should be quite still.

Use about 2 cm depth of oil in a roomy frying pan and do not crowd in too many fillets at one time. Allow 2–4 minutes for each side depending on the thickness of the fish. Drain on paper towels and keep hot. Serve with lemon wedges and French-fried potatoes. Tartare sauce is delicious with crisp deep-fried fish *(see p. 307)*.

FRITTER BATTER •

1 cup plain flour
a pinch of salt
2 eggs, beaten lightly
1 cup beer or soda water

Sift flour and salt into a bowl, make a well in the centre and pour in eggs and beer or soda water. Stir flour in gradually and beat to a smooth batter. Stand for an hour before using if possible.

note: self-raising flour can be used and it gives a particularly light batter that many love.

TO BAKE FISH

This method is excellent for whole fish, fish steaks or fillets. The prepared fish is placed in a baking dish, brushed with melted butter or oil, seasoned with pepper, salt and a squeeze of lemon juice for flavour then sprinkled with paprika for colour.

The fish can be covered with baking paper, but remember to baste once or twice during cooking to prevent drying out. Bake until tender. This will depend on the thickness of the fish, not on the weight. Times vary from 10 minutes for thin fillets to 30 minutes for a large thick fish.

Less delicate fish can be marinated before grilling or baking.

TO POACH FISH

Fish should never be boiled but poached gently until tender. This can be done on top of the stove or in the oven. The cooking liquid may vary from salt and water for a simple dish, to a court bouillon for a more elaborate and fully flavoured one. Poaching is suitable for whole fish, fish steaks, fillets or shellfish.

To test if the fish is cooked, pierce with a fork at the thickest part. The flesh should flake easily. Allow 6–10 minutes for every 500 g.

COURT BOUILLON •

2½ cups water with 1 tablespoon vinegar or
1 cup white wine with 1½ cups water
4 peppercorns
1 onion
2 slices carrot
1 stalk of celery
1 bay leaf
1 teaspoon salt
2 stalks of parsley
a sprig of dill (optional)

Bring the ingredients to the boil in a medium saucepan. Lower heat and simmer for 15 minutes. Strain and use liquid for poaching fish, or put fish in the cold liquid, add remaining ingredients and simmer until cooked.

TO GRILL FISH

This method is simple and is excellent for whole fillets or steaks. Preheat the griller. Butter or oil the griller rack or line with buttered foil. Wipe fish with paper towels. Dust with flour and brush with melted butter or oil and season with sea salt and pepper. Grill until lightly browned. If you have preheated the grill, it is not necessary to turn the fish while grilling. If thin, the fish will be completely cooked when brown. For thick fish, reduce heat and cook until the fish flakes easily when tested with a fork. Baste frequently with the melted butter and the juices in the pan to prevent the surface of the fish drying out. Sprinkle with parsley and serve at once with lemon wedges.

TO PAN-FRY OR SEAR FISH

Heat a well-seasoned or non-stick frying pan until very hot, then add a little oil or butter. Fry the thinner fillets for 2–3 minutes on each side and thicker cuts for 4–5 minutes on each side.

To pan-fry steaks and fish cutlets such as tuna or salmon, heat the frying pan until very hot. Brush fish with olive oil and season with a little pepper. Fry, skin-side down first, for 3–5 minutes on each side.

FISH À LA MEUNIERE •

This is an excellent and simple way of cooking delicate fish. The cooking is gentle, and the fat used is clarified butter or half oil and half butter, so that no residue gathers in the pan to burn or discolour the flesh.

6 fish fillets
plain flour seasoned with salt and pepper
clarified butter or half oil and half butter
extra 1 tablespoon butter
juice of 1 lemon
1 tablespoon chopped parsley
lemon slices, to garnish

Dust the fish lightly with seasoned flour. Use enough butter or oil and butter mixture to cover the base of the frying pan. Melt slowly and do not allow to colour. When butter is hot, place fish in it and cook first one side to a delicate brown for about 2–3 minutes, then turn and cook other side.

Arrange on a serving plate and keep warm. Add extra butter to pan and, while foaming, add the strained lemon juice and the parsley. Pour immediately over fish and serve at once. Sliced lemon is the classic garnish for this dish.
Serves 4.

FISH FLORENTINE •

The word 'Florentine' with food usually means the dish includes English spinach. This dish has no spinach but is a classic way of cooking fish fillets in Florence. Have the fish, seasoned flour and beaten egg all at the ready and the vegetables you plan to serve prepared. Cook the fish at the very last moment. Fish cooks much quicker than many of us realise. An average steak about 2cm thick cooks in 8 minutes. A thinner fillet will be cooked in 4–5 minutes, depending on thickness.

750 g fish fillets, boned and skinned
plain flour seasoned with salt and pepper
1 egg, beaten
light olive oil, for frying

Wash the fillets and dry with paper towels. Dip them into the seasoned flour, for a light coating, then in the beaten egg and again in the flour.

Heat a small amount of the oil in a heavy-based frying pan and cook the fish gently for about 3–4 minutes on each side, until golden brown. Drain on paper towels. Serve with steamed potatoes and lemon wedges or tartare sauce (see p.307). Serves 4–6.

GRILLED SALMON WITH MANGO SALAD ••

This is a lovely dish for warm weather entertaining.

4 thick salmon fillets
1 small onion, finely sliced
2 cloves garlic, peeled and finely chopped
1 red bird's eye chilli, seeded and finely chopped
2.5 cm piece ginger, grated
1 tablespoon fish sauce
1 tablespoon white wine vinegar
1 tablespoon sweet chilli sauce
2 tablespoons vegetable oil
½ cup water

to serve:
1 mango, peeled and cut into thin strips
1 teaspoon lime juice
mixed salad greens
125 g snow peas, blanched, and refreshed

Rinse the salmon very lightly and pat dry with paper towels. In a mixing bowl, add the onion, garlic, chilli, ginger, fish sauce, vinegar and sweet chilli sauce. Add the salmon fillets and allow to marinate for 1 hour.

Meanwhile, place mango strips in a small bowl with the lime juice and marinate for 30 minutes. Heat a grill until hot, then brush the rack or pan with oil. When hot but not smoking, add the fish, reserving marinade and cook for about 6 minutes, turning once. Remove the fish and keep warm. Add the water and marinade to a small saucepan and boil a few minutes to form a sauce. To serve, peel away the skin and cut the fillets in half. Arrange on plates piled with salad greens. Spoon over the sauce and strew with snow peas. Serves 4.

STEAMED FISH WITH CORIANDER ••

Aromatic oils and seasonings are heated and poured piping hot over steamed fish.

1 whole fish weighing about 1.5 kg, cleaned
salt
3 spring onions, sliced
4 x 4 cm-long slices fresh ginger, peeled
roots and stems of 1 bunch fresh coriander, washed thoroughly
2 cups water

garnish:
4 spring onions
2 cm piece fresh ginger, peeled and finely shredded
½ cup fresh coriander leaves
1 tablespoon sesame oil
2 tablespoons peanut oil
2 teaspoons light soy sauce

Slash the fish two or three times in the thickest part of each side and lightly salt inside and out. Place half the spring onions, ginger and coriander roots and stalks in cavity. Lay the fish on a roasting rack in a flameproof baking dish. Scatter remaining spring onions, ginger and coriander on top. Pour in the water. Cover loosely with foil. Over a moderate heat, steam for 15 minutes, or until the flesh is opaque and flakes easily when tested with a skewer.

To prepare garnish, wash and trim the spring onions, leaving 2 cm of the green tops with the white parts. Cut each spring onion into 3–4 cm lengths, then shred each length finely. Shred the ginger into similar-sized strips. Set aside with the coriander leaves.

To finish, remove the steamed fish to a heated serving platter and scatter with the garnish. In a small frying pan, heat the oils and pour when sizzling over the fish. Garnish and sprinkle with soy sauce. Serve immediately. *Serves 4.*

BAKED FISH FILLETS WITH PINE NUT CRUST ••

3 tablespoons pine nuts
½ cup dry breadcrumbs
¼ cup black olives, pitted and finely chopped
2 spring onions, finely chopped
½ teaspoon dried tarragon
3 tablespoons olive oil
salt
4 blue-eye fillets (or other white fish)
juice of 1 lemon
¼ cup dry white wine
½ red onion, sliced
250 g baby English spinach leaves
1 cup peeled, seeded and diced tomatoes

Chop pine nuts fairly finely and mix with the breadcrumbs. Combine the olives, spring onions and tarragon in a bowl and stir in 2 tablespoons olive oil to make a spreadable paste. Season with salt to taste.

Preheat oven to 220°C. Lightly oil a baking dish just large enough to hold the fish. Spread one side of each fillet with about 2 teaspoons of the olive paste and lightly press a quarter of the crumb mixture on top. Place fish in baking dish crumb-side up and carefully pour the lemon juice and wine around the fish. Bake for 6–10 minutes depending on the variety and thickness of the fish.

While the fish is baking, heat remaining olive oil in a large frying pan and sauté onion until soft. Add the spinach and tomatoes and cook until the spinach wilts. Season to taste and arrange on warm plates. Top with fillets of baked fish. *Serves 4.*

SEARED TUNA SALAD ••

4 tuna steaks
¼ cup plain flour seasoned with salt and pepper
1 tablespoon olive oil
125 g green beans, topped and tailed
8 cherry tomatoes, halved
1 small red onion, halved and sliced
1 soft lettuce such as green or red oak leaf, cos leaves or radicchio
6–8 black olives

dressing:
juice of 1 lemon
1 tablespoons Dijon mustard
1 clove garlic, crushed
¼ cup olive oil
salt and freshly ground black pepper

Lightly dust the tuna steaks with the seasoned flour. Heat the olive oil in a frying pan and fry the tuna until lightly browned on the outside but still pink in the middle. Break or slice the flesh into bite-size pieces.

Drop the green beans into a little salted boiling water and cook until tender-crisp. Drain immediately and refresh under cold water. Combine the beans with the tomatoes, salad onion and tuna and lightly toss. Wash and dry the lettuce leaves well and arrange on 4 serving plates. Pile the tuna and beans mixture over the leaves. Scatter over the olives and drizzle the salad with the dressing.

to make the dressing: Mix the lemon juice, mustard and garlic in a small bowl. Gradually beat in the olive oil slowly to ensure dressing remains thick and amalgamated. Season to taste with salt and a good grinding of pepper. Serves 4.

BAKED STUFFED WHOLE FISH ••

¼ cup olive oil
2 spring onions, finely chopped
1 large tomato, peeled and diced
2 cups breadcrumbs
½ cup pitted black olives, roughly chopped
½ cup chopped parsley
¼ cup pine nuts *(optional)*
1 whole fish (1.5–2kg) such as jewfish, snapper or barramundi, scaled and gutted
1–2 teaspoons flaked sea salt
1 red onion, sliced
1–2 bay leaves
a few sprigs of fresh thyme

Preheat the oven to 220°C. Heat the oil, reserving a tablespoon for later, in a frying pan and sauté the spring onions gently for a few minutes until softened and beginning to colour. Add the tomatoes, cook another minute then remove from heat. Stir in the breadcrumbs, olives, parsley and pine nuts.

Pat the fish dry with paper towels and fill cavity with the breadcrumb mixture. Press into a neat shape. Put in a large oiled baking dish, placing any leftover stuffing under the fish. Rub a little sea salt over the fish and scatter with the red onion and herbs. Drizzle with a little extra oil. Bake for 30–35 minutes or until just tender. Serves 4–6.

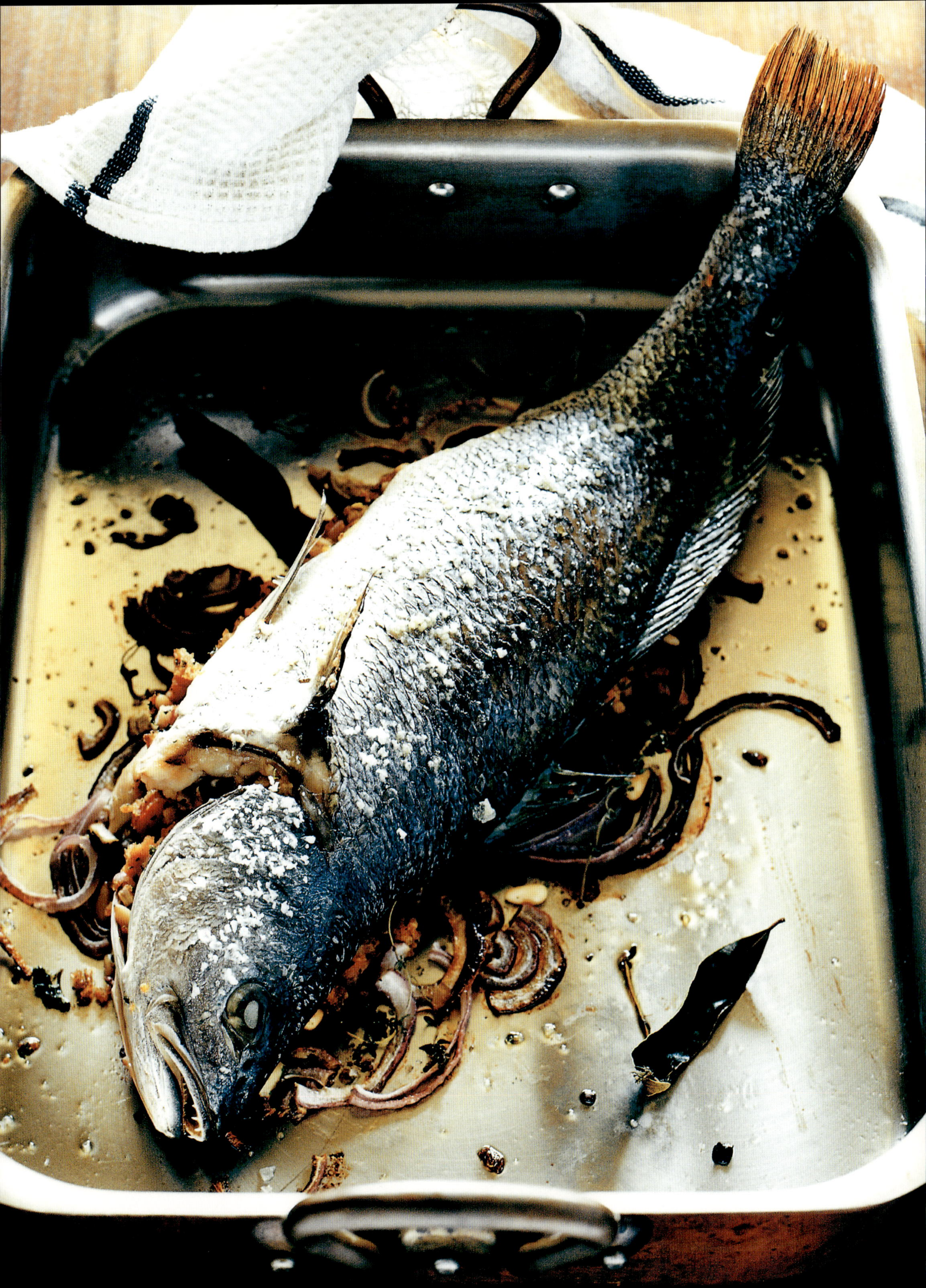

SHELLFISH

Shellfish add a note of luxury to a meal and are readily available. I've included some of the best-loved ways of serving them.

CRAB

The blue swimmer is one of the smallest and best crabs to eat. It is also called sand or blue manna crab. The long legs, paddles and claws are cobalt blue, hence the name, but its colour changes to a deep orange red when cooked. Queensland mud crab is a world famous delicacy with its huge claws and large, bulky body. Use frozen crab when fresh is not in season.

to prepare crab: Place crabs on a board near sink. Grasp live crab from the rear with a good hold on the back and place with back on board. Put point of knife in shell between eyes. Hit the back of the knife with a hard, quick blow which kills the crab instantly. Firmly grasping hold of a front claw, twist off where it joins the body, repeat with the other claw and legs. Scrub and rinse well. Pull off the top shell with knife, if necessary. Remove gills and spongy parts under shell. Wash body and leg pieces thoroughly. Crack each claw with a mallet to open each section and make it easy to lift out all the meat.

CRAB CAKES ••

2 slices bread, crusts removed
 milk, to cover
500 g crabmeat
1 tablespoon mayonnaise
½ teaspoon salt
1 tablespoon Worcestershire sauce
1 tablespoon baking powder
1 tablespoon chopped parsley
flour, for dusting
light olive oil, for frying

Soak the bread in milk to cover for 15 minutes. With a hand, squeeze out excess milk gently and place bread in a bowl with the crabmeat, mayonnaise, salt, Worcestershire, baking powder and parsley. Work into a combined mixture. Using slightly wet hands, shape mixture into small cakes, dust with flour and fry in light olive oil on each side until golden. Drain on paper towels. Serve as soon as possible and offer with lemon wedges. Makes 8–12 cakes, depending on size. Serves 4.

DEVILLED CRAB ••

4 spring onions, chopped
60 g butter
1 tablespoon brandy
4 tablespoons cream
4 tablespoons breadcrumbs
1 teaspoon Dijon mustard
1 teaspoon Worcestershire sauce
1 teaspoon anchovy essence
½ teaspoon salt
a pinch of cayenne pepper
500 g crabmeat

Preheat the oven to 200°C. Sauté spring onions in butter until soft. Remove from heat, add brandy, cream, breadcrumbs and seasonings. Mix well and add flaked crabmeat. Put into greased ramekins, sprinkle with breadcrumbs and dot with butter. Bake for 5 minutes or under grill until lightly browned and heated through. Serves 2-4.

CRAYFISH (LOBSTER)

The Australian rock lobster (spiny lobster or crayfish) with its long antennae is one of the delights of the crustacean world. The meat, most of which is found in the tail, is sweet, firm-textured and very white when cooked.

Wrap live crayfish in newspaper and chill in refrigerator for a hour or so. This numbs the nerves. Place the chilled crayfish shell-side up on several layers of newspaper. Hold securely with a large pointed knife and pierce through shell at the head and between the eyes to kill. Plunge into boiling, salted water and simmer for 15 minutes per 500 g and cool in the liquid.

Drain, wipe the shell and rub with a little olive oil. Cut in half lengthwise with a meat cleaver and remove the 'stomach' in the head. The small claws can be used as a garnish or, if time permits, the sweet flesh can be pushed out with a skewer.

CRAYFISH (LOBSTER) MAYONNAISE •

1 crayfish, cooked
1 lettuce heart, quartered, or watercress
1 Lebanese cucumber, peeled and sliced
lemon wedges
⅔ cup mayonnaise (see p. 306)

Cut the crayfish in half lengthwise. Lift out the flesh from each half and cut in thick slices. Replace in the opposite half-shell. Serve on a plate with lettuce heart quarters, cucumber slices and lemon wedges. Serve the mayonnaise separately. Serves 2.

CRAYFISH (LOBSTER) MORNAY ••

Prepare cooked crayfish in shell as before, coat with mornay sauce (see p. 302), sprinkle with cheese and place under grill until browned and heated through. Lightly poached scallops can be treated the same way using scallop shells or ramekins.

CRAYFISH (LOBSTER) THERMIDOR ••

1 crayfish, cooked
30 g butter
2 tablespoons plain flour
1¼ cups milk
1 tablespoon tomato paste
1 teaspoon salt
1 teaspoon sugar
a dash of Tabasco
⅓ cup cream
1 tablespoon brandy
2 tablespoons grated Gruyére cheese
½ teaspoon ground paprika

Cut the crayfish in half lengthwise and remove the legs and tail meat. Cut tail meat into neat pieces and set aside. Discard head and trim half-shells. Set shells aside with the legs. In a frying pan melt the butter, add the flour and cook for a few minutes without browning. Add milk and stir over a gentle heat until smooth and thickened. Add tomato paste, salt, sugar and Tabasco and simmer for 10 minutes. Stir in crayfish flesh, cream and brandy. Keep hot but do not boil. Fill the half-shells with crayfish mixture. Sprinkle cheese and paprika over and place under grill or in a 190°C oven until brown. Garnish with reserved legs. Serves 2.

MUSSELS

It is worthwhile making an effort to pick over mussels at the markets to find small to medium ones that feel heavy for their size. The essential rule is they must be alive. Live mussels hold their shells together so tightly it is difficult to pry them apart. Discard any with open shells.

to prepare and clean mussels: Thoroughly scrub mussels to remove any seaweed or dirt clinging to them. Pull off the beard that clings to them *(see p. 52)*. Soak them in water to thoroughly cover, preferably for 3–4 hours, with a good handful of oatmeal added to encourage the mussels to disgorge any sand.

MUSSELS POULETTE ••

2 kg mussels, prepared and cleaned
6 spring onions, finely chopped
4 sprigs of parsley
1 bay leaf
a sprig of fresh thyme
freshly ground black pepper
1 cup dry white wine
2 egg yolks
½ cup cream
½ cup chopped parsley

Prepare and clean the mussels, *(see illustration p. 52)*. Put mussels into a wide saucepan with spring onions, herbs, pepper and the wine. Cover and cook over a high heat for 5 minutes, shaking the pan now and then.

Remove the mussels as soon as they open, discarding half of each shell, and pull off any beard. Arrange mussels on the remaining shells on warm soup plates. Strain the cooking liquid and measure 1½ cups, making up with water if necessary.

Beat egg yolks and cream together and place in a small saucepan. Add measured cooking liquid and whisk over moderate heat to thicken slightly. Add the parsley. Pour over the mussels and serve at once with crusty bread. Serves 4.

mussels pernod: Spike the sauce with a tablespoon or two of Pernod before pouring over mussels.

OYSTERS

There are many varieties of oysters available though rock oysters are one of the most highly regarded by connoisseurs. Select on the half-shell from reliable suppliers. They should be plump, creamy and smell of the sea.

OYSTERS AU NATUREL • *(see p. 6)*

OYSTERS CATALINA •

oysters on the half-shell
cayenne pepper
cocktail sauce *(see p. 6)*
lemon wedges, to garnish

Sprinkle oysters with cayenne pepper. Place a small bowl of cocktail sauce on a plate of ice and surround with the prepared oysters. Garnish with lemon wedges and serve with buttered brown bread sandwiches.

OYSTERS MORNAY •

24 oysters on the half-shell
1¼ cups mornay sauce *(see p. 302)*
¼ cup grated Parmesan cheese

Remove oysters from shells and set aside. Place a little sauce on each shell, return oysters and cover with remaining sauce. Sprinkle with cheese and place under grill until lightly browned. Serve at once. Serves 4.

MUSSELS POULETTE

PRAWNS

Prawns are a delicacy enjoyed all over the world. Cooked prawns are used in salad recipes but when cooking it is best to use fresh green (raw) prawns. The delicate flesh of prawns does not stand up to being cooked twice.

FRIED PRAWNS •

500 g shelled green (raw) prawns
salt and freshly ground pepper
a dash of Tabasco sauce
fritter batter (see p. 54)
oil, for frying

Devein prawns. Season with salt, pepper and a dash of Tabasco. Dip prawns in batter and drop separately into hot oil. Cook only a few at a time. When golden, drain and serve very hot with lemon wedges. Serves 3–4.

SEAFOOD COCKTAIL •

A favourite first course for dinner parties. (see p. 6)

SKEWERED SEAFOODS •

This versatile recipe may be served as a first course. As a main course, serve with hot buttered rice. It is also good for barbecues and cooks successfully over hot coals.

500 g scallops
500 g shelled green (raw) prawns
lemon wedges for serving

marinade:
¼ cup olive oil
¼ cup dry sherry
1 teaspoon grated fresh ginger
2 cloves garlic, crushed
1 teaspoon salt
freshly ground pepper
4 spring onions, finely chopped

Devein prawns, remove any dark portions of scallops, but leave coral intact. Combine marinade ingredients. Place seafood in a bowl and pour over marinade. Cover and leave at least 1 hour. Drain, reserving marinade. Thread scallops and prawns alternately on skewers. Put under preheated grill, brushing frequently with marinade until lightly browned and cooked. Serve with lemon wedges. Serves 4–6.

SHELLFISH THERMIDOR • •

Prawns, crabmeat and scallops are delicious served in a thermidor sauce. Allow 375 g prepared shellfish to serve 2. (See crayfish thermidor, p. 61)

SCALLOPS

Scallops need only 2–3 minutes cooking time. The bright orange coral is considered a delicacy, so do not discard it. The small tough white membrane containing a dark vein however, should be removed. Any of the recipes for lobster, crab or prawn may be used for scallops. They are particularly good in a light curry sauce.

SCALLOPS PROVENÇAL (see p. 8)

FRIED SCALLOPS •

250 g scallops
1 teaspoon salt
1 tablespoon plain flour
30 g butter

Wash and dry scallops well. Mix flour and salt and roll scallops in seasoned flour. Melt butter in a heavy frying pan, add scallops and fry very gently until golden. Serve with hollandaise (page p. 303) or tartare sauce (p.307). Serves 1–2.

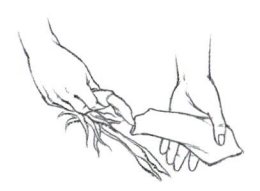

Pull the head with the tentacles from the tube of the squid at the same time pulling out the intestines.

Cut away the tentacles in 1 piece just above the eyes. Discard the head and intestines.

Pull the translucent quill from the tube of the squid and discard. Cut the tube into rings or squares, or if small, leave whole.

SQUID (CALAMARI)

Squid is one of the most sustainable seafoods we can eat.

cleaning squid: Pull the head and body of the squid apart, the intestines will pull out with the head. Discard head and intestines. Cut off tentacles just above the eyes and remove the transparent quill from inside the body sac. Rinse the sac well and pull off the back fins. Reserve tentacles, sac and fins and use as recipe directs.

BABY SQUID WITH GARLIC •

1 kg prepared baby squid
¼ cup olive oil
2 cloves garlic, smashed (not crushed)
salt and freshly ground pepper
½ cup chopped parsley
juice of ½ lemon

Cut the prepared squid into rings or lengthwise into quarters. Retain the tentacles. Heat the olive oil with the garlic gently until it begins to colour, then discard garlic. Add pieces of squid, season with salt and pepper and cook over brisk heat for 1–2 minutes. Sprinkle with parsley and lemon juice and serve very hot with crusty bread. Serves 4.

SALT AND PEPPER CALAMARI ••

Keep calamari tubes each wrapped individually in the freezer. Take them out and thaw them only slightly so that they are still solid enough to cut into very thin rings. This thinness makes all the difference.

500 g squid (calamari) tubes
1 cup plain flour
½ teaspoon sea salt
2–4 cups light olive oil
3 cups baby rocket leaves, washed and dried
freshly ground pepper

Cut the squid into thin rings. Dry thoroughly using paper towels. Place the flour in a large bowl with salt. Toss the calamari in the flour and remove, shaking off excess flour. Set aside. Pile the rocket leaves in the centre of plate. Heat a deep frying pan with the oil and fry the calamari rings in several lots until they begin to turn golden. Remove and drain on paper towels. Season with salt and pepper and pile on top of the rocket leaves. Serve with lemon wedges. Serves 4.

CLAMS

Clams are saltwater bivalves and are available fresh all the year round; they can also be bought canned or bottled in a brine. Soak fresh clams in plenty of water to cover to encourage them to disgorge as much sand as possible. They are opened much like mussels or oysters – with a flat knife inserted between the 2 shells in front of the muscle that holds them together; then they are dipped in water to remove sand. They may also be steamed open. Clams are a great addition to risotto and chowders or they can be simmered in a thick tomato sauce for serving with crusty bread or pasta. Italians love tiny clams (which they call vongole) as a sauce with pasta.

SPAGHETTI WITH CLAMS ● ●

1.5 kg clams
1 cup white wine
5 small ripe tomatoes,
   cut into large dice
½ small chilli, seeded and finely sliced
1 large clove garlic, finely chopped
2 tablespoons extra virgin olive oil
¼ cup chopped parsley
salt and freshly ground pepper
375 g spaghetti

Wash the clams thoroughly in several changes of water. Discard any that do not shut when tapped. Soak them in cold water for 1 hour, then drain them to remove the sand, rinsing them thoroughly again. Heat the wine in a large saucepan. Add one-third of the clams, cover and cook until all are open. Make sure you shake the pan to mix the clams several times during cooking. Repeat with remaining clams in 2 more lots. When cool enough to handle, remove the clams from the shells, leaving just a handful intact for the garnish. Discard the shells, reserving the flesh.

Meanwhile, combine the tomatoes, chilli and garlic in a bowl with the olive oil. Add the clams and season well with salt and pepper. Stir in the parsley. Boil the spaghetti in a large saucepan of boiling, salted water until done to the bite, al dente. Drain thoroughly, return to the saucepan and toss with the clam sauce over a moderate heat, until heated through. Serves 4–6.

FRESH CLAM CHOWDER ● ●

4 rashers bacon, diced
2 medium onions, finely chopped
2 stalks celery, diced
1 large carrot, peeled and diced
1 leek, washed thoroughly and diced
½ bay leaf
2 tablespoons plain flour
6 cups hot fish stock or water
2 medium potatoes, peeled and diced
1.5 kg clams, soaked in water
   to cover to disgorge sand
500g skinned fish fillets such as
   blue eye or snapper, cut into chunks
¼ cup cream
sea salt and freshly ground pepper
1 tablespoon chopped dill or parsley

In a large saucepan sauté the bacon, onions, celery, carrot, leek and bay leaf. Cook stirring, until the vegetables are soft, about 5–7 minutes. Stir in the flour and cook for 1 minute. Add the stock and cook, stirring until the liquid thickens. Add the potatoes and simmer for 15 minutes, until tender. Drain the clams, rinse and add to the chowder. Simmer until the shells open, 1–2 minutes. Add the fish and simmer until tender. Discard the bay leaf. Add the cream and season to taste. Sprinkle with dill or parsley and serve. Serves 8.

SPAGHETTI WITH CLAMS

poultry

My mother's Sunday dinner was invariably one of two things —
rare roast beef or a roast chicken, big and fat and crisp and brown.
There were no fancy trimmings and no surprise stuffings,
but we used the best china and sat down to dinner in our best Sunday clothes.
The whole house took on a special atmosphere.

For 18 years this was the cosy pattern of our household and it might have continued
had not my sister Jean gone to live in Italy, France and other 'foreign parts'.
She returned to live with us when the Second World War broke out and she was now a
sophisticate. We soon learned that the French *poulet*, the Spanish and Italian *pollo*, the
Indian *murgh* and the Chinese *gai* all meant chicken, and chicken began to appear on
the Sunday table in completely new guises.

The plump familiar shape had sometimes a garland of unfamiliar vegetables,
sometimes the shape wasn't there at all. Chicken sautéed the French way,
cut up before cooking and served with a creamy sauce, exotic seasonings and
a lacing of wine was soon accepted by the whole family
for one reason — it tasted so good.

Poultry is no longer a special occasion dish and it's natural that the prices
have come down with mass production. Something of the old-fashioned flavour of
poultry has been lost, which has brought about a new approach to cooking methods.
The cook has to put the flavour back into the bird.

I like to buy free-range poultry, even better if it is organic.
I believe a bird that has spent time scratching around and pecking the ground will
taste as it should and has also had some sort of life. Such a bird you pay extra for,
but I would prefer to eat chicken less often and make the meal more special.

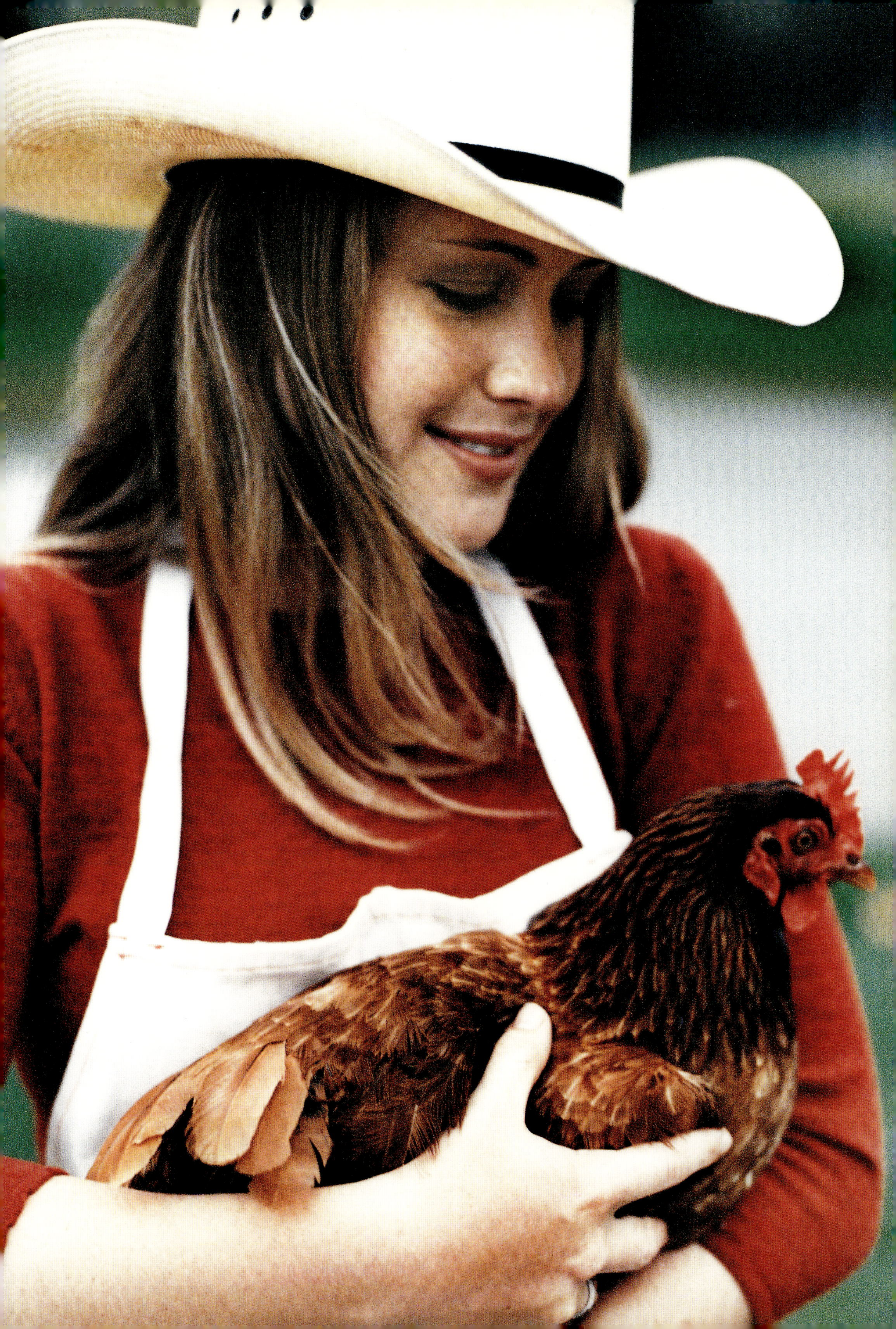

CHICKEN

Chicken is always best when fresh but is often sold frozen. The weight is clearly marked and is also classified by numbers with the metric weight. Organic chickens are best. Look for Enviroganic, just one of the many good organic chickens available.

what size to buy:

450–500 g
These are perfect for splitting and grilling or roasting whole. Serve 1.

750 g – 1 kg (size 10)
May be grilled or roasted and will serve 2. May also be split for the barbecue or grill.

1 – 1.25 kg (size 12)
The perfect size for sautéed dishes. Will serve 3–4. Buy 2 birds for serving 6.

1.5 – 2 kg (size 15–20)
For roasting or to joint and use in sauté dishes. Serves 4–6.

TO JOINT OR CARVE A CHICKEN

- Place the bird on a board with the neck end facing you. Using a sharp knife and holding the bird firmly with one hand, cut the skin around the leg with the knife against the carcass and press the leg joint gently outwards to expose the joint. Cut through and slip the point of the knife under the back to release the 'oyster' with the thigh meat. You should now have a maryland, which can be cut in half to make a drumstick and a thigh. The 'parson's nose' can be cut from the thigh. Repeat with the other leg.

- To cut the wing joints with some breast meat attached, make a cut into the breast running parallel with the wishbone. Pull the wing away from the carcass and cut against the ribs until you reach the ball joint. Now cut through the joint and detach.

- Cut through the centre of the breastbone then cut away each side of the breast. If carving, you may like to carve the breast.

- Trim the joints, removing any excess fat and scraggly skin on bones. Keep back and neck to use later for stock.

Cut the skin between the leg and breast of each side. Twist legs briskly to break the joints then cut away each leg together with the thigh (marylands).

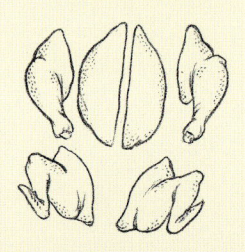

Keeping breast-side up, imagine the breast as an elongated diamond taking some of the breast meat for each wing joint. Use scissors or a sharp knife to remove these from the rib cage. Cut the remaining breast into two sections. This gives 6 good-sized portions.

buying chicken pieces:
breast: Sold either halved, boned and skinned or left whole with bone and skin attached. Boned half breasts can also be cut with the wing attached. True chicken breast fillets are the long thin pieces of meat that lie beneath either side of the breast. Ideal for grilling, baking or pan-frying, it can also be poached and served with a sauce or used for salads. Take care not to overcook the breast as it is less fatty than other parts of the chicken and can quickly become dry.

drumsticks: Fry, grill or barbecue. Good for a crowd, roasted in the oven.
chicken marylands: Includes thigh and drumstick. Fry, grill or roast, or make chicken casseroles.
wings, necks and giblets: Also sometimes sold as a soup pack, good for flavoursome soups or stock.
chicken livers: Make a pâté, sauté in butter, wrap in bacon and grill, or add to a spinach salad. Before using in any recipe, cut away tubes and any discoloured spots with a sharp knife.

FRENCH ROAST CHICKEN

1 size 18 (1.8 kg) chicken
60 g butter
salt and freshly ground pepper
a good pinch of dried tarragon or fresh parsley stalks
a few strips of orange or lemon rind
2 cups chicken stock

Cut a long piece of string and loop the centre under the tail end and around the knuckles. Tie a knot to secure the legs.

Pull the string along both sides towards the wings. Pull string tightly over the wings and turn the chicken over.

Bring the string around the wings and tie the ends together to secure the bird into a neat shape.

Preheat the oven to 190°C. Wipe the cavity of the chicken with a paper towel. Remove excess fat. Place a little butter, a little salt and pepper, tarragon or parsley stalks and strips of orange or lemon rind inside chicken cavity. Truss with string (see illustration).

Wipe outside of bird, spread with remaining butter and place breast-side up in a small baking dish, preferably on a rack. Pour 1 cup of water in with ½ cup of the stock and place in the oven for 10 minutes, basting once or twice with the liquid underneath. Turn on side and baste well with stock. Continue to cook for a further 20 minutes, basting and adding more stock as necessary. Turn chicken to other side and cook, basting for a further 20 minutes.

Turn bird on its back a further 15 minutes or so to brown the breast. There should be just enough stock to keep the juice in the dish from scorching, if not add more water. To test, run a fine skewer into the thigh joint of the chicken. If the juice that runs out is clear and colourless, the chicken is cooked. Take chicken from dish and remove string. Keep in a warm place.

gravy: Pour off all but 2 tablespoons fat from the dish. Add 1 tablespoon flour and stir well until lightly browned. Add remaining 1½ cups chicken stock, stir until thickened. Season with salt and pepper.

cream gravy: Make as above but just before serving stir in 3 tablespoons cream and cook a little until thickened. Serves 4–5.

STUFFING FOR CHICKEN •

Chicken roasted in butter (see right) or French roast chicken (see p. 71) may be filled with this stuffing and secured with poultry pins before roasting.

2 rashers bacon, diced
1 onion, chopped
¼ cup chopped celery
2 cups fresh white breadcrumbs
½ cup milk
2 mushrooms, chopped
2 tablespoons chopped parsley
2 teaspoons chopped thyme or sage leaves
salt and freshly ground pepper
1 egg

Lightly fry bacon in its own fat, remove and add onion and celery and cook gently until soft and golden. Soak breadcrumbs in milk, add all other ingredients and stir in beaten egg. The stuffing should not be too moist. Fill cavity of chicken and use a poultry pin to secure stuffing.

MEDITERRANEAN CHICKEN •

1 French roast chicken *(see p. 71)*
8–10 button mushrooms
4–6 tomatoes, halved or quartered
2 red onions, peeled and quartered
½ cup pitted black olives
2 tablespoons roughly chopped parsley

Prepare the chicken. While the chicken is cooking, prepare the garnish. Place the mushrooms with the tomatoes, onions and olives around chicken for the last 20 minutes of cooking. Serve the chicken surrounded by vegetables. Scatter with parsley. Serves 4.

CHICKEN ROASTED IN BUTTER •

1 size 18 (1.8kg) chicken
salt and freshly ground pepper
a little chopped fresh or dried tarragon
60 g butter
extra butter for rubbing over bird
  and for basting
½ cup chicken stock

Preheat the oven to 190°C. Wipe the cavity of the chicken with a paper towel. Remove excess fat. Mix about 1 teaspoon salt and pepper, to taste, with the tarragon and butter and place half inside the chicken. Put the chicken breast-side up in a well-greased baking dish and rub remaining butter over exposed surface. Place in oven. After 20–25 minutes turn the bird on its side and baste with the pan juices. After 20 minutes turn again and baste well. In 1 hour 5 minutes the chicken will be cooked and a beautiful golden brown all over. Remove from oven, take chicken from pan and keep in a warm place, lightly covered with foil while making the sauce. Add chicken stock to pan. Stir to lift off chicken drippings and bring to the boil. Allow to simmer for a few minutes before checking for seasoning, adding salt and pepper if necessary. Strain into a sauce boat and serve separately. Serve with roast potatoes and a green vegetable or a salad. An English favourite with roast chicken is bread sauce *(see p. 304)*. Serves 4.

MEDITERRANEAN CHICKEN

SAUTÉED CHICKEN AND OTHER CHICKEN DISHES

SAUTÉING IS A QUICK WAY TO COOK CHICKEN AND THERE ARE AN ENDLESS NUMBER OF SAUCES TO ADD VARIETY TO THIS RELATIVELY SIMPLE DISH. WE PREFER TO JOINT AN ORGANIC CHICKEN OURSELVES, BUT REMEMBER IF YOU ARE BUYING CHICKEN PIECES THAT A SELECTION OF DIFFERENT CUTS WILL MAKE A MORE INTERESTING DISH TO PLEASE EVERYONE.

BASIC CHICKEN SAUTÉ ••

1.6 kg chicken pieces or a size 16 chicken, jointed
60 g butter
1 tablespoon oil
salt and freshly ground pepper
1–2 teaspoons chopped parsley (optional)
extra butter

Pat chicken pieces well with paper towels and remove any excess fat. Heat the butter and oil in a heavy-based sauté pan or frying pan. When foam has almost subsided, add chicken pieces skin-side down, in one layer. Sauté for 2–3 minutes and, when chicken is golden, turn and sauté other side. As chicken browns, remove to a warm plate and add more pieces to the pan until all are browned.

Season with the salt and pepper and add the parsley, if using. Return leg and thigh joints to the pan, adding a little more butter if necessary, and cook slowly for 8–9 minutes. Add breast and wing joints. Cover and continue cooking for about 10 minutes, turning and basting several times.

To test if the chicken is cooked, pierce with a fine skewer. The juice that runs out should be clear, not pink. Remove the chicken to a hot serving dish and keep warm while making the sauce.

sauce:
1 tablespoon chopped spring onions or shallots
¾ cup dry white wine
¾ cup chicken stock
salt and freshly ground pepper
2 teaspoons softened butter
1–2 tablespoons chopped parsley (optional)

Retain about 1 tablespoon fat used in cooking the chicken. Add the spring onions and cook slowly 1 minute. Pour in wine and stock. Scrape crusty pieces from the bottom of pan and boil rapidly, until reduced to about ¾ cup. Taste and season if necessary with salt and pepper. Remove from heat and just before serving, swirl in the butter and add the parsley, if using. Pour the sauce over chicken and serve. Serves 4.

CHICKEN SAUTÉ A LA CRÈME ••

Prepare as above recipe but, in making sauce, use ⅔ cup stock or stock and wine, as well as ⅓ cup cream.

COQ AU VIN •••

1 size 18 (1.8 kg) chicken,
  cut into serving pieces
1½ cups red wine
1 clove garlic, crushed
bouquet garni
2 tablespoons plain flour
salt and freshly ground pepper
60 g butter
8–12 small onions such as pickling onions
125 g thickly sliced speck or bacon,
  cut into strips
12 button mushrooms
½ cup brandy

Dry chicken pieces well with paper towel and remove any excess fat. Place wine in a china or glass bowl with garlic and bouquet garni. Add chicken pieces, turn to cover the chicken with the wine mixture, cover and leave in refrigerator overnight to marinate.

The next day, remove chicken from wine and pat dry with paper towels. Reserve marinade. Dust chicken pieces with flour seasoned with salt and pepper. In a large, heavy-based saucepan heat butter slowly until it sizzles slightly. Brown chicken pieces in several lots until browned all over, turning. Remove and set aside.

Add onions to pan and brown them lightly. Remove and set aside. Do the same with the speck and mushrooms, separately. Return the chicken, onions, speck or bacon and mushrooms to pan. Add brandy and ignite, shaking pan gently. Add marinade. Bring slowly to a simmer, cover and simmer over gentle heat for 1 hour. Add salt and freshly ground pepper if needed. Delicious served with creamy mashed potato. Serves 4–6.

OVEN-FRIED CHICKEN •

1.8kg chicken pieces or a size 18 chicken,
  jointed
¾ cup plain flour
1 teaspoon salt
¼ teaspoon pepper
1 egg, lightly beaten
2 tablespoons water
1 cup dried breadcrumbs or corn meal
olive or vegetable oil, for frying

Dry chicken pieces well with paper towel and remove any excess fat. Combine the flour, salt and pepper then lightly dust each piece with the seasoned flour. Shake off excess flour, dip in beaten egg and water and coat with the breadcrumbs. Heat enough oil to make a shallow layer in a frying pan. Place a few pieces of chicken in at a time and brown on all sides. Place in a baking dish and bake for 45 minutes at 180°C. Serves 4.

note: oven-fried chicken is delicious with cream gravy (see French roast chicken, p. 71). A few sautéed mushrooms may be added to the gravy.

GRILLED CHICKEN •

2 x size 10 (1 kg) chickens
salt and freshly ground pepper
juice of 1 lemon
60 g butter, melted,
　or 3 tablespoons olive oil

Split chickens in halves lengthwise and put skin-side up on large piece of greased foil. Sprinkle with salt and pepper and a squeeze of lemon juice. Brush with a little melted butter. Place under heated griller and cook for about 8 minutes, brushing several times with butter. Turn over. Brush with butter, add a squeeze of lemon juice and grill for 8 minutes then turn again so the chicken is skin-side up. Continue to grill until tender and brown. Serve with the reserved juices from the foil, and with vegetables of your choice. Serves 4.

CORIANDER CHICKEN ••

1 cooked Chinese white chicken *(see right)*
6 spring onions
2.5 cm piece fresh ginger
2 tablespoons toasted sesame seeds
1 cup carefully picked fresh coriander sprigs
2 tablespoons light vegetable oil
1 teaspoon sesame oil
3 tablespoons light soy sauce

Prepare and chop Chinese white chicken, and arrange on serving plate. Cut the spring onions into 2.5 cm lengths, including some of the green tops, then cut the lengths into thin shreds. Slice the ginger lengthwise and cut it into thin shreds. Scatter the prepared spring onions, ginger, sesame seeds and coriander sprigs over the chopped white chicken. Just before serving, heat oils and, when smoking, pour evenly over the chicken. Sprinkle with soy and serve with steamed rice. Serves 4–6.

CHINESE WHITE CHICKEN ••

This is the common name given to chicken steamed in the Chinese way. The flesh should be firm, white, tender and juicy. Keep in mind that this method takes some time to prepare. Serve quite plain as suggested here or turn into coriander chicken (see left).

1 size 16–18 (1.6–1.8 kg) chicken
a few slices of fresh ginger
1 teaspoon salt
2 spring onions, roughly chopped
1 teaspoon sesame, peanut or light olive oil

Place chicken in a large, heavy-based saucepan and add water to cover. Now remove the chicken, set aside and bring the water left in pan to the boil with the ginger, salt and spring onions. Once water is boiling, carefully lower the chicken back into the water, return to the boil and simmer gently for 10 minutes. Cover the pan, remove from heat and leave to stand and cool in the water for 2 hours. Remove the chicken from the pan, drain thoroughly and pat dry with paper towels.

Brush skin all over with the oil and sprinkle generously with salt. When cool, just before serving, chop chicken with a Chinese cleaver into small serving pieces and arrange on serving plate. Serves 4–6.

CORIANDER CHICKEN

BASQUE CHICKEN ••

Lavish use of capsicum and tomatoes is a characteristic of the Basque cuisine.

1.8 kg chicken pieces or a size 18 chicken, jointed
2 tablespoons olive oil
8 cloves garlic
3 red capsicum, seeded and cut into quarters
12 baby new potatoes, boiled for 8–10 minutes
salt and freshly ground pepper
2 medium ripe tomatoes, skinned, seed and quartered
¾ cup dry white wine or chicken stock
chopped parsley

Preheat the oven to 190°C. Dry chicken pieces well with paper towels and remove any excess fat. Heat half the oil in a heavy-based flameproof baking dish over a moderate heat. Slowly brown the chicken pieces, turning them once or twice. Add the remaining oil to the dish with the garlic, capsicum and potatoes, tossing together. Season with the salt and pepper and bake for 45 minutes, turning the chicken and vegetables several times. Add tomatoes for last 15 minutes of cooking.

Arrange the chicken pieces in a serving dish. Surround with vegetables and keep warm. Add wine to dish over heat, scrape up crusty pieces and allow to simmer for a few minutes. Spoon sauce over chicken and scatter with parsley. *Serves 4–6*.

note: a red onion cut into eight can be added with the potatoes.

DEVILLED GRILLED CHICKEN ••

4 large chicken marylands or 2 spatchcock
2 teaspoons salt
2 teaspoons sugar
1 teaspoon ground pepper
1 teaspoon ground ginger
1 teaspoon dry mustard
1 teaspoon mild curry powder
15 g butter
2 tablespoons tomato ketchup
1 tablespoon Worcestershire sauce
1 tablespoon light soy sauce
1 tablespoon fruit chutney

Dry chicken pieces well with paper towels and remove any excess fat. Cut the drumsticks from the thighs to speed cooking. If using spatchcock, split down the back, using poultry scissors and remove most of the backbone. Flatten out by covering with cling wrap and using a rolling pin or meat bat. Mix salt, sugar and dry spices together and rub well into the surface of the chicken. This can be done ahead of time and left to marinate.

Arrange the chicken pieces on a foil-lined griller rack and brush with the butter melted in a small saucepan. Grill under a preheated griller for 10 minutes, turning once after 6 minutes. Keep a careful eye on the chicken to watch for burning and cover with foil where necessary until chicken is cooked.

Meanwhile, heat the remaining ingredients in pan until butter is melted. Spoon over the chicken. Continue to grill, basting with the mixture for a further 2 minutes or until the juices run clear when a thigh is pierced with a skewer. Good served with Indian ghee rice (*see p. 173*). *Serves 4*.

BASQUE CHICKEN

SPECIAL POULTRY

IT ALWAYS SEEMS LIKE A PARTY WHEN DUCK OR TURKEY COMES TO THE TABLE BUT, LIKE CHICKEN, THESE BIRDS ARE NOW APPEARING ON THE MARKET AT A PRICE MOST PEOPLE CAN AFFORD MORE THAN ONCE A YEAR. THIS MEANS TURKEY OR DUCK NEED NOT BE KEPT ONLY FOR CHRISTMAS OR SUCH FESTIVE OCCASIONS. HOWEVER, AS WITH CHICKEN, I PREFER TO EAT THESE BIRDS LESS OFTEN AND CHOOSE ORGANIC AND FREE-RANGE TURKEYS AND DUCKS.

ROAST TURKEY FOR CHRISTMAS •••

Turkey is an all-time favourite for Christmas with its two stuffings, crispy skin, moist tender white meat and richly flavoured dark meat, plenty of gravy and crispy roast potatoes. Order the turkey well before you need it. If buying a frozen turkey, you will need to collect it 3 days in advance.

1 x 3.5–4 kg whole turkey
1 quantity pork, apple and pistachio stuffing (see p. 82)
1 quantity of parsley and lemon stuffing (see p. 82)
2 tablespoons butter
freshly ground pepper
turkey gravy (see p. 83)

If frozen, thaw turkey completely by leaving on a large plate, still in the wrapper, in the refrigerator for at least 2 days (the slower the better). Remove giblets if any from cavity. Wipe thoroughly dry with paper towels. Spoon the pork stuffing inside the crop (breast) and press outside of breast to mould to a good shape. Bring neck flap over to the back and secure it with a poultry pin or small skewer.

Preheat the oven to 160°C. Spoon the parsley and lemon stuffing into body cavity. Shape bird nicely with both hands. Place turkey on its back, legs facing you. Place centre of piece of string below breast at neck end, bring ends down over wings then down underneath the bird. Cross string underneath, then bring it forward and up, to tie ends of drumsticks and parson's nose together (*alternatively, tie as for the chicken on p. 71*). Wipe bird with a paper towel and spread the 2 tablespoons butter over, being sure to cover breast and legs well. Season with a little pepper. Place on a rack in a large baking dish, propping up legs with crumpled foil if necessary. Cover pan with a tent of greased foil.

Roast until done (see p. 82 'is the turkey cooked?'), about 2–2½ hours. Baste every 25 minutes with juices in dish and remove foil for last 30 minutes to allow turkey to brown. Remove the turkey to a heated serving platter or carving board and allow to rest in a warm place for 20–30 minutes while finishing off vegetables and gravy.

Carve the bird, serving a little white and a little dark meat to each person with some stuffing. Serve the vegetables in separate dishes, letting everyone help themselves. Have a jug of gravy for those who like plenty and a bowl of cranberry sauce, if liked. Serves 8–10.

ROAST TURKEY FOR CHRISTMAS

PORK, APPLE AND PISTACHIO STUFFING •

A good butcher will prepare the pork mince. Otherwise, buy pork with a little fat, cube it and mince in a food processor.

½ cup apple juice or cider
4 slices white bread, cubed
500 g pork mince
3 stalks celery, finely chopped
2 apples, peeled, cored and diced
1 small onion, chopped
1 tablespoon chopped parsley
2 teaspoons chopped thyme
½ cup shelled unsalted pistachios
1 egg, beaten
salt and freshly ground pepper

Pour the apple juice or cider over bread cubes and allow to stand for 30 minutes. Mix together pork mince, celery, apples, onion, herbs and pistachios with the soaked bread. Blend well together with egg and season well with salt and pepper. Use to stuff the crop (breast) of turkey.

PARSLEY AND LEMON STUFFING •

A wonderful fresh-tasting stuffing, ideal for the cavity.

1 small onion, finely chopped
30 g butter, melted
3 cups fresh breadcrumbs
¾ cup freshly chopped parsley
2 teaspoons grated lemon rind
1 egg, beaten
salt and freshly ground pepper
lemon juice or chicken stock

Combine the onion, butter, breadcrumbs, parsley and lemon rind. Store in the refrigerator in a covered bowl until ready to use. Add the beaten egg, salt and pepper and a little lemon juice or stock to moisten. Toss lightly with a fork, don't over mix.

STUFFING A TURKEY

For some, the stuffing is the favourite part of the roast turkey. As well as adding flavour, stuffing can help the cooking of the bird by holding it in shape, keeping it moist and making it go further. Here are some pointers:

- Mix and handle stuffings lightly, so as not to compact them, leaving room for the stuffings to expand during cooking and stay light. If some stuffing is left over after filling the bird, cook it separately for 45 minutes in a greased baking dish, covered with foil.

- Make fresh breadcrumbs for stuffings, using 2–4 day-old bread. If you have a blender or food processor, beautiful breadcrumbs can be made very easily, by processing chunks of bread until turned into crumbs.

- Stuff the turkey just before cooking, never ahead of time. The stuffing may be made ahead but store separately in refrigerator until required.

- Take care not to overstuff the turkey as the stuffing expands and may cause the skin to burst during cooking. Stuff the crop first. Fold over the skin of the neck and secure with a poultry pin. Finally, stuff the cavity.

is the turkey cooked? The turkey is cooked if a meat thermometer put into the thickest part of the thigh registers 90°C. If you don't own a meat thermometer, pierce the thickest part of the thigh with a skewer. The turkey is cooked if it is easily pierced and clear, not pink, juice runs. Some turkeys come with a little pin on the breast, the red changes colour or pops out when the bird is cooked. Instructions are on the wrapping.

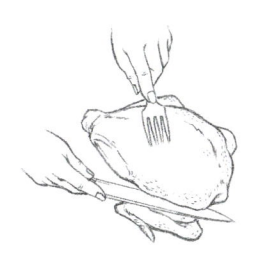

Carving a turkey is made easier by first making a horizontal cut just above the wing into the breast.

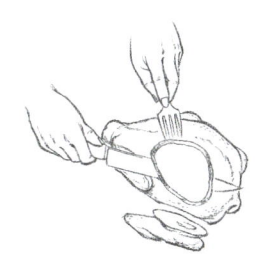

Then carve slices of turkey easily from the centre of the breast downwards.

CARVING THE TURKEY

Remove the trussing string and poultry pin. Place a long-bladed sharp knife between the thigh and the body of the bird and cut through the joint. Remove the leg by pressing it outward with the knife and bending it back with the fork. Separate the thigh and drumsticks and slice off the dark meat. Repeat with the other leg. Remove the wings. Carve the breast with straight, even strokes. Carve the stuffing in the crop into thin slices and remove stuffing from the body with a spoon.

to serve: Each guest gets slices of white meat and some of the dark meat. Stuffing is put on each plate – a little of each. Pass the vegetables and gravy, for guests to help themselves.

store leftovers carefully: After any meal, store leftovers promptly. If the stuffing is involved, remove from bird and store separately. Cut meat from the carcass in large pieces and then store in smaller containers, leaving valuable refrigerator space clear.

TURKEY GRAVY •

30 g butter
2 tablespoons plain flour
3 cups turkey giblet stock or chicken stock

Pour off excess turkey drippings, leaving about 3 tablespoons. Place the baking dish on the heat and stir in the butter and flour until lightly browned. Stir in the stock, scraping up all the crusty pan residue. Bring to the boil. Simmer for 2 minutes. Adjust the seasonings if necessary and skim the excess fat from top. Strain into a jug and serve piping hot.

turkey stock: Gently simmer turkey giblets and neck with 1 halved onion, 1 bay leaf, 1 stick celery and 5 cups water until reduced to 3 cups. Strain and use to make gravy.

VEGETABLES FOR CHRISTMAS DINNER

The vegetables served with the Christmas bird are important to the success of the meal. Choose two or three from the following selection to make your meal complete.

CRISP-ROASTED POTATOES AND PARSNIPS *(see p. 138)*
PEAS, FRENCH-STYLE *(see p. 137)*
CARROTS VICHY *(see p.131)*
GLAZED SWEET POTATOES *(see p. 140)*

DUCK

Duck is prized by gourmets for its rich flavour and succulence and can be prepared in a variety of ways. Don't be misled by the size of a duck. A duck has more fat, a larger frame and less meat than a chicken of the same weight, so allow about 375–500 g raw weight per person.

DUCK A L'ORANGE ••

This is the best loved of all duck dishes. The duck is roasted and then served with an orange sauce. This recipe includes port as well as Cointreau, which makes a particularly delicious sauce.

2 x 2.5 kg ducks
salt and freshly ground pepper
2 oranges

orange sauce base:

4 tablespoons sugar
1½ cups duck or chicken stock
1½ tablespoons arrowroot slaked with 2 tablespoons port
¼ cup brandy
½ cup port
2 tablespoons Cointreau liqueur
salt and freshly ground pepper
15 g butter
¼ cup vinegar

Preheat the oven to 200°C. Season ducks with salt and pepper. Remove the rind from 1 orange and place a few strips in the cavities, reserving leftover rind for the orange sauce base. Truss the ducks with string into a neat shape as for chicken *(see p. 71)*. Prick the skin using a metal skewer or the tip of a paring knife held almost parallel to the duck to avoid piercing the meat, in several places on the thighs, back and tail to allow the fat to release. Pierce a few times during cooking as well to help give a crisp skin. Place on a rack in a large baking dish. Roast for 15 minutes, until the duck has browned lightly and released some of its fat. Remove from oven and pour off the excess fat. Cover duck loosely with foil, reduce heat to 180°C and cook a further 1–1½ hours, until tender.

Meanwhile, peel the rind as thinly as possible from the other orange with a vegetable peeler. Cut the rind into very fine shreds then cover with hot water in a saucepan. Simmer for 3 minutes, strain, cool and reserve for garnish. Remove and discard white pith from both oranges and cut between the membrane into segments. Sprinkle with brandy and set aside.

When the duck is cooked, remove the trussing string, place on a serving dish and keep warm. You may find it easier to carve the duck in the kitchen *(see opposite)*. Remove all the fat from the baking dish, leaving all the juices in the bottom. Place on the heat and stir in the port, scraping up all the pan juices. Allow liquid to reduce to half. Strain into the prepared orange sauce base and bring to a gentle simmer, then stir in the Cointreau. Adjust the seasoning and when ready to serve, remove the sauce from the heat, add orange segments and swirl in the butter. Spoon a little of the sauce over the duck to give it an attractive glaze, and serve the rest in a sauce boat. Serve with creamy mashed potatoes or buttered rice.

orange sauce base: Boil the sugar and vinegar over a high heat until it forms a caramel syrup. Remove from the heat and gradually stir in the duck or chicken stock. When smooth, place back on the heat and bring to the boil. Gradually add the arrowroot mixture and the prepared orange rind strips. Simmer the sauce for about 4 minutes or until the sauce is clear and thickened. *Serves 4–6.*

to carve a duck:

- Remove the trussing strings and set the bird on a board.

- Cut straight down through the breastbone and back into halves. Use scissors, or poultry shears to cut through bone.

- Lay each half on the board and make a slanting cut between the ribs to separate the wing and leg, making two good portions of each half. With scissors, trim away any carcass bone. The four portions should be two wings and two legs with a good piece of breast attached to each.

GRILLED DUCK BREAST WITH MANGO SALSA ••

Duck breasts are available at many good butchers, the legs often being used for duck confit. This recipe gives a medium-rare but delicious meat.

4 duck breasts
salt and freshly ground pepper

mango salsa:
1 mango, peeled and cut into 1 cm cubes
2 small red onions, finely chopped
**½ fresh bird's eye chilli,
   seeded and finely chopped**
1 tablespoon light olive oil
1 teaspoon water
¼ cup mint leaves
2 tablespoons lime juice
salt and freshly ground pepper

First make the mango salsa. Place the mango in a mixing bowl. Combine the onion, chilli, oil and water in a saucepan. Cover and cook over a gentle heat until onion is transparent without colouring, about 10 minutes. Cool before adding to the mango. Drop the mint leaves into boiling water for 1 minute. Drain, refresh in iced water, drain and squeeze dry then finely chop. Add to the onion and mango mixture and stir in the lime juice, salt and pepper. Leave to stand for 1 hour before serving.

Preheat the griller to very hot or the oven to 230°C. Season the duck pieces with salt and pepper and place skin-side up on a rack in a pan. Grill or roast for 10 minutes to render some of the fat from under the skin. Drain off the fat, reduce the oven to 180°C and continue to cook the duck until tender, a further 5–10 minutes, according to taste.

Let the duck rest in a warm place for 5 minutes to allow the juices to be reabsorbed into the meat. To serve, slice the breasts slightly diagonally across and arrange on warm plates. Spoon some mango salsa on each plate. Follow with a green salad. *Serves 4.*

QUAIL

A small game bird, quail is white-fleshed and has a deliciously gamey taste. It is usually tender and should be cooked quickly either in a hot oven, or on a grill or barbecue. Allow 1 or 2 per person for a main course.

BARBECUED QUAIL •

These delectable birds are split, then barbecued for 10 minutes with a herb marinade.

4–6 quail
2 cloves garlic, crushed
2 tablespoons olive oil
4 tablespoons lemon juice
a sprig of fresh rosemary, chopped
salt and freshly ground pepper

Split the quail lengthwise with a sharp, pointed knife. Flatten with the heel of the hand and fasten with thin skewers to keep the legs close to the body. Combine garlic, oil, lemon juice and rosemary and brush over the birds. Season well with salt and pepper. Place the quail skin-side up on a greased barbecue rack and grill for 5 minutes before turning and brushing with the marinade. Cook for another 5 minutes, brushing frequently. When cooked, remove the skewers and serve with lemon wedges. Serves 4–6.

QUAIL IN VINE LEAVES ••

There are two ways of enjoying this dish. One is in a rather rustic fashion without the grape garnish and sauce. This way, fingers are quite in order and there should be plenty of crusty bread to mop up the juices. The other more formal way, with bacon and vine leaves removed, muscat grapes added and a sauce made to finish the quail. In this case, you may like to halve the quail with poultry scissors and cut away the backbone for your guests. Polenta is a traditional accompaniment for quail cooked this way.

6 quail
12 blanched grape leaves, or preserved vine leaves
6 rashers streaky bacon
2 tablespoons melted butter
salt and freshly ground pepper
250 g muscat grapes (optional)
1 tablespoon cognac or brandy
1 cup good brown beef stock
1 tablespoon orange liqueur
45 g butter

Preheat the oven to 200°C. Wipe the quail and cover the breasts with vine leaves. Wrap a bacon rasher around each one and secure with a toothpick. Place in a baking dish with the melted butter and bake for 7–10 minutes on each side, basting every now and then until they are tender. The bacon and vine leaves can be left intact or removed. Season the quail with salt and pepper.

Surround the quail in the pan with the grapes. Roast for a further few minutes. Transfer quail and grapes to a platter and keep warm while making sauce. Deglaze the baking dish with the cognac, scraping up the brown bits clinging to the base, and add the stock and orange liqueur. Bring the liquid to the boil over a high heat and season with salt and pepper.

Reduce heat and whisk in the butter, cut into small pieces, until sauce has thickened slightly. Pour the sauce over the quail and grapes. Serves 4.

to blanch grape leaves: Simply pick large undamaged leaves from a grapevine, wash and plunge into a large saucepan of boiling water until wilted. Remove then rinse under cold water and drain.

PROSCIUTTO-WRAPPED ROASTED QUAIL ••

This is a delectable dish for a special occasion. Think of offering finger bowls in case fingers are used to help eat the quail.

6–8 quail
salt and freshly ground pepper
2 strips orange rind
a few sprigs of fresh thyme and parsley
60 g butter
2 tablespoons olive oil
3–4 slices prosciutto, halved

pea purée:
500 g shelled green peas, fresh or frozen
1 small lettuce, shredded
60 g butter
salt and freshly ground pepper
¼ cup cream

Preheat the oven to 230° C. Wipe the quail with damp paper towels and season with salt and pepper. Put a small piece of orange rind and a sprig of thyme and parsley inside each bird. Place a half-slice of prosciutto on the breast of each bird and tie with string into a neat shape. Heat the butter and oil in a flameproof casserole and brown the quail all over. Cover the casserole and bake the birds in the preheated oven for 15–20 minutes, basting several times during cooking with the juices.

Place the peas in a heavy-based saucepan with the shredded lettuce and butter. Cover and cook over a gentle heat until tender, shaking the pan from time to time. Season with salt and pepper, to taste, and purée in a food processor or push through a sieve. Return to the pan, taste and adjust the seasoning. Stir in the cream and heat gently. This may be done ahead and reheated when ready to serve.

Spoon the pea purée into an ovenproof serving dish. Take the quail from the oven, remove and discard the string and arrange on the pea purée. Return to a 180°C oven for 10 minutes. Serves 6.

meat

Most families have their favourite meals and they usually centre
around the meat dish. Roast beef with crisp baked potatoes,
savoury Yorkshire pudding and gravy is the first choice for many English people.
Or, a common favourite is roast pork with crisp crackling,
roasted apples and heavenly gravy.

In France, the choice may be a leg of lamb, scented with rosemary
and a hint of garlic, sitting on a bed of sliced potatoes. A claim from the Irish for
Irish stew, with its delicate wholesome flavour, is a reminder that it is not
necessary to use the grander, more expensive cuts of meat to make a memorable dish.
And, surely, no one has found a better dish than steak and
kidney pie with its rich, brown peppery gravy, tender beef and delicious crust.

While the demand for expensive cuts of meat grows,
good cooks everywhere agree that the more economical cuts can compete.
They just require longer and slower cooking which,
in addition to tenderising the meat, blends the multitude of flavours
into one magnificent whole.

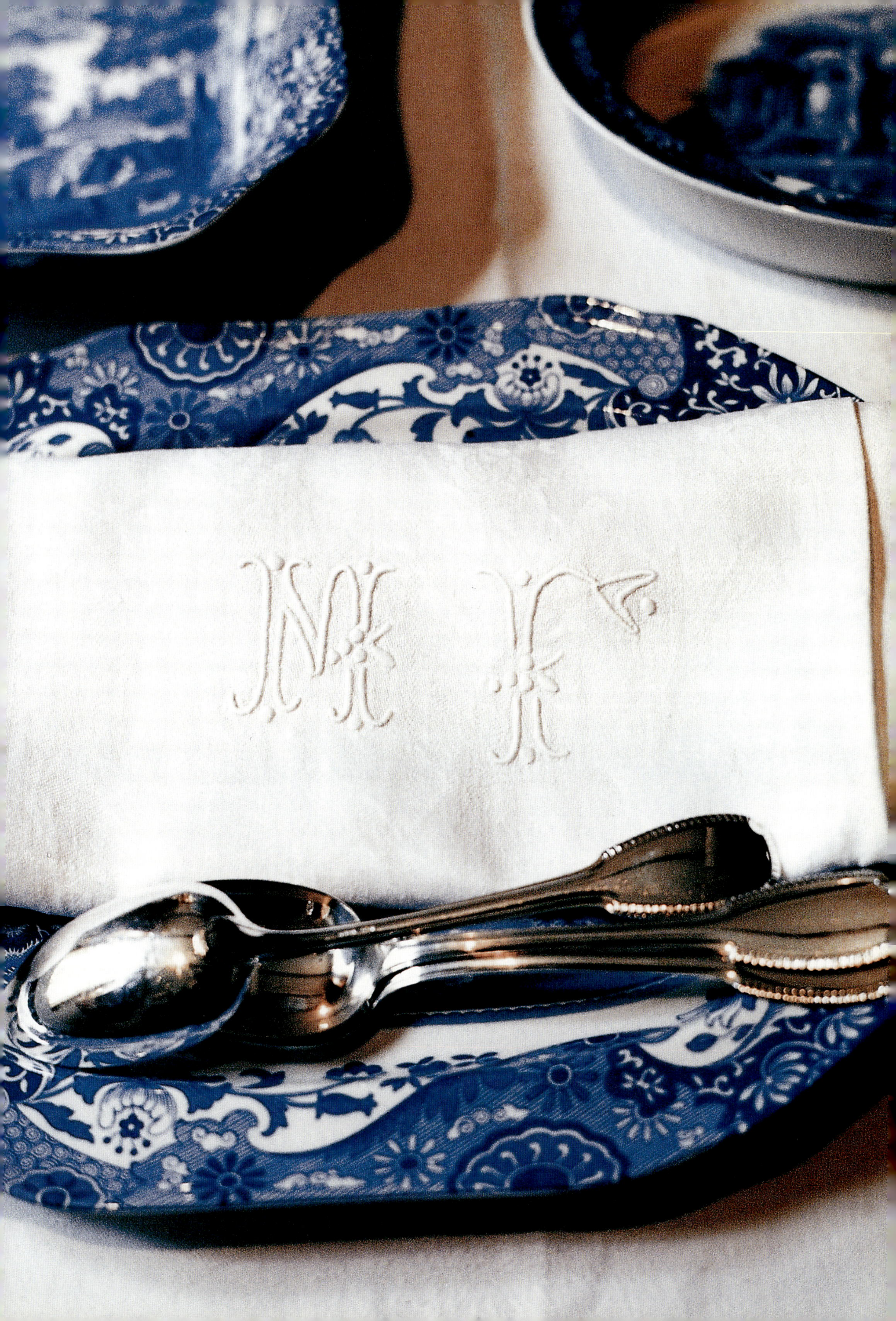

BEEF

BEEF IS ONE OF THE PRIME MEATS, FULL OF FLAVOUR AND FOOD VALUE. IN GENERAL, THE CHARACTERISTICS OF GOOD FRESHLY CUT BEEF ARE A RICH RED TO DARK RED COLOUR, A FIRM AND ELASTIC TOUCH AND A FAIRLY FINE GRAIN. THERE SHOULD BE MARBLING WITH FLECKS OF FAT THROUGH THE THICKER PARTS AND FIRM, SMOOTH FAT WHICH IS CREAMY WHITE OR YELLOWISH, ACCORDING TO THE BREED OF ANIMAL, AGE AND THE WAY IT WAS FED. STORE IMMEDIATELY BY REMOVING THE WRAPPING AND PLACING IN THE MEAT TRAY IN THE REFRIGERATOR OR ON A PLATE COVERED LOOSELY WITH FOIL.

A sirloin of beef is excellent for roasting. Slices can be either grilled, barbecued or pan-fried.

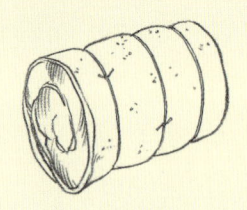

A rolled rib of beef is excellent for roasting or for pot-roasting with vegetables.

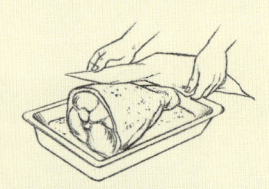

Roasted meats are easier to carve if allowed to 'rest' after cooking. Cover the meat loosely with foil and leave in a warm place for about 15 minutes.

BEEF CUTS

sirloin: Best for roasting. If cut thick, slices can be either grilled or pan-fried. It usually contains part of the fillet.

t-bone steaks: Cut from the sirloin, containing a piece of the fillet. Grill, pan-fry or barbecue.

rib and rolled rib: Good for roasting. Two or three ribs make a good roast for a small family, although a larger piece allows for leftover cold beef, which is excellent for salads or sandwiches.

rump: An excellent cut for grilling, pan-frying or the barbecue. Best cooked in a piece then cut into portionss.

topside, silverside, round, chuck or stewing steak: Use for braising or boiling. Good too in stews and casseroles. Can be roasted in oven but requires larding with little strips of fat. Suitable for pot-roasting with vegetables.

fillet: The classic undercut of the sirloin may be trimmed and oven roasted whole, cut into steaks and pan-fried or grilled.

brisket: A fatty cut that is often salted for boiled beef. Unsalted, it is a good buy for pot roasts it is often rolled.

minced beef: For hamburgers, meat loaves and pasta sauces.

shin of beef: Mostly used with bones for stock. Requires very long, slow cooking in stews or casseroles. Good flavour with gelatinous texture.

oxtail: For stews or soups. Ask the butcher to cut it into suitable joints.

tongue: Mostly salted but can be fresh or smoked. Boil and serve cold or hot .

how much to buy: Allow approximately 185–250 g per person for boneless meat such as steak, meat for casseroles and stews, hamburgers and rolled roasts. Allow 250–315 g for meat with a large amount of bone.

BEEF STEAK

Charcoal-grilled steaks are hard to beat, but pan-frying or grilling, if done properly, will produce the same result; a crisp savoury crust on the outside and juicy, tender beef on the inside.

The tender, choice cuts of beef, such as good quality rump, fillet and porterhouse, require only to be seasoned with salt and pepper.

When using tougher cuts such as oyster blade, round or topside, it is best to marinate the meat. This helps to tenderise as well as provide extra flavour. Marinate for at least 2 hours.

marinade: Combine 1 sliced carrot, 1 sliced onion, 3 cloves garlic, 1 teaspoon peppercorns, 1 bay leaf, 4 sprigs parsley, 2 sprigs thyme, 4 tablespoons oil and 1 cup red wine. Pour over the meat in a glass or china bowl. Sufficient for 1–1.5 kg steak. For white meats you may use white wine in place of the red wine. For large joints to be roasted, increase the wine to 2 cups.

PAN-FRIED STEAK •

Allow 185–250 g rump steak, boneless sirloin or 1 piece fillet per person, each cut 2.5 cm thick. Remove from the refrigerator at least 30 minutes before cooking. Slit fat in a few places to prevent the meat from curling.

Season the steak with salt and pepper. If it has been marinated, dry well on paper towels. Cover the base of a heavy-based frying pan with a thin layer of oil and heat. When smoking, put in the seasoned steak. Leave for about 1 minute, turn over and leave for another minute. Both sides should be covered with a brown crust. Now lower the heat and continue to cook for 6–8 minutes for a fillet and 7–10 minutes for medium-done sirloin or rump. Allow extra time for well-done or less for rare.

For gravy, add ½–¾ cup seasoned stock or wine to the pan, scraping up the drippings. Add a nut of butter, swirling to create a liaison in the gravy. Spoon a little over each steak.

GRILLED STEAK •

Prepare the steak as above. Preheat the grill to very hot. Brush steaks with a little olive oil or melted butter and grill, following the method for pan-fried steak. If the surface appears to dry out, brush with a little extra oil. Cooking times are much the same as for pan-frying. Turn the meat with tongs or two spoons. Parsley butter (*see p. 304*) is good with grilled steak.

STEAK AU POIVRE ••

4 steaks (porterhouse or fillet)
1 tablespoon coarsely cracked black pepper
2 teaspoons oil
4 teaspoons butter
a dash of Tabasco (*optional*)
a dash of Worcestershire sauce
lemon juice
2 tablespoons brandy (*optional*)
chopped parsley
chopped chives

Sprinkle both sides of each steak with pepper and press well into the meat with the heel of your hand. Let stand for 30 minutes. Heat the oil in a heavy-based frying pan and, when the pan is hot, add the steaks and cook until well browned on one side. Turn the steaks and cook until brown on other side. Continue to cook until done to taste. Put 1 teaspoon of the butter on each steak and add the sauces and lemon juice, to taste. Warm the brandy, if using, ignite and pour over the meat. Sprinkle with the parsley and chives and serve at once. For a creamy sauce, swirl about 2 tablespoons cream with the pan gravy. Serves 4.

TOURNEDOS WITH BÉARNAISE SAUCE •••

4 slices bread
60 g butter
4 tournedos (trimmed thick fillet steak)
1 quantity béarnaise sauce (see p. 304)

Prepare the croûtes by cutting out rounds from the bread slices that are the same size as the steaks. Heat half the butter in a heavy-based frying pan and fry the bread on both sides, until golden. Set aside. Heat the remaining butter and add the tournedos to the pan when the butter is sizzling. Sauté 4–5 minutes each side. Place the cooked steaks on the croûtes and spoon the béarnaise sauce over, or serve the sauce separately. Serves 4.

BEEF STROGANOFF ••

750 g fillet steak
salt and freshly ground pepper
1 tablespoon plain flour
60 g butter
2 medium onions, finely sliced
185–250 g button mushrooms, finely sliced
1 tablespoon tomato paste
⅔ cup sour cream

Cut the steak into thin strips (5 cm x 1 cm), toss with the salt and pepper and flour. Melt half the butter in a frying pan. Add the onions and fry slowly for about 10 minutes until golden. Add the mushrooms, and fry a few minutes, adding more butter if needed. Remove the onions and mushrooms, add the remaining butter and, when hot, add the beef strips and fry briskly for 3–4 minutes. Return the mushrooms and onions with salt and pepper, to the pan. Shake over the heat for 1 minute then add the tomato paste and sour cream. Cook until heated through and serve with boiled rice. Serves 4–6.

MALAY BEEF SATAYS ••

If using bamboo skewers, soak them first for several hours in water to prevent them burning during cooking.

1 kg sirloin, rump or blade steak
⅓ cup light soy sauce
⅓ cup vegetable oil
2 onions, finely chopped
2 cloves garlic, crushed
3 tablespoons toasted sesame seeds
2 teaspoons ground cumin
1 tablespoon lemon juice
salt and freshly ground pepper

Cut the steak into 2.5 cm cubes. Put the meat in a glass bowl and add the soy sauce, oil, onions, garlic and sesame seeds. Turn to coat the meat thoroughly with the seasonings, then cover and leave in a cool place for 3 hours to marinate. Drain, reserving the marinade. Thread the steak cubes onto skewers and brush with a mixture of the cumin and lemon juice. Grill the meat over hot coals or under the grill, basting with the marinade and turning frequently for 6–8 minutes for rare, 8–10 minutes for medium and 10–12 minutes for well-done. Season with salt and pepper and serve. Serves 4–6.

RUMP ROAST ••

Allow about 250 g per person (a whole rump may weigh 3–4 kg). Preheat the oven to 230°C. Rub the fat with sea salt. Place in the oven and reduce the heat to 200°C. After 20 minutes, turn the oven down to 180°C.

If 2 kg of meat is used, keep the oven at the high temperature for less time – say 15 minutes; 3 kg of meat would be ready after 1½ hours at 180°C; and 2 kg of meat after 1 hour. This results in the meat being well-done on the outside and rare in the middle. Adjust times according to taste. Slice the meat and serve with hot English mustard.

GRILLED STEAK WITH PARSLEY BUTTER

ROAST SIRLOIN OF BEEF ••

1.5–2 kg sirloin or prime rib of beef, boned and rolled
salt and freshly ground pepper

yorkshire puffs:
1 egg
1 cup milk
1 cup flour
½ teaspoon salt

gravy:
1 tablespoon plain flour
1½ cups of stock or water
salt and freshly ground pepper

Rub beef with salt and pepper and put on a rack in a baking dish. A meat thermometer will help determine how long to cook the roast, although the weight before cooking can also be a reliable guide. Sear the meat in a 230°C oven for 15–20 minutes, turning once. Decrease the heat to 180°C and bake for 20 minutes per 500 g. For underdone beef, allow 15 minutes to the 500 g. For well-done beef, allow 30–35 minutes per 500 g. Baste every 15–20 minutes.

Half an hour before the meat is cooked, turn the oven to 200°C and put in the Yorkshire puffs, if making. Remove the meat, cover loosely, and leave to rest in a warm place while making the gravy. Continue to bake the Yorkshire puffs for a further 20–25 minutes. Transfer the beef to a serving dish and slice with a sharp knife across the grain.

yorkshire puffs: Beat the egg slightly, add milk, flour and salt and beat briskly for 2 minutes, until smooth. Allow to stand for 1 hour. Grease 10 muffin pans generously with either fat from the roast or butter. Divide the batter evenly among cups, filling about one-third full.

Bake at 200°C for about 45 minutes, until a rich golden colour. Serve immediately.

gravy: Skim off the fat in the baking dish, leaving only 1 tablespoon. Blend in a little flour and cook until brown. Stir in the stock. Cook, stirring and scraping the crust from the pan, until the gravy thickens slightly. Boil for 1 minute. Season with salt and pepper.
Serves 6–8.

ROAST FILLET OF BEEF ••

This roasted fillet of beef is excellent served cooled and sliced for a party dish accompanied with salads.

1.5 kg fillet of beef
salt and freshly ground pepper
90 g butter
¼ cup brandy

Preheat the oven to 200°C. Trim the fillet and remove all the tissue and skin with a sharp knife. Rub the meat with salt and pepper. Heat the butter in a heavy-based frying pan and sauté the fillet until brown on all sides, turning constantly with 2 spoons for about 10 minutes. Warm the brandy, ignite and pour over the fillet. Shake the pan and cook until the flame dies down. Baste with juices and cook for a further 1 minute. Transfer the fillet with the juices to a roasting pan. Bake for 15–20 minutes. Remove from the oven and stand, covered loosely with foil, for 5–8 minutes. Serve cut into slices and serve with béarnaise sauce *(see p. 304)* or pan gravy.

pan gravy: Add ½ cup wine or stock to the pan over a moderate heat. Scrape up the drippings, add a nut of butter and swirl around pan. Season with salt and pepper and pour over beef.
Serves 6.

BEEF PROVENÇALE ••

Chuck steak, gravy or shin and blade or beef cheek are all good for the long, slow cooking of this beautiful French dish. Make the day before and chill, allowing the fat to set on the top and be lifted away.

750 g lean beef, cut into large cubes
2 cloves garlic, finely chopped
3 tablespoons olive oil
1½ cups red wine
bouquet garni
125 g pancetta, thickly sliced (*optional*)
1 large onion, finely chopped
2 carrots, sliced thickly, across
2 tomatoes, peeled and quartered
½ cup beef stock
1–2 strips orange rind
salt and freshly ground pepper

Place the beef in a large bowl with the garlic, 1 tablespoon olive oil, wine and bouquet garni. Marinate in a cool place for at least 3 hours. Cut the pancetta, if using, into small cubes. Heat the remaining oil in a flameproof casserole and sauté the pancetta for 3 minutes.

Drain the beef, pouring the marinade into a separate saucepan. Boil rapidly until reduced by half. Meanwhile, add the beef to the pancetta and cook until coloured over a brisk heat. Add the onions and carrots and cook for a further 5 minutes. When the marinade has reduced, add to the pan with the bouquet garni. Add the tomatoes, stock and orange rind and season with the salt and pepper. Cover and simmer gently for 2–2½ hours, until meat is tender. Turn the meat into a serving dish. Remove the bouquet garni and any excess fat. Pour over the meat and sprinkle with chopped parsley. Serves 4.

note: to thicken gravy, combine 30 g butter with 1 tablespoon flour and whisk into the sauce. Bring to the boil and simmer for a few minutes.

BEEF BOURGUIGNONNE ••

1.25 kg stewing beef such as chuck, topside or blade
125 g pancetta or speck
1 tablespoon olive oil
30 g butter
24 small white onions, peeled
1 onion, finely chopped
1 tablespoon plain flour
2 cups red wine
about 1 cup beef stock or water
salt and freshly ground pepper
bouquet garni
1 clove garlic
10 button mushrooms
freshly chopped parsley

Preheat the oven to 150°C. Cut the beef into large cubes and the pancetta or speck into thin strips. Heat the oil with the butter in a flameproof casserole. Brown the small onions, then remove and set aside. Add the beef cubes in several lots and brown thoroughly, removing as each is done. Add the pancetta strips and the chopped onion and cook until softened and lightly coloured. Stir in the flour and cook another minute. Add the wine, stirring. Return the meat to the casserole and add enough beef stock or water to cover. Season with salt and pepper, adding bouquet garni and garlic. Bring slowly to a simmer then cover and cook in the oven for about 2 hours. Meanwhile, sauté the mushrooms in a little extra butter until lightly cooked. Add the onions to the beef for the last 30 minutes of cooking. Scatter with parsley and serve. Serves 6.

BEEF POT ROAST ••

2 tablespoons flour seasoned
  with salt and pepper
1.5 kg piece topside or rolled brisket
1 tablespoon olive oil
3 onions, finely chopped
3 tomatoes, peeled and quartered
1 carrot, peeled and diced
1 tablespoon parsley, chopped
1 bay leaf
1 tablespoon tomato paste
500 g new potatoes
2 tablespoons sour cream *(optional)*

Preheat the oven to 150°C. Rub the flour into the beef. Heat the oil in a frying pan and brown the meat well on all sides. Add the remaining ingredients, except the sour cream, mix well and baste the meat with this sauce. Place in a casserole, cover tightly and bake for 1 hour.

Add the potatoes and cook for a further hour or until tender. Baste frequently or turn the meat over halfway through cooking time. Just before serving, stir the sour cream into the gravy. Serves 8.

CARBONNADE OF BEEF ••

750 g round or chuck steak
1 or 2 tablespoons olive oil
2–3 onions, sliced thinly
1 tablespoon plain flour
1 clove garlic, crushed with salt
1 cup hot water
1 cup beer
bouquet garni
salt and freshly ground pepper
a pinch of ground nutmeg
a pinch of sugar
a dash of vinegar *(optional)*
8 rounds of baguette
Dijon mustard

Preheat the oven to 180°C. Cut the meat into large cubes. Heat the oil in a saucepan and brown the meat quickly on both sides. Add the sliced onions to the pan and brown well. Pour off a little of the fat, dust the meat with the flour and add the garlic. Add the hot water to the beer and then pour over the meat. Add the bouquet garni and season with the salt, pepper, nutmeg, sugar and vinegar, if using. Place in a casserole, cover tightly and cook gently in the oven for about 1½ hours. About 15 minutes before it is done, skim off any surface fat from the gravy and pour it on the rounds of bread. Spread these lightly with Dijon mustard and put on top of the casserole, pushing bread down below the surface to soak with the gravy. They will float again to the top. Remove the lid and bake for a further 15–20 minutes or until the bread is nicely browned. Serves 4.

BEEF POT ROAST

BASIC STEAK AND KIDNEY ••

1 kg chuck, blade or rump steak
1 ox kidney or 2 lamb kidneys
1 tablespoon plain flour
1½ teaspoons salt
1 teaspoon ground black pepper
½ teaspoon dried herbs
1 cup water

Remove any gristle from the beef and cut into large cubes, leaving a little fat. Core the kidney and cut into small pieces. Sprinkle with the flour, salt, pepper and herbs. Place in a bowl and pour water over. Cover with a double layer of greased baking paper or foil and tie with string. Place in a large saucepan, sitting on an upturned saucer, and fill with enough boiling water to come halfway up the sides of the bowl.

Steam for 3½–4 hours or until the meat is tender, replacing the water with more boiling water as it evaporates. Taste and correct seasoning. Serve hot. Serves 4–6.

note: basic steak and kidney may also be cooked in a flameproof casserole on top of the stove over a low heat for about 2 hours or in a 180°C oven for about 2 hours. The quickest method is to pressure cook it for 1 hour. Add a little more water if necessary.

STEAK AND KIDNEY SPONGE ••

This topping is light and tender and, I believe, a great improvement on the old-fashioned suet crust, particularly in a warm climate.

1 quantity basic steak and kidney *(see above)*
1 cup S.R. flour
½ teaspoon salt
2 eggs, separated
1 cup milk
60 g butter, melted

Cook the basic steak and kidney and keep hot by standing in a saucepan of hot water, while preparing the topping. Sift the flour and salt into a bowl, then make a well in the centre. Beat the egg yolks and stir in the milk. Pour into the flour mixture. Add the butter and stir until smooth. Beat the egg whites until stiff and fold into the mixture. Hold a large cooking spoon over the meat and gently pour the sponge mixture onto the spoon so that the topping spreads over the steak and kidney. Put into a large saucepan, sitting on an upturned saucer, and add enough boiling water to come halfway up the sides of the bowl.

Put the lid on the saucepan and bring the water to a fast boil. Boil for about 20 minutes. Serve immediately with a napkin tied around the bowl. Serves 4–6.

variations:
steak and kidney pudding: Mix 1 cup S.R. flour, 60 g shredded suet, a pinch of salt and about 4 tablespoons cold water into a soft dough. Roll out the dough on a lightly floured board to cover the basic steak and kidney mixture in the bowl. Steam, as above, for 1 hour. Serves 4–6.

steak and kidney pie: Spoon the cooked basic steak and kidney into an oval ovenproof dish and allow to cool. Preheat the oven to 200°C. Roll out 250 g puff pastry on a lightly floured board into an oblong shape 2 cm larger than the top of dish. Cut out to fit dish and cut another strip 2 cm wide. Place the strip on the edge of the dish, then brush with a little beaten egg and cover with the pastry top. Trim the edge. Cut an air vent from centre. Brush with egg and bake for 20–30 minutes. Reduce the heat to 180°C and bake for a further 30–40 minutes. Serves 4–6.

LAMB

For sheer simplicity, a plump, sizzling, grilled lamb chop takes a lot to beat. Unless you prefer a tender leg of lamb cooked 'to the pink', or does your heart really long for an old fashioned Irish stew?

WHEN BUYING LAMB

The flesh is a pinkish colour, lighter in colour than beef and there should be an even coating of firm white fat. Very lean lamb is seldom good.

leg: For roasting, braising or stewing. Sometimes the chump end is sold separately. If using mutton, make a curry or boil and serve with caper or parsley sauce (see p. 302).

loin: Served whole for roasting or cut into chops for grilling. If whole, ask the butcher to cut through the chop bones for easier carving. It can also be boned and rolled for easy roasting.

best neck: Cutlets are cut from the best end of the neck. They may be grilled or pan-fried.

middle or scrag neck: Cheap and good for stews, casseroles or broth. There is a high proportion of bone to flesh so you need to allow 375 g per serve.

shoulder: For roasting, it is often boned and filled with a stuffing, then rolled. Because it is a juicy and succulent joint, some prefer it for curries and stews.

breast: Very fatty and requires careful preparation. I like to cook it, then cool it and remove the excess fat before using it in Irish stew and other casserole dishes.

tongue: Often salted, then boiled and served hot with caper or parsley sauce (see p. 302). It can also be pressed and served cold.

CRUMBED LAMB CUTLETS •

about ½ cup plain flour seasoned with salt and pepper
2 eggs, beaten
1½ cups dry breadcrumbs
8 lamb cutlets
2 tablespoons oil
30 g butter
1 lemon, cut into wedges

Place the flour in a shallow bowl. Beat the eggs in another bowl and put the breadcrumbs in a third bowl. Trim excess fat off the cutlets and dust with the flour. Dip, one at a time, into the eggs, then coat evenly with the breadcrumbs. Set aside. This can be done beforehand and the crumbed cutlets kept chilled until ready to cook.

In a large frying pan, heat the oil with the butter. When sizzling, fry the cutlets until golden, about 3 minutes. Turn and cook the other sides, until golden. Drain on paper towels and keep in a warm place until all the cutlets are done. Serve immediately with lemon wedges. Serves 4.

GRILLED LAMB CHOPS •

8 thick short loin lamb chops
salt and freshly ground black pepper

Preheat griller for 5 minutes on a high setting. Trim off excess fat. Curl the fat edge of the tails into the meat to make a neat shape of each chop. Season and put the chops on a rack and grill. After about 5 minutes, turn with tongs and grill for another 5 minutes or until done. Serves 4.

GRILLED TANDOORI LAMB CUTLETS ••

The secret of this dish is the yoghurt marinade — the longer the meat is left in the marinade, the more flavoursome and succulent the finished dish will be. The tandoori mix can be prepared at home or, alternatively, there are some excellent commercial tandoori mixes available.

12 lamb cutlets, well trimmed of fat
½ teaspoon salt
1 tablespoon grated fresh ginger
1 cup plain yoghurt
1 tablespoon lemon juice
½ teaspoon paprika
1–2 tablespoons oil

tandoori mix:
2 teaspoons turmeric
1 teaspoon ground paprika
½ teaspoon ground chillies
1 teaspoon garam masala
½ teaspoon ground cardamom
a good pinch of saffron threads or powdered saffron

First, put the tandoori mix ingredients together and set aside. Scrape the cutlet bones of any fat. Combine the salt, ginger, tandoori mix, yoghurt, lemon juice and paprika into a wide glass or ceramic dish. Add the cutlets and turn to coat thoroughly with the marinade. Cover and chill for at least 6 hours, preferably overnight.

Preheat a griller or have glowing coals ready in a barbecue. Brush the racks with the oil and arrange the cutlets, not too close together, under or over the heat. Cook for 5 minutes on each side or until done to taste, brushing a few times with oil. *Serves 4–6.*

ROASTING LAMB

In countries where lamb is plentiful, good and relatively inexpensive, the shoulder and leg seem to be the favourite cuts for what is often referred to as a 'baked dinner'. In many homes, this was the Sunday family dinner. I say 'was' because times have changed, although there is a resurgence of this great treat as something we all want to be able to do.

A leg of lamb may be roasted on a rack, surrounded by potatoes, pumpkin and onions and is usually served with a gravy and mint sauce. Alternatively, it can be served Mediterranean-style with the colourful vegetables of that part of the world. A shoulder of lamb is treated in much the same way. The French like their lamb 'pink', while in Australia and England the taste is often for well-done lamb, although many of us now accept pink lamb and rather like it. It's just a matter of taste. Loins and racks of lamb are often roasted, but they don't seem to constitute the 'roast' of family meals.

timing for a roast of lamb: Allow a total roasting time of approximately 20 minutes per 500 g, plus 20 minutes for lamb pink in the centre or 30 minutes for well-done lamb. Always rest the lamb for 15 minutes in a turned-off oven, with door ajar, or another warm place before carving. A shoulder of lamb requires less time.

ROAST LEG OF LAMB WITH VEGETABLES ● ●

2 kg leg of lamb
1 large clove garlic, peeled and sliced
salt and freshly ground pepper
olive oil
6 small or 3 large potatoes
750 g pumpkin (optional)

gravy:
1 tablespoon plain flour
1 cup stock or vegetable water

Preheat the oven to 220°C. Wipe the lamb clean and trim off the excess fat. Cut 6–8 small incisions in the lamb with a pointed knife and insert the slivers of garlic. Rub the lamb generously with the salt and pepper before putting into a baking dish and drizzle with oil. Sear in the oven for 20 minutes. Meanwhile, peel the potatoes and pumpkin, if using, and cut into chunks.

After 20 minutes, remove from the oven and baste well with the drippings. Place the vegetables around the meat and season with salt. Reduce the oven temperature to 180°C and cook for a further 1¼–1½ hours, basting the lamb every 20–30 minutes and turning the vegetables. When cooked, place lamb on a serving platter. Cover loosely with foil and rest in a warm place for 15 minutes. Return the vegetables to the oven, increase the heat to 200°C and cook until golden and tender.

gravy: Drain off all but 1 tablespoon of fat from the juices in the dish. Add flour and stir over a moderate heat until well browned. Add stock or vegetable water and stir until mixture boils. Lower the heat and simmer gently, stirring occasionally, until it thickens. Strain into a gravy boat or jug. Serves 6–8.

FRENCH ROAST LAMB ● ●

Prepare as before, but omit vegetables and cook as follows: Place lamb on a rack in a baking dish, put 1 cup water, 1 tablespoon butter and 1 teaspoon salt in the dish. Roast in a moderate 180°C oven for 17–20 minutes per 500 g. French roast lamb is always served, with the flesh still pink. Baste lamb every 15 minutes.

gravy: Add a little water to the baking dish after the meat has been removed. Scrape the juices in the bottom of the dish. Strain and serve with roast.

ROAST LAMB CORIANDER ● ●

Deep diamond cuts on the surface of the lamb, in this dish, allow the spicy seasonings to penetrate and flavour the meat. Carve the lamb in thick but small slices and serve with rice pilaf and any of the sambals, chutneys or pickles that usually accompany curried food.

2 kg leg of lamb
1½ tablespoons lemon juice
2 cloves garlic, chopped
2 tablespoons oil
1 teaspoon turmeric
1 tablespoon ground coriander
2 teaspoons ground cumin
1 cup water

With a sharp knife, score the leg of lamb in a diamond pattern in cuts about 5 mm deep. Combine all other ingredients and rub well into lamb. Cover and allow to stand for 1 hour in the refrigerator. Preheat the oven to 180°C. Put the lamb into a shallow baking dish without the rack. Pour the water into the dish and roast in the oven for 1½ hours, basting with the cooking juices. Serves 6.

RACKS OF LAMB WITH CUMIN CRUST ••

4 small racks of lamb, consisting of 3 or 4 cutlets each
1½ cups fresh white breadcrumbs
2 tablespoons chopped parsley
1 tablespoon ground cumin
2 cloves garlic, finely chopped
1 tablespoon extra virgin olive oil
sea salt and freshly ground black pepper

roasted stuffed tomatoes:

4 roma tomatoes, halved
2 sun-dried tomatoes or red capsicum, quartered
4 black olives, pitted and finely chopped
1 teaspoon capers

Preheat the oven to 200°C. Trim the racks of excess fat and score the fat in several places. Mix the breadcrumbs, parsley, cumin, garlic and oil in a small bowl and season with salt and pepper. Cover the scored side of the lamb with a thick layer of the crumb mixture, pressing onto the meat.

Place the halved tomatoes on a baking tray and top each with a the quartered sun-dried tomato or capsicum, sprinkle with the olives and capers and set aside. Place the lamb in a baking dish and roast for 15–20 minutes, until the meat is pink and juicy. Allow a further 5–10 minutes for well-done. Leave to rest for 5 minutes.

Drizzle a little olive oil over the stuffed tomatoes and season with salt and pepper. Place in the oven to roast while the lamb is resting. Transfer the meat to 4 heated plates and surround with the roasted tomatoes. Serve if liked, with roast potatoes. Serves 4.

LEG OF LAMB WITH HARICOT BEANS ••

The French often serve a bowl of haricot beans with their roasted leg of lamb.

500 g dried haricot beans
2 large onions, quartered
bouquet garni
1 clove garlic, peeled
a few peppercorns
2 kg leg of French roast lamb *(see p. 101)*
30 g butter
4 golden shallots, chopped
1 teaspoon salt
2 tablespoons chopped parsley

Soak the beans overnight in water to cover, then drain. Place in a large saucepan with fresh water to cover, adding the onions, bouquet garni, garlic and peppercorns. Bring slowly to the boil, skim and cover. Cook gently for 1½ hours or until tender.

Meanwhile, put the leg of lamb on to roast. Melt the butter in a saucepan 30 minutes before the lamb is due to finish cooking. Add the shallots and cook until softened, about 4 minutes. Drain the cooked beans and add to the pan, shaking to toss them with the butter and shallots. Add ½ cup of the lamb juices from the pan. Cover and simmer gently for a further 15 minutes. season with salt. Place the lamb on a serving platter and strain the juices from the dish into a gravy boat or jug. Toss the haricot beans with parsley and serve separately. Serves 6–8.

note: add a peeled and diced tomato to the shallots before the cooked beans, if desired.

RACKS OF LAMB WITH CUMIN CRUST

LOIN OF LAMB WITH ARTICHOKES AND POTATOES ● ●

1 x 1.5 kg loin of lamb in one piece
1 x 440 g can artichoke hearts or
　3–6 artichokes in oil, drained
4 large potatoes, peeled and
　sliced into thin rounds
30 g butter
salt and freshly ground pepper
1 tablespoon olive oil

Ask your butcher to bone the loin of lamb. Remove the skin and any excess fat then roll and tie securely. Preheat the oven to 200°C. Slice each artichoke into thirds and arrange in alternate layers with the sliced potatoes in a well-buttered oval casserole or small baking dish. Sprinkle each layer with salt and pepper, dot with butter. Bake for 15 minutes.

Heat the oil in a frying pan and brown the loin of lamb on all sides over a moderate heat. Put on top of the vegetables in the casserole, cover tightly with lid or foil and return to the oven. Bake for a further 40–50 minutes or until the meat is tender but still pink inside. Serves 6.

LAMB PILAF ● ●

500 g boned shoulder of lamb, cubed
2 onions, chopped
60 g butter
1 cup long-rice
3 cups beef stock
1 teaspoon oregano
salt and freshly ground pepper
2 tablespoons tomato paste
1 tablespoon melted butter
½ cup seeded raisins

Sauté the lamb cubes and onions in the butter, until the meat is brown and the onions are golden. Add the rice and cook, stirring, for 1 minute. Add the stock, oregano and seasoning. Cover and cook slowly for 40 minutes or until the meat and the rice is tender. Combine the tomato paste and melted butter and add to the pan. Stir in the raisins and serve. Serves 4.

IRISH STEW ●

Authentic Irish stew has 1 kg potatoes and 250 g onions to each 500 g meat. Equal quantities of meat and potatoes can be used, but the gravy may need to be slightly thickened before serving.

1 kg lamb neck chops
2 kg potatoes, peeled
500 g onions, thickly sliced
2 cups water
a bunch of herbs such as parsley and thyme
2 bay leaves
salt and freshly ground pepper

Trim excess fat from the chops. Slice a few of the potatoes and halve the rest. In a deep saucepan, layer the sliced potatoes, then the meat, then the halved potatoes with the other ingredients. Cover tightly and simmer gently for 1½–2 hours. This stew should be thick, well seasoned and creamy. Serves 6.

BRAISED LAMB SHANKS ••

6 lamb shanks, French-trimmed
plain flour seasoned with salt and pepper
1 tablespoon olive oil
1 garlic, crushed
1 onion, chopped
1 cup thickly sliced carrots
2 tomatoes, peeled, seeded and quartered
¾ cup red wine
¾ cup stock
grated rind of 1 lemon
1 tablespoon chopped fresh oregano

Preheat the oven to 180°C. Wipe the shanks with a damp cloth. Dredge with the seasoned flour. Heat the oil in a flameproof casserole and brown the shanks a few at a time. Remove and set aside. Add the garlic, onion and carrot to casserole and cook, stirring, for 5 minutes. Add the tomatoes, wine, stock, lemon rind and oregano and boil, stirring well, for a few minutes. Return the shanks to the casserole.

Cover and bake for 1½ hours or until the meat is tender. If liked, thicken the gravy with a tablespoon of flour blended with 2 tablespoons water, adding this a little at a time. The lamb should be very tender and almost falling from the bone. Serve with steamed rice or mashed potatoes. *Serves 4–6.*

SPICED LAMB STEW ••

1½ cups dried haricot or kidney beans, or chickpeas
1 tablespoon olive oil
1 large onion, sliced
500 g boneless lamb, cut into 2 cm cubes
1 tablespoon ground chillies
1 teaspoon turmeric
2 cloves garlic, crushed
2 carrots, diced
salt and freshly ground pepper
2 cups water
8 cherry tomatoes
1 bunch parsley, chopped
1 small bunch mint, finely chopped
lemon juice

Soak the dried beans or peas overnight in plenty of cold water to cover. Drain and place in a large saucepan with fresh water to cover. Bring to the boil and cook for about 20 minutes. Drain.

Meanwhile, heat the oil in a large frying pan and sauté the onion gently, remove and set aside. Add the lamb cubes in a few lots and brown all over. Add the chilli and turmeric and return the sautéed onions with the garlic and carrots. Season with salt and pepper and stir. Add about 2 cups water to the drained beans then cover and simmer gently for about 1 hour. Add the cherry tomatoes, parsley and mint and continue to cook a further 30 minutes. Sprinkle with lemon juice just before serving. *Serves 4–6.*

PORK

A favourite in just about every country in the world, pork is at its best during the cold winter months. From a simple pork roast with crackling to Chinese barbecued pork, Italian pork involtini or Hungarian goulash, pork turns up in all kind of dishes.

WHEN BUYING PORK

Look for pale pink flesh that is finely grained, with pearly white fat and thin skin.

leg: For roasting. Make sure that you ask your butcher to score the skin.

fillet: For roasting, grilling or, if cut into thin steaks, pan-frying.

loin: For roasting, but score the skin first. Loin chops may be cut off this for pan-frying.

shoulder: May be boned and rolled or purchased whole. Suitable for roasting or casseroles.

spare ribs: Demand for spare ribs has encouraged butchers to prepare these for Chinese dishes and barbecues. As there is a high proportion of bone to flesh, allow about 375 g per serve.

belly: Often sold salted, for boiling. If not too fat, fresh belly of pork is ideal for some Chinese dishes and for stuffing and roasting.

hand and spring: This lower part of the shoulder is often sold salted for boiling. Can be boned and rolled for a roast. Requires long, careful cooking.

liver: Makes an excellent pâté.

PORK INVOLTINI ••

6 thin pork schnitzels
1 clove garlic, finely chopped
2–3 sage leaves, chopped
6 tablespoons fresh white breadcrumbs
⅓ cup Parmesan cheese shavings
2 tablespoons olive oil
½ cup dry white wine
salt and freshly ground pepper
½ cup chicken stock

Flatten the pork schnitzels if necessary, then cut in half. Mix the garlic with the sage and breadcrumbs and sprinkle, with the cheese shavings, on each piece of pork. Roll up and secure each with a toothpick. Heat the oil in a large, heavy-based frying pan and brown the rolls on all sides. Add the wine and season with the salt and pepper. Bring to the boil, then add the stock. When simmering, reduce the heat and cook gently for about 5 minutes,stirring occasionally. Remove the pork rolls, keeping them warm, and continue cooking the liquid until syrupy and reduced, for about 3 minutes. Remove the toothpicks from the rolls before serving 2 or 3 per person, with the sauce spooned over. Good with new potatoes and a green salad. *Serves 4.*

PORK CHOPS WITH PRUNES, APRICOTS AND SPINACH ••

Thick pork chops, slit on one side, make perfect pockets for filling with an exotic fruit mixture. A gentle wine sauce finishes the dish admirably.

¼ cup pitted prunes
¼ cup dried apricots
1½ cups white wine
12 English spinach leaves
4 thick pork medallions or loin chops
¼ cup flour
salt and freshly ground pepper
30 g butter
2 tablespoons olive oil
1 clove garlic, finely chopped
2 spring onions, including some green, chopped

Soak the prunes and apricots overnight in the wine or, if time is short, simmer very gently in the wine until soft. Remove from the liquid and set aside. Reserve the liquid. Thoroughly wash and trim the spinach. With a very sharp knife, carefully cut a slit through the top (the lean part, not the fatty edge) of the pork medallions, just enough to make a pocket for filling. Spoon the prunes, apricots and spinach evenly into each piece of pork. Secure with a toothpick, if desired.

Dust each medallion with the flour, seasoned with salt and pepper. Heat the butter and oil in a large, heavy-based frying pan and gently fry the pork medallions until golden on each side. Add the garlic and spring onion and continue to cook gently until soft, for about 1–2 minutes. Increase the heat, add the reserved liquid to the pan and bring to the boil. Cover and simmer gently until tender, for about 8 minutes. Serve the pork with the sauce spooned over. Serves 4.

ORIENTAL PORK SPARE RIBS ••

These spare ribs are simmered gently in Oriental spices then finished off in the oven to crisp the edges.

1.5 kg pork spare ribs
2 tablespoons oil
5 tablespoons light soy sauce
½ cup chicken stock or water
2 tablespoons hoisin sauce
1 teaspoon sugar
4 slices fresh ginger, shredded
2 onions, thinly sliced
5 tablespoons dry sherry

Preheat the oven to 180°C. Blanch the spare ribs in boiling water for 5 minutes, then drain and pat dry with paper towels. Put the ribs and oil into a flameproof casserole. Heat until the oil just begins to bubble, then stir-fry for 5 minutes over a moderate heat to brown the ribs. Add soy sauce, stock or water, hoisin sauce, sugar, ginger and onions. Stir until well blended, turning the ribs.

Cover the casserole and put into the oven for 45 minutes–1 hour, stirring every 20 minutes. At the first stirring, add the sherry. Take the dish from the oven, remove the spare ribs and place them side by side on the bottom of a baking dish lined with foil. Put them into the oven and increase the temperature to 220°C. Roast for 12–15 minutes until crisp and golden brown. These are delicious warm with rice. Serves 4–6.

ROAST PORK ••

Put a loin or leg of pork into a very hot 250°C oven for 30 minutes and then reduce the heat to 180°C. This ensures a crisp crackling. Allow 1 hour cooking time per kg, plus 30 minutes for the piece.

1 loin of pork weighing about 2 kg, or 1 leg of pork
coarse salt

Ask your butcher to score the skin of the pork. Preheat the oven to 250°C. Rub all over with coarse salt. Roast for 30 minutes or until the skin is crisp and golden. Reduce the heat to 180°C and roast until cooked through. Serve hot with vegetables and apple sauce *(see p. 304)* or fried or baked apples.

ROASTED STUFFED BELLY OF PORK ••

This is an economical pork roast, with lots of flavour and crunchy crackling.

about 1.25 kg pork belly in one piece, boned and scored
4 delicious apples, peeled and cored
15 g butter

stuffing:
2 medium onions
4 cloves garlic
30 g butter
250 g cooked English spinach, chopped finely
1 cup fresh breadcrumbs
½ cup cream
500 g pork mince
1 large egg
½ teaspoon chopped thyme leaves
½ teaspoon chopped fresh rosemary
salt and freshly ground pepper
¼ teaspoon grated nutmeg
grated rind of ½ lemon

gravy:
2 tablespoons flour
2 cups stock
salt and freshly ground pepper

Ask your butcher to bone the pork and score the rind. Preheat the oven to 230°C. Cut a slit right through the centre of the meat to form a pocket for the stuffing. It is easier to start cutting from the short ends, meeting in the middle, and leaving long sides intact to hold stuffing. Fill the cavity of pork with the stuffing and close each end with a large skewer.

Grease a baking dish large enough to hold the pork lying flat and place the meat in it, skin-side up. Rub the skin with a little salt and bake for 25–30 minutes, until the skin has blistered. Reduce the heat to 190°C and continue cooking for a further 45 minutes.

Remove the meat and place on a hot serving platter. Leave to rest for at least 5 minutes. Meanwhile, cut the apples into slices and fry lightly in a little butter. Cut across the pork into slices, taking a piece of crackling for each serving. Serve with the apples and gravy.

stuffing: Cook the onion and garlic in the butter for about 5 minutes or until softened. Add the spinach and cook, stirring, until the liquid has evaporated. Meanwhile, soak the breadcrumbs in the cream. In a large bowl, combine the spinach mixture, breadcrumbs and the pork mince with the egg, seasonings and lemon rind.

gravy: Pour off all but 1½ tablespoons of fat from the baking dish, add the flour and stir over moderate heat until browned. Pour in the stock and stir until thick and smooth. Season with salt and pepper and pour into a gravy boat or jug. *Serves 4–6.*

ROAST PORK

PORK CHOPS WITH SAGE •

4 thick pork chops or steaks
2 tablespoons plain flour
1 teaspoon finely chopped onion
1 teaspoon finely chopped parsley
1 teaspoon chopped sage leaves
1 egg
salt and freshly ground black pepper
1 cup fresh breadcrumbs
olive oil, for frying

Trim the excess fat from the pork. Dredge the pork in flour. Combine the onion, parsley, sage and egg in a bowl. Beat well and season with salt and pepper. Dip the pork in the egg mixture. Drain and dip into the breadcrumbs, pressing them well onto the pork. Stand for 20 minutes. Fry for 10 minutes in the oil, turning once. *Serves 4.*

HUNGARIAN GOULASH ••

30 g butter
1 tablespoon olive oil
2 cups chopped onion
1 kg boneless shoulder pork, cut into cubes
2 tablespoons paprika
1 tablespoon flour
1 tablespoon tomato paste
salt and freshly ground black pepper
1 x 440 g can sauerkraut, drained
½ cup sour cream or natural yoghurt

Heat the butter and oil in a large flameproof casserole and cook onions until golden. Add the pork and paprika and sauté for 5 minutes. Stir in the flour and cook a further minute. Add water to cover and stir in the tomato paste. Bring to the boil and season with salt and pepper. Cover and cook over a very gentle heat for 30 minutes. Remove the cover and stir in the sauerkraut. Cook for a further 30 minutes. Stir in sour cream, cover and cook for 25 minutes. *Serves 4–6.*

VEAL

THIS DELICATE MEAT IS VERSATILE AND PRACTICALLY EVERY CUT CAN BE MADE INTO THE MOST DELICATE DISH, BUT IT DOES REQUIRE VERY CAREFUL COOKING. LUCKILY, THE REWARDS ARE WELL WORTH ANY PAINS YOU MAY HAVE TO TAKE.

when buying veal: The flesh should be very pale with just a tinge of pink. There is very little fat, which should be white and satiny. There should be no unpleasant odour.

fillet: For roasting. As it is very lean, baste regularly during cooking or wrap with a little bacon. The fillet is often cut into steaks or escalopes (scaloppini) and flattened for the thinner schnitzel.

shoulder: For roasting. It may be bought on the bone or boned ready for stuffing and rolling. Good also for stews and goulash.

nut: Cut from the thick part of the leg whole. Roast or use for casseroles and goulash.

loin: Great for roasting or cutting into chops for pan-frying or casseroles.

WIENER SCHNITZEL ● ●

4 veal steaks, thinly cut and flattened
salt and freshly ground black pepper
2 tablespoons plain flour
1 egg, beaten
1 cup fine fresh breadcrumbs
olive oil, for frying
30 g butter
lemon slices
capers

Flatten the veal steaks until very thin. Halve or leave whole. Season with salt and pepper and dip into the flour, egg then breadcrumbs. Press with the heel of your hand to firm the coating. Chill for 30 minutes.

Heat sufficient oil to cover the base of a frying pan. Add half the butter and, when hot, add half the veal. Cook about 1½ minutes on each side, until golden brown. Drain on paper towels and keep warm on a heated platter. Repeat with remaining veal. Serve with slices of lemon and a few capers. Serves 4.

VEAL CORDON BLEU ● ●

4 veal steaks, thinly cut and flattened
salt and freshly ground black pepper
4 thin slices Gruyère cheese
4 thin slices ham
2 tablespoons plain flour
2 eggs, beaten
1 cup fresh breadcrumbs
60 g butter

Flatten the veal steaks and sprinkle with salt and pepper. Put a slice of cheese and ham on one half of each steak and fold the steak over to hold the filling. Press edges together. Dip into the flour, eggs and finish with the breadcrumbs. Press firmly and chill for 30 minutes. Heat the butter in a large frying pan and fry the steaks for 4 minutes on each side, until golden. Serves 4.

VEAL WITH MUSHROOM SAUCE ● ●

4 thin veal steaks
flour, for dusting
60 g butter
12 button mushrooms, quartered or sliced
2 tablespoons brandy or dry sherry
½ cup cream
salt and freshly ground pepper

Flatten the veal steaks, cut in two if large, and dust with flour. Heat half the butter in a shallow frying pan and, in batches, fry the veal on each side until brown, for about 3 minutes. Remove from the pan and keep in a warm place. Add remaining butter and the mushrooms, cover and simmer for 4 minutes. Warm the brandy or sherry, ignite and pour over. Shake the pan until flames subside. Stir in cream, season with salt and pepper and simmer for a few minutes. Spoon over the veal. Serve with noodles or steamed rice. Serves 4.

SALTIMBOCCA ●

This dish tastes so good and literally 'jumps in the mouth', as the Italian name implies.

8 sage leaves
4 thin veal steaks, halved
4 slices prosciutto, halved
45 g butter
¾ cup dry white wine
salt and freshly ground black pepper
extra butter *(optional)*

Place a sage leaf on each slice of veal, top with prosciutto and secure with toothpicks. Melt the butter in a frying pan, add veal in several lots, and brown quickly on both sides, turning carefully. Arrange the veal on a warm serving dish. Add the wine to the pan, with a little salt and plenty of freshly ground pepper, and scrape base well. A nut of butter may be swirled in for a richer sauce. Spoon the sauce over and serve. Serves 4.

GRILLED VEAL CHOPS WITH BASIL BUTTER ••

A ribbed grill pan does a lovely job of cooking the chops with just a brushing of olive oil. A good grill, that you trust to get hot, does the job too.

2 tablespoons olive oil
6–8 rib veal chops, French-trimmed
salt and freshly ground pepper

basil butter:
90 g unsalted butter
1 teaspoon grated lemon rind
1 teaspoon lemon juice
1 tablespoon finely chopped spring onion
2 tablespoons chopped basil leaves
salt and freshly ground pepper

Heat the grill pan or griller and brush with the olive oil. Pat the veal chops dry with paper towels and season with salt and pepper. Cook on a moderately high heat for 5 minutes on each side until golden and still slightly pink inside. Top each veal chop with one or two thin slices of the basil butter to serve.

basil butter: Cream the butter in a small bowl and beat in the lemon rind, then the juice, spring onion, basil and salt and pepper. Shape into a roll, wrap in a piece of foil then chill until firm. This may take an hour and can be done well in advance. Serves 4–6.

ROAST SHOULDER OF VEAL ••

2.5 kg shoulder of veal, boned and rolled
3 tablespoons oil or butter
2 onions, chopped
1 large carrot, diced
1 cup diced celery
2 bay leaves
10 peppercorns
1 clove garlic, crushed
1 teaspoon salt
½ teaspoon paprika
2 teaspoons each plain flour and butter, mixed together

Preheat the oven to 160°C. Heat the oil or butter in a flameproof heavy-based baking dish over a high heat. Sear the meat until brown all over. Lift out the meat and add the remaining ingredients except for the butter and flour mixture. Cook for 2 minutes over a moderate heat, until the onions begin to soften. Put the meat on a roasting rack over the diced vegetables. Add enough water to cover the vegetables, cover with foil or a lid and roast for 2½ hours. Uncover and cook a further 20 minutes adding more water, if necessary, to prevent drying out.

Thicken cooking liquid by whisking in flour and butter mixture and simmering for 5 minutes, stirring, until smooth. Remove string and cut into slices. Serve with the gravy. Serves 8.

OFFAL OR VARIETY MEATS

In many countries offal is just as prized as choice cuts of meat. Cervelles au beurre noir, or in english, brains in black butter sauce, is considered a dish fit for gourmets. As for myself, lamb's fry with bacon when properly prepared is one of the best dishes.

LAMB'S FRY WITH BACON •

8 rashers bacon, rind removed
1 lamb's fry, thinly sliced
plain flour seasoned with salt and pepper
60 g butter
1 cup stock
a little wine (optional)

Fry the bacon and keep warm. Melt the butter in the frying pan and fry, in batches, the lamb's fry dipped in the seasoned flour. Allow only 1–2 minutes on each side. Arrange on a hot dish with the bacon. Add the stock and wine to the pan and bring to the boil. Pour over the lamb's fry to serve. Serves 4.

KIDNEYS IN WINE SAUCE ••

2 veal kidneys or 6 lamb's kidneys
plain flour seasoned with salt and pepper
60 g butter
2 tablespoons chopped spring onions
2 teaspoons Dijon mustard
½ cup dry white wine
2 teaspoons lemon juice
¼ cup chopped parsley

Skin the kidneys, remove core and slice thinly. Dust with seasoned flour and brown in half the butter. Remove to a warm dish. Add the spring onions to the frying pan and cook. Add the mustard with the remaining butter and then add the wine and lemon juice. Return the kidneys to the pan and cook gently, until the liquid is reduced by half. Add the parsley and cook for 1 minute. Serve with fluffy boiled rice, noodles or with toast. Serves 4.

BRAINS IN BLACK BUTTER SAUCE ••

4 sets lamb's brains
1 tablespoon vinegar
1 teaspoon salt
4 peppercorns
4 whole cloves
1 clove garlic
bouquet garni
1 cup water

black butter sauce:

90 g butter
2–3 tablespoons chopped parsley
1 tablespoon wine vinegar

Soak the brains for 2 hours in cold water, changing the water at least twice. Clean carefully by removing loose pieces of skin and fibres. Combine the vinegar, salt, peppercorns, cloves, garlic, bouquet garni and water in a saucepan. Add the brains and bring slowly to boiling point. Cook gently for 10 minutes. Remove the brains. Halve and serve on a heated dish with black butter sauce.

black butter sauce: Melt the butter until it is a nut-brown colour, taking care not to let it burn. Add the parsley and allow to fry for 1–2 minutes. Pour over the brains, return the frying pan to the heat and add the vinegar. As soon as the vinegar is hot, spoon it over the brains. Serve immediately with steamed rice or creamy mashed potatoes. Serves 4.

MINCED MEAT

For flavour and economy, rissoles or meatballs are a favourite. Minced meat is just as rich in protein as expensive cuts and so has an important place in the diet.

HAMBURGERS •

3 slices bread, crusts removed
½ cup cream, evaporated milk or milk
1 kg minced steak
2 teaspoons salt
freshly ground pepper
½ teaspoon dry mustard powder
¼ cup grated onion
2 eggs
4–6 hamburger buns
shredded lettuce
2 tomatoes, sliced

Cut bread into squares and soak in the cream for 10 minutes, then beat with a fork. Mix with the meat, salt, pepper, mustard and onion in a large bowl. Mix in the eggs with a fork.

Shape into 8 even-sized patties with wet hands. Preheat the griller and brush the rack with oil. Grill hamburgers for about 5–8 minutes on each side or until brown. Serve hamburgers inside buttered hamburger buns with shredded lettuce and tomatoes. Serves 4–6.

hamburger variations:
herbed: To the meat mixture, add a little chopped fresh marjoram and thyme, ½ cup diced celery and 1 tablespoon chopped parsley.

onion: Sauté onion slices in butter until golden and heap on each hot hamburger.

cheeseburger: Top each hamburger, after turning and just finishing cooking, with 1–2 thin slices of cheese of your choice.

SWEDISH MEATBALLS •••

500 g lean, minced steak
250 g lean, minced pork and veal
1½ cups fresh breadcrumbs
½ cup cream
½ cup milk
1 onion, finely chopped
60 g butter
1 egg, beaten
salt and freshly ground pepper
¼ teaspoon ground ginger
a pinch of grated nutmeg
1 tablespoon plain flour
½–1 cup light sour cream

Mix the minced meats together well. Soak the breadcrumbs in the cream and milk. Cook the onion in half the butter until softened. Mix the meats, breadcrumb mixture, egg, onion and seasonings. Beat vigorously until fluffy, chill and form into small balls.

Melt the remaining butter in a frying pan and brown the meatballs, a few at a time. Shake the pan constantly to keep the balls round. Remove and keep warm. Stir the flour into the butter in the pan and cook, stirring, for 2 minutes without browning. Remove from the heat and blend in the sour cream. Cook, stirring, for 5 minutes. Season with salt, pepper and a little grated nutmeg, then spoon over the meatballs. Serve with hot boiled rice. Serves 6.

CABBAGE ROLLS ••

This version of cabbage rolls has a good lemon flavour and uses more meat than rice.

1 small cabbage
1 large onion, finely chopped
1 tablespoon olive oil
500 g minced beef or lamb
½ cup short-grain rice
1 tomato, peeled and chopped
3 tablespoons chopped parsley
1 teaspoon chopped mint or dill
¼ teaspoon ground allspice
¼ teaspoon ground cinnamon
salt and freshly ground pepper
juice of 2 lemons

Remove about 24 leaves of the cabbage without breaking them. It is best to have a saucepan large enough to drop the whole cabbage in boiling, salted water and blanch for about 7 minutes, until the leaves have softened enough to remove easily. Otherwise, blanch the separated raw leaves in salted boiling water for about 5 minutes and drain. Cut out thick centres of large leaves and cut very large leaves in half.

Gently fry the onion in the oil until soft and pale golden. Cool slightly and mix in a bowl with the meat, uncooked rice, tomato, parsley, mint or dill and seasonings. Place a tablespoon of filling on the base of each leaf, turn up at base end to cover filling, fold in sides and roll firmly into a neat cylinder. Squeeze lightly before arranging in one layer in the base of a saucepan which is lined with any torn or extra cabbage leaves. Continue rolling and filling the pan, separating each layer of rolls with the spare blanched cabbage leaves, until the entire filling is used. Add the lemon juice and hot water to cover then invert a heavy plate on top. Cover and simmer for about 1½ hours. Drain well and serve piping hot. *Serves about 6.*

EGGPLANT AND POTATO MOUSSAKA ••

4 tablespoons olive oil
750 g potatoes, peeled and sliced
1 eggplant, sliced
1 kg minced lamb
1 large onion, finely chopped
1 tablespoon chopped fresh oregano or 1 teaspoon dried
1 x 250 g can peeled, chopped tomatoes
2 cloves garlic, crushed
freshly ground pepper and salt
4 tablespoons grated Parmesan cheese

sauce:
30 g butter
2 tablespoons flour
1¼ cups milk
1 egg, lightly beaten
salt and freshly ground pepper

Heat 2 tablespoons of oil in a frying pan and cook the potatoes 4–5 minutes on each side. It will be necessary to cook these in a couple of batches. Remove and set aside. Heat the remaining oil in the frying pan and fry the eggplant on both sides for about 5 minutes. Remove and set aside. Add the meat, onion, oregano, tomatoes, garlic, salt and pepper and cook these gently together for 15 minutes, stirring from time to time. Preheat the oven to 180°C. Line a buttered 8-cup casserole with the potato slices. Put half the meat mixture in the casserole, cover this with a layer of eggplant and potatoes. Add the remaining meat mixture then the last of the vegetables.

Pour the sauce over the layered meat and vegetables, cover with a lid or foil and bake for 45 minutes. Remove foil, sprinkle the cheese over top and bake until golden. Serve hot or cold.

sauce: Melt the butter, blend in the flour and cook for a minute. Add milk, stirring over a moderate heat until sauce thickens. Add the egg and season to taste. *Serves 6.*

COLD MEATS

MEATS FOR SUMMER MAY BE COOKED IN THE COOL OF EVENING AND REFRIGERATED TO FORM THE BASIS OF EASY MEALS WITH SALADS, SAUCES AND CRISP RELISHES. THESE RECIPES INCLUDE OLD FAVOURITES LIKE CORNED BEEF, ABERDEEN SAUSAGE AND TONGUE, AS WELL AS SAUCES TO SERVE WITH THEM.

COUNTRY TERRINE •••

Anyone who has been to France will remember with nostalgia the magnificent pâtés and terrines. One can choose from an enormous selection of these meats for a simple lunch, eaten with the incomparable crusty batons and a glass of wine. These meats are commonly made at home in France, each household having its own recipe, which is often called pâté maison.

250 g pork fat
500 g pork belly
500 g veal neck
¼ cup each port and brandy
1 teaspoon thyme leaves, chopped
1 teaspoon fresh rosemary leaves, chopped
15 g butter
1 small onion, finely chopped
3 cloves garlic, peeled
500 g chicken livers
1 egg, lightly beaten
1 teaspoon salt
freshly ground black pepper
100 g pistachio nuts, blanched and peeled
a few sprigs of thyme

Slice some of the pork fat thinly and use to line a terrine mould, saving some for the top. Dice the remaining fat and half the pork belly. Dice half the veal. Marinate the diced meats together with the port, brandy and herbs for several hours.

Meanwhile, melt the butter in a small frying pan and cook the onion and garlic very gently for about 5 minutes until soft, without colouring. Cool this mixture. Cut the remaining veal and pork belly into pieces and mince, using a food processor. Remove and set aside. Remove any sinew from the chicken livers, place in the processor and mince. Preheat the oven to 140°C.

In a bowl, combine the minced meats with the minced livers, egg, diced meats with marinade, salt and a good grinding of black pepper. Fold the pistachio nuts through the mixture. Turn into the prepared terrine mould and top with the reserved slice of pork fat and thyme. Cover with a lid and place the terrine in a baking dish half-filled with hot water. Bake for 1¼ hours. Remove from the oven, take off the lid and place a light weight on top (about 750 g). This is for easier slicing. Leave for 2 days before eating to allow the flavours to develop. Cut into thick slices and serve with crusty bread and cornichons. Serves 8.

note: some cooks use what is called a luting paste, a mixture of plain flour and water to make a soft dough which is put around the edge of the lid to seal between the lid and the mould. It bakes into a crust and protects the terrine from too much shrinkage.

COUNTRY TERRINE

VITELLO TONNATO • • •
6 anchovy fillets
2 kg boned and rolled leg of veal
1 onion, sliced
2 stalks celery, sliced
2 carrots, sliced
2 sprigs parsley
2 whole cloves
salt and freshly ground black pepper
2 or 3 bay leaves
1 cup dry white wine (optional)
lemon slices

tuna sauce:
½ cup mayonnaise
200 g can tuna in oil
6 anchovy fillets
1 teaspoon capers
2 tablespoons lemon juice
freshly ground black pepper

Cut the anchovy fillets into small pieces. With a sharp pointed knife, make holes in the surface of the meat and insert the anchovy pieces. Place the meat in a flameproof casserole with the onion, celery, carrots, parsley and cloves. Season with salt and pepper. Put the bay leaves on top.

Pour in the wine and sufficient water to cover the meat. Bring slowly to the boil, cover and simmer very gently for 1½–2 hours. When the veal is tender, allow to cool in the stock. Drain and reserve the stock. Remove the string and place the veal in a ceramic, glass or stainless steel bowl. Cover with the tuna sauce and marinate overnight in the refrigerator.

A few hours before serving, remove the veal from the sauce and slice thinly. Arrange the slices on a serving platter and spoon over the sauce, thinned with a little of the reserved veal stock. Chill again until ready to serve. Garnish with sliced lemon.

tuna sauce: Make a thick mayonnaise (see p. 306). Pound the tuna with the anchovy fillets, capers and lemon juice until smooth. Season with the black pepper. Combine with the mayonnaise in a blender, adding a little of the veal stock if the sauce is too thick. **Serves 8**.

ABERDEEN SAUSAGE • •
250 g rashers bacon, rind removed
500 g lean minced steak
1 cup fresh breadcrumbs
1 tablespoon tomato ketchup
  or 2 teaspoons Worcestershire sauce
1 tablespoon chopped parsley
freshly ground pepper
1 teaspoon salt
a little ground nutmeg
grated rind of ½ lemon
1 egg
plain flour, for dusting
extra breadcrumbs

Mince the bacon and blend with the minced steak. Add the breadcrumbs, ketchup or Worcestershire sauce, parsley and seasonings and mix well with beaten egg. Form into a long roll. Flour well, roll in a scalded floured cloth, tie both ends with string and plunge into a saucepan of boiling water. Boil for 2 hours. The sausage may also be steamed in a greased pudding bowl. While still hot, roll in extra breadcrumbs and place in a 120°C oven to dry for about 15 minutes. Serve in slices when cold. **Serves 6–8**.

POTTED HOUGH ••

Potted hough is a dish as old as time and one known to every true Scot. It is a simple dish of chopped meat, set in its own jelly. When served with a little vinegar and hot English mustard, it's a great dish.

1.5 kg beef shanks, cut into thick slices
2 large knuckles of veal or pig's trotters
1 onion, peeled and sliced,
¼ teaspoon mixed spice
6 black peppercorns
1 bay leaf
3–4 anchovy fillets, mashed
salt and freshly ground black pepper
cucumber slices, to garnish

Put the beef shanks, veal knuckles or pig's trotters, onion, mixed spice, peppercorns and bay leaf into a large, heavy-based saucepan and cover with cold water. Bring to the boil and skim the top. Reduce the heat, half cover and simmer gently for 3 hours. Cool and remove the meat from the broth. Strain the broth. Trim away the fat and gristle and remove the bones from the meat. Chop the meat finely. Return the chopped meat to the broth. Boil uncovered, until reduced, for 20 minutes. Add the anchovies and season with salt and pepper. Boil for a further 5 minutes to blend the flavours. Pour into 1 large or 2 small bowls, which have first been rinsed with cold water. Cool, cover with cling wrap and chill until firm.

To serve, turn out onto a serving plate and garnish with cucumber slices. Accompany the potted hough with small bowls of malt vinegar and hot English mustard. Serve with a bowl of pickled gherkins or tiny cornichons, tomatoes, cucumber and a potato salad. Serves 6–8.

CORNED BEEF ••

1 large onion, peeled
6 whole cloves
1.5–2 kg corned beef, silverside or rolled brisket
1 tablespoon lemon juice or white vinegar
12 black peppercorns
1 blade mace
2 stalks celery
1 bay leaf
bouquet garni
2 tablespoons brown sugar
1 carrot

Halve the onion and stud with the cloves. Put the meat into a large saucepan with all other ingredients then add enough cold water to cover. Cover and simmer for approximately 1 hour per kg after it has reached simmering point. The cooking time will vary according to the cut and age of the meat.

If the meat is cooked, a fine metal skewer inserted through the thickest part of the meat will come out easily. Turn off the heat and allow the beef to cool in the liquid. Chill and slice thinly. Serves 6.

note: mace is the slightly more pungent layer between a nutmeg and its outer shell.

OX TONGUE ••

1 ox tongue
6 whole allspice
6 whole cloves
1 onion, sliced
bouquet garni
1 carrot, quartered
1 bay leaf
1 stalk celery
6 peppercorns
1 tablespoon salt

Curl the tongue into a saucepan. Add water to cover, the allspice, cloves, onion, bouquet garni, carrot, bay leaf, celery and peppercorns. Add the salt only if the tongue is unsalted or not smoked. Bring to the boil, cover and simmer for 2–3 hours or until the tongue, tested at the root end with a skewer, is tender. Allow to cool 1 hour in liquid. Lift out of the pan, remove the root and bones of tongue and peel off the skin. Serve cold in thin slices. Serves 6.

note: use this method for cooking an unsalted, salted or smoked tongue.

PRESSED TONGUE ••

Rinse the salted, unsalted or smoked tongue with fresh cold water then cook it as in the previous recipe. Put the trimmed tongue into a small round bowl and pour in a little of the cooking liquid. Put a plate on top, making sure it fits just inside the bowl, and put a heavy weight on the plate. Chill overnight. Serve cold in thin slices.

PORK RILLETTES ••
(SHREDDED PORK PÂTÉ)

1 kg pork belly
1 large clove garlic
sprig thyme
salt and freshly ground pepper
good pinch of grated nutmeg

Remove the rind and small bones from the pork belly. Cut the meat into small pieces and place in a heavy-based saucepan with remaining ingredients. Cover and cook over a very gentle heat for 1½ hours or until pork is very tender. Strain the fat from the pork and remove the thyme. Allow to cool.

Place the pieces of pork on a board and using two forks shred the meat finely. Pack tightly into small pots and cover each with a round of foil. Place a lid on top if possible and keep in the refrigerator. Serve with fresh crusty bread or piping hot toast. Serves 6.

SAUCES FOR COLD MEATS

HORSERADISH CREAM •
Serve with tongue, corned beef, Aberdeen sausage (see page 118) or cold roast beef.

1 cup sour cream
1 teaspoon grated onion
¼ cup lemon juice
1–2 tablespoons grated horseradish relish
1 teaspoon salt
a pinch of cayenne pepper

Combine all ingredients and beat with whisk until stiff.

CUCUMBER SAUCE ••
This sauce is suitable for tongue and corned beef, as well as salmon mousse (see p. 286).

1 cup peeled, seeded and finely diced cucumber
½ teaspoon salt
½ cup mayonnaise
¼ cup whipped cream
1 tablespoon lemon juice
2 teaspoons snipped dill

Place the cucumber in a colander with the salt and mix. Leave to drain for 30 minutes. Combine the mayonnaise, cream, lemon juice and salt, to taste. Drain the liquid from the cucumber then stir into the sauce with the dill. Serve chilled.

GRIBICHE SAUCE •
3 hard-boiled eggs
1 teaspoon Dijon mustard
½ teaspoon salt
freshly ground pepper
1½ cups of olive oil
½ cup of white wine vinegar
½ cup of capers and gherkins, mixed
1 tablespoon finely chopped mixed parsley, tarragon and chives

Halve the eggs and rub the yolks through a sieve. Mix with the mustard salt and pepper. Add the olive oil gradually as if making a mayonnaise and then add the vinegar stirring constantly. Finally add the egg-whites, capers and gherkins and finely chopped herbs. This is a rich sauce resembling mayonnaise and is good with cold beef, tongue, chicken and shellfish.

SOUR CHERRY SAUCE •
Delicious with either tongue or ham.

¼ cup sugar
1 x 440 g can pitted sour red cherries
2 teaspoons cornflour, blended with little cold water
a pinch of salt

Combine all the ingredients. Cook and stir over a low heat until the syrup is thick and clear. Serve hot or cold. Makes 2 cups.

SPICED MUSTARD SAUCE •
Suitable for corned beef, tongue and potted hough.

3 tablespoons cider or white wine vinegar
4 tablespoons oil
1 teaspoon hot English mustard
½ teaspoon salt
½ teaspoon ground black pepper
2 tablespoons brown sugar
a pinch of ground cloves or nutmeg

Mix all the ingredients together well.

vegetables

At any time of the year, there is always some vegetable at its peak.
Use them not only as an accompaniment, but let them take star billing.

For vegetables to be tempting, they must be cooked with
care and imagination. Try cooking in a very small amount of stock
with a little butter or oil added for flavour and lustre.

Seasonings make the difference to vegetables, especially frozen ones.
Fresh herbs added for flavour, browned butter poured over,
or toasted almonds sprinkled on for texture contrast,
are little touches that make a good cook an outstanding one.

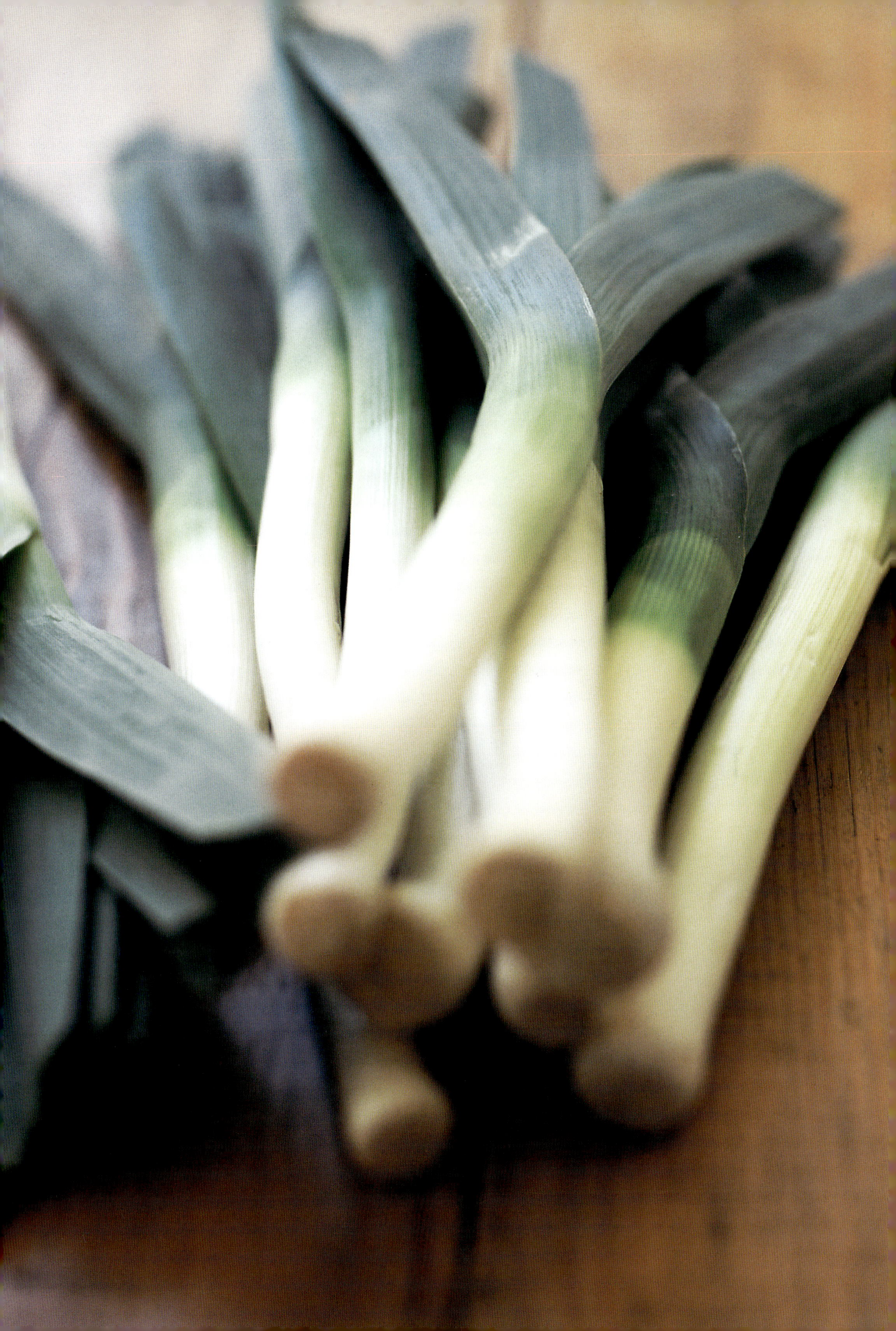

MAKE AN INTERESTING FINISH WITH:

- Slivered, toasted almonds for beans, broad beans, asparagus, broccoli or brussels sprouts.

- Crumbled crisp bacon pieces for carrots, peas, beans or broccoli.

- Chopped parsley is good with all vegetables.

- Diced roasted capsicum for peas, cauliflower, beans or mixed vegetables.

- Crisp buttered breadcrumbs and chopped hard-boiled eggs are delicious with cauliflower and asparagus.

- Creamed vegetables make a good dish at any time. Use 1 or 2 varieties. Allow 1 cup béchamel or mornay sauce (see p. 302) to 3 cups vegetables to make 4 servings. Add the hot sauce directly to hot vegetables, brown under griller or in oven, or serve sauce separately.

- A purée of vegetables is now very easy with today's electric appliances. There's the hand-held 'magic wand' and the food processors that are designed for small or family-size meals. These machines process, chop, or purée a wide range of foods and are a great help in the kitchen.

GLOBE ARTICHOKES

The leafy bud of a plant of the thistle family, globe artichokes are one of our most elegant vegetables. They can be boiled or braised as in artichokes in wine (below). To prepare, trim the stalk and outer leaves, cutting the points off each leaf. Cut one-third off the top of the artichoke. (see p. 10).

As each is prepared, place in a bowl of cold water into which is squeezed some lemon juice, to prevent discolouring. Artichokes are cooked when a leaf pulls out easily. To eat artichokes, pull off the leaves one at a time, bite on the base and pull the leaf, through your teeth, for the fleshy morsel. When you get through the leaves, remove the fuzzy choke and enjoy the choice base of the artichoke. At the beginning of the season the Italian elongated artichokes are available. They have hardly any choke and, even if they do have, are usually not worth worrying about. They are usually quartered or halved then fried or braised in stock or wine.

ARTICHOKES IN WINE ••

4–6 globe artichokes
2 tablespoons olive oil
1 onion, sliced
a sprig of oregano
2 large cloves garlic
1 bay leaf
½ cup white wine
1 tablespoon freshly chopped parsley
salt and freshly ground pepper

Prepare the artichokes (see p. 10). If large, cut into quarters and put into acidulated water, to cover. Drain and dry thoroughly. In a heavy-based saucepan combine the onion, oregano, garlic, bay leaf, white wine and parsley with the salt and pepper. Add the artichokes, cover and simmer slowly for 40 minutes. Serve warm. Serves 4–6.

ASPARAGUS

The first breath of spring is when asparagus makes its appearance in the greengrocer's shelves. Special pans for cooking asparagus are available, although a wide, not too shallow, frying pan with a lid is ideal. Take care to wash asparagus thoroughly and snap off the tougher ends.

STEAMED ASPARAGUS •

asparagus (allow 6–8 stalks per person)
salt

Rinse the stalks thoroughly under running water to dislodge any grit. Trim the ends if necessary and, with a vegetable peeler, peel off any tough skin.

Half-fill a wide pan with boiling, salted water. Lay the asparagus in the pan. Keep the heat high until the water boils again and cook for about 6–8 minutes, depending on the thickness of the stalks. Remove the asparagus and lay the spears on a clean, folded tea towel to drain.

Place on serving dish, and serve as soon as possible after cooking. Delicious with hollandaise sauce *(see p. 303)*, melted butter, olive oil, vinaigrette or just a squeeze of lemon juice and grinding of pepper.

BEANS

There are a great variety of green beans on the market and, with many of these now stringless, they are a vegetable to be enjoyed often. The old snap test is still the best assurance of age and freshness. Top and tail beans (if very young, tails may be left on) and if they have strings, run a knife or vegetable peeler down the sides to remove them. Leave whole or slice thinly into diagonal strips, or snap in half before dropping into boiling, salted water. Cook for 6–8 minutes or until just tender, drain and toss with butter.

HILL OF BEANS •

When green beans are good, serve plenty of them. A lovely platter of piled green beans makes a good vegetable dish for the table. Serve hot with butter, or cold, drizzled with vinaigrette at the very last moment (or they will turn grey).

1 kg green beans
salt
45 g butter
freshly ground pepper
2 tablespoons chopped parsley

String the beans, if they are the stringed variety, wash and remove their tails. Bring a large pan of boiling, salted water to the boil and cook the beans for 6–8 minutes, or until done to your taste. Drain and refresh immediately under cold water.

Return to the pan with the butter and shake the beans over a low heat, until the butter is melted and the beans have warmed through. Season with pepper, scatter with parsley and serve hot.

If you wish to serve the beans cold, cook as above, refresh them and then toss in vinaigrette *(see p. 306)*. Serves 6–8.

GREEN BEANS WITH TOMATO, GARLIC AND BASIL •

This bean dish is good hot or cold. Use the thin French beans or look for the longer, flatter runner green beans, favoured by Italians.

¼ cup olive oil
2 cloves garlic, finely chopped
500 g ripe tomatoes, peeled and chopped roughly
500 g green beans, trimmed at stalk end only
a pinch of salt
10 basil leaves
a good grinding of black pepper

In a large sauté pan, heat the oil and sauté the garlic gently, until softened, without colouring. Add the tomatoes and cook over a high heat for a minute or so. Add the prepared beans and salt, and cover the pan to cook the beans for about 10 minutes, or until tender but still with a little bite to them. A minute or so before the end of cooking add the whole basil leaves and a grinding of pepper. Stir-fry a few times during cooking, to mix the tomato mixture through the beans. Serve as a vegetable accompaniment or as a light vegetable dish on its own with crusty bread. Serves 4–6.

BEETROOT

Wash beetroot, cut tops off leaving a little stalk. Do not damage skins or tap root. Boil in unsalted water for 30–45 minutes. To bake, wrap in foil and cook in a 180°C oven for 1–1½ hours. Beetroot is as delicious served as a hot vegetable as it is as a salad.

BEETROOT AND ENDIVE SALAD •

8–12 baby beetroot
3 heads of Belgian endive (witlof)
lemon juice
extra virgin olive oil or walnut oil
salt and freshly ground pepper
chopped parsley (*optional*)

Cut off the stems of the beetroot leaving only 5 cm attached. Wash, leave whole and do not peel. Cover with cold water in a large saucepan. Cook, covered for 20–30 minutes, or until tender. Drain, and slip off the skins, pulling away the root and pull off, or re–trim the stem ends.

Discard the outer leaves of the endive. Break off the crisp leaves or cut through into 2.5 cm lengths or have a mixture of both whole leaves and sliced. Squeeze just a little lemon juice over to prevent discolouration. Season with good olive or walnut oil, salt and pepper and roll gently until all leaves are glistening. Arrange on a salad platter. Leave the baby beetroot whole and just before serving arrange over the endive. Scatter with parsley, if liked. Serves 4.

HOT BUTTERED BEETROOT •

2 bunches beetroot, cooked and peeled (altogether weighing about 1 kg)
45 g butter
1 tablespoon wine vinegar
salt and freshly ground pepper
½ teaspoon sugar

Slice or dice the beetroot, or cut into wedges. Melt the butter in a saucepan, add the beetroot and toss over a gentle heat until reheated. Add the vinegar with the salt, pepper and sugar to season. Turn into a heated serving dish. Serves 6–8.

BEETROOT AND ENDIVE SALAD

BROAD BEANS

Fresh broad beans, with their large lumpy pods, are usually shelled just before going into the pot. When the beans are large it is necessary to remove the skins after boiling. If the beans are very young, they can be eaten with the skins.

To cook, drop into boiling, salted water and cook until just tender. Drain and add a little butter, salt and freshly ground black pepper.

BROAD BEANS WITH MINT AND PANCETTA •

3–4 cups freshly podded broad beans or
  1 packet frozen broad beans
3 tablespoons extra virgin olive oil
1 small onion, finely chopped
100 g pancetta or bacon, cut into strips
1 tablespoon chopped mint
salt and freshly ground pepper

Drop the beans in a saucepan of boiling, salted water. Cook for 5 minutes or until tender, drain, and remove the white skins to reveal the bright green beans inside.

Heat the oil in a large saucepan and sauté the onion until soft, add the pancetta strips and cook for 2–3 minutes. Add the beans and mint then season with salt and a good grinding of pepper, tossing. Cook over a gentle heat for 1 minute. Serves 4–6.

BROCCOLI

Choose rich-green florets without any yellow buds. Trim tough ends and peel stems. Make cross-shaped slits in the stalks to speed cooking. Stand the stalks of broccoli upright in a deep saucepan, add 2.5 cm boiling, salted water, cover and cook until stalks are just tender, for 6–8 minutes. Drain well.

BRAISED BROCCOLI ROMANA •

The Romans offer this dish as a separate course, but it may be offered with grilled chicken or lamb as a vegetable. If you don't have wine, use water.

1 kg broccoli
4 tablespoons oil
2 cloves garlic, crushed
1½ cups dry white wine
salt and freshly ground black pepper

Remove the tough outer leaves of the broccoli and then cut off the stalks, about 5 cm below the heads. Peel the stalks, cut any thick stalks in half lengthwise, or, if they are very thick, quarter them. Heat the oil in a large frying pan over a moderate heat, add the garlic and cook until the garlic begins to colour. Add 1 cup of the wine and the broccoli stalks, season with a little salt and pepper, cover the pan, and simmer for 5 minutes. Lay the heads of the broccoli on top of the stalks, season again with a little salt and pepper, and cook uncovered for about 8 minutes longer, or until the stalks and the heads are tender. If too much wine evaporates, add a little more as it cooks, but 5 minutes before the broccoli is tender, raise the heat slightly and allow the wine to reduce to about ½ cup. Arrange the broccoli on a hot serving dish and pour the liquid in the pan over it. Serves 6.

BROAD BEANS WITH MINT AND PANCETTA

CABBAGE

Cabbage is one of the least expensive vegetables and it's also low in kilojoules and high in potassium and vitamin C, amongst other good things. There are so many light and flavourful ways of cooking cabbage. Ideal for stir-frying, braising and steaming, its leaves are also delicious in salads or used to encase savoury fillings.

To cook cabbage, start by removing the tough outer leaves and then quartering the head. Cut away the core and hard centre portions at the base. Using a long sharp knife, shred the leaves into long thin strips. Either steam the cabbage or blanch it in enough boiling, salted water to barely cover. Boil uncovered for 5 minutes, by which time it should be al dente. Drain and add melted butter or olive oil to the saucepan then toss, covered, over a gentle heat until tender. Season with salt and a good grinding of black pepper.

BRAISED RED CABBAGE •

1 small red cabbage
45 g butter
1 tablespoon vinegar
1 onion, finely chopped
2 apples, peeled and cut into thick slices
1 tablespoon sugar
salt and freshly ground pepper

Cut the cabbage in quarters, remove the hard cores, and cut the cabbage into fine shreds. Melt the butter in a heavy-based saucepan that has a tight-fitting lid. Add the shredded cabbage, vinegar, onion, apples and sugar. Season with the salt and pepper. Cover the pan and simmer for 1–1½ hours, stirring every now and then. Check for moisture during the cooking and add a little water if the cabbage is starting to catch. Serve hot. Serves 6.

CAPSICUM (SWEET PEPPERS)

Ripe and red, yellow, orange or green, capsicum are like precious jewels when used properly. A simple way to cook capsicum is to halve them, flick out the seeds, remove the ribs and cut the flesh into strips. Fry in a little olive oil, perhaps flavoured with garlic. Season with salt and pepper and serve with grills.

Many recipes call for the capsicum to be skinned. To do so, first char over a gas flame or under a very hot grill, turning all the time. Place in a paper bag and leave to cool. Scrape away the charred skin and rinse lightly in cold water. Halve and remove the seeds and membranes.

FRIED CAPSICUM •

6 medium red capsicum
3 tablespoons oil
2 onions, chopped
4 ripe tomatoes
salt and freshly ground pepper
½ cup pitted black olives

Cut the capsicum in halves, remove the ribs and seeds, and cut into wide strips. Heat the oil in a large frying pan over a moderate heat, add the onion and capsicum strips and cook until the onion begins to colour. Peel and seed the tomatoes and roughly chop. Add the tomatoes, season with the salt and pepper, and cook for 15 minutes. Add the olives then put the mixture in a hot serving dish. Serve warm or cold with crusty bread for mopping up the delicious juices. Serves 6.

STUFFED CAPSICUM PIEDMONT-STYLE •

Add chopped black olives to this mixture if you like. Serve the stuffed capsicum quarters at room temperature as a lunch with crusty bread or part of an antipasto.

4 red capsicum
½ cup fresh breadcrumbs
4 anchovy fillets, finely chopped
1 tablespoon chopped capers
2 tablespoons pine nuts
3 tablespoons sultanas
2 tablespoons chopped parsley
freshly ground pepper
olive oil

Preheat the oven to 190°C. Skin the capsicum (see opposite), if liked, and cut each one in quarters, lengthwise. Mix together the breadcrumbs, anchovies, capers, pine nuts, sultanas, parsley and pepper. Add enough oil to bind the mixture lightly. Stuff a little mixture into each capsicum quarter and arrange in a baking dish. Drizzle with a little olive oil and bake for 30 minutes, until the crumbs are crusty golden. Serves 6.

CAULIFLOWER

Choose a firm white cauliflower with compact flower clusters. Wash, remove coarse outside leaves, and trim the stalk level with the head. Make a crosswise cut in the stalk. Plunge the cauliflower, stalk down, into boiling, salted water. Cook uncovered until just tender, about 10 minutes. It is cooked when a knife pierces the stems easily. Small florets may be cut off the whole cauliflower in quantities needed and cooked for 6–8 minutes. Serve with melted butter flavoured with lemon juice and pepper. Cauliflower masked with mornay sauce (see p. 302) and gratinéed under the grill may be served as a separate vegetable course.

CARROTS

Carrots add a marvellous sparkle to meals. Cook them so they still have a bite to them, in a small amount of boiling, salted water, or try them vichy style, evaporating the water so that none of the fabulous flavour is lost. Or try cooking them a similar way but with peas added, or puréeing them with nutty parsnips. These are all great vegetable dishes.

CARROTS VICHY •

Carrots develop their best flavour cooked in a covered saucepan with butter, seasonings and a small amount of liquid.

500 g young carrots
60 g butter
1 tablespoon water
½ teaspoon sugar
salt
chopped parsley

Scrub or scrape the carrots, then cut into slices. Melt the butter in a saucepan and add the water, sugar and the carrots. Cover and cook gently until tender, turning them occasionally and taking care not to break them.

Sprinkle with a little salt and parsley just before serving. The carrots may also be cut into quarters, then into lengths or, if they are small carrots, they may be used whole. Serves 4.

EGGPLANT

Deep rich purple, slick and glossy, choose smooth firm eggplants with a nice squeak to them like a fresh apple. Avoid extra large ones as they can be watery and lack taste. Salting or blanching eggplant before cooking removes any bitterness and prevents it from drinking up too much oil in frying. Salting is not necessary for very young, fresh eggplant.

EGGPLANT CAVIAR •

2 medium eggplants
½ cup chopped parsley
2 cloves garlic, crushed
1 teaspoon salt
½ teaspoon freshly ground pepper
¼ teaspoon ground cinnamon
2 tablespoons vinegar
1 tablespoon lemon juice

Wash the eggplants and bake in a 180°C oven for about 40 minutes or until cooked through. When soft to the touch, remove from the oven and allow to cool slightly. Halve and scoop out the flesh from the eggplant skin. Chop the flesh, add the parsley, crushed garlic and remaining ingredients, and mix well. Chill thoroughly and serve on crisp toast or crackers as a first-course appetiser. Alternatively, arrange in a bowl and use as a dip. Serves 3–4 as a first course.

STUFFED EGGPLANT ••

Eggplant is excellent stuffed. Use 2 medium eggplants, scoop out some of the inside, leaving a 1.25 cm thickness of shell. Chop the scooped-out centre, and sauté in a little oil until tender. Proceed as for stuffed capsicum, Piedmont-style *(see p. 131)*, adding the sautéed eggplant with the other ingredients. Serves 4.

ESCALAVIDA • (SPANISH-ROASTED VEGETABLES)

This delicious, warm dish of colourful vegetables is served with a generous chunk of bread. Look for the baby eggplants, often long and finger-shaped.

500 g medium or baby eggplants
1 bunch salad onions,
  peeled and trimmed
2 red onions, peeled and quartered
2 red capsicum, halved and seeded
3 large cloves garlic, peeled
½ cup extra virgin olive oil
1 teaspoon sea salt
chopped parsley and pitted,
  halved black olives, to garnish

In a baking dish, roast the vegetables and garlic with half the olive oil in a 180°C oven, until very soft. Cover tightly with a lid or foil and leave for 10 minutes or so to cool slightly. Uncover and skin the capsicum and eggplants, if liked, and cut into long strips. If the eggplants are baby ones, you may prefer to leave them unpeeled and whole or halved. Leave the onions whole.

While still warm, dress with the remaining olive oil and season with the salt. Turn into a serving dish and scatter with parsley and olives. Serves 4–6.

ESCALAVIDA

EGGPLANT PARMIGIANA ••

2 medium eggplants
salt
3 tablespoons flour
freshly ground pepper
olive oil
2 cloves garlic, crushed
500 g ripe tomatoes, peeled and diced
250 g mozzarella cheese, sliced
basil or oregano leaves, to garnish

Peel the eggplants and cut into thick slices. Arrange in a colander, sprinkling layers liberally with salt. Leave to drain for about 30 minutes, then rinse and pat dry. Dredge each slice in the flour seasoned with salt and pepper.

Preheat a grill and arrange the eggplant slices on an oiled grilling rack. Brush with the oil. Grill, turning once and brushing again with oil as they cook, until coloured and tender. Alternatively, pan-fry the slices in oil until light golden and tender. Heat 2 tablespoons of the oil in a saucepan, add the garlic and tomatoes and cook over a brisk heat until the tomatoes are soft and thick, resembling a sauce. Season with salt and pepper.

Preheat the oven to 190°C. Lightly oil a large, shallow ovenproof dish and spoon over half the tomato sauce. Arrange a layer of eggplant slices on top and spoon over the remaining tomato sauce. Top with thin slices of mozzarella cheese. Bake for about 10 minutes, until the cheese is melted and bubbling, or place under a preheated griller. Garnish with basil or oregano leaves before serving. Serves 4–6.

LEEKS

Leeks make an excellent cooked vegetable. Before cooking, the roots and the green tops must be trimmed off; only the white part and 5 cm or so of the green is worth eating. Leeks usually have a great deal of grit between their leaves at the base of the stalks and they must be washed very thoroughly. They can be halved lengthwise, almost to the centre then washed under running water, while gently spreading their leaves apart to help flush out any grit.

LEEKS NIÇOISE •

A favourite French way of cooking leeks. Serve as a first course or a light lunch with crusty bread.

8–10 small to medium leeks
½ cup olive oil
1¼ cups water
1 tablespoon tomato paste
1 teaspoon sugar
salt and freshly ground pepper
lemon juice
1 cup small black olives
chopped parsley

To prepare the leeks, cut off all but 4–5 cm of the green tops. Trim off the roots. Slit down the middle to within about 2.5 cm of the root end and wash very thoroughly under running water. Leave the leeks whole or cut into 5 cm lengths. Place in a heavy-based frying pan in which the whole leeks will fit in one layer, or use a deeper pan if sliced. Add the oil, water, tomato paste and sugar. Season with salt and pepper and cook, covered, for about 15 minutes, until very tender. Add the lemon juice, to taste, and sprinkle with olives and parsley. Serve warm or at room temperature. Serves 4–8.

LEEKS NIÇOISE

MUSHROOMS

Fresh mushrooms have a very subtle flavour and must be cooked gently so that they will not shrivel and become dry.

to sauté: Use just enough butter or oil to cover the surface of the pan. A dash of lemon enhances the flavour. Cook over a moderate heat for no longer than 4 minutes to preserve their shape and flavour.

to grill: Brush with melted butter or olive oil before grilling.

to stew: Heat a little butter in a pan, add the sliced mushrooms and a little cream or stock and season with salt and pepper. Cover and simmer gently for 5–8 minutes.

MUSHROOMS IN CREAM •

Cooked this way, mushrooms can be eaten as a course on their own if served with triangles of toast or thick slices of crusty bread. This dish is also delicious served as a vegetable or sauce with chicken, fish or veal.

500 g firm button mushrooms
30 g butter
⅓ cup cream
salt and freshly ground pepper
2–3 tablespoons finely chopped herbs such as parsley, chervil or chives

No need to wipe, or even trim, the mushrooms. Heat the butter in a heavy-based frying pan and sauté the mushrooms gently for 10 minutes or so. Stir in the cream and simmer gently for several minutes to form a sauce. Season with the salt and pepper then add the herbs. Serves 4–6.

ONIONS

SWEET AND SOUR ONIONS ••

A lovely addition to a tray of antipasto or many hors d'oeuvre dishes, it's worth making a big batch of these onions as they keep very well in the refrigerator and are great for giving a lift to a quickly made meal.

½ cup light olive oil
1 kg pickling onions or small onions (or larger onions, peeled and quartered)
juice of 1 medium lemon
¾ cup dry white wine
2 tablespoons wine vinegar
a few sprigs of parsley
2 large cloves garlic
1 cup raisins
1–2 tablespoons sugar
1 teaspoon black peppercorns
1 teaspoon coriander seeds

Heat the oil in a large frying pan and add the onions when the oil starts to smoke. Sauté until golden all over and add the lemon juice, wine and vinegar. Let it bubble and add the remaining ingredients. Return to the boil, cover and cook over a moderate heat until the onions are crisp-tender. Remove the lid and allow the liquid to reduce, until a syrupy sauce has formed. Cool and serve at room temperature. Serves 6.

FRIED ONION RINGS •

4 large onions
1 egg white, slightly beaten
flour seasoned with salt and pepper
oil, for frying

Slice the onions and separate into rings. Dip the rings into egg white, then toss in the flour. Repeat the process once more. Drop into hot oil and cook until crisp and golden brown. Ideal to serve with grills. Serves 4–6.

GREEN PEAS •

1 kg peas
salt
a sprig of mint
a little sugar
2 teaspoons butter

Shell the peas. Have sufficient boiling, salted water to cover the peas. Add the peas, mint and sugar. Simmer gently until soft for 6–8 minutes. Drain well. Reheat with butter and serve in a hot vegetable dish. Serves 4–6.

note: if the peas must be shelled some time before cooking, put them in a bowl and cover them closely with washed pea pods.

GREEN PEAS, FRENCH-STYLE ••

30 g butter
1 onion, sliced
5–6 lettuce leaves, finely shredded
½ teaspoon salt
2 teaspoons sugar
3 sprigs of parsley
500 g fresh shelled peas
1 rasher bacon, diced (optional)
½ cup water
1 teaspoon butter
1 teaspoon plain flour

Put the butter in saucepan. Add the onion, lettuce, salt, sugar, parsley, peas and bacon, if using. Mix all well together. Add the water. Bring to the boil, cover and cook gently for about 20 minutes, or until very tender. Discard herbs. Blend butter with flour and stir into peas. Return to the heat, shaking to roll the peas around until the butter and flour mixture has combined with the liquid. As soon as it is boiling again, remove from the heat and serve.

note: frozen peas are also delicious cooked this way.

POTATOES

Possibly the best-loved vegetable of all, the potato has been a valuable source of nutrition for centuries.

CREAMY MASHED POTATOES •

Potatoes will get soggy and lose all their flavour if overcooked or cut into small pieces. They should break under the pressure of a fork, but not be too mushy. Always add hot milk for fluffy mashed potatoes. Adding cold milk to potato makes it sticky.

6 medium potatoes
½–1 cup milk
30 g butter
salt and freshly ground pepper

Peel the potatoes and put into a saucepan of cold, lightly salted water to cover. Cook with the lid on the pan until the potatoes are easily pierced with a fork, for about 15 minutes. Drain thoroughly, then shake the pan over the heat for a minute, until all surplus moisture has evaporated and the potatoes are quite dry. Mash with a potato masher or put through a potato ricer.

Beat the potatoes with a wooden spoon until very smooth. Scald the milk. Add the butter to the potatoes, gradually beat in the hot milk until the potatoes are light and fluffy. Season with the salt and pepper. Serves 4–6.

to keep mashed potatoes hot without spoiling: Cook the potatoes as described above, then mash and press down well in a saucepan with a potato masher. Pack tightly, levelling the top. Add butter, spoon about 4 tablespoons hot milk over, cover with tight-fitting lid and leave in a warm place. Before serving, beat well, adding more hot milk if necessary. The potatoes will keep this way for up to 20 minutes.

To prepare onions: Halve the onion lengthwise. Trim the stem ends and peel the outer skin.

To dice, place the onion cut-side down and make lengthwise slits, not quite to the root end. The more slits you make, the more finely chopped your onion will be.

Starting from the stem end, cut across the onion and it will fall into diced pieces.

To slice onions, trim and halve as in the first step then cut across into thick or thin slices.

CRISP-ROASTED POTATOES AND PARSNIPS •

1.5 kg potatoes, choose firm and floury ones
3–4 parsnips, lightly peeled and halved
¼ cup olive oil
sprigs of fresh rosemary
coarse sea salt
freshly ground pepper

Preheat the oven to 200°C. Choose medium even-sized potatoes and peel and halve or quarter. In a saucepan, add the potatoes and enough water to cover and boil for about 5 minutes, until just slightly tender. Drain and cool slightly. Scratch the surface of the potatoes with a fork, if liked, to give them a great crispy finish.

Place the oil, rosemary sprigs, salt and pepper in a bowl. Add the potatoes and parsnips and toss them thoroughly in the mixture, until well coated. Place the vegetables in a single layer in a baking tray. Bake for 1 hour, or until very crisp, turning occasionally. Serve immediately. Serves 8–10.

OVEN-ROASTED POTATOES •

Choose small even-sized potatoes for an attractive appearance, otherwise halve or quarter large ones. Preheat the oven to 200°C. Peel the potatoes and boil for 5 minutes. Drain and mark surface with a fork. Put into a roasting pan containing 6 mm of hot fat or oil, sprinkle lightly with salt and roast for 40–50 minutes or until golden and crusty, turning and basting occasionally.

POTATOES BAKED IN JACKETS •

These potatoes have a crisp skin, but if a softer finish is preferred, rub all over the surface with a little oil before baking. Another method is, after scrubbing and drying, to roll the potatoes in coarse salt.

It is important to choose even-sized potatoes. Preheat the oven to 200°C. Scrub under cold water, drain, dry and pierce each potato 4–6 times with a skewer to prevent splitting during baking. Put on a shelf in the oven and cook for 1–1½ hours, depending on the size of the potatoes. To test, pierce with a fork. When done, cut a cross on the top with a pointed knife, and squeeze gently to open. Put a pat of butter in opening.

These potatoes are also delicious served with a spoonful of sour cream and sprinkled with snipped chives.

SCALLOPED POTATOES ••

A variation of gratin dauphinois, a rich, filling regional dish from France. Some recipes include eggs, but the authentic recipe is made only with potatoes and thick fresh cream. Here is a simpler version.

1 kg potatoes
1 clove garlic, halved
1 cup milk (or half cream, half milk)
grated nutmeg
salt and freshly ground pepper
½ cup grated Gruyère cheese
60–90 g butter

Preheat the oven to 180°C. Peel the potatoes and slice thinly. Rub a shallow ovenproof dish with the cut clove of garlic, then butter dish generously. Arrange the potato slices in layers in dish. Scald the milk and add the nutmeg, salt and pepper, to taste. Pour over the potatoes in the dish. Sprinkle with the cheese and dot with the butter. Bake for 50–60 minutes until the potatoes are tender and golden. If potatoes seem to be browning too quickly cover loosely with foil for 30 minutes of cooking time. Serve in the dish. Serves 6.

FRENCH-FRIED POTATOES ••
(CHIPS)

There's a special cooking technique that gives French fries their inimitable outside crispness that seals in the soft centres. The secret is twice-frying in deep fat or oil at the right temperature.

6 large even-sized potatoes
oil or fat, for deep-frying
salt

Peel the potatoes and cut into 5 cm-long strips, 6 mm wide. Rinse well, soak in ice cold water, then drain. Dry thoroughly using a large tea towel. Heat the oil or fat in a deep heavy-based saucepan and, when a thin blue haze rises from surface (or when a small cube of bread turns brown in less than 1 minute), lower the potatoes into it. For easier handling use a frying basket.

Cook until soft but not brown. Lift from the fat. Reheat the fat to a higher temperature. Gently lower the basket again and the potatoes will immediately crisp and brown, and puff slightly. Drain on paper towels, sprinkle with salt and serve immediately. Serves 6.

BUTTERED SPINACH •

Wash spinach in several changes of cold water. The water clinging to the leaves is all the liquid that is necessary to cook tender young spinach.

1 bunch English spinach
salt and freshly ground pepper
30 g butter
a pinch of nutmeg

Remove the stalks and wash the spinach. Put into a large saucepan and season with the salt. Cover and simmer gently until just tender, 5–8 minutes. Drain and press out as much water as possible. Heat the butter in a pan, add the spinach and toss well to heat through. Add pepper and nutmeg to taste, and serve. Serves 4–5.

SWEET POTATOES

Light coloured skin and flesh are characteristic of sweet potatoes, while a darker red-brown skin and bright orange flesh are referred to as yams or kumera.

GLAZED SWEET POTATOES •

2–3 sweet potatoes
60 g butter
1 tablespoon oil
1 tablespoon honey
a pinch of ground ginger

Preheat the oven to 180°C. Peel the sweet potatoes and cut into even-sized pieces. Put into a saucepan of boiling, salted water, cover and simmer for 5 minutes. Drain. Melt half the butter in a baking dish with the oil. Stir in the honey and ginger. Put the sweet potatoes in a dish and spoon the honey mixture over. Dot with the remaining butter. Bake for 40 minutes, or until tender. Brush with the glaze in the pan every 15 minutes, and turn occasionally. Serve immediately. Serves 4–5.

TOMATOES

Tomatoes are a great standby in the kitchen. They have many uses in providing a quick snack, a first course or a vegetable dish. It pays to buy the best red ripe tomatoes you can find. Tomatoes are best stored at room temperature. Only keep in the refrigerator when they look like going soft.

TOMATOES PROVENÇALE •

2 medium tomatoes
salt and freshly ground pepper
¼ cup fresh breadcrumbs
1 tablespoon melted butter
1 small clove garlic, crushed

Halve the tomatoes, season with salt and freshly ground black pepper. Mix the breadcrumbs with the butter and garlic, and then season with the salt and pepper. Spoon onto the tomatoes and grill under moderate heat until the crumbs are brown and the tomatoes heated through, or bake in a 190°C oven for 10–15 minutes. Serves 2.

ZUCCHINI

Zucchini or baby marrows should be about 10 cm long and very firm to the touch. Spongy ones will be bitter. Do not peel, but cut off the stem end. Wash well and slice. Drop into boiling, salted water for 3–5 minutes, until just tender. Drain. Put the saucepan back on the heat, add a little butter and the zucchini slices. Season to taste, toss well and serve. Small baby patty pan or yellow squash may also be cooked this way, though halve if largish.

ZUCCHINI, BEAN AND TOMATO MEDLEY ••

This is a dish that is good on its own or served as an accompaniment. Topped with grated cheese, it becomes a meal in itself.

1 large onion, sliced
1 clove garlic, crushed
2 tablespoons olive oil
a large pinch of salt
freshly ground black pepper
¼ cup chopped parsley
1 teaspoon chopped thyme or oregano
500 g green beans
500 g zucchini, or patty pan or yellow squash
4 large tomatoes, quartered
¼ cup water

Saute the onion and garlic in the oil in a heavy-based frying pan. Season with the salt and freshly ground black pepper and add the herbs. Cut the beans into lengths, and the zucchini into chunks. Add the beans, zucchini, tomatoes and water to the pan and simmer, covered, for 8 minutes or until just tender. Serves 4–6.

RATATOUILLE ••

Serve cold as an hors d'oeuvre or warm as a vegetable accompaniment with grills.

2 medium eggplants
salt
2 large onions, finely chopped
⅓ cup olive oil
2 green capsicum, halved and seeded
4 zucchini
2–3 cloves garlic, peeled
a generous amount of freshly ground pepper
4–6 tomatoes, quartered
freshly chopped parsley

Cut the eggplants into large cubes and place in a colander, sprinkling lightly with salt. Allow to stand and drain for 30 minutes. Meanwhile, cook the onions in oil until soft and golden. Add the eggplant and cook a further 2 minutes. Cut the capsicum into strips and add to the pan with the zucchini, which have been cut into thick slices. Add the garlic and season with the freshly ground pepper. Cover and cook gently for about 15 minutes. Add the tomatoes and cook for a further 5 minutes. Salt, to taste, and serve warm or chilled, sprinkled with parsley. Serves 4–6.

OLLA GITANA ••

1 quantity ratatouille
4–6 eggs
½ cup pitted black olives, to garnish

Preheat the oven to 180°C. Transfer the ratatouille to an ovenproof dish, mixing lightly to combine. Make slight depressions in the top and break an egg into each. Bake for about 15 minutes, or until the eggs are set. Garnish with the olives. Serve warm. Serves 4–6.

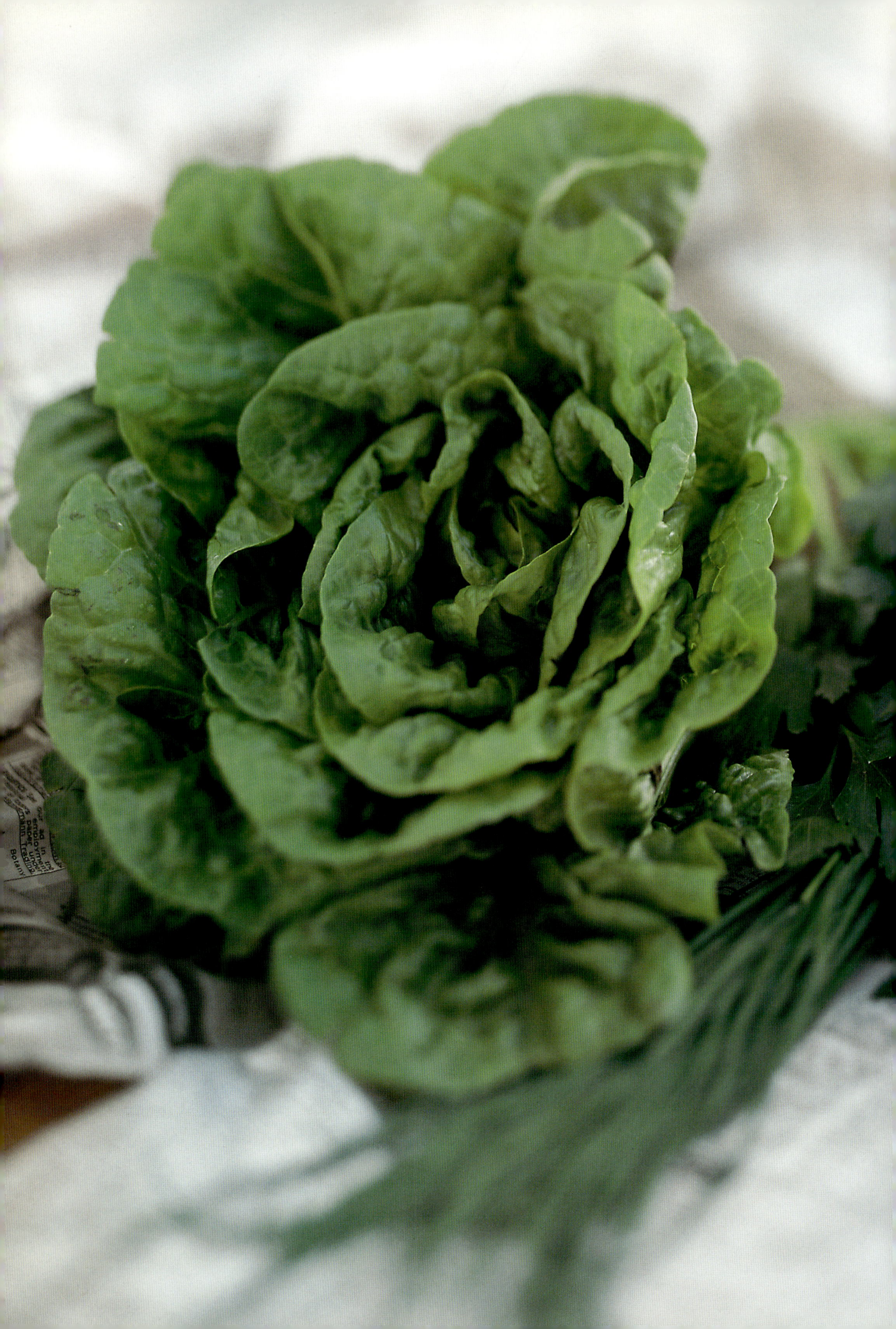

salads

We all have an instinctive need to eat fresh greens. Salads provide that wonderful feeling of sunshine. It may be a simple salad of carefully selected and prepared greens dressed with a good olive oil, a good vinegar, salt and a grinding of pepper. Or, there are times when an elaborate salad of luscious and varied seafood, rare roast beef or perfectly poached chicken fits the bill. There is hardly an edible food that cannot be made into a salad, but it is worth using only the best.

SALADS

Today the search is on for a wide variety of greens. There's a choice of mignonette, oak-leaf, coral, tiny corn salad (also known as lamb's lettuce or mache), watercress, witlof, rocket, escarole or frisée. Fresh garden herbs also add interest and distinction to salads.

Take the time to see what's available at the supermarket. You will be amazed at the wide range of oils, vinegars, mustards, anchovies and canned goods that can make your salads a standout success.

cos lettuce

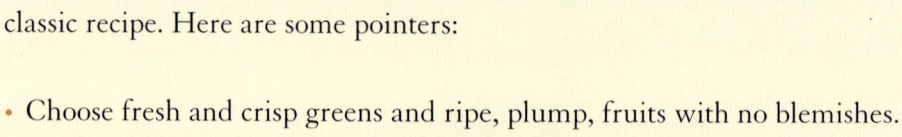

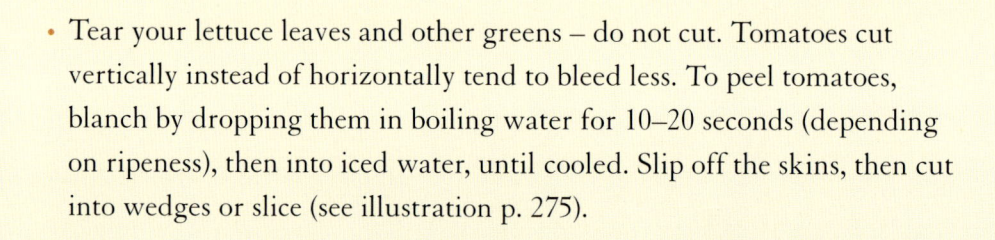

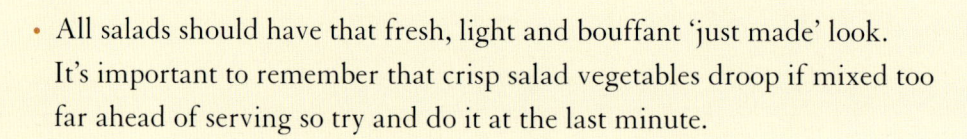

radicchio

rocket

A good salad needs the subtle attention to detail that a chef devotes to a classic recipe. Here are some pointers:

- Choose fresh and crisp greens and ripe, plump, fruits with no blemishes. Fruits should not be washed until ready to use.

- Before using, wash salad vegetables in plenty of water. Rinse well to get rid of any grit or earth. Dry in a salad spinner or shake in a large tea towel. Place in plastic bags and chill in a refrigerator crisper.

- Fresh herbs, cress, parsley, garlic and seasonings all help a salad.

- Keep a special bowl and servers exclusively for salads, a stainless knife with a special cutting blade, and a plastic or stainless steel whisk for dressings.

- Tear your lettuce leaves and other greens – do not cut. Tomatoes cut vertically instead of horizontally tend to bleed less. To peel tomatoes, blanch by dropping them in boiling water for 10–20 seconds (depending on ripeness), then into iced water, until cooled. Slip off the skins, then cut into wedges or slice (see illustration p. 275).

- All salads should have that fresh, light and bouffant 'just made' look. It's important to remember that crisp salad vegetables droop if mixed too far ahead of serving so try and do it at the last minute.

TOMATO AND BASIL SALAD •

Use the large red beefsteak tomatoes in this fresh-tasting salad. Remember not to keep tomatoes in the refrigerator as it is detrimental to their flavour. They should only go into the refrigerator if they are getting too soft.

4 large ripe tomatoes
1 large spring onion with green part intact
8 basil leaves, roughly torn
2 tablespoons extra virgin olive oil
a light drizzle of balsamic or wine vinegar
sea salt and freshly ground pepper

Slice across the tomatoes thinly (if large, halve vertically first), and lay them out on a large plate or platter. Slice the onion very thinly and lay over the tomatoes. Scatter with the basil leaves and dress with olive oil, vinegar, salt and pepper. Serves 4.

RADICCHIO SALAD WITH SHAVED PARMESAN •

1 large head radicchio
2 tablespoons balsamic vinegar
salt and freshly ground pepper
¼ cup light olive oil
60 g shaved Parmesan cheese

Separate the radicchio leaves, wash, dry and tear into bite-size pieces, before placing in a salad bowl. In a small bowl mix together the vinegar, salt and pepper.

Gradually add the oil in a slow stream to form a dressing, whisking all the time with a fork, until well amalgamated. Drizzle the salad with half the dressing and toss gently. Add the Parmesan shavings before serving. Serves 4.

note: try making this salad with rocket leaves in place of the radicchio.

TOSSED GREEN SALAD •

Many salads use a variety of young greens and sprigs of fresh herbs. The essence of a good salad is to mix with a lavish hand all the lovely leaves and herbs you can find at the greengrocer, or if one green is superb just use that.

The list given here is simply an inspiration for your version. For enough salad greens for a number of people, use a mixture chosen from: iceberg, cos and mignonette lettuce, young English spinach or rocket leaves, radicchio, coral or oak-leaf lettuce, frisée and witlof. Include one or more of these herbs: sprigs of tarragon, green basil, purple basil, flat-leaf parsley, chervil and watercress.

mustard vinaigrette:
2 tablespoons white wine vinegar
1 tablespoon Dijon mustard
salt and a good grinding of pepper
⅓ cup extra virgin olive oil

Use fresh, unblemished salad greens. Wash and dry thoroughly, using a salad spinner or clean tea towel to shake off all water. Tear large lettuce leaves into attractive pieces. Cover and chill in green salad bags, until required. Break herbs into sprigs. Wash well, drain and dry. Arrange the salad in a large salad bowl. A wooden, glass or china bowl should be used and kept exclusively for salads. Pour over the dressing at the last minute and toss until every leaf is glistening. Serve immediately.

To make vinaigrette: Beat vinegar and mustard together with a fork or small whisk, until well mixed. Add salt and pepper, then oil a little at a time, beating constantly until dressing thickens a little.

note: a ⅓ cup of dressing is sufficient for 1 lettuce plus a mixture of 1–2 cups of other greens.

CAESAR SALAD ●●

This is the authentic recipe made for me by the Cardini family in Mexico, the creators of the caesar salad. Particular care was taken to lay the tender, elongated cos leaves all in the one direction.

1 cos lettuce
1 small baguette
2 anchovy fillets
1 clove garlic, crushed
15 g butter

dressing:
juice of 1 lemon
⅓ cup olive oil
1 teaspoon Worcestershire sauce (Lea & Perrins)
salt and freshly ground black pepper
¼ cup freshly grated or shaved Parmesan cheese
1 coddled egg (see below)

Remove tough outer leaves of the lettuce. Wash the tender leaves, spin dry and place in a plastic bag in the refrigerator to crisp. Preheat the oven to 180°C. Make croûtes by cutting the baguette into thick slices. Mash the anchovy fillets and garlic with the butter and spread over the bread slices. Place on a baking tray and bake until pale gold and crisp.

Mix all the ingredients for the dressing together, except the coddled egg. Arrange the crisp lettuce leaves in a bowl. Add the croûtes, break in the coddled egg, add the dressing and turn the salad gently, until the dressing coats the lettuce leaves evenly. Serves 4.

coddled egg: Lower the egg into a small saucepan of simmering water and simmer for 1 minute. Lift out.

FRIED ZUCCHINI SALAD WITH MINT ●●

Zucchini flavoured with mint might sound an unusual combination, but this Italian antipasto salad is delicious.

1 kg young firm zucchini
2–3 tablespoons extra virgin olive oil
1 garlic clove, peeled and sliced finely
1 cup roughly torn mint leaves
1 tablespoon white wine vinegar
1 clove garlic, sliced finely
¼ teaspoon salt
freshly ground pepper

Trim the zucchini and cut each one lengthwise into 3 or 4 slices. In a large heavy-based frying pan, heat the oil and fry the zucchini slices, a few at a time, until tender and golden brown on both sides. Remove from the pan and place on a serving platter. Gently fry the garlic slices, to soften without colouring, and add to the zucchini with the mint. Drizzle with the vinegar, season with the salt and pepper then toss lightly. Leave to marinate for an hour or so before serving. Serves 4.

CAESAR SALAD

FENNEL AND ORANGE SALAD •

a selection of salad greens
2 naval oranges
½ bulb fennel
¼ red salad onion, cut into lengthwise strips
½ cup black olives

vinaigrette:
4 teaspoons balsamic vinegar
4 teaspoons red wine vinegar
⅓ cup olive oil
salt and freshly ground pepper

Wash the salad greens, drain very well, and whirl in a salad spinner or tea towel, or pat dry with paper towels. Store in a plastic bag in the refrigerator, until ready to use.

With a sharp knife, carefully follow the curve of the orange and cut away the white pith and rind. Cut the flesh into thin slices. Remove the core from the fennel and shave it thinly with the grain, using a very sharp knife.

Arrange the salad greens on each of four serving plates, and top with the orange slices, fennel and onion. Scatter with olives and drizzle with vinaigrette. Serves 4.

vinaigrette: In a small bowl, whisk together the vinegars. Gradually whisk in the oil until the dressing is thickened. Season with salt and pepper.

ITALIAN CAPSICUM SALAD ••

Take the trouble of charring and peeling capsicum, as it makes an enormous difference to their flavour.

4 medium red capsicum
2 tablespoons wine vinegar
1 clove garlic, crushed
salt and freshly ground pepper
1 teaspoon Dijon mustard
6 tablespoons olive oil
4–6 anchovy fillets
¼ cup black olives, pitted
1 tablespoon capers
snipped or torn basil leaves and parsley, to garnish

Preheat the griller to very hot. Grill the capsicum about 2.5 cm from the heat, until the skin blackens and blisters, turning them frequently. As they are done, place them in a paper bag or wrap in a cloth. Leave for several minutes then scrape away all the blackened skin. Rinse lightly with cold water, if liked. Halve the capsicum, remove the ribs and seeds, and cut lengthwise into 1 cm-wide strips.

Meanwhile, have a bowl ready in which you have beaten together the vinegar, garlic, salt, pepper and mustard. Gradually whisk in the olive oil until a thickened dressing is formed. Add the capsicum strips to the dressing, making sure they become well coated, and leave for at least 15 minutes. To serve, toss the capsicum strips, anchovy fillets, olives and capers in a serving bowl. Garnish with basil and parsley. Serves 4–6.

ITALIAN CAPSICUM SALAD

LETTUCE WEDGES WITH YOGHURT DRESSING •

1 large iceberg lettuce
1 egg yolk
½ teaspoon salt
¼ teaspoon dry mustard powder
½ teaspoon paprika
¾ cup natural yoghurt
2 teaspoons lemon juice

Have lettuce washed and well chilled. In a small bowl, with a fork, beat the egg yolk, salt, mustard and paprika, until thick. Gradually beat in the yoghurt and lemon juice, and then chill. Cut the lettuce into wedges, arrange in a salad bowl and spoon the dressing over. Serves 6.

AMERICAN POTATO SALAD •

Splash the still-hot potatoes with dry white wine to make a very special just-warm potato salad. The best potato salad has never been in a refrigerator.

1 kg new potatoes
⅓ cup dry white wine
½ cup vinaigrette (see p. 306)
1 red onion, sliced into rings
1 stalk celery, sliced
2 dill pickles or gherkins, thinly sliced
1 teaspoon capers
4 hard-boiled eggs, peeled and sliced
2 tablespoons chopped parsley
salt and freshly ground pepper

Scrub then simmer the potatoes gently, until tender, in salted water. Peel, if liked, and slice them while still hot into a bowl. Sprinkle with white wine, turning the potato slices carefully. Now, sprinkle with the vinaigrette and gently fold through the remaining ingredients. Season with salt and pepper. Serves 4–6.

HERBED POTATO SALAD •

1 kg potatoes, unpeeled
salt and freshly ground pepper
2–3 tablespoons good wine vinegar
6–7 tablespoons extra virgin olive oil
4 tablespoons stock or hot water
2 tablespoons chopped parsley
2 tablespoons snipped chives
2 spring onions, thinly sliced
½ cup mayonnaise (see p. 306)

Boil the potatoes in salted water to cover until they are tender. Drain, peel and cut into thick slices. Spread over a shallow dish. While the potatoes are still hot, season with salt and a little pepper, then sprinkle with the vinegar and oil.

Add the herbs with the spring onions. Let the salad stand at room temperature until most of the dressing is absorbed. Turn the potato slices carefully to ensure even seasoning. Serve the salad without chilling. For a creamy salad, spoon the mayonnaise over the potatoes. Top with extra chopped herbs, if liked. Serves 4–6.

CUCUMBER AND YOGHURT SALAD •

Popular throughout the Middle East as a mezze (appetiser), this is great used as a dip for flat bread. It is also excellent as a sauce with grilled meat dishes.

3 Lebanese cucumbers
1 teaspoon salt
1 cup natural yoghurt
1–3 cloves garlic, crushed
salt and freshly ground pepper
a few sprigs of fresh mint or dill, finely chopped
olive oil (optional)

Peel the cucumber thinly, leaving as much of the green under the skin as possible. Cut into tiny cubes or thin slices (or grate coarsely). Place in a colander with a teaspoon of salt, and leave to drain for 30 minutes or so. Rinse well in cold water and drain thoroughly.

Beat the yoghurt in a bowl until smooth. Mix in the cucumber and garlic. Season with salt and pepper, to taste. Scatter over the mint and dill and, if you like, drizzle with a little olive oil. Serves 6.

MUSHROOM SALAD •

250 g firm button mushrooms
1 tablespoon lemon juice
3 tablespoons vinaigrette (see p. 306)
2 cups watercress sprigs
2 tablespoons finely snipped parsley or dill (optional)

Slice the mushrooms thinly and sprinkle with the lemon juice. Place in a salad bowl and toss with the vinaigrette and watercress. Cover and chill. Sprinkle with parsley or dill. Serves 2–4.

SOUR CREAM COLESLAW •

A young green sugar loaf cabbage or savoy is ideal for this lovely coleslaw.

¼ medium cabbage, finely shredded
½ cup mayonnaise (see p. 306)
½ cup diced celery
½ cup diced red or green capsicum
¼ cup finely chopped spring onions
¼ cup finely chopped parsley
a dash of tabasco
½ cup light sour cream

Place the cabbage in a large bowl. Combine the remaining ingredients, and pour over the cabbage. Toss and chill well before serving. Serves 6.

DANISH CUCUMBER SALAD •

This side salad is my favourite to serve with cold poached salmon.

2 Lebanese cucumbers
½ teaspoon salt
1 tablespoon white wine vinegar
1 tablespoon water
1 teaspoon sugar
2 tablespoons snipped dill

Slice cucumber thinly. Place in a colander and sprinkle with the salt. Press lightly and drain. Make a dressing with the vinegar, water and sugar. Steep the cucumber slices in the liquid for an hour before serving, and then mix in the dill. Serve with cold meats or fish. Serves 4.

FRENCH WHITE BEAN SALAD ••

1½ cups dried haricot beans
1 onion, quartered
bouquet garni
2 tablespoons olive oil
2 tomatoes, cut into cubes
2 tablespoons halved and pitted black olives
2 tablespoons torn basil leaves
1 clove garlic crushed with a little salt
½ cup mayonnaise *(see p. 306)*
1 tablespoon vinegar
salt and freshly ground black pepper

Soak the beans overnight, or at least several hours, in water to cover, and then drain. Place in a large saucepan with the onion and bouquet garni. Slowly bring to the boil, skim and cover. Cook gently for 1–1½ hours or until tender – dried beans vary greatly in cooking time. Drain the beans and discard the bouquet garni and onion. Toss the beans in the olive oil and leave to cool.

In a bowl, combine the cooled beans with the tomatoes and the olives, then toss with the basil. Combine the garlic, mayonnaise and vinegar together and toss with the salad, adding salt and plenty of freshly ground pepper. Serve at room temperature. Serves 4–6.

GREEK SALAD ••

1–2 tablespoons lemon juice
¼ cup extra virgin olive oil
salt and freshly ground pepper
2 small Lebanese cucumbers
½ punnet red cherry tomatoes, halved
mixed salad greens such as mignonette, oak-leaf or butterhead lettuce
150 g feta cheese, crumbled
¼ cup black olives, pitted and slivered
¼ cup whole mint leaves

In a small bowl, add the lemon juice and gradually add the oil, whisking until thickened. Season with salt and pepper.

Lightly peel the cucumbers, leaving the pale green under the skin intact. Halve, lengthwise, and cut across into thick slices. In a large bowl, combine the cucumber and tomatoes.

Pour over half the dressing and toss to coat. Just before serving, place the salad greens with the cucumber mixture in a large bowl.

Add remaining dressing, a little at a time, and toss gently, coating the leaves evenly. Divide the salad between 4 individual serving plates, scatter with feta, olives and the mint leaves. Serve immediately. Serves 4.

WALDORF SALAD •

3 red apples, unpeeled
juice of 1 lemon
¼ cup mayonnaise (see p. 306)
1 tablespoon cream
1 cup sliced celery
½ cup chopped walnuts
crisp lettuce leaves
walnut halves, to garnish

Unpeeled apples make the most attractive looking salad, but the apples can be peeled. Keep a few unpeeled slices as a garnish. Dice the apples, squeeze the lemon juice over the fruit. Combine the mayonnaise, cream, celery and walnuts and serve on the lettuce leaves. Decorate with apple slices and the walnut halves. *Serves 4–6.*

note: refresh and crisp the walnuts by toasting in a dry pan over a moderate heat. The crisp walnuts make a lovely contrast to the apples and creamy dressing.

CORIANDER EGGPLANT SALAD ••

Resist any temptation to process this mixture in a blender or food processor, so that the texture of the eggplant is retained. Serve this as a spread on fresh crusty bread.

6 garlic cloves, unpeeled
1 large eggplant
1 teaspoon cumin seed
½ teaspoon fennel seeds
½ teaspoon coriander seeds
2 medium tomatoes, peeled, seeded and finely diced
3 tablespoons chopped fresh coriander
2 tablespoons lemon juice
2 tablespoons olive oil
½ teaspoon paprika
4 tablespoons chopped mint leaves
sea salt

Preheat the oven to 180°C. Wrap the garlic in foil. Prick the eggplant all over. On a baking tray, roast the garlic and eggplant in the middle of the oven for 30–40 minutes, or until the garlic is tender. Transfer the garlic to a plate and continue to roast the eggplant, until blackened and softened, for about 30 minutes longer.

Meanwhile, dry-fry the spice seeds in a small frying pan over a moderate heat, shaking the pan and taking care not to let them burn. Remove from the heat when the seeds are fragrant. Grind the seeds finely with a mortar and pestle or in a clean coffee grinder.

Use a spoon to scrape the eggplant flesh from the skin, and chop coarsely. Slip the garlic cloves from their skins and mash to a paste. In a bowl, stir together the eggplant, garlic, spice mixture, tomatoes, coriander, lemon juice, oil, paprika and half the mint. Season with salt, to taste, and stir until well combined. Sprinkle the salad with the remaining mint and serve at room temperature. *Serves 6.*

SALAD MEALS

Salads are what we all look to for easy living, especially when time is short and the days are warm. Those that aren't tumbled together at the drop of a hat, using whatever is at hand, can usually be made with ingredients prepared beforehand.

These salads make a meal on their own, and all celebrate the wealth and diversity of fresh produce readily available these days.

SALADE NIÇOISE ••

A salad like this makes a fabulous meal on its own, either for an evening meal or a weekend lunch. Salade niçoise is a rustic country salad and, like all good salads, is made with ingredients on hand and in season. For this version, use a good quality canned tuna in olive oil.

500 g new potatoes, scrubbed
2 eggs, at room temperature
250 g green beans, tailed
2 x 210 g cans tuna in oil
3 tomatoes
1 red onion, thinly sliced
¼ cup black olives, (preferably kalamata)

dressing:
1 tablespoon white wine vinegar
1 tablespoon lemon juice
1 clove garlic, finely chopped
salt and freshly ground pepper
¼ cup olive oil
1 tablespoon chopped herbs
  (parsley, chives, and oregano)

Put the potatoes in a saucepan and cover with boiling water. Add a little salt and bring to the boil. Cook uncovered, until the potatoes are tender, drain.

Lower the eggs carefully into warm water and bring the water slowly to the boil, stirring all the time so as to centre the yolks. Once the water is simmering, allow to cook for 10 minutes. Drain, lightly crack the shells, and leave to cool completely in cold water. Drop the prepared beans into a little boiling, salted water, and cook until crisp-tender. Drain immediately and refresh in iced water. Drain again.

Drain the tuna and flake into large chunks. Slice the tomatoes and arrange on serving plates with the sliced onion. Slice the potatoes thickly and place on top. Arrange the beans, olives and shelled eggs, which have been quartered, on top and around, and then top with the chunks of tuna. Drizzle the dressing over the salad.

dressing: Mix together the vinegar, lemon juice, garlic, salt and pepper. Beat in the olive oil slowly, to ensure dressing remains thick and amalgamated. Beat again before using, adding herbs at the end. Serves 4.

COBB SALAD ••

A hearty salad meal created by Robert Cobb at Hollywood's Brown Derby Restaurant in 1936.

1 whole chicken breast fillet, poached
salad greens such as cos, oak- or coral-leaf lettuce
1 bunch of asparagus, trimmed and blanched
4 hard-boiled eggs, quartered
2 avocados, peeled and cut into cubes
3 rashers bacon, cooked and cut into large pieces
⅓ cup stuffed green olives
1 red onion, finely chopped

dressing:
1 tablespoon white wine vinegar
salt and freshly ground pepper
1 teaspoon Dijon mustard
1 clove garlic, crushed
3–5 tablespoons olive oil

Shred the poached chicken into thin strips. Tear the salad greens into small pieces and place a bed of greens on each plate. Place the chicken on top of each in a row. Arrange the asparagus, eggs, avocado, bacon, olives, and onion on either side of the chicken rows. Drizzle with the dressing and serve.

dressing: Put the vinegar in a small bowl with the salt, pepper and mustard. Add the garlic and mix well with a fork or whisk. Gradually add the oil, whisking until the dressing has thickened. Serves 4.

WILTED SALAD ••

Use your own choice of greens for this French country salad 'wilted' with hot bacon.

a selection of salad greens including chicory and frisée
2 hard-boiled eggs
1 cup bread cubes, fried until golden then drained
100 g speck, bacon or pancetta
2 teaspoons wine vinegar
freshly ground pepper
1 tablespoon chopped parsley

Wash the greens and dry thoroughly. Tear into bite-size pieces and place in an oiled salad bowl. Shell and roughly chop the eggs and scatter over the greens with the croutons. Meanwhile, dice the bacon and fry in its own fat, until golden and the fat is transparent. Add to the salad with the vinegar, ground pepper and the parsley. Toss and serve immediately. Serves 4.

SPANISH RICE SALAD ••

This is a favourite in Spain. A similar salad is made in France by omitting the prawns and using 1–2 cups freshly cooked peas instead of the capsicum. Both versions are great.

1½ cups long-grain rice
¼ cup olive oil
3 cups chicken stock
1 teaspoon salt
½ teaspoon saffron threads
8 spring onions, sliced
250 g prawns, shelled
2 cups cubed ham or cooked chicken
1 small red capsicum, diced
1 small green capsicum, diced

dressing:

1 tablespoon white vinegar
3 tablespoons olive oil
2 teaspoons paprika

In a large saucepan with a tight-fitting lid, sauté the rice in the oil for a few minutes, stirring, then add the stock, salt and saffron. Stir well, cover tightly, and cook over a low heat for 25–30 minutes. When cooked, fluff up with fork and leave uncovered until cooled. Mix the dressing ingredients and add to rice a little at a time, tossing lightly but thoroughly to distribute evenly. Mix in the spring onions, prawns, cubed meat and half the diced capsicum reserving some prawns for the garnish. Pile the rice mixture in a bowl and garnish with the prawns and remaining capsicum. *Serves 6.*

BEEF AND VERMICELLI NOODLE SALAD ••

250 g rice vermicelli noodles
1 Lebanese cucumber
1 large carrot, grated coarsely
½ cup mint leaves
⅓ cup fresh coriander leaves
500 g thick rump steak
1 tablespoon chopped toasted peanuts (optional)

dressing:

2 tablespoons brown sugar
¼ cup lime juice
1 tablespoon fish sauce
1 red chilli, seeded and chopped

In a bowl, pour over the noodles enough boiling water to cover. Leave to stand for 5 minutes, then drain, rinse and set aside. Noodles should be tender but firm. Repeat with fresh boiling water if not quite soft enough.

Slice the cucumber thinly. Make the dressing by mixing the sugar, lime juice, fish sauce and chilli, stirring well.

Toss the noodles together with the carrot, cucumber, herb leaves and dressing, and set aside. Slice the steak thinly and stir-fry quickly over a high heat until the colour changes. Pile the beef over the noodles and finish with a few reserved herb leaves and peanuts, if using. *Serves 4.*

BEEF AND VERMICELLI NOODLE SALAD

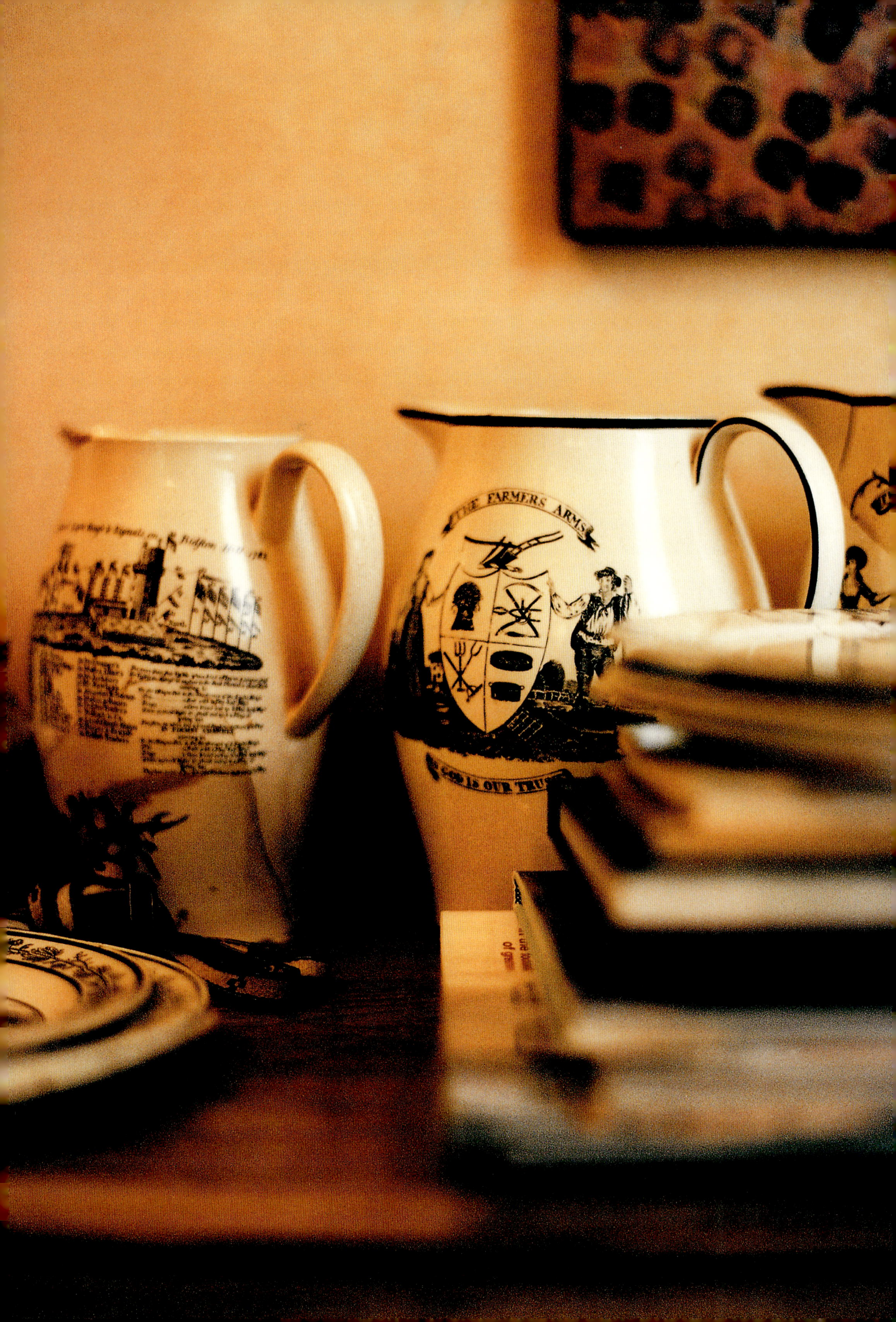
THE FARMERS ARMS

pasta, rice, other grains & pulses

Rice, pasta, couscous and pulses are staple foods, along with vegetables, for much of the world's population. Learn to cook these essentials and you have the base for hundreds of dishes.

Combine them, spice them, learn some of the great traditional dishes, and you are on the way to a fascinating and healthy lifestyle.

PASTA

Many varieties of pasta are available, such as fettuccine flavoured with tomato, saffron, and black squid ink, as well as egg. Each has its own inimitable flavour and colour. There are also many different pasta shapes — the catalogue of one large pasta company lists over 50 varieties. Take your pick from penne and the corkscrew-shaped fusilli to concheglie (shells) and the small cartwheels called rotelle. The choice is enormous and no pasta lover will ever want for variety.

The size or shape of pasta is as important as the sauce. It may be a simple sauce of melted butter, or butter with mashed anchovies and garlic. Pesto, the green sauce from Genoa is another classic, made by pounding basil, pine nuts, oil and parmesan cheese to a paste. The favourite is perhaps the rich meat ragu known to the world as bolognese. The quality of the pasta and the sauce is the key to most dishes, but learning to cook pasta correctly is just as important.

HOW TO COOK PASTA

Use a large saucepan, with plenty of room for the pasta to cook separately, and allow the water to bubble briskly. Use lots of water for cooking, measure 5 litres water (many Italians recommend 6 litres) for 250 g pasta. Add about 1 teaspoon salt for each litre (4 cups) of water, and have the water boiling vigorously before adding the pasta.

Be careful not to overcook pasta, it must be tender, but still firm. As the Italians say, the pasta must be al dente, which means just firm enough to bite comfortably, but not so soft that it is mushy to the bite. When it reaches this stage, remove from the heat, pour a cup of iced water into the pan to stop boiling, and drain immediately.

Follow the cooking times for different varieties on the manufacturer's instructions. As soon as the pasta is added to the boiling water, stir well to prevent sticking. When cooking spaghetti, curl it around in the pan as it softens, until the whole length is submerged. Do not cover. Approximately 500 g of pasta serves 4 people as a main course, and 6 people for a first course.

TO SAUCE PASTA

Place the drained pasta in a warm serving bowl, add most of the sauce, and sprinkle with Parmesan cheese, if liked. With 2 forks, or spaghetti tongs, lift the spaghetti so that the sauce coats the strands, in the way one would toss a salad. Top the spaghetti with the remaining sauce, and offer more cheese separately.

TO KEEP PASTA HOT

The drained pasta can be returned for a short while to the empty cooking saucepan with a good tablespoon of butter, then covered and kept warm. Another method to keep cooked pasta warm is to drain in a colander and set over a saucepan containing a small amount of simmering water. Coat the pasta with 2 tablespoons butter or olive oil (for 500 g) to keep the strands from sticking together, and cover. However, pasta is always best served immediately.

Pasta is delicious served with extra virgin olive oil or butter, chopped fresh herbs and freshly ground black pepper.

SAUCES FOR PASTA

FRESH TOMATO SAUCE ••

This sauce can be used as a base for many pasta dishes with various ingredients added, such as mushrooms, shellfish, tuna and salami.

3 tablespoons olive oil
½ stalk celery
1 small onion, finely chopped
1 clove garlic, crushed
1 kg ripe tomatoes, cut into chunks
2 tablespoons tomato paste
½ teaspoon salt
freshly ground pepper
1 bay leaf
2 tablespoons chopped fresh herbs such as parsley, oregano, basil

Heat the oil in a large saucepan, add the celery, onion and garlic, and sauté lightly. Add the tomatoes and the tomato paste. Season with the salt and pepper and simmer gently for about 45 minutes. Add the bay leaf and herbs. Cook for a further 10 minutes. Rub through a coarse sieve. This is enough sauce for 500 g pasta. Serves 4–6.

GARLIC OIL SAUCE •

4–6 cloves garlic, finely chopped
½ cup olive oil
salt and freshly ground pepper

Cook the garlic gently in the oil without browning. Drain the pasta well and pour the garlic and oil over. Stir thoroughly, season, and serve at once. This is ample sauce for 500 g pasta. Serves 4–6.

BOLOGNESE SAUCE (RAGU) ••

This is how the classic dish of Bologna is made. It freezes very well.

45 g butter
2 tablespoons olive oil
1 medium onion, finely chopped
1 medium carrot, finely chopped
1 stick celery, finely chopped
2 cloves garlic, finely chopped
90 g pancetta, coppa or bacon, finely chopped
500 g minced beef, pork or veal mince (or a mixture of both)
1 cup dry red wine
salt and freshly ground pepper
3 tablespoons tomato paste
1 cup beef stock
¼ cup cream (optional)

Heat the butter and oil in a deep frying pan, add the vegetables and fry until softened and browned lightly. Add the pancetta and minced meat and fry until the meat changes colour. Add the wine, let it bubble hard for a few minutes, and then add the salt, pepper, tomato paste and a little stock to moisten.

Simmer, covered, stirring every now and then, and adding the remaining stock as necessary, for 1½ hours. Add the cream, if liked, and cook, uncovered, for 5 minutes longer. Serve with hot drained pasta. This is ample sauce for 500 g of pasta. Serves 4–6.

PASTA PRIMAVERDE ••

This beautiful pasta dish is brimful of the healthy goodness of a variety of green vegetables.

500 g spaghetti
2 tablespoons cream
1 cup chicken stock
a pinch of ground nutmeg
freshly ground pepper
1 cup blanched or frozen peas
1 cup sugar snaps or snow peas
1 bunch asparagus
4 young zucchini, cut into thick sticks
½ cup chopped parsley or mint leaves, to garnish (optional)

Bring a large saucepan of salted water to the boil. Add the pasta and cook until tender to the bite or al dente. Drain and transfer to heated bowl, cover. Meanwhile, in another saucepan, place the cream, chicken stock, nutmeg and pepper and warm over a low heat, stirring constantly. Stir in the blanched peas. Keep the sauce warm over a gentle heat.

Bring a saucepan of water to the boil. Drop in the sugar snaps and blanch until tender, for about 1 minute. Remove, drain and refresh in a bowl of iced water. Break the asparagus into short lengths and halve lengthwise, if liked. Drop in the pan and boil until tender, for about 2 minutes. Remove and drain well. Repeat with zucchini, cooking for 2 minutes, draining and refreshing.

Place the pasta, the sugar snaps, halved lengthwise if large, and the asparagus and zucchini in a large saucepan. Toss well over a gentle heat. Add the sauce with the peas and toss again, until well heated. Garnish with parsley or mint leaves. Serve immediately. Serves 4.

PASTA PRIMAVERDE

PESTO •

This famous Italian sauce from Genoa is excellent with pasta in summer, when fresh basil is available.

2–3 cloves garlic, chopped
4–6 tablespoons finely chopped basil
4 tablespoons chopped parsley
1 tablespoon pine nuts or chopped walnuts
½ cup grated Parmesan cheese
about 1 cup olive oil
freshly ground pepper
500 g pasta
30 g butter
extra grated Parmesan cheese

Using a mortar and pestle, pound the garlic, basil, parsley, pine nuts and Parmesan until smooth. Gradually add the oil, beating between additions. Add enough oil, beating all the time, until the sauce is thick and smooth. Season with the pepper.

To serve pesto, cook the pasta as directed on the manufacturer's packet. Drain and return to pan. Spoon the sauce over and add the 30 g butter. Toss well over a gentle heat until deliciously fragrant and serve with extra Parmesan. Serves 4–6.

note: this sauce may be made in a blender or food processor fitted with a steel blade, and can be stored in the refrigerator in a jar.

LASAGNE • • •

315 g lasagne sheets or wide noodles
500 g mozzarella cheese, very thinly sliced or grated

meat sauce:
500 g minced steak
1 clove garlic, crushed
2 teaspoons shredded basil
1½ teaspoons salt
2 cups cooked or canned tomatoes
1 cup tomato purée
2 tablespoons tomato paste

cheese filling:
3 cups fresh ricotta cheese
½ cup grated Parmesan cheese
1 tablespoon chopped parsley
2 eggs, beaten
1 teaspoon salt
½ teaspoon pepper

Preheat the oven to 180°C. Cook the lasagne, following the manufacturer's instructions, in a large amount of boiling, salted water. Drain. Place a layer of lasagne sheets in a 33 cm x 23 cm x 5 cm ovenproof dish, spread with half the cheese filling, cover with half the mozzarella and half the meat sauce. Repeat in layers, finishing with a layer of meat sauce topped with mozzarella. Bake for 30 minutes. Stand for 10 minutes then cut into squares. The filling will set slightly.

meat sauce: In a large frying pan, brown the meat slowly. Spoon off the fat and add the remaining ingredients. Simmer, partially covered for 30 minutes, stirring occasionally.

cheese filling: Mix the ricotta and Parmesan, parsley, eggs, salt and pepper. Serves 4–6.

LASAGNE

Fill the cannelloni with the mixture, using a pastry bag and tube.

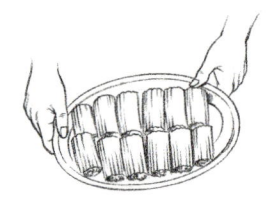

Arrange side by side in the sauce.

BAKED CANNELLONI ••

250 g cannelloni
1 quantity fresh tomato sauce (see p. 161)

filling:
500 g minced steak
2 eggs, beaten
2 tablespoons oil
2 tablespoons grated Parmesan cheese
1 tablespoon chopped parsley
1 teaspoon salt
freshly ground pepper

Cook 3 or 4 pieces of cannelloni at a time in plenty of boiling, salted water, following the manufacturer's instructions for timing. Rinse in cold water and drain.

filling: Preheat the oven to 180°C. Mix the steak, eggs, oil, Parmesan, parsley, salt and pepper to taste. Fill the cannelloni with the mixture, using a pastry bag and tube, or a small teaspoon. Arrange side by side in the sauce. Cover with the remaining sauce and bake for about 45 minutes. Serves 4.

SPAGHETTI AND MEATBALLS ••

500 g finely minced steak
1 cup breadcrumbs
1 small onion, finely chopped
½ cup grated Parmesan cheese
1 egg, lightly beaten
salt and freshly ground pepper
2–3 tablespoons oil for frying
1 quantity fresh tomato sauce (see p. 161)
500 g hot, cooked spaghetti
extra grated Parmesan cheese

Put the minced steak in a bowl with the breadcrumbs, onion, Parmesan, egg, salt and pepper. Mix lightly and evenly with a fork. Roll into 20 small balls and chill while preparing the sauce. Heat the oil in a frying pan and cook the meatballs, shaking the pan to brown evenly. Drain and gently stir into the tomato sauce in a large saucepan. Simmer for a further 10 minutes. Serve on hot, cooked spaghetti, accompanied by extra grated Parmesan. Serves 4–6.

HUNTER'S MUSHROOM PASTA SAUCE ••

Dried porcini mushrooms are available at most delicatessen shops, though they can be omitted if you can't find them. Look for a good selection of fresh mushrooms at your supermarket. Shiitake mushrooms have a good strong flavour and could be used in place of the porcini. Along with prosciutto, brandy and cream the mushrooms make a rich hunter's style sauce that is delicious with any pasta.

10 g dried porcini mushrooms
2 tablespoons olive oil
250 g field mushrooms,
  wiped clean and thinly sliced
4–5 oyster mushrooms (optional)
125 g sliced prosciutto, cut into strips
¼ cup brandy
1 cup cream
100 g peas
salt and freshly ground pepper
¼ cup grated Parmesan cheese

Place the porcini mushrooms in a small bowl and cover with boiling water. Allow to stand for 20 minutes and drain, reserving the water. Rinse the porcini several times as they can contain sand. Chop finely and set aside.

In a frying pan combine the olive oil, mushrooms and prosciutto and cook over a moderate heat until the mushrooms are soft, about 6 minutes. Add the brandy and cook for 1 minute. Stir in the cream and peas, simmer for about 6 minutes, or until the sauce has thickened slightly. Season to taste with salt and pepper. Serve poured over cooked pasta and sprinkle with the Parmesan. This is enough sauce for 500 g pasta. *Serves 4–6.*

SPAGHETTI ALLA CARBONARA •

500 g spaghetti, rigatoni or penne
3 eggs
½ cup cream
200 g rashers bacon, rind removed
60 g butter, softened
⅓ cup chopped parsley
about ½ cup grated Parmesan cheese
freshly ground pepper

Cook spaghetti in a large pan of boiling, salted water for about 15 minutes or until tender but still firm. Drain and turn into a heated serving bowl. Cover to keep warm. Beat eggs lightly with the cream and set aside. Meanwhile, cut bacon into thin strips and cook gently in a pan in a little of the butter until crisp and golden.

Just before serving, stir eggs into bacon and mushrooms and cook over a very gentle heat just until eggs start to thicken. Pour into the spaghetti, tossing well with the remaining butter and parsley. Add grated Parmesan, season well with freshly ground pepper and toss again. *Serves 4-6.*

note: it is important to drain the pasta before cooking the bacon and egg mixture. The eggs must not overcook and they should be moist. The softened butter blends in to produce a soft creamy sauce.

RICE

From Hong Kong to Halifax, Madrid to Mandalay, Bali to Baltimore, people the world over love rice. From an exotic pilaf to a simple creamy pudding, rice cooking is as varied as the nations cooking it.

Pilafs or pilaus are dishes in which the rice absorbs the flavour of the meats and spices, while they are all cooking together. Rice for curries is usually aromatic basmati rice with saffron or turmeric often added so that the rice assumes a golden hue.

Risotto is made with either arborio, carnaroli or vialone rice which is first cooked in butter before hot stock is added, a ladleful at a time. The rice becomes plump, tender and deliciously creamy.

The Chinese cook rice in a minimum of water. For fried rice, Thai fried rice and nasi goreng, it is best that the rice is cooked the day, or at least several hours before, and spread out on a large tray to dry.

HOW TO COOK RICE

BOILED RICE •

This is a failure-proof method for boiling rice to perfection, so that the grains are white, fluffy and separate. This quantity makes 4–4½ cups of cooked rice. Lemon helps to keep the rice white.

1½ cups long-grain rice
12 cups water
3 teaspoons salt
2 slices lemon

Wash the rice well in several changes of water. Bring the water, salt and lemon slices to a rolling boil in a large saucepan. Add the rice slowly, so that water continues to boil. Boil for 12–15 minutes, uncovered, until the grains are tender and have no hard centre when pressed between fingers. Keep the water boiling rapidly during the entire cooking process. Drain at once through a colander. The rice may need cold water poured through, to separate the grains and wash out any clinging, excess starch. Make about 8 holes in the rice mass with the handle of a wooden spoon to drain well and allow the steam to escape. *Serves 4–6.*

to keep hot: Put the colander of drained rice over a pan of simmering water. Cover the rice.

variations: A number of different things can be added to cooked rice with a nut of butter. Try raisins, snipped chives, cooked peas, diced capsicum, sliced olives, toasted pine nuts and almonds or sliced mushrooms and finely chopped onion cooked in a little butter.

STEAMED RICE •

The absorption method of cooking rice results in well-defined grains, which are never sticky or lumpy. The cooking time and the amount of liquid required vary slightly with different types of rice.

3 cups water
1½ teaspoons salt
a squeeze of lemon juice
1½ cups rice

Wash the rice in several changes of cold water in a bowl, until the water is clear. This removes any excess starch. Pour into a strainer, and allow to drain well.

Bring the water to the boil in a medium saucepan. Add the salt and lemon juice, then sprinkle in the rice. Allow the water to return to the boil, stir once, turn the heat as low as possible, cover with a well-fitting lid, and steam gently for 20–25 minutes. Do not lift the lid or stir during the steaming time. Remove from the heat, and uncover for a few minutes to allow steam to escape. Fluff up with a fork. Serves 4–6.

note: for added flavour, use stock instead of water. A small nut of butter may also be added to the water.

RISOTTO MILANESE ••

The method of cooking risotto results in a creamy rice, with each grain separate and still firm to the bite. The hot liquid is added slowly, while the rice is stirred constantly, and must be absorbed after each addition before more is added.

Use a heavy-based saucepan, preferably with rounded edges at the base to prevent the rice sticking in the corners. It needs to be big enough to accommodate the rice, which will swell as much as three times. The stock for adding must be kept simmering next to the risotto pan, to prevent any slowing down of the cooking process. The cook has to devote 15–20 minutes at the stove, gently stirring the rice, but it is worth every minute.

6 cups chicken stock
½ teaspoon saffron threads
90 g butter
1 small onion, finely chopped
350 g arborio, carnaroli or vialone rice
½ cup dry white wine
½ cup grated Parmesan cheese

Bring the chicken stock to a simmer and keep hot. Take out ½ cup and use it to steep the saffron. In a heavy-based saucepan, melt half the butter, add the onion and cook gently, stirring until softened. Add the unwashed rice and stir for 3–4 minutes. Stir in the wine and, when evaporated, add a ladle of simmering stock. Cook over a moderate heat, stirring until the stock is absorbed. Repeat this process, adding the stock a ladle at a time, until the rice absorbs the stock, stirring constantly. The rice should be cooked after 20 minutes. Lastly, add the saffron-steeped stock. At this stage, remove the pan from the heat, cover and, without stirring, allow the rice to absorb the last liquid. Just before serving, fold in the remaining butter and Parmesan. Taste for seasoning and serve immediately. Serves 4.

NASI GORENG ••

2 cups rice
4 cups water
1 teaspoon salt
½ cup peanut or vegetable oil
2 onions, chopped
½ teaspoon dry shrimp paste (trasi or blachan)
1 clove garlic, crushed
1 fresh chilli, seeded and sliced
250 g beef or pork fillet, diced
2 half chicken breasts, diced
250 g prawns, shelled
2 tablespoons light soy sauce
4 eggs

Wash the rice in several changes of water. Bring the water to the boil, and then add the salt and rice. Reduce the heat, cover tightly, and simmer for 20–25 minutes. Uncover, and allow to get quite cold. It is a good idea to cook the rice the day before.

Heat half the oil in a large frying pan. First fry the onions, shrimp paste, garlic and chilli, stirring constantly, for 2–3 minutes. Add the beef or pork and fry until cooked, about 3–4 minutes. Add the remaining oil when necessary. Add the chicken and prawns and cook 2 minutes longer, then add the rice and fry, stirring constantly, until heated through and the rice is golden. Sprinkle with soy sauce and toss together well.

Fry the eggs individually, or prepare an omelette separately and cut into thin strips. Heap the rice on a serving plate and garnish with the eggs or omelette strips. Serves 4.

For parties or special occasions, any of the following garnishes may accompany the nasi goreng:

- crisp fried onion (see following)
- fried egg
- slices of unpeeled Lebanese cucumber
- small fried meatballs *(see following)* served on skewers and topped with a little chilli sauce
- fried sardines or sprats
- fried pappadums or prawn crisps fried in oil

crisp fried onion: Peel and thinly slice an onion lengthwise. Toss with 2 tablespoons of oil, place on microwave-proof plate and cook on high, stirring frequently until browned. Drain on paper towel.

fried meatballs: Combine 250 g finely minced steak, 1 small finely chopped onion, a dash of Tabasco, 1 egg white and salt and pepper, to taste. Mould into small marble-sized balls. Fry in a little oil in a frying pan, tossing, until browned and cooked. Arrange on the rice.

NASI GORENG

RICE WITH BROAD BEANS •

Although broad beans are strictly a summer vegetable, the frozen product is excellent for other times of the year. This is a lovely Egyptian way of cooking them, with rice. It's also a way of stretching a little meat to make a meal.

3 cups long-grain rice
1 kg blanched or frozen broad beans
60 g butter
salt
chicken or other meat stock
¼ cup blanched almond halves
1 tablespoon oil
250 g minced steak

Wash the rice and drain. Simmer the beans in salted boiling water for 2–3 minutes, drain and, if liked, peel the white skin from each bean. Heat the butter in a saucepan, add the rice, and stir for a few minutes, until the rice becomes transparent. Add salt to taste and enough stock to cover. Bring to the boil and simmer, covered, for about 15 minutes, or until the rice is almost tender and the broth has absorbed. Add the beans and simmer a further 5 minutes. Fork the rice and let it rest, still covered, while the remaining moisture is absorbed and the grains become separated.

Toast the almonds in a dry frying pan then remove and set aside. Heat the oil and fry the minced steak until well browned, mashing and stirring it into small pieces. Sprinkle the almonds over the dish with the fried minced steak before serving. *Serves 6*.

SAFFRON RICE ••

Saffron is one of the most common spices of mediaeval cookery. It is an essential ingredient of risotto Milanese (see p. 169) and many Spanish rice dishes such as the traditional paella valenciana (see p. 275). It is also widely used in Indian cookery, especially in rice dishes.

Saffron comes from the stigmas of a variety of crocus flower, native to Asia and parts of Europe. It is available either as the dried stigma threads or as a powder. The former may be ground, crumbed, or used whole before being mixed with the hot stock or liquid called for in a recipe, while the powder is simply infused in the liquid. Ground turmeric is not a substitute for saffron, the flavour being quite different, even though it is often used to give a golden hue to rice. Turmeric may replace the saffron for a yellow rice.

3 cups water
1½ cups rice
2 teaspoons salt
6 cloves
1 stick cinnamon
3 bay leaves
4 black peppercorns
½ teaspoon saffron threads
1 teaspoon butter

Bring the water to the boil and put all the ingredients into the pan. Bring back to the boil, then reduce the heat to very low, cover tightly, and steam for 20–25 minutes. Do not uncover during the cooking time. Remove from the heat, uncover to allow the steam to escape, and then fluff up with fork. *Serves 4–6*.

INDIAN GHEE RICE •

60 g ghee or butter
2 onions, finely sliced
1 teaspoon turmeric
2 cups rice
3½ cups stock
8 peppercorns
2 cloves
4 bruised cardamom pods
1 stick cinnamon
2 teaspoons salt
1 cup cooked peas

Heat the ghee or butter in a saucepan with a lid. Fry half the onions until golden brown, add the turmeric, and stir well for a minute. Add the rice and fry for a few minutes, stirring until it is golden in colour. Add boiling stock, spices, salt and remaining onions. Stir well, cover tightly, and cook on very low heat for 20–25 minutes. Turn off the heat, and keep covered until ready to serve. A few minutes before serving, uncover the pan to allow the steam to escape. Fluff up with a fork. Garnish with the peas. Serves 4–6.

ARROZ CON POLLO ••

1 x 1.5 kg chicken
½ cup olive oil
1 clove garlic, chopped
2 onions, chopped
1 green capsicum, chopped
1 bay leaf
1 x 440 g can tomatoes
3 cups chicken stock
1 teaspoon salt
½ teaspoon saffron threads
2 cups rice
125 g green beans, cut into short lengths
1 small can artichoke hearts, drained (optional)

Preheat the oven to 180°C. Cut the chicken into serving pieces and wipe dry with paper towels. Heat the olive oil in a flameproof casserole dish. Brown the chicken pieces on all sides then remove from the dish. Add the garlic, onions and capsicum to the juices in the dish and sauté until the onions are golden. Add the bay leaf, whole tomatoes and chicken stock. When the stock boils, add the salt, saffron and rice. Arrange the chicken on the rice and cover the casserole. Bake for 20 minutes or until the rice is tender. Add the beans and artichokes, if using, during the last 10 minutes of cooking. Serves 6.

THAI FRIED RICE ••

Fried rice is best made with rice cooked several hours, or even a day before, and allowed to dry out to ensure a good-looking rice dish with separate grains. Red curry paste is available from most supermarkets. You'll find this dish is almost a meal in itself.

about 5 cups cooked long-grain or
    jasmine rice
3 tablespoons vegetable oil
2 small brown onions or
    6 golden shallots, finely chopped
2 cloves garlic, finely chopped
2 teaspoons red curry paste
1 chicken half breast or ½ pork fillet cubed,
    or 1 cup shelled and deveined green prawns
2 eggs, lightly beaten
2–3 tablespoons Thai fish sauce (nam pla)
freshly ground pepper
chopped fresh coriander, sliced Lebanese
    cucumbers, sliced spring onions and
    lemon wedges, to garnish

Spread the cooked rice out on a baking tray or plastic tray to cool and air. This can be done the day before. When ready to cook the dish, heat the oil and stir-fry the onion or shallots for a few minutes, until softened. Add the garlic and continue to stir-fry until the onions are golden. Add the red curry paste and fry until the aroma is released. Add the rice and chicken, pork or prawns and stir-fry for about 4 minutes. Add the beaten egg, continue to stir-fry to thoroughly mix until cooked. Sprinkle with the fish sauce and season well with the pepper.

Turn onto a large serving platter and garnish liberally with the coriander, cucumber, spring onions and lemon wedges. Serves 4–6.

DOLMADES ••

Vary the flavour by using sultanas or chopped dried apricots instead of currants, and oregano in place of mint. If you have access to a grapevine, pick the medium-sized, tender leaves and blanch for a few minutes before draining and cooling.

25 blanched grape leaves,
    or vine leaves packed in brine
¾ cup rice
¼ cup olive oil
2 medium onions, finely chopped
½ cup chopped dill
¼ cup currants
salt and freshly ground pepper
½ teaspoon ground cinnamon
1 cup water
juice of 1 lemon
lemon wedges to serve

Wash the grape leaves in a colander and drain thoroughly. Cover the rice with cold water, soak for 5 minutes and drain. Heat half the oil in a frying pan and gently fry the onions until pale golden. Add the rice, dill, currants and seasonings. Add the remaining oil and ⅓ cup water. Cover and simmer for about 15 minutes, until the liquid is absorbed. Cool.

Put about 2 teaspoons of the rice stuffing on the dull side of each prepared leaf at the stem end. Trim and discard the stem. Fold in the sides and roll up the leaf tightly. Line the base of a flameproof casserole with several unstuffed vine leaves. Pack the stuffed leaves fairly tightly so they will not unwrap.

Pour 1 cup of water and the lemon juice over the dolmades and cover with a small plate. Cover with a lid and cook over a gentle heat for about 1 hour, or until tender. Cool and serve with wedges of lemon. Serves 4–6.

KICHADI ••

One of the healthiest dishes, this is a delicious mixture of fresh vegetables, a grain and a legume.

4 tablespoons light olive oil
2 cloves
1 small piece of cinnamon stick
4 cardamom pods, split
1 teaspoon ground turmeric
1 teaspoon ground cumin
2 onions, chopped
1 green capsicum, seeded and diced
2 cups rice, brown or white
6 cups water
1 teaspoon salt
1 cup yellow split peas
1 large tomato, peeled and diced
1–2 cups cauliflower florets or green peas

Heat half the oil in a large, heavy-based saucepan. Add the spices and sauté gently until fragrant. Add the onions and capsicum and cook, stirring, until the onions are soft. Stir in the rice and cook for about 5 minutes, or until the rice begins to turn glossy.

Add the water and salt and bring to the boil. Cover and cook the white rice over a gentle heat for 10 minutes. If using brown rice, cook a further 10 minutes. Sauté the yellow split peas and tomatoes in the remaining oil. Add the split peas and tomato to the rice and continue cooking for 15 minutes. Add the cauliflower or green peas, cover, and cook for a further 15 minutes. Serves 6.

BURGHUL

A cracked wheat used in the Middle East, particularly Lebanon. Available from health food stores and most supermarkets, it is always soaked in cold water before use to soften and swell the grains. It is the essential base for tabbouleh.

TABBOULEH •

This Middle Eastern salad is good for packing into flat bread pockets or into scooped-out tomatoes, or as part of a casual buffet meal or barbecue.

¾ cup burghul
½ cup finely chopped spring onion
salt and freshly ground pepper
2 cups finely chopped parsley
½ cup finely chopped mint
3 tablespoons salad oil
½ cup lemon juice
2 firm tomatoes, diced

Soak the burghul in cold water for 1 hour; it will expand considerably. Drain well and press out the excess water. Spread out on a clean tea towel to dry.

Place in a bowl and refrigerate for an hour or so. Mix the burghul with the onion, salt and pepper, crushing onion juice into the burghul with your fingers. Add the parsley, mint, oil and lemon juice and mix thoroughly. Finally, add the tomatoes. Taste and adjust seasoning. It should be distinctly lemony. Serves 4–6.

COUSCOUS

A cereal dish originating in North Africa, couscous consists of fine semolina combined with flour, salt and water which is formed into tiny pellets. Instant couscous is available at most supermarkets, simply follow the instructions on the packet.

COUSCOUS WITH VEGETABLES ••
Try experimenting with different vegetables as they come into season.

6–8 tablespoons olive oil
2 cloves garlic, crushed
1 small eggplant
1 teaspoon salt
1 teaspoon ground cumin
freshly ground black pepper
½ teaspoon ground ginger
1 bay leaf
1–2 fresh red chillies
4 medium carrots, scraped, cut into quarters lengthwise, then across into 5 cm lengths
4 zucchini, cut the same size as the carrots
200 g green beans, topped (*optional*)
500 g potatoes, peeled and cut into 5 cm lengths (*optional*)
500 g instant couscous

Heat half the olive oil in a large heavy-based saucepan. Add the garlic and eggplant and sauté for 1–2 minutes, until softened. Add salt, cumin, black pepper, ginger and bay leaf and stir well. Add the whole chillies and vegetables with just enough water to cover Bring to the boil, cover, and simmer gently for about 20 minutes, or until tender.

Meanwhile, prepare couscous according to manufacturer's instructions then, when ready to serve, place the swollen couscous in a heavy-based pan to moisten with the remaining oil. Reheat gently and fluff up the couscous occasionally with a fork, until ready. To serve, pile the couscous onto a large serving platter and pile the vegetables into the centre, removing the chillies. Serve immediately with harissa, a Moroccan spice paste, if liked. Serves 6.

SPICY COUSCOUS WITH CHICKPEAS ••

1 cup instant couscous
2 tablespoons olive oil
6 spring onions, chopped
1 clove garlic, finely chopped
6 patty pan squash, quartered
4 zucchini, sliced
1 cup cooked or drained canned chickpeas
½ teaspoon ground cumin
½ teaspoon curry powder
½ teaspoon salt
freshly ground pepper
¼ cup freshly chopped parsley

Prepare couscous according to manufacturer's instructions and set aside. Heat the oil in a large frying pan and sauté the spring onions and garlic for 1 minute. Add the squash and zucchini and continue to stir-fry for about 5 minutes, until just tender. Stir in the chickpeas and spices and stir-fry a further minute. Gently fold through the prepared couscous and keep over a gentle heat until heated through, for about 5 minutes. Scatter with the chopped parsley. Serves 4.

COUSCOUS WITH VEGETABLES

GRILLED LAMB WITH LEMON COUSCOUS ••

3 cups chicken, beef or vegetable stock
1 cup diced zucchini
1 cup diced pumpkin
2 tablespoons olive oil
2 cups instant couscous
2 tablespoons finely diced preserved lemon (see p. 249)
freshly ground pepper
4 pieces backstrap lamb fillets
8–12 snipped mint leaves (optional)

white bean purée:
1 x 440 g can white cannellini beans
3 cloves garlic, crushed
juice and rind of 1 lemon
1 tablespoon olive oil

Make the white bean purée first and set aside. Bring the stock to the boil in a saucepan with the vegetables and simmer until just tender. Add the oil, reserving a little for cooking the lamb. Stir in the couscous, remove from the heat and leave to stand, covered, for 5 minutes. Add the preserved lemon and fluff the couscous with a fork. Meanwhile, season the lamb with pepper and brush with olive oil. Have ready a preheated grill or heavy-based frying pan and cook until tender, about 4–5 minutes each side. Cover and rest for 5 minutes. To serve, spoon the couscous onto serving plates. Top with thick slices of lamb and finish with a dollop of white bean purée. Garnish with mint leaves, if using. Harissa could also be offered with this.

white bean purée: In a blender, purée the drained beans (saving the liquid) with lemon juice and garlic. Transfer to a small saucepan, add the oil and simmer gently for 5 minutes. If too thick, stir in a little of the reserved liquid. Serves 4.

HUMMUS WITH TAHINA •

A Lebanese spread served with flat bread. Chickpeas, which are used in this dish, are sometimes called garbanzos, and are available dried or canned. They are readily available from health food shops and delicatessens. Tahina is a paste made from ground sesame seeds.

1 cup chickpeas, soaked overnight in water to cover or 1–1½ cups canned chickpeas
juice of 1–2 lemons
2 large cloves garlic, crushed
salt
½ cup tahina paste
a little olive oil
a sprinkling of ground cayenne pepper or paprika
rounds of pita bread

Boil the soaked chickpeas in plenty of water for about 1 hour, or until very soft. Drain and set aside a few whole peas, to garnish the dish. Save at least ½ cup of the cooking liquid. Purée the peas in a blender or food processor. Pour in a little of the lemon juice, adding enough cooking liquid to blend the peas to a smooth paste.

Add the crushed garlic, salt and more lemon juice, and slowly beat in the tahina. Blend to a creamy paste, adding more lemon juice and salt, to taste.

Spoon into a shallow serving bowl and make a slight depression in the centre. Pour in a little olive oil, decorate with the reserved chickpeas and sprinkle with the cayenne or paprika. Serve with wedges of pita bread. Serves 4–6.

note: hummus can be used instead of the white bean purée for the grilled lamb (see left).

ROASTED CAPSICUM WITH COUSCOUS ● ●

4 tablespoons olive oil
2 teaspoons ground cumin
1 teaspoon paprika
1 cup water
1 cup instant couscous
6 red capsicum
¾ cup chopped red onion
1 cup diced carrots
1 cup diced zucchini
1 teaspoon dried oregano leaves
salt and freshly ground pepper
3 tablespoons chopped fresh parsley
3 tablespoons pine nuts

Heat 1 tablespoon of the olive oil, cumin, paprika and water in a small saucepan until boiling. Stir in the couscous and cook gently until most of the water has been absorbed, about 2 minutes. Remove from the heat, cover the pot, and allow to stand for 10–15 minutes. Slice the tops from the capsicum, halve if large. Flick out the seeds.

Preheat the oven to 180°C. Heat the remaining 3 tablespoons of the olive oil in a frying pan. Add the onion, carrots, zucchini and sauté for 5 minutes. Stir in the oregano and the couscous and season to taste with salt and pepper. Stir in the parsley and pine nuts. Spoon the couscous mixture into the capsicum shells. Place in an ovenproof baking dish and bake for 35 minutes, covering with foil if the couscous mixture seems to be drying out on top. Serve immediately. Serves 6.

COUSCOUS WITH FRUIT COMPOTE ● ●

This is a lovely comforting breakfast cereal dish. Try a spoonful of natural yogurt with it.

250 g mixed dried fruit, such as apples, pears, peaches, apricots and prunes
pared rind of ½ orange
1 stick cinnamon
1 vanilla bean
sugar
1½ cups freshly squeezed orange juice
1 cup instant couscous
¼ cup raisins

Place the fruit in a large bowl, cover with water and soak overnight or for several hours before cooking. Place the fruit with the water in a saucepan. Add the rind, cinnamon and vanilla. Bring the mixture gently to the boil, reduce heat and cover. Simmer for 15–20 minutes or until the fruit is soft and plump. The length of time depends on the type and size of the fruit. This can be done days beforehand and stored in the refrigerator. Drain, reserving the liquid. Set the fruit aside.

Measure the liquid and return to the saucepan. Add half as much sugar as liquid and simmer until syrupy. Pour the syrup over the fruit. Meanwhile, bring the orange juice to the boil in a large saucepan. Stir in the couscous, remove the pan from the heat and let the couscous stand for about 5 minutes, covered. Add the raisins and fold through, covered for 5 minutes. Fluff the couscous with a fork before serving. To serve, pile the couscous into serving bowls, spoon the cooked fruit over and drizzle with the syrup. Serves 4.

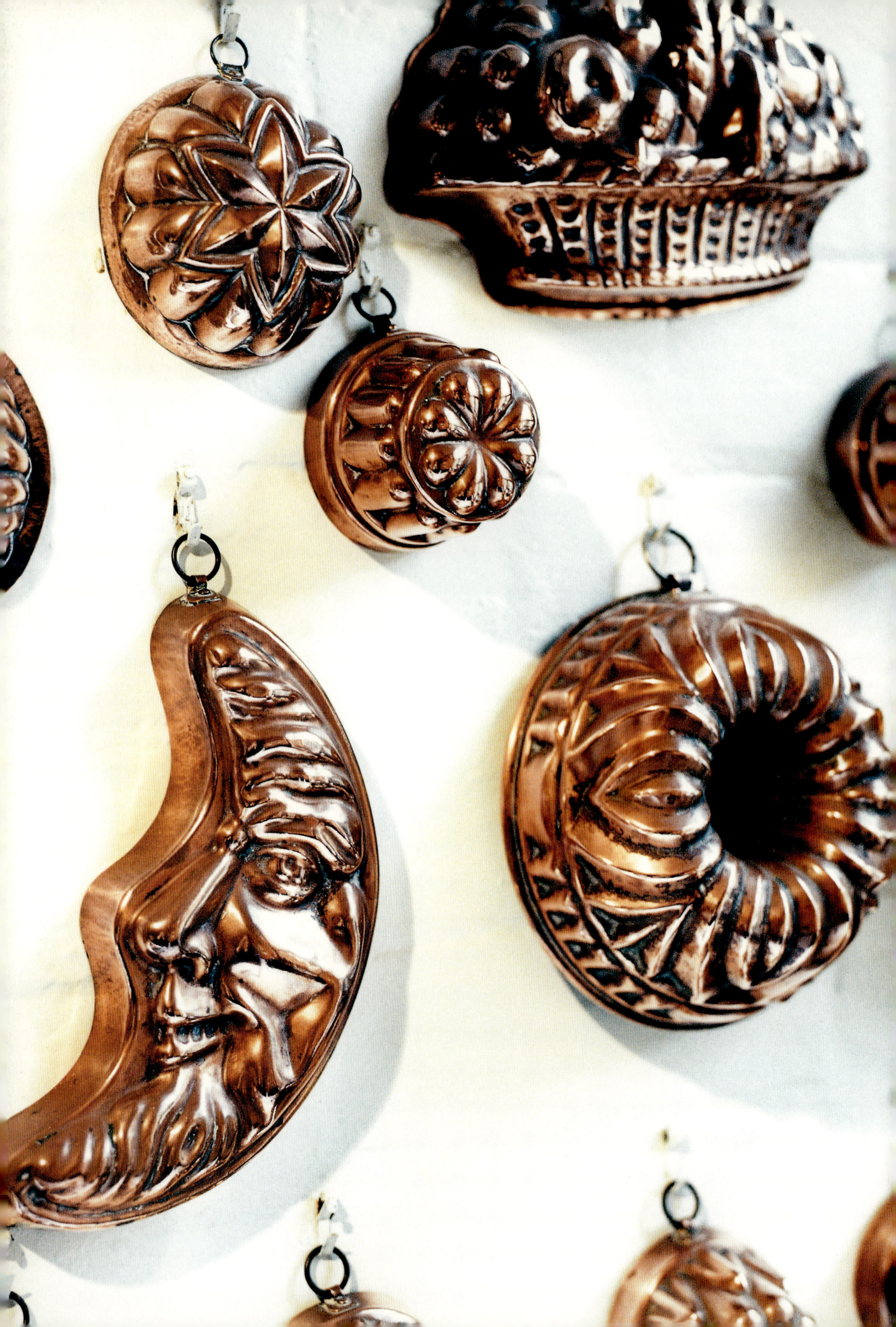

desserts

For years I was content to finish an evening meal with a
perfect piece of fruit, a sweet juicy apple perhaps, a few freshly picked strawberries,
or one of the peaches my sister had preserved from her orchard.

A turning point came when Suzanne returned from London
with her Cordon Bleu Diploma and 12 months' experience as the dessert and cake
chef at the Cordon Bleu Restaurant in Marylebone Lane. The restaurant was famous
for its food, fine cakes and exquisite desserts. I learnt from Suzanne that a good
dessert is worth waiting for and can be the crowning glory to a meal.

DESSERTS

The world of soufflés, crêpes, fruit tarts and pies, custards and creams, mousses and beautiful fresh fruit desserts is accessible to the home cook and make a lovely way of treating the special people in our lives.

SOUFFLÉS

The charm of a soufflé, apart from its delectable flavour and airy texture, is its spectacular appearance. Rising magnificently above the rim of the dish, its height is determined by the size of the dish. Sizes vary from individual serving dishes through to 5- and 6-cup dishes and larger.

To prepare a dish for a hot soufflé, brush with melted butter and dust inside with a little caster sugar. Remove excess sugar by turning the dish upside down and tapping lightly on the work surface.

For a high soufflé, tie a double band of baking paper around the dish to give it extra height. Cut a strip of baking paper 15 cm wide and wrap it around so that it stands like a collar above the edge of the dish (see p. 42).

BASIC HOT SWEET SOUFFLÉ ••

45 g butter
1 tablespoon plain flour
1 cup milk
¼ teaspoon salt
½ cup sugar
a piece of vanilla pod
4 egg yolks
5 egg whites

Prepare a 6-cup soufflé dish *(see left)*. Preheat the oven to 180°C. Melt the butter in a saucepan, blend in the flour, and cook for 1 minute. Remove from the heat and add the milk, stirring constantly. Add the salt, sugar and vanilla pod. Heat, stirring constantly, and when the sauce is thick and smooth, remove from the heat and cool. Remove the vanilla pod and stir in the egg yolks. Whisk the egg whites until stiff and fold into the mixture.

Turn into the prepared soufflé dish. Bake for 35 minutes until well-risen and golden. Serve immediately. Serves 6.

variations
passionfruit: Add ½ cup sieved passionfruit pulp, retaining 1 teaspoon of seeds to add to the sauce with the egg yolks.

orange liqueur: Add 2 tablespoons Grand Marnier or Cointreau to the sauce when adding the egg yolks.

chocolate: Finely chop 60 g dark chocolate and melt over hot water. Add to the sauce when slightly cooled.

SOUFFLÉ OMELETTES

These are closely related to the soufflé proper, but they offer fewer problems to the cook, other than a few minutes absence from the table.

For a spectacle, the soufflé omelette often comes to the table enveloped in the blue flames of rum, brandy or a liqueur of some kind. Best made for two or three people – don't attempt this dish for a larger crowd.

SOUFFLÉ OMELETTE •

3 eggs
1 tablespoon caster sugar
2 teaspoons plain flour
1 tablespoon cream
1 teaspoon grated lemon rind
a pinch of salt
15 g butter
1 tablespoon strawberry or raspberry jam
icing sugar, to dust

Separate eggs and place the whites in a china or clean copper bowl. In a small bowl, combine the yolks with the sugar, flour, cream and rind. Whisk the whites with the pinch of salt until stiff peaks form. Pour in the yolk mixture and fold through gently with a large metal spoon.

Heat butter in a large ovenproof frying pan, without browning, and pour in mixture. Smooth over and place in preheated oven for 12–15 minutes, or until risen and golden. Slide onto a heated serving plate and spread with jam. Fold over and sprinkle with dusted icing sugar.
Serves 2–3.

note: this omelette looks special with a caramelised lattice worked on top. To do this, mark with a red-hot skewer on the icing sugar to burn it. Serve immediately.

variations
Prepare the soufflé omelette as before and try the following additions.

rum: Add 1 tablespoon rum to the egg yolk. Put on a hot dish, pour over 3–4 tablespoons warmed rum, ignite and serve immediately.

apricot: Add the grated rind of an orange to the mxture. Spread heated, thick apricot purée over, before folding, and dust with caster sugar.

peaches and brandy: Heat sliced, fresh peaches in a little brandy. Spoon over omelette. Dust with cinnamon. Fold omelette and sprinkle with cinnamon and caster sugar.

flaming the omelette
A flamed omelette should be flavoured with the liquor that will later envelop it in flames. A tablespoon of rum or brandy is sufficient to beat in with the egg yolks. The platter should be hot, the omelette straight from the stove, and 2–3 tablespoons of rum or brandy heated with a pinch of sugar and ignited as it is poured on.

CHOCOLATE ROULADE ••

This beautiful light-as-air dessert cake has no flour; it's really a chocolate soufflé omelette.

3 x 60 g eggs, separated
½ cup caster sugar
2 tablespoons sifted cocoa
1 teaspoon vanilla essence
¾ cup cream, whipped
1 punnet fresh strawberries or raspberries (*optional*)

Preheat oven to 180°C. Line a 30 cm x 25 cm Swiss roll tin with baking paper. Beat the egg yolks with a whisk or electric beater until thick and creamy. Gradually beat in sugar. Sift cocoa then fold into the egg yolk mixture with the vanilla essence.

Beat egg whites until soft peaks form and fold into cocoa mixture. Pour at once into prepared tin and bake for 15 minutes, until the cake has drawn away from sides and springs back when gently touched in the middle.

Have ready a tea towel liberally sprinkled with caster sugar. Turn the cake out onto the towel and carefully peel away the base paper. While still warm, roll the cake up, including the towel, and leave on a wire rack to cool. When completely cooled, unroll and spread with whipped cream. Scatter over sliced strawberries or raspberries, if using. Roll the cake up and chill in the refrigerator for 30 minutes. **Serves 4–6.**

note: don't be alarmed if the cake starts to crack when you shape it into a roll as the cream will bind it well. The melt-in-the-mouth quality of this roulade is worth a crack or two.

COLD SOUFFLÉS

The charm of a cold soufflé is that it looks spectacular and can be made ahead, unlike a baked soufflé. A cold soufflé uses gelatine to hold the air in the egg whites and cream. Three-egg soufflés are made in the 15 cm or 5-cup capacity dishes, while the larger sweet sherry soufflé is made in a large 18 cm or 8-cup capacity dish.

LEMON SOUFFLÉ ••

3 eggs, separated
1 cup caster sugar
grated rind and strained juice of 2 small lemons
2 teaspoons powdered gelatine
3–4 tablespoons water
1 cup cream, lightly whipped
extra whipped cream and finely chopped toasted nuts, to decorate

Prepare a 15 cm soufflé dish (*see p. 182*) Using vegetable oil in place of the butter. Put the egg yolks in a bowl and beat in the sugar gradually, then add rind and juice. Whisk over simmering water until thick and light. Remove from the heat and whisk for a few minutes longer.

Soak the gelatine in water for 5 minutes, dissolve over a saucepan of simmering water, and add to the lemon mixture. Fold the cream into the mixture then the stiffly beaten egg whites. Turn at once into a prepared soufflé dish and chill until set. When ready to serve, peel off the paper carefully, decorate it with extra cream and press the nuts around the sides of the soufflé. **Serves 5–6.**

CHOCOLATE ROULADE

VANILLA SOUFFLÉ •••

1 vanilla pod
2 cups milk
3 eggs, separated
¼ cup sugar
1 tablespoon powdered gelatine
2–3 tablespoons water
½ cup cream, whipped
1 punnet strawberries
caster sugar
a dash of kirsch
shaved chocolate or extra whipped cream, to decorate

Prepare a 15 cm soufflé dish (see p. 182), greasing with vegetable oil instead of the butter. To make a custard, split the vanilla pod and scald in the milk. Cream the egg yolks with the sugar and pour into the milk. Thicken over low heat, without boiling, and strain and cool. Soak the gelatine in water for 5 minutes, dissolve over hot water and add to the custard.

Stir the mixture over ice and, when beginning to set, fold in the cream then the stiffly beaten egg whites. Put a small oiled jam jar or bottle in the centre of prepared soufflé dish. Pour the mixture into the soufflé dish and chill until set. Before serving, remove the jar and fill the centre of soufflé with whole or sliced sugared strawberries, flavoured with kirsch. Carefully peel off the baking paper and decorate with the shaved chocolate or whipped cream. Serves 5–6.

liqueur soufflé: Add 1–2 tablespoons of your favourite liqueur, such as Grand Marnier or Cointreau plus the same amount of rum or brandy.

SWEET SHERRY SOUFFLÉ •••

This is a great dish for a crowd.

savoy (sponge) fingers
1 tablespoon powdered gelatine
½ cup cold water
1½ cups sweet sherry
6 eggs, separated
¾ cup sugar
1 scant tablespoon lemon juice
1¼ cups cream
extra whipped cream, to decorate (*optional*)

Prepare an 18 cm soufflé dish (see p. 182) and line the inside with savoy fingers. Soak the gelatine in the cold water for 5 minutes. Stand over boiling water and stir until dissolved. Remove from the heat and add the sherry. Cool the mixture. Chill for 30 minutes or until the mixture begins to thicken.

Meanwhile, beat the egg yolks until frothy, gradually add ¼ cup sugar, and beat until the yolks are thick and lemon-coloured. Whip the egg whites until soft peaks form. Add ½ cup sugar gradually, beating constantly. Add the lemon juice and beat until the mixture is stiff, but not dry.

Add the slightly thickened sherry and gelatine mixture to the egg yolks and combine well. Whip the cream and fold in. Lastly, fold in the egg whites gently but thoroughly. Pour into the prepared soufflé dish. Chill until firm. Remove the collar from the dish and serve decorated with the additional whipped cream, if desired. Serves 12.

CUSTARDS AND CREAMS

Velvet smooth crème caramel, with its glistening golden top, is the custard classic of world cuisine. It stars with other delectable rich creams and simple custard desserts.

PLAIN BAKED CUSTARD ••

2 cups milk
2 eggs
1 egg yolk
2 tablespoons sugar
a pinch of salt
½ teaspoon vanilla essence or grated nutmeg

Preheat the oven to 160°C. Heat the milk in a heavy-based saucepan over a low heat. Mix together the eggs, egg yolk, sugar, salt and vanilla or nutmeg. Mix well, but do not beat. When small bubbles appear around edge of milk pan, pour about one-third into the egg mixture and mix until well blended, then add this mixture to remaining milk left in the pan and mix again. Put 6 buttered custard cups or 1 large dish in a baking tin and fill the cups with the strained custard. Carefully pour hot water into the baking tin to come halfway up the sides and bake for 30 minutes, or until a knife inserted in centre of the custard comes out clean. Remove from the water and cool. Serves 6.

CRÈME CARAMEL ••

Most good cooks have perfected this lovely dish. It is luscious and has the added virtue that it can be made a day ahead.

½ cup water
1 cup sugar
1 cup cream
1 cup milk
2.5 cm piece vanilla bean
3 eggs
2 egg yolks
⅓ cup caster sugar

Preheat the oven to 160°C. Put the water and sugar in a small saucepan over a low heat until the sugar dissolves. Bring to the boil and cook quickly, until golden brown (caramel stage). Take care not to make the caramel too dark or it will taste bitter; too light, and it will taste too sweet. Pour into an 18 cm mould or 6 individual moulds. Hold with a cloth and quickly rotate the mould until the caramel coats the sides and base. If using individual moulds, pour a little caramel into the base of each.

Scald the cream and milk with the vanilla bean. Cool slightly and remove the vanilla. Beat the eggs, egg yolks and caster sugar until well blended, and then pour in the cooled milk gradually, stirring constantly. Strain through a fine sieve. Pour the custard mixture into the caramel-lined mould or individual moulds and set in a pan of hot water. Bake the single mould for about 50–60 minutes, or until the custard is set and a knife inserted near the centre comes out clean. If using individual moulds, bake only for 45 minutes. Cool, then chill in refrigerator for several hours or overnight. Unmould onto a serving dish or plates. Serves 6.

CRÈME ANGLAISE •
(ENGLISH CUSTARD)

Many French cooks say this is the greatest sauce of England.

1½ cups milk
1 vanilla bean
4 large or 5 small egg yolks
½ cup sugar
1 teaspoon cornflour

Place the milk and the vanilla bean in a small saucepan. Bring slowly to a simmer then remove from the heat, cover and leave to infuse until cooled.

Beat the egg yolks lightly, then gradually beat in the sugar. Continue to beat for 2–3 minutes until pale yellow. Beat in the cornflour then gradually stir in the strained milk. (The vanilla bean can be rinsed and stored for another use.) Pour the mixture into the top of a double-boiler, over barely simmering water, and stir slowly and continuously until the custard thickens sufficiently to coat the back of the spoon. Keep the custard itself well under simmering point.

Remove from the heat, stir for a minute or two to cool slightly, and then strain. Serve warm or cooled. If serving cooled, cover the surface with damp greaseproof paper to prevent a skin forming on top. Serves 6.

CRÈME BRÛLÉE •••

Make as recipe for crème anglaise *(see left)*, but using only ¼ cup sugar and substituting cream for the milk. Pour into 4 individual or 1 larger serving dish and chill well. Preheat grill. Just before serving, stand the custard in a shallow baking dish, surrounded with ice to keep the custard chilled. Sprinkle caster sugar in a 3 mm layer over the top and put under the preheated grill until the sugar melts and forms a toffee glaze. Alternatively, use a small portable gas blowtorch to caramelise the sugar to a toffee. (Blowtorches are available from most hardware stores – make sure you read the instructions carefully first.) Serve immediately. Brown sugar can be substituted for caster. Serves 4.

RICE CUSTARD •

2 tablespoons short-grain rice
2½ cups boiling water
3 eggs
3 tablespoons sugar
3½ cups milk
½ teaspoon vanilla essence
1–2 teaspoons butter
grated nutmeg

Preheat the oven to 160°C. Wash the rice and cook in the boiling water for 20 minutes, until tender. Drain well and put into a buttered ovenproof dish. Beat the eggs until well mixed, add the sugar, milk and vanilla. Stir into the rice, top with the butter and sprinkle with the nutmeg. Bake for 45 minutes or until set. Serves 6.

FRUIT PIES AND TARTS

Apple pies, in one form or another, figure prominently among the favourite dessert recipes of the world. The French favour the classic tarte aux pommes, with its traditional top of overlapping slices and sweet pastry enclosing a vanilla-flavoured apple purée. Everyone loves a strawberry tart.

GLAZED STRAWBERRY TART ••

1 quantity sweet flan pastry *(see p. 301)*
2 x 125 packets cream cheese
2 tablespoons sugar
1 teaspoon grated lemon rind
1 tablespoon orange juice
1 tablespoon cream
1 punnet strawberries
½ cup redcurrant jelly
1 tablespoon water
2 teaspoons Cointreau or
   2 tablespoons orange juice

Preheat the oven to 190°C. Roll pastry out on a lightly floured board. Fit into a 20 cm or 23 cm flan ring or case and prick well. Chill until firm. Line with greaseproof paper and half-fill with pie weights or dried beans and bake blind for 15 minutes. Remove the paper and beans, reduce the temperature to 180°C and bake for a further 5–10 minutes, until the crust is golden. Allow to cool.

In a bowl, beat the cream cheese with the sugar, rind, orange juice and cream until just smooth. Turn the mixture into the flan case, spreading to make even. Chill for 30 minutes. Top with hulled whole strawberries. In a small saucepan, melt the redcurrant jelly with the water and Cointreau or juice, and then beat slightly until smooth. Brush the glaze over the strawberries and cream cheese filling. Leave to set for 30 minutes before serving. Serves 8.

APPLE STRUDEL ••

This version of the famous continental dessert is simplified by using commercial puff pastry, rolled as thinly as possible.

4 large cooking apples, peeled and cored
2 tablespoons brown sugar
1 tablespoon vanilla essence
250 g commercial puff pastry
   (preferably made with butter)
125 g unsalted butter
½ cup fresh breadcrumbs
2 tablespoons redcurrant jelly
½ cup chopped almonds
icing sugar, to dust

Preheat the oven to 190°C. Quarter the apples. Cut into thin slices. Sprinkle with sugar and vanilla essence. Toss well to coat and leave to stand for 1 hour. Put the pastry on a well-floured tea towel and roll out as thinly as possible to an oblong shape of about 35 cm x 51 cm, or make 2 separate strudels by rolling each out half the size.

Melt half the butter in a saucepan and sauté the breadcrumbs until golden. Melt remaining butter, brush over the pastry and sprinkle half of the breadcrumbs in an even layer over half the pastry, leaving a 5 cm margin at each side and one end. Spread half the apples over the breadcrumbs. Dot with 1 tablespoon redcurrant jelly. Sprinkle with half the almonds. Top with the remaining apples, redcurrant jelly, almonds and breadcrumbs. Fold in the edges of the pastry. Brush the folds with the melted butter. Starting with the filled end, roll up as you would a Swiss roll. Put the strudel on a greased large baking tray. Curl the roll slightly to fit the tray, if necessary. Brush with melted butter. Bake for 45 minutes, brushing with remaining butter every 10 minutes. Dust with icing sugar. Serves 6–8.

Spread the cooked apple in the prepared flan case.

Peel and core the reserved apples and slice very thinly. Arrange slices in a pattern on top of the cooked apple.

TARTE AUX POMMES (APPLE TART) ••

1 quantity sweet flan pastry (see p. 301)
6–8 medium cooking apples
1 tablespoon water
½ cup sugar
¼ cup brandy or 2 teaspoons vanilla essence
30 g butter
1 teaspoon lemon juice
1 extra tablespoon sugar

apricot glaze:
½ cup apricot jam
1 tablespoon water

Preheat the oven to 190°C. Line an 20 cm flan ring or case with pastry, then prick well and chill until firm. Line with greaseproof paper and half-fill with pie weights or dried beans and bake 'blind' for 10 minutes. Remove the paper and beans. Reduce temperature to 180°C and bake for a further 5–10 minutes until the crust is golden. Allow to cool.

Reserve 2 or 3 apples for the top of the tart. Peel, core and quarter the others. Slice roughly and put into a saucepan with the water, sugar, brandy or vanilla and half the butter. Cover and cook over a gentle heat for about 20 minutes, stirring occasionally, until tender. Raise the heat and boil, stirring, until thick enough to hold in a mass in the spoon. Push through a sieve if necessary. Taste and add more sugar if not sweet enough. Spread in pastry shell.

Peel and core reserved apples and slice very thinly. Sprinkle with lemon juice and extra sugar. Arrange slices in a pattern on top of the cooked apple. Brush with the remaining butter, melted. Bake for about 30 minutes until the apples are tender and browned lightly.

Slide onto a rack or serving dish and brush the top and pastry with the apricot glaze. Serve the tart warm or cold with a bowl of whipped cream.

apricot glaze: Heat the jam and water in a saucepan over a low heat and stir until dissolved. Pass through a sieve, then return to the pan and bring to the boil. Cook gently until the glaze is clear and the desired consistency is obtained. *Serves 6.*

TARTE AUX POMMES

RHUBARB AND STRAWBERRY CRUMBLE ••

½ cup sugar
juice and grated rind of 1 orange
1 bunch rhubarb, trimmed and cut into 5cm lengths
1 punnet strawberries, washed and halved

crumble topping:
1 cup plain flour
60g butter
¼ cup sugar
a pinch of ground cinnamon

Preheat the oven to 180°C. Combine the sugar and orange juice in a saucepan. Stir over a moderate heat until sugar dissolves. Bring to the boil, lower the heat and add the rhubarb and orange rind. Cover and simmer for 5 minutes, or until tender but not mushy. Stir in the strawberries.

Spoon into a well-greased ovenproof dish. Sprinkle with the crumble topping and bake until golden brown, about 30 minutes. Serve with cream, yoghurt or vanilla ice-cream.

crumble topping: Sift the flour into a bowl and rub in the butter until the mixture resembles coarse breadcrumbs. Add the sugar and cinnamon and mix well. Serves 4–6.

note: this crumble topping can be used for other stewed fruit bases, for example, apple, plum, pear. Just make sure your fruit base is not too liquid.

PUDDINGS FOR WINTRY DAYS

CANARY PUDDING •

125 g butter
grated rind of 1 lemon
¾ cup caster sugar
2 eggs
1½ cups S.R. flour, sifted
¼ cup milk
warmed jam

Cream the butter with the rind. Add sugar gradually, beating until light and fluffy. Beat in the eggs, one at a time, with a teaspoon of flour. Fold in the remaining flour alternately with enough milk to make a dropping consistency. Spoon into a well-buttered pudding bowl, cover with a double thickness of baking paper and tie firmly with string. Place in a saucepan half-filled with boiling water, cover and steam for 1½–2 hours, adding extra boiling water when necessary. Turn out onto heated serving dish and spoon the jam over. Serves 6.

SULTANA PUDDING •

1½ cups S.R. flour
a pinch of salt
125 g butter
⅔ cup brown sugar
2 eggs, slightly beaten
½ teaspoon vanilla essence
⅓ cup sultanas
4 tablespoons milk

Sift the flour and salt together. Cream butter and sugar then gradually beat in eggs and vanilla (adding a little flour with the last few additions). Fold in remaining flour, the sultanas and milk. Spoon into a well-buttered pudding bowl, cover with a double thickness of baking paper and tie firmly with string. Place in a saucepan half-filled with boiling water, cover and steam for 1½–2 hours, adding boiling water when necessary. Serves 6.

LEMON DELICIOUS •

This light sponge pudding makes its own lemon sauce.

60 g butter
¾ cup sugar
2 eggs, separated
4 tablespoons S.R. flour
grated rind and juice of 1 lemon
1½ cups milk

Preheat the oven to 180°C. Cream the butter and sugar, add the egg yolks and beat well. Add the sifted flour, lemon rind and juice. Add the milk slowly to the creamed mixture, stirring well. Beat the egg whites until stiff, then fold into the mixture and put into a buttered shallow casserole. Bake for about 45 minutes. Serves 4-6.

CREAMY RICE PUDDING •

The best rice pudding is rich and creamy with a good proportion of milk to rice. It should be watched while baking and stirred occasionally.
Add milk from time to time, if necessary.

1 teaspoon butter
2 tablespoons short-grain rice
grated nutmeg
3 cups milk
2 tablespoons sugar

Preheat the oven to 160°C. Butter a deep ovenproof dish and put in all the ingredients, stir. Bake until the rice is quite soft and the milk is thickened and creamy. Stir every half an hour during cooking and add more milk if necessary. After 1½-2 hours the milk should be absorbed and a golden crust formed. Serve warm with pouring cream. Serves 4–6.

note: a vanilla bean or a few bruised cardamom pods can be added at the beginning for extra flavour.

CHOCOLATE SAUCE PUDDING ••

¾ cup S.R. flour
2 tablespoons cocoa
1½ teaspoons instant coffee
a pinch of salt
125 g butter
⅔ cup caster sugar
2 eggs, slightly beaten
½ teaspoon vanilla essence
2 tablespoons milk
1 tablespoon chopped walnuts *(optional)*

sauce:

1 tablespoon cocoa
⅔ cup firmly packed brown sugar
1 cup hot water

Preheat the oven to 190°C. Sift together the flour, cocoa, instant coffee and salt. Cream the butter and sugar until light, and gradually beat in the eggs and vanilla. Add a little flour mixture with the last few additions of egg. Fold in the remaining flour and enough milk to mix to a fairly soft consistency. Spoon the mixture into a buttered ovenproof dish and sprinkle with the chopped walnuts, if using. Pour the sauce over and bake for 40 minutes. Serve warm with whipped cream.

sauce: Mix together the cocoa and brown sugar in a small bowl. Stir in the hot water and mix until the sugar is dissolved and the sauce is smooth. Serves 6.

OTHER LOVED DESSERTS
PROFITEROLES WITH CHOCOLATE SAUCE ••

1 quantity choux pastry *(see p. 301)*
1 cup cream, whipped and lightly sweetened

chocolate sauce:
¾ cup milk
200 g dark chocolate
2 tablespoons sugar
2 teaspoons cornflour
a pinch of salt
extra cold milk
30 g unsalted butter
½ teaspoon vanilla essence

Preheat the oven to 200°C. To form puffs, use a pastry bag and plain tube to shape the pastry. Hold the bag directly over a greased tray and pipe small high mounds, leaving space for spreading. Alternatively, use a spoon to make mounds of pastry about 3 cm in diameter. There should be about 16.

Bake for 20 minutes, then reduce to 190°C and bake until golden brown and crisp, about 10 minutes longer. If necessary, slit puffs with tip of a sharp knife and stand in a warm oven for 10 minutes until centres are dry. Remove from oven and slit open slightly in order to scoop out any uncooked centre with a spoon. Just before serving, slit puffs open and fill with cream. Serve drizzled with chocolate sauce.

chocolate sauce: Heat the milk and chocolate over gently simmering water. When melted, beat until perfectly smooth. Combine the sugar, cornflour and salt, blend with a little extra milk and stir into the chocolate mixture. Cook for 5 minutes, stirring, until thickened. Remove from heat and add butter and vanilla. Serves 6.

CHOCOLATE MOUSSE •
Instant coffee can be used in this delicious mousse.

125 g dark chocolate, chopped
1 tablespoon strong black coffee
4 eggs, separated
1 teaspoon rum, brandy or
  few drops vanilla essence

Melt the chocolate with the coffee in a heatproof bowl set over a saucepan of hot, but not boiling, water. Stir until smooth.

Remove from the heat and mix in the egg yolks one at a time, stirring until well blended. Stir in the rum, brandy or vanilla essence. Beat the egg whites until stiff and fold gently into the chocolate mixture. Spoon into 6 mousse pots or ramekins. Chill in the refrigerator for 4 hours or overnight. Serve each with a dollop of cream, if liked. Serves 6.

MANGO MOUSSE •
1 tablespoon powdered gelatine
½ cup water
1 cup canned or frozen mango pulp, thawed
½ cup orange juice
2 tablespoons rum *(optional)*
2 egg whites
2 tablespoons sugar
½ cup cream, whipped

Soak the gelatine in the water for 5 minutes, and then dissolve over gentle heat. Combine the mango pulp, orange juice and optional rum, mix in gelatine, and chill until slightly thick. Beat the egg whites until peaks form, add the sugar gradually and beat until thick and glossy. In a chilled bowl, whip the cream until soft peaks form. Fold the cream and egg whites into the mango mixture, turn into a serving bowl and chill. Serves 4–5.

PROFITEROLES WITH CHOCOLATE SAUCE

EGGNOG TART ••

125 g butter
⅓ cup caster sugar
1 egg yolk
1 cup plain flour
½ cup S.R. flour
1 tablespoon cornflour

filling:
3 egg yolks
⅓ cup sugar
3 teaspoons powdered gelatine
¼ cup cold water
1 cup hot milk
300 ml cream, whipped
3 egg whites, stiffly beaten
2 tablespoons rum
whipped cream, to decorate
ground nutmeg, to sprinkle

Cream the butter and sugar well, add the egg yolk and beat in. Sift in the flours and cornflour and mix lightly. Knead, cover in cling wrap and chill for 1 hour. Roll out and line a 23 cm tart plate and prick the base to prevent rising. Chill again. Preheat the oven to 190°C. Line the pastry case with greaseproof paper and half-fill with pie weights or dried beans. Bake blind for 15 minutes. Remove the paper and beans, reduce the temperature to 180°C and bake for further 5–10 minutes, until crust is golden. Allow to cool.

filling: Beat the egg yolks and sugar in a double-boiler over gentle heat until thick and pale. Soak the gelatine for 5 minutes in the water and milk and stir it into the mixture. Continue to cook, stirring constantly, until smooth. Stir the mixture over ice until it is cool and begins to set. Fold in whipped cream, egg whites and rum. Turn into the tart shell. Chill until set, decorate with whipped cream and sprinkle with nutmeg to serve. Serves 8.

PAVLOVA ••

4 egg whites
a pinch of salt
1½ cups caster sugar
1½ teaspoons vinegar
1 teaspoons vanilla
300 ml cream, whipped
pulp of 3 passionfruit or 1 cup sliced strawberries

Preheat the oven to 200–210°C. Place a piece of baking paper on a baking tray and mark a 20 cm circle (the pavlova will spread a little).

Beat the egg whites and salt in an electric mixer until they stand in stiff peaks. Sift the sugar and gradually sprinkle in 1 tablespoon at a time, beating at full speed only until all sugar has been added. Lastly, fold in the vinegar and vanilla. Spoon large dollops inside the circle on the baking sheet and smooth over the top lightly. Place in the oven (reducing the temperature to 150°C) for 1 hour. Turn off the heat and leave pavlova in the oven until cold. If using a gas oven, bake at 150°C for 1 hour, reduce heat to 120°C for a further 30 minutes and then turn oven off and leave the pavlova in oven until completely cooled.

When pavlova is cooled, slide onto a large, flat cake plate and remove the baking paper. Don't worry if the pavlova collapses slightly, also expect cracks on the surface. Whip the cream until stiff and spoon over the top of pavlova. Spoon over the passionfruit pulp or strawberries to serve. Serves 8–10.

CRÊPES SUZETTE •••

To be served crêpes suzette in a restaurant is one of those classic dining experiences. And what a production it is, with gleaming copper pans, leaping flames and a waiter chosen for his expertise. At home, the crêpes can also be flamed at the table for a touch of restaurant theatrics.

1¼ cups plain flour
2 tablespoons sugar
a pinch of salt
3 eggs, beaten
1½ cups milk
2 teaspoons melted butter
1 tablespoon brandy
a little butter, for frying

sauce:

4 sugar cubes
1 orange
75 g unsalted butter
a few drops of lemon juice
½ cup Curaçao, Cointreau
   or Grand Marnier
½ cup brandy

Sift flour, sugar and salt into a bowl. Combine the eggs and milk, stir into the dry ingredients until the batter is smooth. Stir in the melted butter and brandy then let the mixture stand for 2 hours. In a frying pan, heat a little butter and, when bubbling, pour in sufficient batter to cover the bottom of the pan in a thin layer. Rotate the pan quickly to spread the batter as thinly and evenly as possible. Cook the crêpe for about 1 minute on one side. Flip and cook another minute. Stack the crêpes flat, one on top of the other, on a warm plate. Each crêpe should be about 14 cm across.

sauce: Rub the sugar cubes on the rind of the orange until they are well-impregnated with the zest. Crush the sugar in a small bowl with half the butter, using a fork, and mix until creamy. Place the remaining butter in a chafing dish or frying pan and add the juice of the orange, the lemon juice and liqueur. Bring to the boil and stir in the creamed butter and sugar. Place the crêpes in the pan, spooning the sauce over them liberally. Fold each crêpe in quarters like a handkerchief. Sprinkle with heated brandy and ignite. Serves 4.

PANCAKES WITH LEMON •

1 quantity of crêpe batter (see recipe
   opposite)
caster sugar
lemon

Make batter as for crêpes, omitting the brandy and sugar. Cook pancakes in a medium rather than thin layer, until golden on both sides. Serve piping hot with sugar sprinkled over and lemon juice sprinkled to taste. Serves 4-6.

ZABAGLIONE ••

4 egg yolks
2 tablespoons sugar
½ cup marsala

Beat the yolks and the sugar together until they are white and frothy. Stir in the marsala and put the whole mixture into a double-boiler, or a bowl over a saucepan of hot, but not boiling, water. Place over a low heat and whisk constantly until frothy and slightly thick. Take care it does not boil or it will curdle. As soon as it thickens, pour into warmed glasses and serve immediately with savoy (sponge) fingers for dipping. Serves 4.

DANISH RUM CREAM •

5 egg yolks
½ cup icing sugar, sifted
½ cup rum
1 tablespoon powdered gelatine
¼ cup water
2½ cups cream, whipped
5 egg whites, stiffly beaten
raspberry sauce (see p. 305)

Beat egg yolks and icing sugar then stir in the rum. Soak gelatine in the water for 5 minutes and dissolve over a gentle heat. Stir into the rum mixture until well combined. Fold in the cream and egg whites. Chill in a glass bowl for at least 3 hours. Serve with raspberry sauce. Serves 6–8.

FRUIT DESSERTS

Fruit is perfect on its own, with cheese, or as the base for many simple desserts. A large bowl of ice with an assortment of grapes, apples, peaches or just one perfect piece of fruit is very often all that is needed to complete a meal. If you fancy something else, there's a wonderful selection of fruit desserts to choose from.

STRAWBERRIES ROMANOFF •

8 sugar cubes
2 oranges
2 punnets strawberries
6 tablespoons Curaçao
1¼ cups cream, whipped, sweetened and flavoured with vanilla essence, to taste

Rub the sugar over the skins of the oranges, until they are well impregnated with the flavour of the fruit. Crush the sugar. Wash and hull strawberries. Macerate them in the Curaçao and crushed sugar in a covered container, until serving time. Put into a serving bowl or individual dessert dishes in a pyramid shape. Decorate with cream. Serves 6–8.

CARAMEL ORANGES ••

These oranges featured in most French restaurants of the Sixties especially in London, where they were often the centrepiece of the sweet trolley. Serve chilled with a bowl of mascarpone for those who like a touch of cream and a plate of crisp biscuits.

6–8 large oranges
1 cup sugar
⅔ cup cold water
⅔ cup warm water

Thinly pare several strips of rind from one orange and cut into shreds. Drop into boiling water for 1 minute, drain and set aside.

Put sugar and cold water into a heavy-based saucepan and heat, stirring occasionally, until sugar dissolves. Boil without stirring until the syrup begins to colour, then drop in the shredded rind and cook for 3–4 minutes to glaze.

Remove rind with a slotted spoon and continue to cook the syrup, rotating the pan frequently so that it will colour evenly, until it is a rich caramel brown. Remove pan from heat and, protecting your hand with a cloth, add warm water.

Stir to dissolve the caramel, pour into a bowl and leave to cool while preparing oranges. Peel oranges, removing all the pith. Cut across into slices, removing any seeds, and reshape the oranges. Place on a serving dish, top with glazed rind and spoon a little caramel sauce over. Chill oranges and caramel. Pour a little more caramel sauce over each orange as it is served. Serves 6–8.

CARAMEL ORANGES

BAKED PEARS IN RED WINE ••

6 small, firm cooking pears
¾ cup sugar
2 cups red wine
strip of lemon rind
1 small stick cinnamon
1 teaspoon arrowroot (optional)

Preheat the oven to 180°C. Peel the pears, but do not remove the stalks. Dissolve the sugar in the wine in a heavy-based saucepan over a gentle heat. Add the lemon rind and cinnamon stick. Bring to the boil for 1 minute. Place the pears, stalks up, in a casserole and pour over the wine syrup. The pears should just fit so that they all stand up nicely, giving them a better shape when cooked.

Cover the casserole and bake until tender, for about 1 hour. If the pears are very firm they make take up to 2 hours. Remove and strain the syrup. The syrup may be thickened with the arrowroot mixed with a little water. Add the arrowroot mixture to the syrup, and stir until almost boiling and quite clear.

Arrange the pears in a serving dish and spoon over the wine sauce. They should be served warm or at room temperature, and may be accompanied by a bowl of whipped cream.
Serves 6.

GINGER, LIME AND MELON COMPOTE •

You can use half honeydew melon and its equivalent weight in watermelon to create a very pretty pink and green compote as a variation.

rind of 1 lime, pared in strips
⅓ cup lime juice
¼ cup sugar
1 tablespoon grated fresh ginger
⅓ cup water
1 honeydew melon
1 tablespoon chopped mint leaves

In a small heavy-based saucepan, combine the lime rind and juice, the sugar, ginger and water. Bring the mixture to a boil, stirring until the sugar is dissolved, and boil for 5 minutes. Pour the syrup through a fine sieve into a bowl and let it cool.

Meanwhile, remove the seeds from the melon and scoop the flesh into balls with a melon cutter, or cut into cubes. In a serving bowl, turn the melon balls in the syrup and mint. Cover and chill for at least 30 minutes.
Serves 4.

ITALIAN BAKED STUFFED PEACHES ••

The filling for these peaches is made with amaretti biscuits, the Italian almond macaroons.

4 large ripe but firm peaches
2 tablespoons sugar
1 egg yolk
30 g butter
90 g crushed amaretti biscuits
¼ cup white wine or water

Preheat the oven to 180°C. Halve the peaches and remove the stones – there is no need to skin them. Mix the sugar, egg yolk, butter cut into small pieces and amaretti crumbs in a bowl. Scoop out a little pulp from each peach half, chop finely and mix with the stuffing mixture. Use to stuff each peach half.

Arrange the peaches in a buttered shallow ovenproof dish. Add the white wine or water, making sure the base of the dish is covered. Bake for about 30 minutes or until tender. Serve hot with cream. Serves 4–6.

BERRIES WITH YOGHURT CREAM •

300 ml cream
2 cups quality natural yoghurt
demerara or brown sugar
1 punnet each raspberries or blueberries and strawberries

Whip the cream until it holds soft peaks and fold in the yoghurt. Place in a serving bowl and sprinkle thickly with enough sugar to completely cover. Stand the yoghurt cream in refrigerator until required, or until the sugar melts to a luscious sauce.

Wash the berries and hull the strawberries and halve or slice thickly. Divide the berries among 4 to 6 dessert bowls or glasses. To serve, spoon on the yoghurt cream. Serves 4–6.

PASSIONFRUIT FLUMMERY •

1 tablespoon powdered gelatine
¼ cup cold water
1 tablespoon flour
½ cup sugar
¼ cup orange juice
1 tablespoon lemon juice
1 cup hot water
½ cup passionfruit pulp

Sprinkle the gelatine over cold water. Combine the flour and sugar in a saucepan, add enough orange juice to blend to a smooth paste. Add remaining orange juice, lemon juice and hot water. Bring to the boil, stirring until mixture thickens. Add the gelatine mixture and stir until dissolved.

Cool, then transfer to a large bowl and chill until starting to set. Beat well until very thick and at least doubled in volume. Add the passionfruit pulp and beat again. Turn into a serving bowl and chill until set. Serve large spoonfuls on individual dessert plates or bowls. Serves 6.

PEACH AND BERRY COMPOTE ••

One of summer's treats is a compote of stone fruit and berries, flavoured with citrus and the fragrance of honey. Serve with cream, a good natural yoghurt or plain.

¾ cup fresh orange juice
½ cup honey
¼ cup fresh lemon juice
2 sticks cinnamon
½ cup water
6–8 firm ripe peaches, skinned
2 punnets strawberries or raspberries

In a heavy-based saucepan, combine the orange juice, honey, lemon juice, cinnamon and water, and bring the liquid to the boil, stirring. Add the peaches and simmer until just tender. Remove from the heat and leave to stand for 10 minutes.

Transfer the whole peaches, with a slotted spoon, to a bowl. Reduce the cooking liquid over a moderate heat until it is syrupy. Pour the syrup over the fruit and let the mixture cool for 15 minutes. Fold in the berries and chill the compote, covered loosely, for at least 1 hour. Serves 6.

note: peaches can be skinned by first pouring boiling water over them in a bowl, leaving them to stand for 3 minutes, then draining and putting them into a bowl of iced water.

BANANAS WITH RUM •

6 medium bananas
¼ cup brown sugar
½ cup fresh orange juice
¼ teaspoon grated nutmeg
¼ teaspoon ground cinnamon
½ cup sherry
30 g butter
4 tablespoons rum

Peel the bananas and split them in halves, lengthwise. Place in a buttered baking dish. Combine the sugar with the orange juice, spices and sherry. Heat and pour over the bananas. Dot with butter and bake for 10–15 minutes, or until tender, basting once or twice. Remove from the oven and sprinkle with warmed rum. Serve with the rum flaming. Serves 4–6.

FIGS WITH CINNAMON AND MARSALA ••

½ cup marsala or port wine
½ cup water
3 tablespoons soft brown sugar
1 vanilla bean
1 cinnamon stick
4–6 large fresh figs
1 cup mascarpone
4–6 mint sprigs, to garnish

Place the port, water, sugar, vanilla bean and cinnamon in a saucepan. Bring slowly to the boil, stirring, then simmer partially covered for 20 minutes, or until reduced by half. Meanwhile, cut figs into quarters half-way down towards the stem and open each out like a flower. Place figs cut-side up in a flameproof dish. Spoon some of the port mixture over then cook under a preheated hot grill for a few minutes, or until the figs are softened and glazed. Carefully arrange the figs with a scoop of mascarpone on dessert plates then drizzle with juices from the dish. Garnish with mint sprigs. Serves 4–6.

PEACH AND BERRY COMPOTE

RHUBARB AND STRAWBERRY FOOL •
An example of how surprising and delicious the combination of rhubarb and strawberries can be.

1 bunch rhubarb, trimmed and cut into 5 cm lengths
½ cup sugar
grated rind of 1 orange
1 punnet strawberries, washed and hulled
1 cup whipping cream

Place the rhubarb in a saucepan with the sugar, orange rind and a little water, and simmer gently until just tender. Drain, then push through a sieve or purée in a blender. Slice the strawberries and fold them into the rhubarb and leave to cool completely. Whip the cream until firm peaks form and fold into fruit. Turn into a dessert bowl or individual dishes, and serve chilled with crisp dessert biscuits. Serves 6.

note: lighten this combination, if you like, with 1 or 2 stiffly beaten egg whites folded through. The strawberries can be puréed with the rhubarb.

ICE-CREAM
There are a number of good ice-cream makers available that are quite inexpensive and simple to use. However, if you haven't one, it is possible to make a good ice-cream at home using a freezer and an ice tray. For the latter, quick freezing and using a custard base makes smoother ice-cream. Turn the refrigerator control to maximum for 2 hours. When the ice-cream is firm, turn the control to a normal setting.

APRICOT ICE-CREAM ••
Choose Australian dried apricots for preference, their colour and flavour is superior.

125 g Australian dried apricots
1¼ cups cream
3 egg yolks
½ cup sugar

Soak the dried apricots for an hour or so in water to cover and simmer gently until soft. Pour off any water left in the saucepan and purée the apricots in a blender or food processor. Leave to cool.

In the top of a double-boiler, gradually stir cream into the egg yolks. Cook over gently simmering water, stirring constantly, until the custard thickens. Remove from heat and add sugar immediately. Stir until sugar is dissolved. Cool, then stir in apricot purée. Pour into an ice tray and cover well with aluminium foil. Freeze until mixture forms a solid rim about 2.5 cm wide. Transfer to a chilled bowl and beat with an electric or rotary beater until smooth. Return to tray, recover with foil and freeze again until firm and creamy. Serves 4–6.

OLD-FASHIONED VANILLA ICE-CREAM ••

This is a fabulous creamy ice-cream for those who appreciate the sweet fragrance of fresh vanilla. Add a little fruit, such as berries, to the mixture to make a fruit ice-cream. Just remember that if extra sugar or sweet fruit pulp is added, the ice-cream will take longer to freeze.

2 cups milk
1 vanilla bean, split lengthwise
¼ cup caster sugar
6 egg yolks
1 cup cream

Heat the milk, vanilla and half the sugar in a saucepan until it comes to the boil. Cover with a lid and stand for 15 minutes. Beat the egg yolks with an electric mixer and gradually add the remaining sugar until light and fluffy. Bring the milk mixture back to the boil. Cool slightly and stir in the egg mixture. Cook over a low heat until the mixture forms a thin custard and coats the back of a spoon. Remove the vanilla bean and cool the custard.

Beat the cream until firm and fold through the cooled custard. Pour into an ice tray, cover tightly with foil and freeze until a 2 cm solid rim has formed around the edge. Transfer to a chilled bowl and beat vigorously with an electric mixer or rotary beater, until the ice particles have broken up. Return to the tray, re-cover with foil and freeze until firm and creamy. Alternatively, use an ice-cream maker and follow the manufacturer's directions. Serves 8.

ITALIAN COFFEE ICE-CREAM ••

Make the day before required.

3 egg yolks
1½ cups cream, or cream and whole milk
¼ cup freshly roasted coffee beans
½ cup sugar

Beat the egg yolks lightly in a bowl, or on the top of a double-boiler, and whisk in the cream or cream and milk to blend. Add the coffee beans and place mixture over a saucepan of gently simmering water, stirring constantly, until thickened. Remove from the heat and add the sugar immediately, stirring until dissolved.

Allow the custard to stand several hours, to develop a good coffee flavour, and then pour through a sieve into a jug. Pour into an ice tray, cover tightly with foil and freeze until a 2 cm solid rim has formed around the edge. Transfer to a chilled bowl and beat vigorously with an electric mixer or rotary beater, until the ice particles have broken up. Return to the tray and freeze until firm and creamy. Alternatively, use an ice-cream maker and follow the manufacturer's directions. Scoop into glasses to serve and sprinkle, if liked, with chopped roasted nuts or chocolate-coated scorched almonds. Serves 4–6.

cakes & biscuits

RICH CHOCOLATE FUDGE CAKE

BUTTER CAKES, SPONGES, YEAST COOKERY AND CONTINENTAL CAKES

THERE'S SOMETHING ABOUT GOOD HOME-MADE CAKES AND BISCUITS THAT JUST CAN'T BE DUPLICATED IN SHOP-BOUGHT ONES. THEIR FRESHNESS, GOOD INGREDIENTS AND THE CARE THAT GOES INTO THEIR MAKING GIVE THEM A SPECIAL QUALITY.

A GOOD RECIPE IS ESSENTIAL, FOR THIS IS ONE BRANCH OF COOKERY WHERE INDISCRIMINATE INSPIRATION DOES NOT WORK. THE BALANCE OF INGREDIENTS IS CRITICAL. PERHAPS OUR GRANDMOTHERS DIDN'T USE A RECIPE, BUT THEY HAD A SURE EYE AND AN EXPERIENCED HAND. UNTIL YOU HAVE BOTH, DON'T EXPERIMENT. FOLLOW A RECIPE CAREFULLY AND YOU'LL SOON BE TURNING OUT LOVELY TREATS LIKE THE BEST OF THEM.

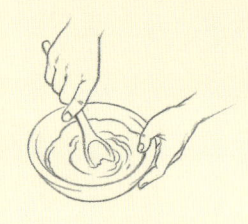

When creaming butter or beating in sugar, use a long lifting motion from the bottom of the bowl to trap as much air as possible into the cake mixture.

Whisk egg whites until stiff but not too dry.

BUTTER CAKES

A butter cake is one of the most popular of all cakes. Most common is the creamed method, where butter and sugar are beaten to a creamy consistency first, then the egg is beaten in, and lastly the flour is added. Then there is the melting method, which for many is easier, where the butter is melted and the remaining ingredients are folded in. Lastly, there is the rubbing-in method, where the butter is rubbed into the flour then the remaining ingredients are added. There are a few basic rules to observe in making a butter cake successfully. With these in mind, it is simple to turn out perfect cakes time after time, and to vary the basic mixture in many ways.

WAYS TO SUCCESS

- Prepare the tins before you start making your cake. Make sure they are the correct size and well greased. For some recipes, you will need to line the bases with baking paper cut to fit. The size of the tin is usually stated but, as a general rule, the mixture should fill the tin by no more than two-thirds. As it bakes, the mixture should rise to the rim or slightly above.

- Set the oven shelf in position and preheat the oven to required temperature. Check the oven temperature guide and also check the chart that belongs to your stove for oven positions and temperatures, as these will vary with different types.

Add a spoonful of whisked egg whites to the cake mixture and mix in thoroughly to soften the mixture.

Then finally, fold in the remaining egg whites with a large metal spoon, using large cut and fold motions to the bottom of the bowl and back to the top.

- Have eggs, butter and milk at room temperature for easy mixing, and good results.

- Maximum creaming of the butter and sugar is the first step to a good butter cake. When this mixture is light and fluffy, add the eggs. Caster sugar gives a fine texture. When using an electric mixer, add a little of the cake's liquid when creaming butter and sugar as it helps dissolve the sugar.

- Eggs are beaten lightly and added gradually. If using an electric mixer, it is not necessary to beat the eggs first, simply add them one at a time. The following recipes use 55 g eggs, unless specified otherwise.

- When folding in the sifted dry ingredients alternately with the liquid, always begin and end with flour. Be careful not to beat and use a large metal spoon, drawing a figure eight through the mixture.

- Learn to test when a cake is cooked. Lightly press the centre of the cake. If it springs back, it is safe to bring it out of the oven. If your finger leaves an impression, leave the cake in the oven a little longer. A well-cooked cake should also shrink just a little from the sides of the tin. There are fine cake testers, which can be inserted into the centre of cake and must come out clean.

- Avoid a draught when taking the cake from the oven.

- If a cake sticks or refuses to leave the tin, place the tin on a damp cloth for a few minutes to help the cake ease.

BASIC BUTTER CAKE •

Follow this basic butter cake recipe and try a few simple variations such as adding grated orange or lemon rind, sultanas, spices or chopped nuts. Vary the cake tins to make a deeper cake, a loaf or a bar.

125 g butter
¾ cup caster sugar
1 teaspoon vanilla essence
2 eggs
2 cups S.R. flour
a pinch of salt
½ cup milk

Preheat the oven to 180°C. Brush 2 x 20 cm sandwich tins with melted butter. Line the tin bases with rounds of baking paper. Cream the butter and gradually beat in the sugar with the vanilla, until the mixture is light and fluffy. Gradually beat in the slightly beaten eggs. If using an electric mixer, add the eggs one at a time and beat well after each.

Sift the flour and salt (some cooks do this 3 times), and then fold into the creamed mixture alternately with the milk, beginning and ending with flour (it is important not to overwork the mixture). Put the smooth mixture into the prepared tins and lightly smooth the top. Bake for 25–30 minutes, or until a skewer inserted in the centre comes out clean. Cool on wire racks. Sandwich with whipped cream, jam or lemon butter and ice as liked.

note: if making one larger cake in a deep 20 cm tin, it will require 45–50 minutes baking time, a loaf tin 23 cm x 13 cm will take 30–40 minutes.

variations:
lemon cake: Add the grated rind of 1 lemon and 2 teaspoons lemon juice, but leave out the vanilla essence.

sultana cake: Fold in ¾ cup sultanas and 1 teaspoon ground cinnamon or mixed spice.

seed cake: Add 1 tablespoon caraway seeds to mixture and sprinkle an extra teaspoon of seeds on top before baking.

spice cake: Sift 1 teaspoon spice (ground ginger, cinnamon, cardamom or mixed spice) with the flour. Add ⅔ cup chopped dates or chopped walnuts to the mixture.

chocolate cake: Add 60 g melted dark chocolate to creamed mixture, before the flour.

LAMINGTONS •

Cook lamington mixture a day before they are required to prevent the cakes from crumbling when iced.

1 quantity basic butter cake mixture
desiccated coconut

thin chocolate icing:
3 cups icing sugar
3 tablespoons cocoa
4–6 tablespoons boiling water
½ teaspoon butter
vanilla essence

Preheat the oven to 180°C. Line the base of a greased 27 cm x 18 cm lamington tin with baking paper. Spread the mixture evenly in the tin and bake for 30–35 minutes until cooked. Cool on wire rack, then cut into small oblong shapes or cubes. Dip in the chocolate icing and immediately roll in desiccated coconut. Leave on a rack to set.

thin chocolate icing: Sift the icing sugar and cocoa into a bowl. Add the boiling water, butter and a few drops of vanilla essence then stir until smooth and shiny. If the icing sets, stand the bowl in hot water.

CUP CAKES •

If the cup cakes are to be iced and smooth tops are required, bake in a moderately hot oven, at 190°C. For peaked tops, necessary for butterfly cakes, increase the heat by 10°C and place the cakes in the hottest part of oven, usually near the top of gas ovens and at the bottom of electric ovens. To make sure, check the guide for your own oven. This recipe is similar to basic butter cake but calls for extra milk.

125 g butter
¾ cup caster sugar
1 teaspoon vanilla essence
2 eggs, beaten
2 cups S.R. flour
a pinch of salt
⅔ cup milk

glacé icing:
1 cup sifted icing sugar
1 tablespoon boiling water
a nut of butter
a few drops of flavouring
colouring, if required

Preheat the oven to 190°C. Place paper cases in patty tins. Cream the butter. Gradually add the sugar and beat until light and creamy. Add the vanilla. Add the eggs gradually, and beat well after each addition. Sift the flour and salt and fold lightly into creamed mixture, alternately with milk, to make a smooth dropping consistency. Spoon into the patty cases. Bake for about 15 minutes and then cool. Ice with the glacé icing and decorate as liked. Makes about 24.

glacé icing: Sift the icing sugar into a bowl, make a well in the centre and add the boiling water, butter and flavouring and stir until smooth and shiny. Colour as desired. Spread the tops with a spoonful of icing and, before it sets, decorate.

to make butterfly cakes: Cut a disc from the top of each cake, fill with a spoonful of sweetened, whipped cream and place the disc, cut in half, in butterfly-wing fashion on top. Dust with icing sugar.

note: there are many possibilities when it comes to decorating cup cakes. For children, try a selection of sweets to decorate, such as fruit jellies and sparkles. A pretty effect is achieved by slicing the fruit jellies first to reveal their shiny centres. Smarties, chocolate sprinkles, hundreds and thousands, nuts and cherries can all be used. Or, top with freshly picked violets, perfect rose petals or johnny-jump-ups. Just remember to add the topping while icing is still not completely set.

COCONUT CAKE •

2 cups plain flour
a pinch of salt
2 teaspoons baking powder
125 g butter
¾ cup caster sugar
⅓ cup desiccated coconut
2 eggs, beaten
¾ cup milk

Preheat the oven to 180°C. Grease a round 20 cm cake tin. Line the base with baking paper. Sift the flour, salt and baking powder into a large bowl. Add the butter and rub in, until mixture resembles breadcrumbs. Stir in the sugar and coconut. Gradually stir the eggs and milk into the flour mixture. Turn into a prepared tin and smooth the top. Bake in the centre of the oven for 1–1½ hours, or until firm to the touch and golden. Turn out on a wire rack to cool.

MARBLE CAKE •

Children love this cake and it's a very popular choice for birthday parties. The colours form intriguing designs in each slice.

125 g butter
1 cup caster sugar
1 teaspoon vanilla essence
2 eggs
2 cups S.R. flour
½ teaspoon salt
¾ cup milk
2 tablespoons cocoa
2 tablespoons boiling water
red food colouring

Preheat the oven to 180°C. Brush a deep 20 cm cake tin with a little melted butter and line the base with baking paper. Cream the butter and gradually beat in the sugar and vanilla until light and creamy. Beat the eggs lightly, and add to the creamed mixture gradually. Sift the flour and salt and fold into the creamed mixture alternately with the milk. Divide the mixture into 3 portions.

Sift the cocoa and blend in the boiling water. Stir this into one portion of the cake mixture. To other portion, add a few drops of red food colouring to colour it pink. The third portion is left plain. Drop the mixture by tablespoons into the prepared tin, alternately pink, plain and chocolate. Run a knife through gently a few times to marble the mixture. Bake for 50–60 minutes. Cool on a wire rack.

ORANGE CAKE ••

This is richer than the basic butter cake and has good keeping qualities. Serve plain or ice with a thin orange icing.

125 g butter
grated rind and juice of 1 orange
½ cup caster sugar
2 eggs, separated
¾ cup S.R. flour
¼ cup plain flour
a pinch of salt

Preheat the oven to 180°C. Brush a 19 cm x 9 cm loaf tin with melted butter, and then dust lightly with flour. Line the base of the loaf tin with baking paper. Cream the butter, add the orange rind, and beat in the sugar until light and fluffy. Add the egg yolks one at a time and beat well. Sift the flours and salt, and fold into creamed mixture alternately with strained orange juice. Whisk the egg whites until soft peaks form and fold into the mixture. Turn the mixture at once into the tin and bake for 35–40 minutes. Turn out on wire rack and cool.

ORANGE CAKE

THERE'S MORE THAN ONE WAY TO BAKE A CAKE

A FRESHLY BAKED HOME-MADE CAKE HAS NO RIVAL WHEN IT COMES TO FLAVOUR. FROM CLOSE-TEXTURED BUTTER CAKES AND DELICATE LIGHT-AS-AIR SPONGE SANDWICHES TO JAM ROLLS AND SPICY GINGERBREADS WARM AND FRAGRANT FROM THE OVEN, THE METHODS OF MAKING THESE CAKES MAY VARY, BUT THE POPULAR APPEAL DOES NOT.

SPONGE CAKES

The lightness of a good sponge depends on beating air into the eggs. Tins should have their bases lined with baking paper and the sides should be lightly greased with melted butter, then floured. All sponge cakes should be baked as soon as they are mixed. To test if a sponge is cooked, look for shrinkage around edge of the tin, and press the centre lightly with fingers. It will spring back when cooked.

SPONGE SANDWICH ♦♦

1 cup S.R. flour
a pinch of salt
3 eggs
¾ cup caster sugar
1 teaspoon butter, melted
3 tablespoons hot water
jam, for filling
icing sugar, for dredging

Preheat the oven to 180°C. Grease 2 x 18 cm sandwich tins and dust lightly with a little flour. Line the bases with baking paper. Sift the flour and salt together 3 times.

Separate the eggs. Beat the whites stiffly, and add the sugar gradually, beating until thick. Add the yolks, and gently fold into the egg mixture. Fold in the sifted flour, lightly and evenly. Fold in the melted butter and hot water quickly and lightly. Turn into the prepared tins and bake for 20 minutes. Turn out and cool on a wire rack. When cool, fill with slightly warmed jam and dredge with icing sugar.

for a 20 cm sponge sandwich:

4 eggs
1 teaspoon butter, melted
1 cup caster sugar
1½ cups S.R. flour
4 tablespoons hot water
¼ teaspoon salt

Preheat the oven to 180°C. Brush 2 x 20 cm sandwich tins with melted butter, dust with flour then line the bases with baking paper. Follow the method for a sponge sandwich. Pour the mixture into the tins and bake for 20–25 minutes. Cool on a wire rack.

for a 23 cm sponge sandwich:

5 eggs
a pinch of salt
1¼ cups caster sugar
1½ teaspoons butter, melted
1¾ cups S.R. flour
5 tablespoons hot water

Preheat the oven to 180°C. Brush 2 x 23 cm sandwich tins lightly with melted butter, dust with flour then line the bases with baking paper. Follow the method for a sponge sandwich. Put the mixture into the prepared tins and bake for 30 minutes, or until the cake springs back when lightly touched.

PASSIONFRUIT CREAM SPONGE ••

Prepare a sponge sandwich, and allow to cool. Whip ¾ cup cream with 2 teaspoons sugar. Lightly mix the pulp of 1–2 passionfruit into the cream to spread as a filling on one half of the sponge. Top with the other half. Dust the top of the cake with sifted icing sugar or ice with passionfruit icing.

passionfruit icing:

1 cup icing sugar
pulp of 1 passionfruit
1 teaspoon butter

Make the icing by sifting icing sugar into a bowl and mixing smoothly with passionfruit pulp until the icing will cover the back of a spoon thickly and smoothly. Beat in the butter and warm slightly over a saucepan of hot water, stirring until glossy. Spread over the cooled cake.

GLAZED STRAWBERRY SPONGE ••

Prepare a sponge sandwich, and allow to cool. Whip ¾ cup cream with 2 teaspoons sugar. Lightly mix 1 cup sliced strawberries into the cream to spread as a filling on one half of the sponge. Top with the other half. Top with washed and hulled strawberries to cover. Brush with redcurrant jelly melted over a gentle heat with a little water. Leave to set before serving.

SWISS ROLL ••

½ cup S.R. flour
a pinch of salt
3 eggs
½ cup caster sugar
1 tablespoon hot water
caster sugar, for dredging
3–4 tablespoons warm jam or lemon butter

Preheat the oven to 220°C. Grease a 30 cm x 25 cm Swiss roll tin and line with baking paper, or make a paper case this size.

Sift the flour with the salt 3 times. If using a hand-held whisk, place the eggs and sugar in a bowl and stand over a saucepan of gently steaming water, not boiling. Whisk together well, until mixture is very thick and creamy, about 10 minutes. If using an electric mixer, warm the eggs and sugar slightly first, as above (beating should take less time).

Remove the bowl from the water and continue whisking the mixture until cool. Fold in the flour with a metal spoon. Lastly, fold in the hot water. Pour mixture into prepared tin, shake into corners, and spread evenly using a metal spatula. Bake for 7–10 minutes, until pale golden and springy. Do not overcook as it makes rolling up difficult.

Turn the sponge on to a tea towel sprinkled with caster sugar. Carefully strip off the lining paper. Trim off the crisp edges with a sharp knife. Starting from the wide end of the sponge, roll in a towel then leave to cool before unrolling. Warm jam slightly and spread over sponge, taking it almost to the edges.

Lifting the edges of the sugared tea towel, re-roll the sponge into a neat firm roll. Cool roll on a cake rack with join underneath, away from any draughts.

HONEY SPICED SPONGE ROLL ••

½ cup arrowroot
1 tablespoon plain flour
½ teaspoon ground cinnamon
1 teaspoon mixed spice
1 teaspoon cream of tartar
½ teaspoon bicarbonate of soda
3 eggs
½ cup caster sugar
1 tablespoon honey (at room temperature)

honey cream filling:

125 g butter
2 tablespoons honey
1 tablespoon boiling water

Preheat the oven to 190°C. Line a 30 x 25 cm Swiss roll tin with baking paper, or make a paper case with baking paper. Sift the dry ingredients 3 times.

Beat the eggs until thick and add the sugar gradually. Continue beating, until mixture is thick and holds its shape, about 10 minutes. Fold the dry ingredients into the egg mixture, add the honey, mixing until evenly distributed.

Turn into the prepared tin and gently shake to spread the mixture evenly. Bake in the preheated oven for 15–20 minutes. Turn out on a tea towel, which has been lightly dusted with caster sugar, quickly peel off the paper and trim the edges. Roll up in the tea towel, starting with the narrow end. Allow to cool, then unroll. Fill with honey cream filling, and roll up again. If serving as a dessert, roll the cake, starting with the wide end, and cut into diagonal slices.

honey cream filling: Cream the butter until light, add the honey a tablespoon at a time, and then add the water. Continue beating until the mixture is smooth and creamy.

MADEIRA CAKE •

250 g butter
grated rind of ½ lemon
1¾ cups caster sugar
5 eggs
3¼ cups plain flour
2 teaspoons baking powder
a pinch of ground cinnamon
a pinch of salt
½ cup milk
⅓ cup blanched almonds or
  3 thin slices candied lemon peel

Preheat the oven to 180°C. Grease and line the base and sides of a deep 20 cm cake tin with baking paper. Cream the butter with the lemon rind and add the sugar gradually. Beat until the mixture is light and fluffy. Beat in the eggs, one at a time, with a small spoonful of flour added near the end, then sift the remaining flour with the baking powder, cinnamon and salt, and fold into the mixture with the milk. Turn into the prepared tin, arrange the almonds or the peel on top. Bake for about 1½ hours. After 1 hour, reduce the heat to 160°C. Cool in the tin on a wire rack for 10 minutes, and then turn out to cool completely.

BANANA CAKE •

125 g butter
¾ cup caster sugar
1 teaspoon vanilla
1 egg
2 ripe bananas
1½ cups S.R. flour
¼ teaspoon bicarbonate of soda
¼ cup milk
icing sugar, to dust

Preheat the oven to 180°C. Grease a 23 cm fluted ring tin or a deep 20 cm cake tin. Cream the butter, and then beat in the sugar and vanilla until light and fluffy. Beat in the egg. Mash the bananas and add to the creamed mixture. Fold in the sifted flour. Dissolve the soda in the milk, and then stir into the mixture gently but thoroughly. Turn the mixture into the tin and bake for 40 minutes, or until a skewer inserted in the centre comes out clean. Serve with a light dusting of icing sugar and, if liked, a little whipped cream.

CINNAMON TEA CAKE •

1 egg, separated
½ cup sugar
½ cup milk
½ teaspoon vanilla essence
1 cup S.R. flour
30 g butter, melted

topping:

2 teaspoons butter, melted
1 tablespoon sugar
½ teaspoon ground cinnamon

Preheat the oven to 190°C. Line the base of an 18 cm or 20 cm sandwich tin with baking paper. Beat the egg white until stiff, but not dry, and add the egg yolk. Gradually beat in the sugar, beating well between additions. Mix the milk and vanilla and add a little to the mixture at a time. Gently stir in the sifted flour and melted butter. Turn into the prepared tin and bake for 20–25 minutes. While hot, brush with the butter and sprinkle with the sugar and cinnamon mixed together. Turn out and place top side up on a wire rack. Serve warm or cooled with butter.

GINGERBREAD ••

1½ cups plain flour
½ teaspoon bicarbonate of soda
1 tablespoon ground ginger
1 teaspoon ground cinnamon
¼ teaspoon ground cloves
¼ teaspoon ground allspice
125 g unsalted butter
½ cup brown sugar
½ cup treacle
2 x 60 g eggs
2 teaspoons vanilla essence
½ cup buttermilk

lemon frosting (optional):

30 g butter
1 tablespoon lemon juice
1 tablespoon grated orange rind
2 cups icing sugar, sifted

Preheat the oven to 180°C. Butter and line with baking paper the base of a deep 23 cm round cake tin. Sift the flour, soda and spices into a bowl. In a bowl of an electric mixer, cream the butter and beat in the brown sugar, until the mixture is light and fluffy. Beat in the treacle and then the eggs, one at a time. Beat in the vanilla essence. Lastly, stir in the sifted flour mixture thoroughly, and then the buttermilk.

Turn the mixture into the prepared tin, smoothing the top and making a slight indentation in the centre with a spatula. Bake for 35–40 minutes, or until a skewer inserted comes out clean. Let the gingerbread cool in the tin on a wire rack. Turn out onto a serving plate and serve plain or spread with lemon frosting.

lemon frosting: Cream the butter, juice and rind and beat in the sifted icing sugar, beating until smooth.

AFTERNOON TEA CAKES

Cooking these treats may seem like a labour of love, but they are well worth the time and effort required.

ALMOND FRIANDISE ••

These little French cakes have an unusual method and baking technique. Special deep oval moulds are popular for baking them. As they are larger than a mouthful, they may be cut in two or three for dainty eating. Tiny bite-size oval moulds are also available for after-dinner friandise.

185 g butter
½ cup chopped blanched almonds
1 cup ground almonds
1 ⅔ cups icing sugar
⅓ cup + 1 tablespoon plain flour
5 egg whites

Preheat the oven to 230°C. Grease 10–12 friandise moulds (½-cup size) or 24 small patty tins with butter. Melt the butter in a small saucepan. Cook gently until the butter is pale gold then pour into a small jug. Put the chopped almonds and ground almonds into a mixing bowl, add the sifted icing sugar and flour, and mix lightly. Beat the egg whites just enough to break up the solid consistency, but they should not be frothy. Add the beaten egg whites to the dry ingredients. Add the warm butter and mix well together. Spoon the mixture into the prepared moulds, only half-filling. Place the moulds on a baking tray and bake for 5 minutes. Then reduce the heat to 200°C and bake a further 12–15 minutes. Patty tins will take 8–10 minutes. Turn the oven off and leave the cakes in the oven for 5 minutes. Remove from the oven and turn out to cool on a wire rack. **Makes 10-12.**

CARDAMOM SOUR CREAM CAKE •

This is one of the best cakes I know. Easily made, it has a superb lightness and a spicy cardamom and cinnamon flavour. Be sure your spices are very fresh.

2 eggs, beaten
2 cups sour cream
1½ cups caster sugar
3 drops almond essence
3 cups plain flour
1 teaspoon bicarbonate of soda
½ teaspoon salt
2 teaspoons ground cardamom
½ teaspoon ground cinnamon

Preheat the oven to 180°C. Grease 2 x 20 cm ring tins or a 23 cm gugelhopf, bundt or ring tin, and dust lightly with sugar. Place the eggs, sour cream, sugar and almond essence in a large bowl and mix until combined. Sift the flour with the bicarbonate of soda, salt and spices. Gradually add to the egg mixture, beating until the batter is smooth. Pour into the prepared tin.

Bake for about 40 minutes if making 2 cakes, or 1 hour and 15 minutes for the larger cake. The cake is cooked when a skewer inserted in the centre comes out clean. Leave in the tin for 10 minutes before turning out to cool on a wire rack.

MADELEINES ••

These plump little sponge cakes are baked in special embossed moulds that resemble the 'pleated scallop of the pilgrim's shell' that gives them their characteristic puffed dome. Madeleine tins are available at kitchen shops and most department stores.

2 eggs
¾ cup caster sugar
½ teaspoon finely grated lemon rind
1 cup plain flour, sifted
185 g unsalted butter, clarified
1 tablespoon rum (*optional*)

Preheat the oven to 200°C. Butter the madeleine tins and dust with flour. Beat the eggs and sugar until thick and mousse-like, using a hand whisk and a bowl set over a saucepan of gently simmering water or a very good electric mixer. Remove from the heat (if using that method), and continue to beat until cooled. Add the lemon rind, then fold in the flour, and then the cooled butter, mixing only until everything is blended. Take care not to overwork the mixture at this point, and don't allow the butter to sink to the bottom of the bowl. A metal spoon is the best tool for this job. Lastly, fold in the rum if using.

Spoon the mixture into the madeleine moulds to half-fill. Bake in the preheated oven for 8 minutes, until pale golden. Let stand for 1–2 minutes before removing from the moulds. Repeat until all the mixture is used. Makes 32.

to clarify the butter: Place the butter in a small saucepan and slowly melt. When the butter is clear, remove from the stove for a few minutes and pour into a cup, leaving the sediments in the pan, and allow to cool.

ICED COFFEE CAKES ••

1½ cups S.R. flour
a pinch of salt
125 g butter
¾ cup caster sugar
2 eggs
2 teaspoons coffee essence
2 tablespoons milk

coffee glacé icing:
1 cup icing sugar, sifted
1 tablespoon hot strong coffee
toasted hazelnuts, to decorate

Preheat the oven to 190°C. Sift the flour and salt. Cream the butter, add the sugar gradually, and beat until soft and light. Whisk the eggs and beat, a little at a time, into the creamed mixture. Fold in half the flour with a metal spoon, add the coffee essence and milk and, lastly, the remaining flour. Bake in patty pan cases for about 15 minutes. When cool, top each with coffee glacé icing and a whole hazelnut. Makes 12.

coffee glacé icing: Mix the icing sugar and coffee, until the mixture will cover the back of a spoon smoothly and thickly.

COUNTRY COOKING

COUNTRY COOKING AT ITS BEST IS VERY SIMPLE. THESE RECIPES FROM FARMHOUSE KITCHENS USE THE BEST OF COUNTRY PRODUCE; FRESH EGGS, GOOD BUTTER, STRONG FLOUR, THICK DAIRY CREAM AND THE BEST DRIED FRUITS AND NUTS. ENJOY THE FRAGRANCE AND AROMA OF GOOD WHOLESOME BAKING THAT HAS BEEN DEVELOPED OVER GENERATIONS TO SATISFY THE KEENEST APPETITES.

NUT LOAF •

30 g butter
½ cup honey
1 egg
1 cup plain flour
a pinch of salt
1 teaspoon baking powder
¼ cup milk
½ cup chopped walnuts
½ cup sultanas

Preheat the oven to 180°C. Grease a tube loaf tin. Cream the butter and honey until light. Add the egg and beat in well. Sift the flour with the salt and baking powder. Fold into the creamed mixture alternately with the milk, walnuts and sultanas. Spoon into the prepared loaf tin and cover with a lid (if it has one). Bake for 40–50 minutes, or until a skewer inserted comes out clean. Serve warm or cold, in slices, buttered.

PIKELETS •

1 cup S.R. flour
a pinch of salt
2 tablespoons sugar
¼ teaspoon bicarbonate of soda
1 egg
½ cup each buttermilk and milk (or all milk with 1 teaspoon vinegar added)
2 tablespoons melted butter
extra butter, for frying

Sift the flour, salt, sugar and soda into a bowl. In another bowl, beat the egg with the buttermilk and melted butter. Make a well in the centre with a wooden spoon. Add the egg mixture to the well and stir gradually, drawing in the flour from the sides to make a batter (it should still be slightly lumpy and not over mixed).

Put tablespoonfuls on to a hot, greased griddle or heavy-based frying pan. If the batter thickens, add a little more milk. Cook until bubbly on top and brown underneath. Turn to brown the other side. Transfer to a clean tea towel and lightly cover with a towel, until required. Serve with butter and jam, if liked. Makes about 12.

SCONES •

3 cups S.R. flour
1 teaspoon salt
60 g butter, cut into small pieces
1 cup buttermilk
   (or milk with 1 teaspoon vinegar added)

Preheat the oven to 230°C. Sift the flour and salt into a bowl. Rub in the butter. Make a well in the centre and mix in the milk, adding more milk if necessary to make a soft dough. Knead, handling the dough as lightly as possible, and roll out on a lightly floured surface to 2 cm thickness. Cut into rounds with a floured 4 cm cutter. Place on a lightly greased baking tray. Brush the tops with a little milk. Bake for 10–15 minutes. Transfer to a clean tea towel, and lightly cover with a towel, until required. Serve warm with butter or jam and cream. Makes about 12 scones.

ROCK CAKES •

2 cups S.R. flour
½ teaspoon mixed spice
a pinch of salt
90 g butter
½ cup sugar
2 tablespoons each currants, sultanas and
   chopped mixed peel
1 egg
¼ cup milk

Preheat the oven to 200°C and grease the baking trays. Sift the flour with the spice and salt, rub the butter in lightly, and then mix in the sugar. Add the fruits and mix well. Beat the egg and add the milk, then mix with the dry ingredients to a stiff dough. Put small tablespoonfuls in little rough heaps on the greased baking tin. Bake for 10–15 minutes. Makes about 20.

GEM SCONES •

If you haven't inherited a set of gem irons you may be lucky enough to pick some up at a second-hand shop or garage sale.

45 g butter
2 tablespoons sugar
1 egg
1 cup S.R. flour
a pinch of salt
½ cup milk

Grease the gem irons and heat in a 200°C oven. Cream the butter and sugar until light and fluffy. Add the egg and beat until well incorporated. Lightly fold in the sifted flour and salt with the milk, and combine until just mixed. Spoon enough mixture to half-fill the gem irons. Bake for 10–15 minutes. Serve warm with butter. Makes about 12.

PUMPKIN SCONES •

1 cup cooked pumpkin, drained and cooled
2 cups S.R. flour
½ teaspoon salt
30 g butter, cut into small pieces
¼ cup caster sugar
1 egg, beaten lightly
extra milk, for glazing

Preheat oven to 225 °C. Grease a 23 cm sandwich tin with butter. Sift flour and salt into a bowl. Rub in butter, add sugar, pumpkin and egg. Mix into a dough, knead lightly with a little flour. Pat out to 2.5 cm thickness. Cut into 12 rounds. Arrange in prepared sandwich tin. Brush scones with extra milk, bake in preheated oven for 20 minutes, until risen and golden. Remove from oven and wrap in a clean tea towel for a few minutes before splitting and buttering. Makes about 12.

CONTINENTAL AND DESSERT CAKES

These are the cakes for the times there's something to celebrate, someone to impress or a family to spoil.

SOUR CREAM CHEESECAKE ••

1½ cups plain biscuits, crushed or blended into crumbs
6 tablespoons ground almonds
¼ cup cream
75 g butter, melted

filling:
500 g cream cheese
½ cup sugar
2 eggs
grated rind of 1 lemon
1 teaspoon lemon juice
½ teaspoon grated nutmeg

topping:
1½ cups sour cream
2 tablespoons sugar
½ teaspoon vanilla essence

Line the base of a 23 cm springform tin with baking paper. Stir together the crumbs, ground almonds, cream and melted butter. Using your fingers, press the crumb mixture into the tin. The crumbs should come 5 cm up the sides. Chill the crust well while making the filling.

Preheat the oven to 190°C. To make the filling, beat the cream cheese and sugar with an electric mixer. Beat in the eggs, one at a time, adding the lemon rind and juice. Turn the cream cheese mixture into prepared shell, using a spatula to spread the filling evenly. Bake for about 20 minutes. Remove from the oven and dust with grated nutmeg. Let the cheesecake cool to room temperature. Increase the oven temperature to 220°C.

To make the topping, whisk the sour cream with the sugar and vanilla until smooth. Spread evenly over the top of the cheesecake. Bake in the oven for about 5 minutes, just enough to glaze. Remove from the oven, cool, and refrigerate for 6–12 hours before serving. Dust with extra grated nutmeg and cut into wedges. *Serves 10–12.*

RICH CHOCOLATE FUDGE CAKE ••

Quite the most delicious, melt-in-the-mouth cake. It has a crisp meringue crust and light tender centre with a soft creamy almost sauce light consistency.

250 g plus 1 tablespoon butter
250 g excellent quality dark chocolate, coarsely chopped
6 eggs
¾ cup caster sugar
⅓ cup brown sugar
3 tablespoons plain flour
3 tablespoons ground almonds
½ teaspoon cream of tartar
1 tablespoon sifted icing sugar, for dusting
1 cup cream
few drops of vanilla essence

Set oven temperature at 180°C. Butter the sides and base of a 25 cm springform tin with the tablespoon of butter. Line the base with baking paper and flour the tin. Melt the butter in a large, heavy-based saucepan with the chocolate, stirring constantly over low heat, just until melted and smooth. It should not get much hotter than 50°C. Set aside. Separate the eggs and beat the sugars into the egg yolks, just until mixed. While the chocolate is still warm, >

SOUR CREAM CHEESECAKE

whisk the egg yolk mixture into it, and then stir in the flour and almonds. If chocolate mixture has cooled, warm it over a low heat, stirring constantly, until it is just barely warm. Warm the egg whites slightly by swirling them in a bowl above a gas flame, or over hot water. Add the cream of tartar to the egg whites and beat until they form rounded peaks. Gently fold the whites into the base mixture, without deflating the whites.

Pour mixture into the tin and bake for 35–45 minutes, or until the cake is completely set around the sides but still has a soft and creamy circle, about 12 cm diameter in the centre. The cake should tremble in the centre, just slightly, when you shake the tin gently. Cool thoroughly in the tin.

To serve, dust the cake with the icing sugar. Serve with softly whipped cream flavoured with vanilla and icing sugar. The cake keeps well for 3–4 days. Do not refrigerate or freeze. Cover the cake loosely with foil while it is still in the tin.

LINZERTORTE ••

Most recipes for this torte from Linz in Austria call for a pastry made either with ground almonds or hazelnuts. This version is rich and melt-in-the-mouth. Because the mixture is light, the lattice is piped over the top.

185 g unsalted butter
1 cup caster sugar
grated rind of 1 lemon
2 eggs
1¼ cups plain flour
½ teaspoon ground cinnamon
a pinch of salt
1¼ cups ground almonds
⅔ cup raspberry jam
icing sugar, for dusting

Preheat the oven to 160°C. Lightly butter a 23 cm springform tin and line the base with baking paper. Cream the butter and beat in the sugar with the rind until mixture is light and fluffy. Beat in the eggs, adding one at a time. Sift the flour with the cinnamon and salt, and fold into the creamed mixture with the ground almonds until well mixed.

Spoon one-third of the mixture into a piping bag fitted with a plain 5 mm tube. Spread the remaining mixture into the tin. Gently spread the raspberry jam over the creamed mixture, leaving a 1.5cm edge.

Pipe a ring of mixture around the inside edge of the cake tin, and then use the remaining mixture to pipe a lattice over the top, each strip spaced about 2 cm apart. Bake for 30–40 minutes until golden and firm. Leave to cool a few minutes before removing, with the base, from the tin and cooling on a wire rack. The torte may be served warm or cooled, dusted with icing sugar.

TRADITIONAL CHRISTMAS COOKING

It wouldn't be Christmas without a rich spicy fruitcake or a pudding fairly bursting at the seams with plump fruits and presented with great pomp and ceremony.

Make the cake and pudding, as well as the mincemeat for the tarts, well ahead of time to allow them to mature and develop richness for Christmas day.

SHORTBREAD ••

For good shortbread, made as my Scottish mother did, the dough should be kneaded with a lightness of hand and nice judgement for about 5 minutes, until it becomes smooth and very buttery. Then it is pressed into a tin or directly on to a baking tray into a rectangle or round, and pricked or decorated. This makes a superb shortbread; crisp yet tender. If making ahead, re-crisp in a moderate oven 180°C for 15 minutes before serving. For a lighter shortbread, ¼ cup of the flour could be replaced with the same amount of rice flour. For a gritty texture, use fine ground rice or even fine semolina. It's up to you.

250 g butter
½ cup caster sugar
3 cups plain flour

Preheat the oven to 180°C. Butter 2 x 18 cm sandwich tins or 2 baking trays. Cream the butter, and then add the sugar gradually, beating until mixture is light and fluffy. Work in the flour gradually, and then, with a light hand, knead to form a dough. Divide the dough in half and pat each into a round. Press into the prepared sandwich tins or onto the baking trays. With the heel of the hand, push dough out until you have an 18 cm circle and the mixture is very smooth. Then smooth over the surface and edge with a palette knife. Crimp edges by pressing the edge of the dough with your finger, and then pinching the edge together. If using a sandwich tin, fork the edge for decoration. Prick the surface of the shortbread with a fork. This is done to release moisture as it cooks, making the shortbread crisp.

Bake in the centre of the oven for 10 minutes, and then reduce the temperature to 150°C, and bake for a further 40 minutes. Remove from the oven, dust with a little extra caster sugar, and cool completely on wire racks.

To serve, do as the Scots do and break it into good-size pieces. Makes 2 cakes.

SHORTBREAD FINGERS ••

Make shortbread dough as above, and roll out on a lightly floured board to 8 mm thickness. Preheat oven to 180°C. Prick all over with a fork and cut into oblongs 8 cm x 2.5 cm. Place 10 mm apart on a greased baking tray and bake in preheated oven for 15 minutes, until crisp and straw-coloured. Dredge with caster sugar while still warm.

RICH CHRISTMAS CAKE •••

375 g raisins
375 g sultanas
125 g mixed peel
125 g glacé cherries
60 g glacé apricots
2 slices glacé pineapple
3 tablespoons brandy or rum
3 tablespoons sherry

cake mixture:
250 g butter
1¼ cups brown sugar
grated rind of 1 lemon
1 tablespoon golden syrup
2 tablespoons marmalade
5 eggs
2½ cups plain flour
1 teaspoon mixed spice
1 teaspoon ground cinnamon
¼ teaspoon salt
¾ cup finely chopped blanched almonds
extra almonds
extra brandy

first prepare fruit: Wash the raisins and sultanas separately then dry thoroughly. This is best done by spreading fruit on baking trays lined with paper towels. Place in a 120°C oven for 30 minutes, remove and cool completely. Chop the raisins. Put into a bowl with the finely chopped peel. Cut the cherries, apricots and pineapple into small dice, and then add to the fruit in the bowl. Sprinkle with the brandy or rum and sherry. Cover with cling wrap, then a cloth, and leave overnight.

next day: Preheat the oven to 150°C. Line a deep 20 cm square tin. Beat the butter and brown sugar with the lemon rind, until light and creamy. Add the golden syrup and marmalade. Beat well. Add the eggs one at a time, beating well after each. Add 1 tablespoon flour with the last egg. Sift together the flour, spices and salt and stir into creamed mixture alternately with the fruit and chopped almonds.

Spoon the mixture into the prepared tin and arrange the extra almonds on top. Bake for 3½–4 hours or until cooked. Remove from the oven and immediately sprinkle with about 1 tablespoon extra brandy.

Remove the cake from the tin, leaving the paper on the cake. Wrap in a tea towel and leave until cool.

TO STORE AND MATURE CAKE

Remove the paper. Wrap in cling wrap and then foil. Keep in a cool place, or refrigerate, at least 1 month before using. Refrigerate for up to 6 months.

TO ICE CAKE

If the cake is to be iced, do not arrange the almonds on top. Brush the top of the cake with slightly beaten egg white. On a board dusted with icing sugar, roll out the almond paste and cut out to cover the top and sides of the cake neatly. Trim any excess. Put on the cake and press gently with a rolling pin. Leave several hours or overnight. Make fondant icing (or use commercial soft icing), and roll out to fit the top and sides of the cake. Brush the almond paste with the egg white and cover with the fondant icing on top. Trim any excess and decorate as liked.

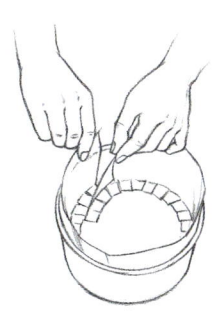

Brush the base and sides of tin with melted butter. Line the sides with a long strip of brown paper. For easy fitting, fold in the paper 2 cm to make a hem and snip as shown.

Place a circle of brown paper cut to fit the base. Repeat these steps using baking paper over the brown paper.

lining the tin

1. Cut a strip of brown paper 10 cm higher than the cake tin and fold a 2 cm hem. Nick the hem with scissors at 2.5 cm intervals and fit this strip around the sides of the tin, making sure the hem lies flat on the base.
2. Cut a square or circle to fit the base of the tin, using brown paper, and fit into the tin.
3. Cut a strip of double thickness baking or greaseproof paper 8 cm higher than the cake tin and make a hem, as for the brown paper, to fit around the sides of the tin. Fit into the tin, making sure the hem lies flat.
4. Cut another square or circle of paper to fit the base of the tin, using baking or greaseproof paper. Fit into tin neatly.

ALMOND PASTE •

This quantity will cover top and sides of one 20 cm cake, or the tops only of two cakes.

500 g icing sugar
250 g ground almonds
juice of ½ lemon
2 tablespoons sherry
1 egg yolk
a few drops almond essence *(optional)*

Sift the icing sugar and combine with the ground almonds. Mix together the lemon juice, sherry and egg yolk, adding the almond essence now, if liked. Mix this mixture into the icing sugar nearly all at once to form a paste, which can be rolled out. If the mixture is too dry, add a little more sherry.

note: a commercial almond icing is available from most supermarkets.

FONDANT ICING •

500 g icing sugar
2 tablespoons liquid glucose
1 egg white
flavouring

Sift the icing sugar, make a well in the centre, and add the glucose, egg white and flavouring. Beat, drawing the icing sugar into the centre, until the mass is a stiff paste. Turn on to a board lightly dusted with icing sugar and knead into a paste. Use to cover top and sides of one cake, or tops only of two cakes.

note: a commercial fondant icing, which is also called soft icing, is available from most supermarkets.

RICH CHRISTMAS PUDDING ••

250 g raisins, chopped
60 g candied peel, chopped
250 g currants
250 g sultanas
3 tablespoons rum or brandy
250 g butter
grated rind of 1 orange and 1 lemon
1¼ cups brown sugar
4 eggs, lightly beaten
½ cup finely chopped almonds
1 cup plain flour
½ teaspoon each salt, mixed spice, ground nutmeg, ginger, cinnamon and bicarbonate of soda
2 cups fresh breadcrumbs

first prepare the fruit: Place the raisins, peel, currants and sultanas in a bowl. Sprinkle with rum and leave overnight.

next day: Cream the butter and the fruit rinds and beat in the sugar until light and fluffy. Add the beaten eggs gradually, beating well. Stir in the soaked fruit and almonds alternately with the flour sifted with the salt, spices and bicarbonate of soda. Add the breadcrumbs.

Turn into a large, well-buttered pudding bowl with the base lined with a circle of baking paper. Cover with another circle of baking paper to fit over the top of the pudding bowl then cover with a pudding cloth that has been scalded, wrung out and floured. Tie firmly with string.

Steam in saucepan of boiling water, on an upturned saucer or metal ring, covered, for 6 hours. Water should come not more than halfway up sides of the bowl. Add more boiling water as necessary. When cold, cover with fresh baking paper, then foil.

STEAMING AND SERVING PUDDING

On Christmas day, put the pudding into a saucepan of boiling water to come halfway up the sides of the bowl, and steam for 2½ hours. Serve with Cumberland rum butter (*see p. 305*), custard or ice-cream. If you wish to flame the Christmas pudding, turn the hot pudding out on to a serving plate, heat a little brandy gently in a small saucepan, ignite, and pour over the pudding at the table. Darken the room and serve immediately.

FRUIT MINCE •

The culinary word 'mince' takes its origin from the French 'emincer' and signifies anything that is chopped finely. This is the filling for everyone's Christmas favourite; mince pies. This quantity makes 6 cups.

375 g seedless raisins
500 g mixed peel
4 apples, cored
60 g glacé cherries
125 g blanched almonds
500 g sultanas
500 g currants
2 cups brown sugar
grated rind and juice of 1 lemon
grated rind of 1 small orange
2 teaspoons mixed spice
½ teaspoon grated nutmeg
125 g butter, melted
½ cup brandy or rum

Finely chop the raisins, mixed peel, apples, cherries, almonds and half the sultanas (alternatively put through a mincer). Add the remaining sultanas with the currants. Stir in the brown sugar, rinds and lemon juice, the spices, butter and brandy. Mix well and put into a large jar. Cover and chill. Stir every day for a week. Fruit mince can be kept for months in the refrigerator.

RICH CHRISTMAS PUDDING

LITTLE MINCE PIES ••

1 cup fruit mince (see p. 228)
extra egg, beaten, for glaze
extra caster sugar (optional)

biscuit pastry:
185 g butter
⅓ cup caster sugar
1 egg
2½ cups plain flour
½ teaspoon baking powder

Preheat the oven to 180°C. First make biscuit pastry. Roll out thinly, and cut into rounds to fit small patty tins. Cut the same number of smaller circles for the tops of the pies. Line the patty tins with larger pastry circles. Put 1 heaped teaspoon of fruit mince into each. Top each filled patty tin with the smaller round of pastry, and glaze with the beaten egg. Make a small slit in each pastry top, or cut with a small star cutter. Sprinkle each, if liked, with a little extra caster sugar. Bake for 20–25 minutes, until pale brown. Remove from the oven and cool on wire racks.

biscuit pastry: Cream the butter and sugar well. Add the egg and beat well. Sift the flour with the baking powder and stir into the butter mixture to form a dough. Knead lightly on a floured board. Chill for 1 hour. Makes about 50.

DUNDEE CAKE

Many a Scottish housewife makes this traditional light fruit cake regularly so that there is always some on hand for family and visitors.

250 g butter
1 cup caster sugar
grated rind of 2 oranges
5 eggs, lightly beaten
2½ cups plain flour
1 teaspoon baking powder
a pinch of salt
¼ cup chopped blanched almonds
1 cup sultanas
1 cup currants
½ cup chopped mixed candied peel
1 tablespoon orange juice
extra blanched almonds, to decorate

Preheat the oven to 150 °C. Grease 20 cm deep round cake tin and line first with brown paper then baking paper *(see p. 227)*. Cream the butter with the sugar and orange rind until light and fluffy. Gradually beat in the eggs. Sift flour, baking powder and salt into the creamed mixture and fold in gently with the almonds, fruit, peel and orange juice. When smooth turn into prepared tin, level the surface and arrange extra almonds on top.

Bake for 2–2½ hours, or until a skewer inserted in the centre comes out clean. Allow to cool in tin before turning out.

YEAST BREADS

ANY COOK USING YEAST FOR THE FIRST TIME COMES UNDER ITS FASCINATING SPELL ONCE THE WARM, SPICY FRAGRANCE OF FRESHLY BAKED BREADS AND BUNS SCENT THE KITCHEN.

Fresh yeast, obtainable in compressed form, and sold by the weight, will keep in the refrigerator for 2–3 days. Dehydrated (dry) yeast, sold in packets, and readily available at most supermarkets, will keep for several months if stored in a cool, dry place. For most, dry yeast, is the easy option.

When the yeast becomes active it creates the gas that gives bread and buns their light, characteristic texture. The temperature of liquid used is most important; it must be lukewarm.

Dry yeast is added to the dry ingredients in a bowl and then the liquid ingredients are added. Compressed yeast is dissolved with a little sugar or liquid before remaining liquid is added.

Sift the dry ingredients into a warm bowl, make a well in centre, and pour in the liquids. Mix into a soft dough. Turn out on a lightly floured board and knead to a smooth, elastic ball, for at 5–10 minutes. Knead in as little extra flour as possible.

Put the ball of dough in a clean, greased bowl and turn the dough over, so that top is lightly greased. This keeps the top soft, allowing it to stretch easily as the dough rises. Cover with a clean tea towel.

'Rising' is the word used to describe the standing time necessary for the dough to double in bulk before it is shaped. The bowl of dough must stand in a warm place free from draughts while it is rising.

A warm place can be:
- In a barely warm oven.
- In a saucepan containing warm water that comes halfway up the sides of the bowl holding the dough.
- On top of an internal hot water cylinder.

Rising the dough will take 1–2 hours, or until it has doubled in bulk. If you are not in a hurry, you can cover the bowl of dough with baking paper, then foil, place in a fridge, and leave overnight. Remember it is heat that kills yeast, not cold. To test, press two fingers lightly and quickly in the top of the dough. If the dent stays, the dough is ready. If it fills up, leave 15 minutes longer and test again.

When ready, knead the dough into its required shape, put into greased tins, and leave to rise again in a warm place for ½–1 hour (this rising is called 'proving'). For buns, allow 15–30 minutes, depending on size. The shaped 'proved' dough should be close to the final size, as it won't rise a great deal more once it is put in the oven.

The shaped dough is always put into a hot oven 200°C for the first 15 minutes so that it kills the yeast and the dough won't over prove. When cooked, the base of the bread or buns will make a hollow sound when tapped with knuckles.

HOT CROSS BUNS ••

Freshly baked, homemade hot cross buns, the traditional Good Friday breakfast, are at their best served warm with butter. If not oven fresh, they are delicious toasted and buttered. Buns keep well wrapped in foil when cool, and stored in the refrigerator. They will keep for weeks in the freezer. Reheat in the oven for about 15 minutes before serving.

4 cups plain flour
1 teaspoon mixed spice
½ teaspoon cinnamon
1 teaspoon salt
60 g butter
½ cup caster sugar
1 sachet (7 g) dry yeast
½ cup lukewarm water
½ cup lukewarm milk
1 egg, slightly beaten
¾ cup currants or sultanas
¼ cup chopped mixed peel (optional)
1 egg white, slightly beaten
warm white icing, for piping crosses

Sift the flour, spices and salt. Rub in the butter and stir in the sugar and dry yeast. Make a well in the sifted flour, and pour in the water and milk and egg. Mix to a soft dough and knead on lightly floured board, until smooth and elastic, for about 5 minutes. Lastly, knead in the fruits lightly to distribute evenly. Put into a clean, greased bowl and cover with a tea towel. Leave to rise in a warm place, until doubled in bulk (about 1¼–1½ hours). Turn out on to a floured board and lightly pat into 2 cm thickness. Cut into 14 even pieces. Knead each into a round shape.

Preheat the oven to 200°C. Put the buns 2.5 cm apart on a greased baking tray. Cover and allow to rise (prove) in a warm place for a further 20–30 minutes. Brush with egg white and bake for about 15 minutes. Alternatively, some buns may be baked packed close together in greased cake tins. These will take 20–25 minutes to cook.

When the buns are baked, remove from the oven and brush with the glaze. When glazed, pipe a cross of white icing on each. (See glaze and icing recipes following.)

If baked-on crosses are preferred, mix 2 tablespoons cold water and 4 tablespoons S.R. flour and beat until smooth. Fill into a greaseproof paper funnel or a piping bag fitted with a narrow round tube. Pipe crosses on the buns before baking.

GLAZE •

¼ teaspoon powdered gelatine
1 tablespoon sugar
2 tablespoons hot water

In a small saucepan combine the gelatine and water, and dissolve over a low heat. Add the sugar and stir until dissolved. Brush over the buns while still hot and leave to dry in the oven, with the door open, for a minute or so.

WHITE ICING •

2 cups icing sugar
about 1 tablespoon hot milk

Sift the icing sugar into a small bowl and stir in enough hot milk to make a firm icing consistency. Fill into a piping bag fitted with a narrow plain tube and pipe crosses on the cooled buns.

RICH SWEET DOUGH ••

This dough, made by an easy method that requires no kneading, makes a rich, tender bread with a flaky texture. It can be prepared up to 3 days before baking, and stored in the refrigerator. It is used for sweet buns and coffee cakes.

¾ cup milk
½ cup sugar
2 teaspoons salt
125 g butter
½ cup warm water
1 egg
1 sachet (7 g) dry yeast
4 cups plain flour

Scald the milk and stir in the sugar, salt and butter. Cool to lukewarm. Pour the warm water into a large, warm bowl. Stir in lukewarm milk mixture, beaten egg, yeast and half the sifted flour. Beat vigorously until smooth. Stir in remaining flour to make a stiff batter. Cover tightly with cling wrap or foil. Chill dough at least 2 hours, or up to 3 days. Shape and bake as described in the following recipes.

ORANGE ROLLS ••

1 quantity rich sweet dough
1 cup sugar
grated rind of 1 orange
½ cup sultanas *(optional)*
60 g melted butter

orange icing:
2 cups icing sugar, sifted
2 tablespoons orange juice

Prepare the dough and chill. When ready to shape, combine the sugar, orange rind and sultanas. Divide the dough in half and roll each half on a well-floured board to a rectangle 46 cm x 23 cm. Brush with the melted butter and sprinkle with sugar and sultana mixture. Roll up from long sides, like a Swiss roll. Cut in thick slices and place, cut-sides up, in 2 x 20 cm sandwich tins.

Cover and let rise in a warm place until doubled in bulk, for about 1 hour. Preheat the oven to 190°C. Bake for about 25 minutes. Remove from the tins and drizzle with the orange icing while warm.

orange icing: Combine the icing sugar and orange juice to make a thin icing.

CINNAMON PINWHEELS ••

Follow recipe for orange rolls above, omitting orange rind and using instead 2 teaspoons cinnamon and a little extra butter.

SPICE CRUMB COFFEE CAKES ••

1 quantity rich sweet dough
2 teaspoons ground cinnamon or cardamom
1 cup plain flour
½ cup chopped almonds
½ cup sugar
125 g butter

Prepare the dough. When ready to shape, divide the dough in two equal portions. Pat into two greased 23 cm square tins. Mix the remaining ingredients until crumbly, and sprinkle over top of dough. Cover and let rise in a warm place, free from draughts, until doubled in bulk, for about 1 hour.

Preheat the oven to 190°C. Bake for about 35 minutes. Remove from the tins and, if liked, drizzle a little glacé icing *(see p. 308)* over the top. Serve warm.

BISCUITS

Freshly baked biscuits, crisp from the oven, are a favourite with the whole family for those tea and coffee breaks or for the packed lunch.

Among these recipes are chilled doughs, to keep and bake as needed, simple doughs that even the children of the household will enjoy making, and some deliciously spiced and iced favourites.

CARDAMOM COOKIES ••

This is a simple biscuit, with the warm fragrance of cardamon.

125 g butter
1 teaspoon bicarbonate of soda
1 teaspoon ground cardamom
¼ teaspoon salt
1 cup light brown sugar, firmly packed
1 egg
2 cups plain flour, sifted
1 teaspoon cream of tartar

Cream the butter and add the soda, salt and cardamom. Mix well and gradually beat in the sugar until the mixture is light and fluffy. Beat in the egg. Sift together the flour and cream of tartar. Gradually stir into the butter mixture to form a dough. Chill until stiff enough to handle, for 3–4 hours. Preheat the oven to 180°C. Scoop out the chilled dough, shaping into small balls. Place on ungreased baking trays. Use a wetted fork to press each cookie into a round shape. Bake for 15–18 minutes, until light golden. Remove from the trays, cool and store airtight. **Makes about 45 cookies.**

APRICOT FINGERS ••

200 g dried apricots
3 eggs, separated
1 cup sugar
1 cup plain flour
½ teaspoon baking powder
a pinch of salt
1 cup chopped walnuts
½ teaspoon vanilla essence
caster sugar

Preheat the oven to 180°C. Cook the apricots in water to cover, and then drain and chop. Beat the egg whites until stiff, gradually add the sugar, and beat well until smooth. Add the egg yolks and beat, then fold in the sifted flour, baking powder and salt. Add the apricots, walnuts and vanilla. Turn the mixture into a greased and lined 27 cm x 18 cm tin. Bake for 30 minutes. Sprinkle with a little caster sugar and cut into fingers while still warm. **Makes about 24.**

ANZAC BISCUITS •

125 g butter or margarine
1 tablespoon golden syrup
2 tablespoons boiling water
1½ teaspoons bicarbonate of soda
1 cup rolled oats
¾ cup desiccated coconut
1 cup plain flour
1 cup sugar

Preheat the oven to 150°C. Melt the butter and golden syrup over a gentle heat, and then add the boiling water mixed with the bicarbonate of soda. Pour into the mixed dry ingredients and blend well. Drop teaspoonfuls of mixture onto greased trays. Bake for 20 minutes. Cool on trays for a few minutes, remove, and store in airtight containers when cool.
Makes about 48.

DATE SURPRISES •

150 g butter
1 cup brown sugar
1 egg
1 teaspoon vanilla essence
2 cups plain flour
¼ teaspoon salt
½ teaspoon bicarbonate of soda
375 g pitted dates

Preheat the oven to 180°C. Cream the butter, gradually add the brown sugar, and cream well together. Add the egg and vanilla and beat well. Sift the flour with the salt and bicarbonate of soda, and mix to make a dough. Chill the dough. Take small pieces of dough and mould around the dates in cocoon shapes, or roll out the dough and cut in 5 cm rounds, and wrap those around the dates. Bake on greased trays for 15–20 minutes. Any remaining dough may be used for plain biscuits. Makes about 36.

OATMEAL RAISIN COOKIES •

250 g unsalted butter
1 cup brown sugar
¼ cup sugar
1 tablespoon vanilla essence
3 tablespoons milk
2 large eggs, lightly beaten
2 cups plain flour
½ teaspoon ground cinnamon
½ teaspoon salt
1 teaspoon baking powder
1 teaspoon bicarbonate of soda
3 cups rolled oats
1 cup raisins

In a bowl of an electric mixer, cream the butter until soft. Beat in the sugars until light and fluffy. Add the vanilla, milk and eggs and beat thoroughly. Sift in the flour with the cinnamon, salt, baking powder and soda, and mix until just combined. Stir in the rolled oats and raisins. Place the bowl with the batter in the refrigerator until firm, for several hours or overnight.

Preheat oven to 180°C. Grease or line several baking trays with baking paper. Scoop out large tablespoons of the batter, shape each into balls, and arrange on the prepared trays, about 8 cm apart. Press down with a wet fork to flatten slightly.

Bake until golden, 15–20 minutes. They will still be slightly soft in the centre. Remove from the oven and transfer to a wire rack to cool completely. Store airtight.
Makes about 36.

GINGER NUTS •

1 cup plain flour
2 tablespoons sugar
1 teaspoon bicarbonate of soda
1 teaspoon mixed spice
1 teaspoon ground cinnamon
1 teaspoon ground ginger
60 g butter
2 tablespoons golden syrup

Preheat the oven to 230°C. Sift the dry ingredients. Melt the butter and syrup, and pour onto the flour mixture. Mix well and roll into balls each about the size of a walnut. Place on a well-greased baking tray, allowing room to spread. Bake for 5 minutes, and then reduce the heat to 180°C and bake for a further 10 minutes. Allow to cool on the tray. Makes 12–16.

BURNT BUTTER BISCUITS •

125 g butter
½ cup caster sugar
1 egg
1 teaspoon vanilla essence
1 cup S.R. flour
½ cup plain flour
a pinch of salt
60 g blanched almonds

Preheat the oven to 180°C. Melt the butter and cook to a light brown over a low heat. Cool slightly, add the sugar and beat well. Stir in the egg and vanilla. Fold in the flours, sifted with the salt. Roll into balls, each about the size of a walnut. Place on a greased tray, allowing room for spreading. Put a blanched almond on top of each. Bake for 10–12 minutes. Makes about 24.

LEMON MELTING MOMENTS ••

Truly melt-in-the-mouth, these are irresistible. There are many recipes for melting moments which are also known as yo-yos. All include cornflour in varying proportions to flour. They can be flavoured with vanilla in place of the lemon if you prefer.

250 g unsalted butter, softened
4 tablespoons icing sugar, sifted
1 tablespoons grated lemon rind
2 cups plain flour
4 tablespoons cornflour

Preheat the oven to 160°C. Butter 2 baking trays or line with baking paper. Cream the butter with the icing sugar and lemon rind, using an electric mixer, until light and fluffy. Sift together the flour and cornflour, add to the butter mixture, and mix until a soft dough is formed. Pinch off pieces of dough and roll into small balls each the size of a walnut. Place on the prepared baking trays about 5 cm apart. Press each one down slightly with the heel of a hand, and then, using a fork dipped each time in cold water, mark biscuits lightly to decorate.

Bake for 15 minutes or until lightly golden. Using a metal spatula, carefully remove from trays on to wire racks to cool. If liked, sandwich the biscuits together with the lemon filling. Store in an airtight container.

lemon filling:

60 g unsalted butter, softened
1½ teaspoons each lemon juice and rind
¾ cup icing sugar, sifted

Beat the softened butter with the lemon juice and rind until pale and creamy. Add the icing sugar and continue to beat until well combined. Makes about 36.

LEMON MELTING MOMENTS

LINZER BISCUITS ••

200 g unsalted butter
1 teaspoon vanilla essence
½ cup caster sugar
2 cups plain flour
1 teaspoon baking powder
¼ teaspoon ground cinnamon
¼ teaspoon cloves
1 egg, lightly beaten
½ cup raspberry jam
½ cup apricot jam
½ cup icing sugar (optional)

Preheat the oven to 180°C. Beat the butter and vanilla essence until creamy. Add the sugar and beat well. Fold in the flour, sifted with the baking powder and spices. Add the beaten egg and mix to combine. Form the dough into a ball, flatten into a disk and chill, wrapped in cling wrap for about 1 hour.

Halve the dough and, one at a time, roll out on a floured board and cut into 4–5 cm rounds. Re-roll the scraps once. Place on ungreased baking trays, allowing a little room for spreading. Using a small cloverleaf or round-shaped cutter, cut out a 15 mm circle from the centres of half the rounds.

Bake for 8–10 minutes or until lightly golden. Remove from the oven and allow to cool on a wire rack. Store in airtight container. Just before serving, spread slightly warmed jam on the plain rounds and top each with a ring. Sprinkle, if liked, with icing sugar. Makes about 36 pairs.

PEANUT CHEWS •

1 cup peanut butter
½ cup honey
¼ cup brown sugar
1 teaspoon vanilla essence
3 cups rice bubbles
½ cup roughly chopped peanuts

Grease a 20 cm or 23 cm square tin. Combine peanut butter, honey and brown sugar in a large saucepan. Cook, stirring over a low heat until melted and thoroughly combined. Remove from heat and stir in vanilla essence, rice bubbles and peanuts until completed coated with peanut butter mixture. Press firmly into the prepared tin. Chill until firm and cut into squares. Makes about 20.

ALMOND FINGERS ••

125 g butter
⅓ cup sugar
1 egg yolk
1 cup chopped almonds
2 cups plain flour
1 teaspoon baking powder
a pinch of salt

icing:

1 egg white
1 cup sifted icing sugar

Preheat the oven to 180°C. Cream the butter and sugar, add the egg yolk and beat well. Add the sifted flour, baking powder and salt and mix to a firm dough. Roll out to 3 mm thickness. Cut into shapes 8 cm x 2.5 cm. Spread the icing on the biscuits and sprinkle with the chopped almonds. Place on a greased baking tray. Bake for 10 minutes.

icing: Beat the egg white then add the icing sugar gradually, until it has a spreading consistency. If necessary, you can add more icing sugar. Makes about 60.

LINZER BISCUITS

VANILLA KIPPELS ••

Little almond shortbread crescents to serve with coffee.

1¼ cups plain flour
a pinch of salt
1¼ cups ground almonds
155 g soft butter
¼ cup icing sugar
2 egg yolks
½ teaspoon vanilla essence
extra icing sugar

Sift the flour with the salt on to a pastry board. Sprinkle the ground almonds over the flour. Make a well in the centre, and put in the butter, sugar, egg yolks and vanilla. Work the ingredients in the centre with your fingertips, until thoroughly blended. Using a metal spatula, quickly draw in the flour and ground almonds to form a dough. Knead the dough lightly, until smooth, and then form into a ball. Wrap in cling wrap and chill for 1 hour.

Preheat the oven to 180°C and butter 2 baking trays. Pinch off small pieces of dough and roll into walnut-size balls. Roll each ball in the palm of the hand to form a small tube, and then curve into a crescent. Arrange on the prepared baking trays.

Bake for 10–12 minutes, until lightly coloured. Transfer the biscuits to a wire rack over a plate. Dredge the kippels heavily with sifted icing sugar, while still warm. Cool and store in an airtight container. *Makes about 40.*

FUDGE BROWNIES •

250 g softened butter
2 cups sugar
1 teaspoon vanilla essence
3 eggs
125g dark chocolate, broken into pieces
1 cup plain flour
½ teaspoon salt
1 cup chopped walnuts or pecans

Preheat the oven to 180°C. Line the base of a 32 x 23 cm tin with baking paper and grease the sides. Cream half the butter and beat in the sugar and vanilla. Beat in the eggs, one at a time. Melt remaining butter with the chocolate in a bowl placed over hot water, stirring. Cool, then stir into butter mixture. Sift the flour and salt into the chocolate mixture. Fold in half the nuts until combined. Spread the mixture into the tin, sprinkle with the remaining nuts. Bake for 45 minutes, or until a skewer inserted comes out clean. Remove from the oven and cool in the tin. Cut into squares to serve. *Makes about 48.*

ALMOND BUTTER BALLS ••

250 g butter
3 tablespoons caster sugar
1 teaspoon vanilla essence
2 cups plain flour
½ teaspoon salt
¾ cup chopped, blanched almonds
1 cup icing sugar

Preheat the oven to 180°C. Cream the butter with the sugar and vanilla. Sift the flour and salt and blend into the creamed mixture with the almonds to form a dough. Shape into balls the size of walnuts, or mould into crescent shapes. Bake on baking trays for about 15 minutes. Remove from the trays and roll in the icing sugar. Cool on a rack and roll again in the icing sugar. *Makes about 24.*

REFRIGERATOR BISCUITS •

This biscuit dough will keep, if wrapped in foil or plastic, in the refrigerator for up to 2 weeks, and in the freezer for months. Slice off the dough as you require it and you will have freshly baked biscuits at a moment's notice.

185 g butter
1 cup brown sugar
1 egg
1 teaspoon vanilla essence
2½ cups plain flour
¼ teaspoon salt
½ teaspoon baking powder

Cream the butter, gradually add the brown sugar and cream well. Add the egg and vanilla, and beat well. Sift the flour with the salt and baking powder. Stir into the creamed mixture. Use the dough as it is or in any of the variations below. Shape into long rolls, about 4 cm in diameter. Wrap in cling wrap then foil and chill until firm. Preheat the oven to 180°C. As needed, slice the dough thinly and put on a baking tray. Bake for 7–10 minutes. Makes 6 dozen.

variations:
Use one-third dough for each variation.
orange: Add 3 teaspoons grated orange rind to the dough then top biscuits with strips of candied orange peel.

chocolate and nut: Add 30 g melted, dark chocolate and 2 tablespoons chopped nuts. Top each with a piece of walnut.

lemon and coconut: Add 1 teaspoon grated lemon rind and 1 tablespoon desiccated coconut.

almond: Add ½ teaspoon almond essence and top each biscuit with an almond before baking.

COCONUT RASPBERRY SLICE

1½ cups plain flour
90 g chilled butter, diced
2 tablespoons sugar
pinch each of salt and baking powder
1 egg yolk
1 teaspoon vanilla essence
1–2 tablespoons water
squeeze of lemon juice
½ cup raspberry jam
60g softened butter
¼ cup sugar
1 egg
¼ cup S.R. flour
1½ cups desiccated coconut

Preheat the oven to 190°C. Place the plain flour, chilled butter, sugar, salt and baking powder in a food processor and process, turning processor rapidly on and off, until butter the mixture resembles coarse breadcrumbs. Mix the egg, vanilla, water and lemon juice together and, with the motor running, pour quickly through the feed tube. Process until a ball of dough forms round the blade. Spread the dough evenly in the base of a 33 x 23 cm Swiss roll tin, lined with baking paper. If necessary, smooth out with the back of a spoon or hand, having first covered the dough with a sheet of cling wrap. Spread evenly with jam.

Cream the softened butter and sugar until light and fluffy. Add the egg and beat well. Fold in the S.R. flour and the coconut. Spread evenly over the jam. Bake for 10 minutes, reduce heat to 180°C and bake for a further 10–15 minutes, or until golden. Remove from tin and set aside for 10 minutes before cutting into squares and leaving to cool on a wire rack. Makes about 20.

MERINGUES ••

The secret to making crisp, light meringues is the timing. You must work quickly once the sugar is added or the meringue will wilt. Avoid damp, humid weather. Most importantly, don't make them while doing other cooking. The moisture in the air will make the meringues weep. The minute they are cooled they should be packed airtight.

Clean utensils are also essential. Fats, oils and grease, even the slightest bit of egg yolk, will reduce the volume of the meringue. Also, have the egg whites at room temperature – this maximises the air they will absorb when beaten.

3 large egg whites
scant 1/8 teaspoon cream of tartar
1 cup caster sugar
1 cup cream

Preheat the oven to 120°C. Use baking paper to line the trays. Beat the egg whites, slowly at first, until frothy. Add the cream of tartar and now beat quickly by hand, or on highest speed of mixer, until the peaks hold their shape. Gradually add 4 tablespoons of the sugar and continue beating for 2–3 minutes. Add all the remaining sugar and fold in lightly and quickly using a large metal spoon.

Pipe on to prepared trays or shape with two spoons. Leave a space of at least 2 cm between each meringue. Bake until crisp, about 1½ hours, then remove from oven. Turn meringues over, then make a hollow indentation in the base of each, by pressing gently with your finger, so that they can hold a little whipped cream and the two halves will not slip when sandwiched together. Return to the oven for about 30 minutes, or until completely dry and a delicate beige in colour. Remove and cool. Whip the cream until thick, and sweeten and flavour if liked. Sandwich the meringues with the whipped cream, or serve the cream separately. Makes about 48 (24 pairs).

MERINGUE FINGERS ••

Put the meringue mixture into a piping bag with a plain nozzle, pipe small finger-lengths on to the prepared baking trays. Bake until crisp and dry, then cool on wire racks for a few minutes. Store airtight until required.

To chocolate-coat one end, have ready a small bowl with a little chocolate first melted gently over hot water, and a saucer of finely chopped nuts. Dip either one or both ends of the cooked meringue fingers into the chocolate, and then sprinkle lightly with the nuts. Return to the rack to set the chocolate.

BRANDY SNAPS ••

60 g butter
1/3 cup caster sugar or brown sugar
1/3 cup golden syrup
1/2 cup plain flour
1 teaspoon ground ginger
grated rind of 1/2 lemon
whipped cream, for filling

Preheat the oven to 180°C. Put the butter, sugar and syrup into a saucepan and heat gently until melted. Remove from the heat, cool to lukewarm, and then stir in the sifted flour and ginger, and the rind.

Grease the baking trays and drop the mixture onto them in teaspoons, leaving 10 cm between each for spreading. Bake for about 10 minutes or until golden brown. Remove from the oven and allow to stand for a few moments to set slightly. Ease from the tray with a broad-bladed knife or spatula and wrap lightly around the greased handle of a wooden spoon. When rolling, keep the smooth side of the wafer to the handle. When set, slip off onto a wire rack to finish cooling. Pipe the whipped cream into either end of the wafers before serving. The brandy snaps may be stored in an airtight container for a few days without the cream. Makes about 20.

SAVOURY BISCUITS

WATER BISCUITS •

1 cup plain flour
½ teaspoon baking powder
½ teaspoon salt
30 g butter
¼–⅓ cup water

Sift the flour, baking powder and salt into a bowl. With your fingers, rub butter into the flour, until evenly distributed. Stir in enough water to make a firm dough. Roll out on a lightly floured board to about 3 mm thickness. Cut with a floured 4 cm biscuit cutter into small rounds. With a rolling pin, roll each round into a very thin round or oval and prick with a fork. Bake on a baking tray in a hot oven 200°C until they are puffed and golden. Makes about 40.

ROSEMARY AND CHEESE BISCUITS ••

Crisp, delicate and savoury, these are perfect to enjoy with drinks. Keep a roll of unbaked dough on hand in the freezer and slice and bake when needed.

90 g cheddar cheese, finely grated
125 g butter
1½ cups plain flour
¼ teaspoon cayenne or ½ teaspoon paprika
¼ teaspoon ground pepper
1 teaspoon salt
1 teaspoon fresh rosemary leaves
2 tablespoons grated Parmesan cheese

Cream the cheddar cheese and butter until soft. Sift the flour, cayenne, pepper and salt together. Add to the creamed mixture and stir together with the rosemary and Parmesan cheese. Mix well and form into a roll, 4 cm in diameter. Wrap in cling wrap and refrigerate for 1 hour. Preheat the oven to 180°C.

Cut into thin discs and place on baking trays. Bake for 15–20 minutes, until golden. Cool on wire racks. Makes approximately 80–100 biscuits.

note: rosemary, the remembrance herb, is lovely in these savoury biscuits. Do not use it freshly picked, leave it 2–3 days to dry out a little or dry it on a paper towel in a microwave oven, set on high for 4–5 minutes, before crumbling. Store in a small jar.

OATCAKES •

1½ cups flour
½ teaspoon baking powder
½ teaspoon salt
125 g butter
1½ cups medium oatmeal
1 egg
2 tablespoons water

Preheat the oven to 180°C. Sift the flour, baking powder and salt into a bowl. Rub in the butter. Stir in the oatmeal, beaten egg and water. Mix and lightly knead to a stiff dough. Roll out thinly to about 3 mm onto a floured surface. Cut out 4–5cm diameter rounds.

Bake on greased baking trays for about 15–18 minutes, but remove before any colouring occurs. Cool on wire racks. Serve with cheese. Makes around 50.

note: a convenient substitute for the medium oatmeal is to grind 2½ cups rolled oats in a food processor for 30–60 seconds.

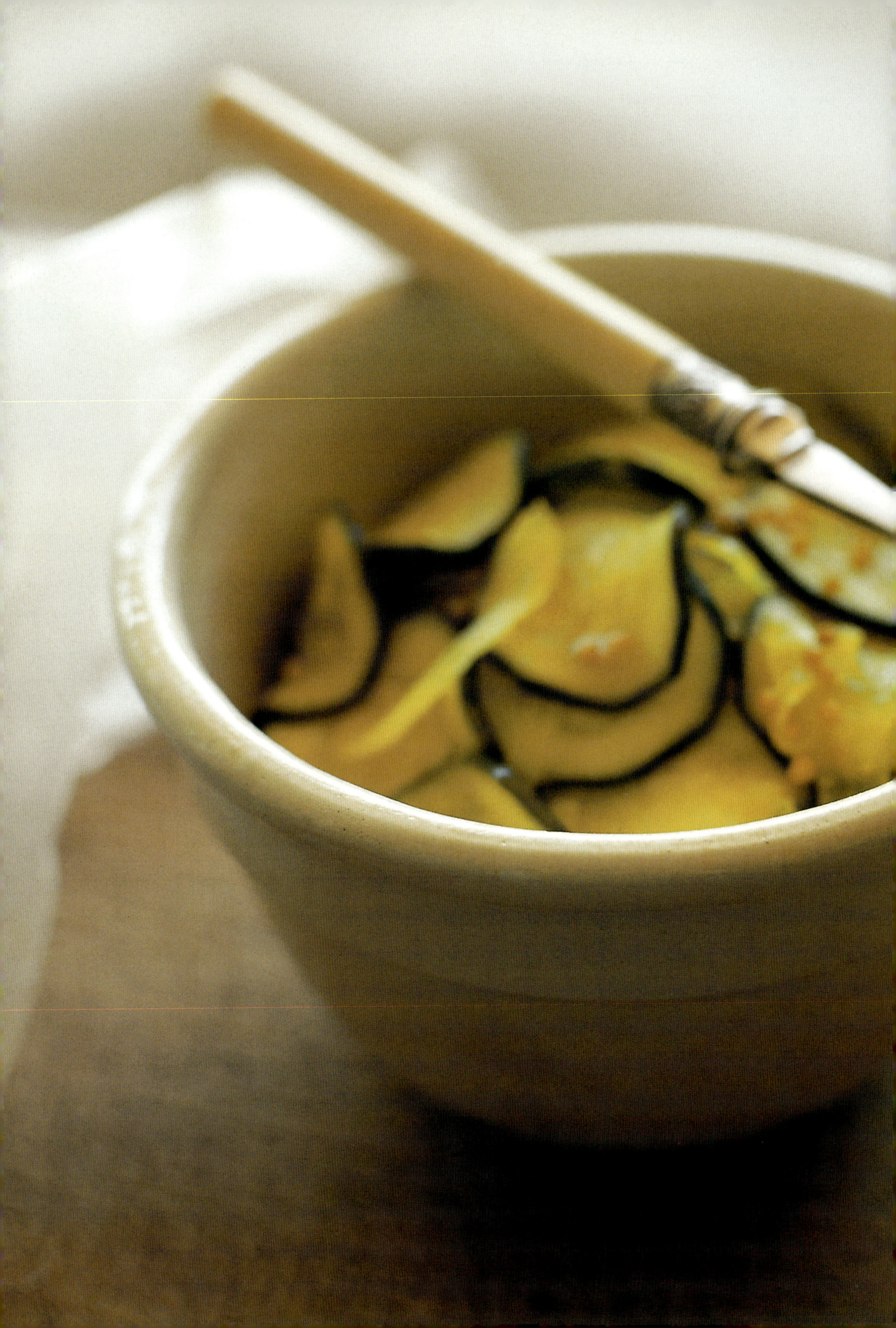

good things for the pantry

Putting down a few jars of a favourite preserve, chutney or jam when certain fruits and vegetables are at their peak can be most rewarding. A new generation of cooks is discovering that making their favourite jam or chutney is easy with a small purchase made from the local greengrocer. Today's homes don't usually boast a large pantry but even a few jars of homemade preserves are enough to add a delicious charm to meals.

BREAD AND BUTTER ZUCCHINI PICKLES

JAMS, CHUTNEYS AND PICKLES

Most of us love mum or grandma's fabulous pickles and chutneys that do so much for cold meats and sandwiches. Even a simple cheddar cheese sandwich takes on another dimension when generously smeared with chutney or pickle. Homemade pickles and chutneys add flavour and variety to all sorts of food. A spoonful of chutney easily enlivens a mayonnaise, dressing or sauce, just as it helps to transform a simple grilled chicken or lamb chop into a dish fit for a maharaja.

On the sweeter side, it is a simple matter to make a few pots of jam and marmalade to preserve the flavour of summer fruits for winter. Where would we be without marmalade for the breakfast toast or jam for our scones? And who could imagine a French apple tart without its glistening apricot jam glaze?

what you should know: No special equipment is needed but, because of the acid factor involved, be sure to use stoneware, pottery or glass bowls for brining. Pans used should be stainless steel, unchipped enamel or silverstone-lined aluminium. Use clean wooden spoons for stirring.

Store pickles and chutneys in clean glass jars, preferably with glass lids, or cover with a round of baking paper, pressing onto the chutney, before adding a metal screw-top lid. Always label and date the jars before storing in a cool, dark place. Leave for several months to allow them to mellow, but all should be used within a year, when it's time to start on a fresh lot.

When cooking a chutney recipe for the first time, it's a good idea to make only a small quantity to start with, for the sake of time and economy. When you are sure you like the result you can invest more in the recipe, making a larger amount. Remember that the flavour of chutneys and pickles needs to mellow for at least a few weeks before opening.

Always use vegetables and fruit in good condition. Spices are best used whole, as ground spices give a muddy look and old spices impart a dusty flavour. Tie spices in a muslin cloth for easy removal as they may cloud the pickle if left in.

Make a few jars of jams, chutneys or pickles as the vegetables and fruit come into season and are at their best and cheapest. You will quickly discover what a difference they make to meals.

PICKLES AND CHUTNEYS

These condiments are a welcome addition to boost the flavours of foods. Cold meats, cheese and toasted sandwiches all taste better with a little chutney or peck of pickle.

BEETROOT CHUTNEY ••

Good with ham, cold pickled pork or corned meats.

1 kg cooked beetroot
500 g onions
2 cups sugar
1 teaspoon allspice
5 black peppercorns
1 tablespoon salt
½ cup plain flour

spiced vinegar:
60–90 g mixed pickling spice
2½ cups vinegar

To cook the beetroot, cut off all but 5 cm of the tops. Simmer in unsalted water until tender. Drain and remove skins when cool enough to handle. Grate or finely chop the beetroot and onion. This can be done in a food processor, in several lots. Use an on and off motion as vegetables must only be finely chopped, not puréed. Combine the beetroot and onion with sugar, allspice, peppercorns, salt and enough spiced vinegar to cover, bring to the boil and gently cook about 25 minutes. Mix the flour to a smooth paste with cold water and add to the beetroot, stirring to thicken. Boil for approximately 5 minutes. When cool, ladle into hot sterilised jars and seal. Label and store in a cool dark place.

spiced vinegar: Boil the mixed pickling spice (a mixture of mustard seeds, allspice and peppercorns available from health food stores) with the vinegar for 5 minutes. Strain when cold. Makes about 6 x 250 g jars.

ROASTED TOMATO AND CHILLI RELISH ••

2 kg ripe tomatoes
1½ tablespoons olive oil
1 large onion, finely chopped
8–20 red chillies,
  seeded and finely chopped
1 red capsicum, finely chopped
2 cloves garlic, crushed
1 cup sugar
1 cup cider vinegar
2 tablespoons balsamic vinegar
salt and coarsely ground black pepper

Preheat the oven to 160°C. Wash the tomatoes and halve, lengthwise. Place cut-side up on baking trays. Drizzle with a little of the olive oil. Bake for 1 hour and 15 minutes. Heat the remaining oil in a large, heavy-based saucepan. Add the onion, chillies, capsicum and garlic. Cook over a moderate heat for 10 minutes, until softened.

Scoop the flesh from the tomato skins and add to the pan, discarding the skins. Stir briskly to break up the flesh. Add sugar and stir to dissolve over a moderate heat. Pour in the vinegars and add the salt and pepper, to taste. Bring to the boil and simmer over a low heat for 1–1½ hours, or until thick and pulpy. Spoon into hot sterilised jars and tap the jars on a hard surface to remove any air bubbles. Wipe the rims with a dampened cloth and seal. Makes about 8 x 250 g jars.

MANGO CHUTNEY ••

This is a great way of making the most of mangoes when they are plentiful. A delectable chutney to enhance cold meats, chicken and lamb curries.

**6 large under-ripe mangoes
  or 3 mangoes and 4 Granny Smith apples
  (peeled and chopped)**
2 cups malt vinegar
1 cup sugar
1 cup firmly packed brown sugar
1 cup finely chopped onion
4 cloves garlic
½ teaspoon cracked pepper
1 teaspoon salt
2 tablespoons grated fresh ginger
1 teaspoon chilli powder
1½ teaspoons ground cinnamon
¼ teaspoon ground cloves
1 teaspoon ground allspice
1 teaspoon mustard seeds
½ cup sultanas and currants

Peel the mangoes and cut into thin strips. Place in a large ceramic or glass bowl with the remaining ingredients. Cover and place in the refrigerator for several hours, or overnight.

The next day, turn the mixture into a large saucepan. Bring slowly to the boil and simmer gently, stirring occasionally, for 30 minutes or until the chutney is thick and syrupy. Spoon into hot sterilised jars and tap the jars on a hard surface to remove any air bubbles. Wipe the rims with a dampened cloth and seal. *Makes about 8 x 250 g jars.*

PEACH AND SAFFRON CHUTNEY ••

Star anise is a star or flower-shaped spice available from Asian grocery stores. This is a fresh-tasting chutney that adds interest to grilled and barbecued meats, and is good, too, with cold meats.

3 firm large yellow peaches
a pinch of saffron threads
¼ cup white wine
2 tablespoons sugar
2 tablespoons white wine vinegar
1 tablespoon Chinese plum sauce
1 bird's eye red chilli
1 piece star anise
1 stick cinnamon
3 tablespoons raisins

Pour boiling water over the peaches in a bowl. Leave them to stand for 3 minutes, then drain and sit in a bowl of iced water. Skin the peaches, halve and remove the stones. Cut into dice. In a bowl, mix the saffron, wine, sugar, vinegar, plum sauce, chilli, star anise and cinnamon. Put the saffron mixture in a saucepan and bring slowly to the boil.

Cook until the liquid has reduced a little, then add the peaches and raisins and cook gently, stirring occasionally. The chutney is ready when the peaches are soft. Spoon into hot sterilised jars and tap the jars on a hard surface to remove any air bubbles. Wipe the rims with a dampened cloth and seal. This one is best kept in the refrigerator. *Makes about 6 x 250 g jars.*

SPICED PRUNES •

Serve with pork, cold meats and terrines.

500 g dessert prunes, pitted
1½ cups cold tea
1½ cups sugar
2 cups white vinegar
4 whole cloves
8 cm cinnamon stick

Soak the prunes with tea to cover, overnight. Add the sugar, vinegar and spices, tied in muslin, to a heavy-based saucepan. Bring to the boil and boil for 15 minutes. Remove from the heat and discard the spices. Pour the prunes and tea into a saucepan and simmer for about 15 minutes, until soft. Drain, reserving 1 cup tea. Pack the prunes into hot sterilised jars. Add the tea to the vinegar mixture and pour over the prunes. Seal and store in a cool, dark place. Leave for 24 hours before using. Makes 5 x 250 g jars.

PRESERVED LEMONS ••

Add chopped or sliced to couscous, rice salads, soups, stews, sauces and to some salads. If you would like an Indian-style pickled lemon to serve with curries, use curry leaves and peanut oil instead of bay leaves and olive oil. A red chilli may be added for a hot pickle.

12 lemons, unpeeled
3 tablespoons rock salt
1 tablespoon paprika
3 bay leaves
12 peppercorns
½ cup olive oil

Boil the lemons for about 20 minutes in water to cover, drain. Cut each into 6 wedges and layer in a large jar with the salt, paprika, bay leaves and peppercorns. Pour in the olive oil, which should cover the lemons. Cover the jar and seal. The lemons will be ready in several weeks. Once opened, store in the refrigerator.

RED CHILLI JAM ••

Just a little of this chilli jam is fantastic and will liven up grilled meats, chicken and rice dishes as well as giving sandwiches a little pep. Tamarind is the acid fruit of a large tropical tree. You can buy tamarind juice already processed or buy the flesh and seeds in packets or plastic containers and make the juice yourself.

1.5 kg red bird's eye chillies
8 brown onions, peeled and quartered
15 cloves garlic
4 cups vegetable oil
½ cup instant tamarind, soaked in
**   1½ cups water**
125 g palm sugar, shaved or coarsely grated

In the bowl of a food processor, add the chillies, onions and garlic and process to a fine paste, adding the oil in a slow stream. In a large, heavy-based saucepan, add the chilli mixture and simmer over a low heat, until the paste changes colour to a dark red. Add the tamarind juice and palm sugar to the chilli paste and cook for 2 hours over a gentle heat. Spoon the jam into sterilised jars, cover with oil, seal and refrigerate.

to make tamarind juice using tamarind pulp: Soak a large piece of tamarind the size of a walnut in 1½ cups hot water for 5–10 minutes or until soft, then squeeze it until it mixes with the water. Strain out the seeds and fibres and use the water.

for less fire: Halve the chillies and discard the seeds. Makes about 8 x 250 g jars.

COUNTRY TOMATO RELISH ••
Home-made tomato relish is lovely with cold meats, grilled chops, cheese or in sandwiches.

1.5 kg ripe tomatoes, peeled and chopped
500 g onions, chopped
2 cups sugar
2½ cups malt vinegar
1 tablespoon plain flour
1 tablespoon curry powder
a pinch of cayenne pepper
1 tablespoon dry mustard
1 tablespoon salt

Prepare the tomatoes and place in a colander over a bowl. Drain, pressing lightly, and reserve the juice in the bowl. Put the tomatoes, onions, sugar and vinegar into a saucepan and simmer, uncovered, until the mixture is thick. Measure the tomato juice and add water to make ¾ cup. Combine the remaining ingredients with the reserved tomato juice and add to the mixture in the saucepan. Stir until boiling and then simmer for 5 minutes. Spoon into hot sterilised jars and tap the jars on a hard surface to remove any air bubbles. Wipe the rims with a dampened cloth before sealing the jars.
Makes about 8 x 250 g jars.

BREAD AND BUTTER ZUCCHINI PICKLES ••
Good with cold meats, in sandwiches, or served at the side of a salad meal.

500 g small zucchini
2 cups white vinegar
1 tablespoon sugar
1½ teaspoons salt
1½ teaspoons black peppercorns
2 tablespoons cold water
125 g small pickling onions

Slice the zucchini thinly. Put the vinegar, sugar, salt, peppercorns and water into a saucepan, bring to the boil and simmer for 5 minutes. Add the zucchini and onions and return to simmering point, stirring. Pack the vegetables into hot sterilised jars and cover with the vinegar. Seal and store for several months in the refrigerator.
Makes about 6 x 250 g jars.

RASPBERRY VINEGAR ••
An antidote for sore throats from Victorian times, it is delicious added to dressings and sauces. Refreshing also as a cordial topped up with chilled mineral water.

500 g fresh raspberries (frozen raspberries can also be used)
2 cups white wine or red wine vinegar
2 cups sugar

Crush the raspberries and tip into a ceramic or glass bowl. Pour the vinegar over and leave overnight. Next day, strain into a heatproof jar and add the sugar. Stand the jar in a saucepan and add water until it reaches halfway up the sides. Simmer over a very gentle heat for an hour and then strain into hot sterilised jars. This vinegar is ready to use immediately and it will become even more lovely and mellow as the months go by.
Makes 4 cups.

RASPBERRY VINEGAR

JAMS AND MARMALADES

Making jams and marmalades requires the same care as pickles, chutneys and other preserves. It is the good fruit that gives each product its special flavour. Full-flavoured, just-ripe fruits are preferred because their flavour is diluted by the large proportion of sugar that is added for good consistency and keeping quality. Over-ripe fruit often lacks the necessary pectin which helps set the jam. This pectin, which is found naturally in most fruits, combines with sugar and natural acid to produce a gel. The perfect jam needs a balance of ripe (for flavour) and under-ripe (for pectin) fruit.

For the time poor, this chapter includes recipes for making scrumptious jam the traditional way, using a heavy-based saucepan on the stove, or the easy way for smaller quantities, using the microwave.

to test for setting:

One of the most essential skills in jam making is knowing when it has reached setting point. The safest test is to simply put a small spoonful of jam on a saucer. Wait 20 seconds, then run a finger through it – if it crinkles at the edges and stays in two separate portions, the jam is ready.

SATSUMA PLUM JAM ••

Satsuma plums make a rich, tart jam which is particularly appealing. They should be barely ripe and in good condition. The addition of the kernels at the end gives the jam a slightly bitter almond flavour that many appreciate.

about 4 kg barely-ripe satsuma plums
500 g sugar to every 500 g of fruit

Wash the fruit and wipe it dry. With a stainless steel knife, split the plums and twist them to break in half. Remove the stones, cracking a few and removing the kernels. Put the kernels aside and tie the remaining stones in a piece of muslin.

Weigh the fruit and measure out the same weight in sugar. Layer the fruit and half the sugar in a large bowl and leave overnight. The next day, put the fruit and sugar into a large, heavy-based saucepan, place on a gentle heat, and bring slowly to the boil, stirring all the time until the sugar has dissolved. Add the muslin bag containing the plum stones and simmer until the plums are tender. Stir in the remaining sugar, which has been warmed, and boil quickly for 20–30 minutes, stirring a few times during the last 15 minutes to prevent scorching. When the jam is on the point of setting (see opposite), skim the surface, remove the muslin bag and add the reserved kernels. Remove from the heat and allow to cool. Fill hot sterilised jars with the slightly cooled jam, seal tightly and label. Store in a dark, cool place. Makes about 8 x 250 g jars.

APRICOT JAM ••

Make as for satsuma plum jam, substituting a mixture of fresh ripe and a few under-ripe apricots for the plums.

BERRY JAM ••

Make as for satsuma plum jam, using berries instead of the plums. Frozen raspberries or mixed berries, which are available in the freezer section of most supermarkets, make an economical choice for jam making.
In place of the kernels, add 3 tablespoons lemon juice for every 500 g of berries to the fruit and sugar.

APRICOT JAM

THREE-FRUIT MARMALADE ••
This well-known English marmalade is so good with morning toast.

2 lemons
1 orange
1 grapefruit
about 1.5 kg sugar

Wash and dry the fruit. Halve the lemons and oranges, and slice thinly. Place the seeds and cores into a muslin bag. Peel the rind, not the pith, from the grapefruit, shred, and add to other fruit. Cut the pith from the grapefruit, cut into small pieces and add to the pips in the muslin bag. Thinly slice the grapefruit flesh and place with the other fruit in a bowl, adding water to cover. Add the muslin bag, put a plate on top to keep the fruit down in the water and leave overnight.

Next day, turn the fruit into a large, heavy-based saucepan and cook gently until the fruit is soft and half the liquid has evaporated, for about 1½ hours. Remove the muslin bag, draining out as much liquid as possible. Measure the pulp. Warm the sugar and for each cup of pulp, add 1 cup sugar. Stir until the sugar has dissolved. Boil rapidly for 20–25 minutes, or until the setting point is reached *(see p. 252)*.

Remove the pan from the heat and cool for about 5 minutes, stir to distribute the fruit evenly. Ladle into hot sterilised jars and seal. Label and store in a dark cool place.
Makes about 8 x 250 g jars.

RHUBARB AND ORANGE JAM ••
(MADE IN THE MICROWAVE)

750 g rhubarb, trimmed and washed
grated rind and juice of 1 orange
500 g sugar

Wash the rhubarb, trim and slice finely. Place in a large 2.5 litre microwave-proof bowl with the rind and juice, cover with microwave cling wrap and cook in the microwave for 10 minutes on high, until very soft. Remove the cling wrap. Add the sugar, stir the fruit and continue to cook on high for 10–15 minutes until a little gels when tested on a cold saucer. If any liquid bubbles out of the dish, simply scrape off the base of the turntable at the end of the cooking. Cool slightly, ladle into hot sterilised jars and seal. Label and store in a cool dark place.
Makes about 4 x 250 g jars.

QUICK STRAWBERRY JAM ••
This jam is cooked in the microwave, which is a practical method when making small quantities. Raspberries can be used instead of strawberries.

2 punnets strawberries
3 tablespoons lemon juice
1½ cups sugar

Wash and hull the strawberries. Place in a large microwave-proof bowl with the juice. Cook on high for 3 minutes. Add the sugar, stir well and cook a further 20 minutes on high, until a little gels when tested on a cold saucer. After 5 minutes or so, give a stir, ensuring that the sugar is fully dissolved. Ladle into hot sterilised jars and seal. Label and store in a cool dark place. Will keep for 3–4 weeks or longer in the refrigerator.
Makes about 4 x 250 g jars.

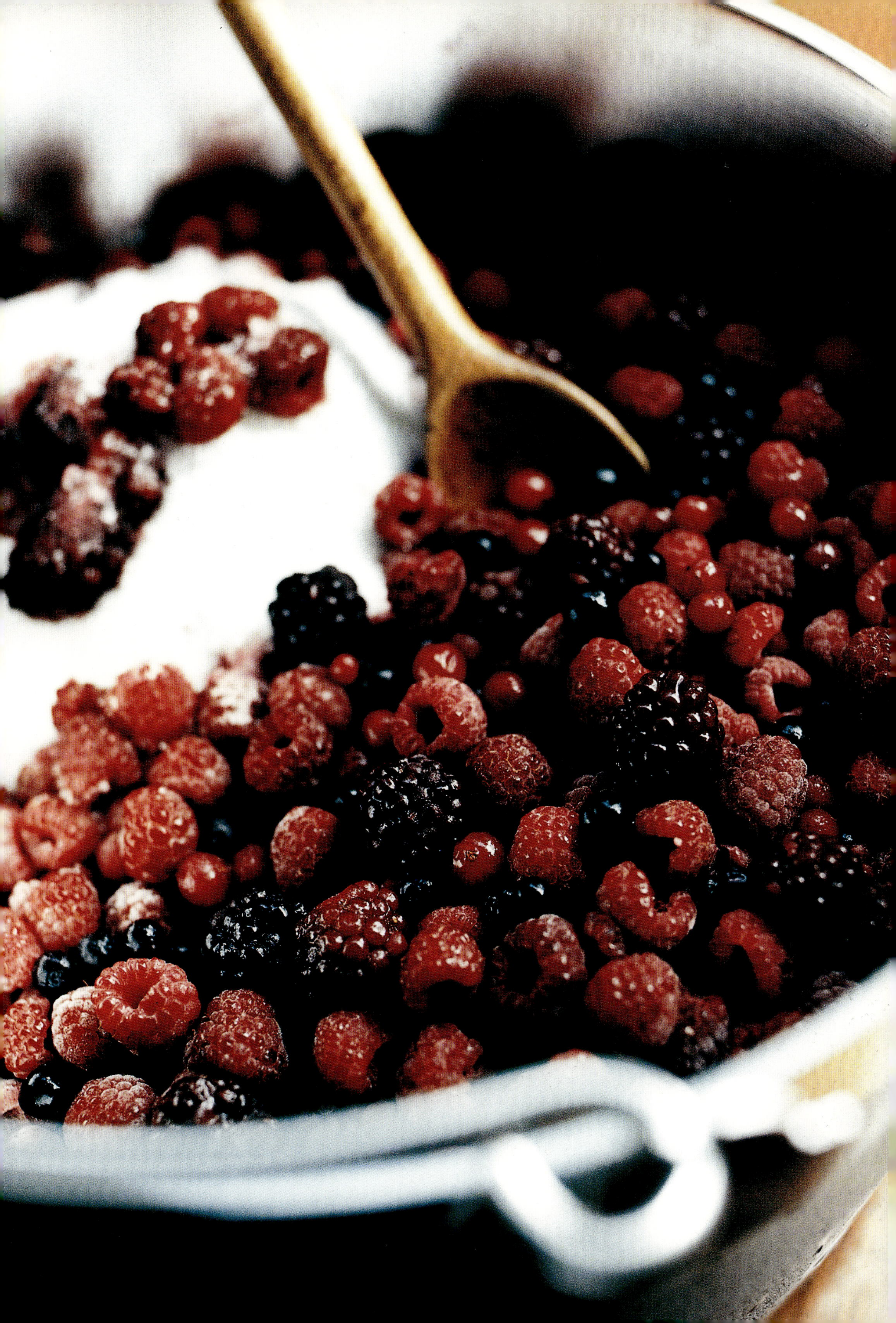

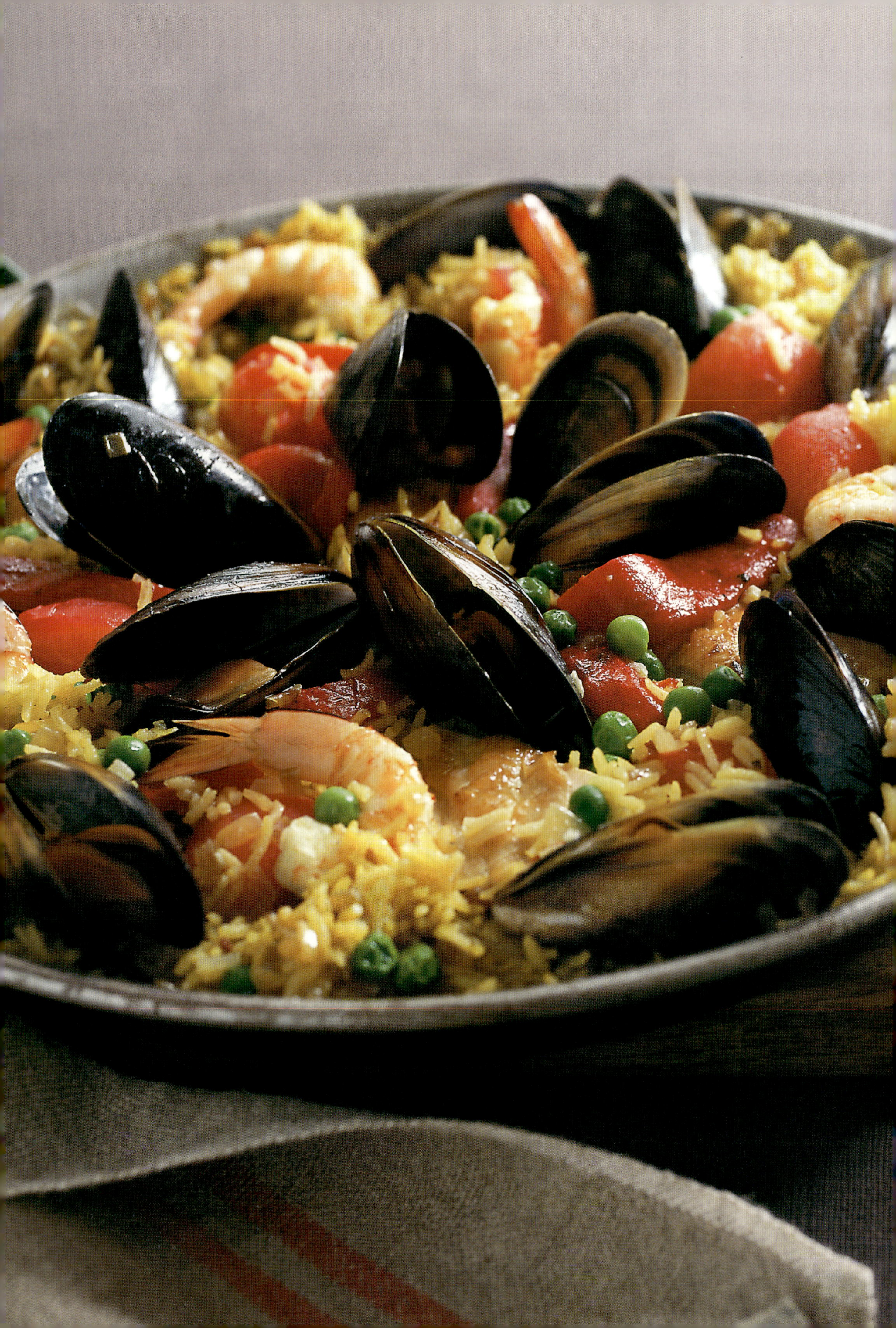

great dishes from my travels

I fell under the spell of travel many years ago — seeing new places, meeting new people and learning of their traditions. My eyes were opened by fascinating tastes, flavours, spices and different cooking techniques. Through my travels I have been privileged to learn what makes each culture unique and this knowledge has become an integral part of my work. It has given me enormous joy to share my understanding of these cultures with my readers over the years through a language we all understand — food and cooking.

PAELLA VALENCIANA

MASTERING CHINESE COOKING

If you are able to shop in a big city, you will find each one has a Chinese quarter where the more unusual ingredients can be bought. In many country towns, a good supermarket will at least have tinned or dried Chinese ingredients. If fresh Chinese vegetables are not available, use local vegetables instead.

Chinese meals are usually planned around several dishes, so these recipes are not designed to feed specific numbers. But, if you remember that two or three dishes and rice are sufficient for four people, your catering will be easy. I believe Chinese food tastes better if eaten from Chinese dishes and bowls. Include tiny dishes for condiments such as soy sauce, chilli sauce, salt and five-spice powder, some china spoons and, of course, chopsticks. Fragrant Chinese green tea is the ideal accompaniment to Chinese food.

CHINESE INGREDIENTS

bamboo shoots: Fresh bamboo shoots are available fresh from Asian grocers. Also, they are readily available in cans. Drain before using.

bean sprouts: The sprouts of mung beans, available fresh. The tails are best removed before cooking. In fine Chinese cooking, the heads are also removed.

black beans: Small soybeans, fermented. If very strong, rinse in water several times. Black bean sauce is often served with crab, lobster, fish, beef or spare ribs.

chilli sauce: A very hot sauce, used mainly for dipping.

chinese pickles: A mixture of ginger, capsicum, leeks and melons. Use shredded in sweet and sour sauce.

chinese rice wine: Also called shao-hsing, this rice wine is used in many recipes. Dry sherry can substitute.

cabbage: There are various types available. They are sliced into lengths, using all stems and a little green leaf. Wash and drain well before using.

shiitake mushrooms: Available fresh and dried. They are dark in colour on top and light underneath. Soak dried mushrooms for 20 minutes in hot water before using. Discard stem.

five-spice powder: Excellent for flavouring duck, chicken or pork.
Mixed with salt, it is served in a bowl for dipping pieces of crisp-skin duck or chicken.

ginger: Use fresh green ginger to flavour food (mainly seafoods) and also to season oil for cooking many dishes.

noodles: There are various types of noodles. They are sometimes boiled, or they may be par-boiled, then finished off in oil. Look for the many types available in supermarkets.

The wok is best for Chinese cookery. It has a rounded base and is used for deep-frying, sautéing and braising.

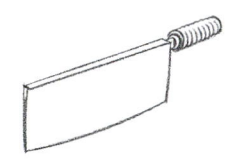

A Chinese cleaver or chopper, made of steel is good for all cutting, chopping poultry into sections and mincing.

Chinese-type ladles with long handles, are useful. The flat type is used to constantly turn all the ingredients in the wok.

peanut oil: Peanut oil is chosen for Chinese cooking because it has a very mild flavour. Substitute with a salad oil if liked but avoid using strong-flavoured olive oil for Chinese dishes. When heating for frying, season with a bruised garlic clove and slice of fresh ginger. Remove these before adding ingredients to be cooked.

sesame oil: A very concentrated refined oil that must be used sparingly. A little is sometimes added to peanut oil for added flavour when frying.

shrimps, dried: Use to flavour dishes like soups and meat dishes.

soy sauce: Most important for Chinese cookery. There are many different grades, some light and some dark.

water chestnuts: Mostly bought in cans, they provide a crisp texture in dishes. Fresh water chestnuts are available from some Asian grocers.

COOKING UTENSILS

The wok, or Chinese cooking pan, is best for Chinese cookery. It has a rounded base and a handle on each side although some do have one long handle. This essential utensil is used for deep-frying, steaming, sautéing and braising.

Knives and choppers are heavy, thick and always of steel. Chinese-type ladles, with long handles, are useful. The flat type is used for many dishes, to turn all the ingredients in the wok. Another ladle has a scoop to hold the liquids for basting. Strainers are a necessary item when deep-frying.

Chinese food is eaten with chopsticks, and they are also used as cooking implements. When using chopsticks for cooking, be sure to use long wooden ones which can tolerate the heat.

A set of rice bowls and inexpensive Chinese plates will add to the enjoyment of eating Chinese food.

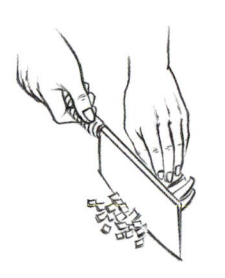

COOKING TECHNIQUES

The main methods of cooking in the Chinese manner are stir-frying, deep-frying, braising, steaming, roasting or barbecuing.

stir-frying: This is the most widely used method in Chinese cookery. The food is cooked in a small amount of oil in a wok or frying pan, and stirred continuously as the food fries.

deep-frying: Cooking with or without batter, in plenty of hot oil.

braising: Brown ingredients in a small amount of oil, add broth or water, cover tightly, and cook slowly over a gentle heat, until food is tender.

steaming: Arrange food to be steamed such as fish or chicken on a heatproof plate and cook, covered, over a saucepan of boiling water for 15 minutes to 1 hour, depending on the dish.

barbecuing and roasting: When this method is used, the food is usually cooked over charcoal, or hung from hooks in the oven. Barbecued pork and duck are cooked in this manner.

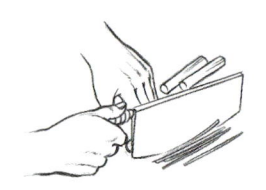

CUTTING METHODS

Ingredients for Chinese cooking are cut into sizes and shapes convenient for picking up with chopsticks. If the food is served whole, such as sweet and sour fish or steamed duck, it is so tender that it can be easily broken off with chopsticks.

Each dish consists of at least two or more ingredients, which are always cut into uniform sizes and shapes. Preparation of ingredients involves more work than the actual cooking. The seasonings and sauces can be mixed together, meat and vegetables cut in readiness.

terms explained:

mince: Chop very finely, then crush with chopper.
wedge: Cut into triangular-shaped sections.
cube: Cut as for dice into 2 cm squares.
dice: Cut into strips, stack, then cut the stack across into 0.5–1 cm cubes.
chop: Cut into very small pieces with chopper or knife.
section: Cut into 1 cm lengths, cutting diagonally. To cut an onion into sections, halve lengthwise, the cut each half into quarters and separate into sections.
shred: Cut into 5 cm lengths, then shred into fine strips. To shred meat, cut into thin slices, then cut each slice into shreds.

The best way to dice vegetables is to first cut into strips, stack, then cut the stack across into 0.5–1 cm cubes.

To shred vegetables such as spring onions, cut into 5 cm lengths, then shred lengthwise into fine strips.

RICE AND NOODLES
how to steam rice, Chinese-style

Rice is the staple food of southern China, and is eaten as westerners eat bread and potatoes. Wheat and other grains are preferred in the north of China in the form of noodles.

Wash 2 cups rice in cold water several times, until water runs clear. Put the rice in a heavy-based saucepan and add cold water to come approximately 2 cm above the level of the rice. Bring to the boil, half-cover the pan, then lower the heat to medium and continue cooking, until the water has almost evaporated and holes form in the rice mass. Reduce the heat to the lowest point, cover with a tight-fitting lid and steam for 15–20 minutes, until the rice is tender. Do not stir during cooking.

HOW TO COOK NOODLES

Noodles should be cooked in boiling, salted water until just tender, then drained. They can be served in a soup, soft-fried or crisp-fried, as for chow mein.

Drop the noodle bundles into boiling, salted water and, when they begin to soften, separate with chopstick or fork. Do not crowd. Drain well, rinse under running water and distribute the noodles as thinly as possible on a damp (not wet) cloth, and place in a cool, airy place to dry for several hours. Prevent the noodles from sticking by tossing lightly with about 1 tablespoon peanut oil.

For crisp-fried noodles, heat 1–2 cups peanut oil in a wok or frying pan. Fry handfuls of cooked noodles separately, turning once to crisp and brown on both sides. Use as a garnish for chow mien. Rice vermicelli and cellophane noodles may be deep-fried in hot oil straight from the packet.

For soft-fried noodles, heat only 2 tablespoons peanut oil and lightly fry handfuls of noodles until just turning brown, but not crisp. Serve with braised meat, seafood or vegetable dishes.

note: the variety of instant noodles available in most supermarkets makes the preparation of noodle dishes much simpler. Just follow the directions on the packet.

COMBINATION FRIED RICE •

6 dried shiitake mushrooms
125 g cooked chicken
125 g barbecued pork or ham
6 tablespoons oil
a pinch of salt
3 eggs, beaten
1 cup chopped spring onions
125 g small prawns, peeled
6 cups cold, cooked rice
½ cup cooked peas
1 tablespoon Chinese rice wine (shao-hsing)
¼ cup stock
1 tablespoon light soy sauce,
or more to taste

Soak the mushrooms in hot water, to cover, for 20 minutes. Drain and cut into dice, set aside. Cut the chicken and pork into dice. Heat 2 tablespoons oil, add a pinch of salt to the eggs and fry like a large omelette, without folding. Roll up the omelette into a cigar-shape, and then cut across into thin slices. Set aside.

Heat the remaining oil and fry the spring onions, mushrooms, chicken, pork and prawns. Add the rice and toss well to mix. Add omelette and the peas. Mix wine, stock and soy sauce and sprinkle over rice. Stir-fry for another minute, until heated through.
Serves 6.

SOUPS

Soup is always part of a Chinese meal. Most soups are clear with floating pieces of cooked meat and vegetables. Thicker soups, which can form a complete meal, are also very popular. A good stock is the base of any well-flavoured soup.

EGG FLOWER SOUP •

Bring 5 cups stock to the boil. Add 1 cup peas, ½ cup quartered, canned straw mushrooms and ½ cup diced, cooked chicken. Beat 2 eggs well. Add to the soup, stirring constantly to cook the eggs into fine shreds. Season with salt, to taste. *Serves 4.*

HOT AND SOUR SOUP •

This simple soup is inexpensive, restorative, healthy, light and also delicious. Also it can be varied. You can use slivers of asparagus spears, when in season.

300 g block bean curd (silken tofu)
4 cups chicken stock
200 g baby English spinach leaves
1 tomato, peeled and diced
1 tablespoon light soy sauce
1 tablespoon cornflour
1 tablespoon water
1 egg, beaten
2 teaspoons vinegar
freshly ground pepper
1 teaspoon sesame oil
2 spring onions, finely shredded

Cut the bean curd into 1.5 cm cubes. In a large saucepan, bring the stock to the boil, add the spinach, bean curd, tomato and soy. Mix the cornflour with the water and stir into the soup. Bring to the boil and slowly stir in the beaten egg, to form fine threads (like egg flower soup). Reheat gently and stir in the vinegar and plenty of black pepper. Finally, stir in the sesame oil and spring onions. Ladle into soup bowls. *Serves 4.*

BEEF AND PORK

Pork is more widely used in Chinese cooking than beef. Pork fillet, used for barbecued pork and sautéed dishes, is popular and cooks quickly. Tender cuts of beef are also ideal.

SHREDDED BEEF WITH CAPSICUM ••

The vegetables used here may be varied, the capsicum can be replaced with 1 cup of carrot strips, green beans, snow peas or bean sprouts.

500 g fillet steak, rump or porterhouse
3 tablespoons light soy sauce
2 tablespoons Chinese rice wine (shao-hsing)
2 cloves garlic, finely chopped
1 teaspoon grated fresh ginger
½ cup vegetable oil
2 onions, cut into eighths, lengthwise
2 red capsicum, seeded and finely shredded
½ red chilli, finely sliced

Trim the fat and sinew from beef and shred finely. Mix the beef with the soy, wine, garlic and ginger in a bowl, allowing about 30 minutes for the seasonings to be absorbed. Heat the oil in a wok or a large, heavy-based frying pan. When very hot, add the beef strips in several batches, and cook until changed colour. Remove and set aside.

Pour off most of the oil, leaving just a little. Reheat the wok and, when very hot, add the onions, capsicum and chilli, tossing and stirring until the vegetables soften, for about 2–3 minutes. Still over high heat, return the beef with the seasonings and continue frying beef 2 minutes longer, stirring and tossing all the while. Serve hot with steamed rice. *Serves 2–4.*

SANG CHOY BOW ••

This dish is fun to eat and delicious. Each person wraps the fried pork and crunchy water chestnut mixture in a lettuce cup to make a fat roll.

1 iceberg lettuce, washed and dried
1 pork fillet
1 tablespoon vegetable oil
6–8 water chestnuts, diced
4 spring onions, finely sliced
½ small red chilli, seeded and finely chopped
1 tablespoon chopped fresh coriander
2 teaspoons cornflour
2 teaspoons light soy sauce
1 teaspoon oyster sauce
1 tablespoon Chinese rice wine (shao-hsing)
1 teaspoon sesame oil

First prepare the lettuce leaves by trimming slightly with scissors to form cups. This can be done hours ahead with the lettuce kept in iced water to crispen. Cut the pork fillet into fine dice (larger than a mince). Heat the oil in a wok or a large, heavy-based frying pan, add the pork and cook over a high heat, stirring and tossing for a few minutes, until changed colour. Add the water chestnuts, spring onions, chilli and coriander, and continue to stir-fry for a further minute. Combine the cornflour, soy sauce, oyster sauce and wine and stir into the mixture. Stir-fry for 30 seconds longer, until a thickened sauce is formed, then stir in the sesame oil. Remove from the heat and turn into a serving bowl.

Arrange the lettuce cups in a large bowl and serve alongside the bowl of hot stir-fried pork mixture. Each person can spoon some of the mixture into each lettuce cup, wrap up the leaf and eat with their hands. *Serves 4.*

BARBECUED PORK •

The marinated pork fillets in this dish are cooked in a spicy red sauce which gives them a unique flavour. Hoisin sauce is available from Chinese food stores and supermarkets.

500 g pork fillet or lean pork
3 tablespoons hoisin sauce
2 teaspoons sugar
3–4 teaspoons light soy sauce
½ teaspoon salt
1 tablespoon five-spice powder
2 tablespoons honey
1 tablespoon Chinese rice wine (shao-hsing)
plum or extra hoisin sauce, for dipping

Preheat the oven to 220°C. Combine all the ingredients and brush over the pork. Allow to stand for at least 1 hour. Put on a rack in a baking dish filled with hot water to come below the rack. Roast for 25 minutes. Turn the meat over, brush with the remaining marinade and cook a further 10 minutes, or until a good caramel glaze has formed over the pork. Serve cut into thin slices with plum or hoisin sauce for dipping. *Serves 2–4.*

POULTRY

Whole chickens are sometimes simmered in soy sauce or deep-fried until crisp then served with salt mixed with five-spice powder. Chickens are cut with a cleaver into bite-size pieces with both flesh and bone. Duck is barbecued, roasted or braised until tender.

CHICKEN AND ALMONDS ••

2 whole chicken breasts,
   skinned and boned
salt
1 tablespoon cornflour
1 egg white
1 teaspoon sesame oil
1 tablespoon Chinese rice wine (shao-hsing)
about ½ cup vegetable oil
1 cup almonds
1 onion, diced
6 dried mushrooms, soaked in hot water
   for 20 minutes and diced
½ red or green capsicum,
   cut into 2 cm squares

sauce:

2 teaspoons light soy sauce
2 teaspoons cornflour
½ cup chicken stock
1 tablespoon Chinese rice wine (shao-hsing)

Cut chicken breasts into small cubes. Mix the chicken with the salt, cornflour, egg white, sesame oil and rice wine. Mix the sauce ingredients together in a small bowl. Heat a pan, add the vegetable oil, and fry the chicken, in several lots, until just coloured. Remove and drain on paper towels. Fry the almonds until golden and set aside. Pour off all but 2 tablespoons oil, sauté the onion, mushrooms and capsicum, until lightly coloured. Add the sauce ingredients and bring to the boil. Return the chicken and mix well. Add the almonds and serve. Serves 4.

CHICKEN CHOW MEIN ••

The technique of boiling and then frying a bed of noodles makes this a Cantonese dish. The outside of the noodles are crisped and lightly browned while the inside should be soft and tender.

250 g Chinese egg noodles
   (instant can be used)
4 tablespoons vegetable oil
1 chicken breast, skinned, boned
   and shredded
1 carrot, peeled and cut
   into thick matchsticks
1 stalk celery, cut into strips
3 spring onions, cut into short lengths
6–8 snow peas, cut into thick strips
2 tablespoons light soy sauce
2 tablespoons oyster sauce
2 tablespoon Chinese rice wine (shao-hsing)
½ teaspoon sugar
1 teaspoon sesame oil
2 teaspoons cornflour mixed with
   2 tablespoons water

Cook the noodles and dry *(see p. 261)* or use instant noodles. Place 2 tablespoons of the oil in a wok or frying pan and heat. Fry the noodles, tossing for 5 minutes, or until crisp and golden. Drain on paper towels.

Heat the remaining oil, add the chicken and stir-fry for a few minutes. Remove and keep warm. Add the vegetables and stir-fry for 1 minute. Return the chicken, and cook for 3 minutes. Then add the sauces, rice wine, sugar, sesame oil mixed together with the cornflour mixture, stirring, until the sauce is velvety and smooth. Arrange the noodles on a serving plate, top with the chicken and vegetables and serve immediately. Serves 4.

CANTONESE ROAST DUCK ••

1 x 2kg duck
2 tablespoons light soy sauce
1 tablespoon honey
½ teaspoon ground ginger
1 tablespoon Chinese rice wine (shao-hsing)
2 teaspoons yellow bean paste
3 cloves garlic, crushed
2 tablespoons chopped spring onion

Preheat the oven to 180°C. Wash the duck and drain well. Mix the soy sauce, honey, ginger, wine and bean paste well, and rub half on the outside of the duck. Place in a shallow bowl, cover with foil and leave in the refrigerator overnight, or at least 2 hours. Mix the garlic and the remaining soy sauce seasoning mixture. Pour this into the duck. Place the duck on a rack in a baking dish half-filled with water, making sure the water does not come over the rack. Cover with foil. Roast for 2 hours. Remove the foil for the last 30 minutes of roasting. Baste the duck with its own sauce several times, after removing foil. Cut into serving portions. Serve while hot. Serves 4.

SEAFOOD

The Chinese make use of a wide variety of seafood, which they cook in many ways, always keeping the flesh juicy and moist even when the outside is crisp and golden. Crisp-skin fish is an example of this technique, as are prawn cutlets. Delicate, braised seafood dishes are also among the most popular Chinese dishes.

PRAWN SICHUAN ••

500 g green (raw) prawns, shelled and deveined
1 teaspoon salt
2 eggs, lightly beaten
½ cup plain flour
oil, for deep-frying
2–3 fresh red chillies, seeded and finely chopped
2 tablespoons finely chopped fresh ginger
2 tablespoons finely chopped onion
2 cloves garlic, crushed
4 tablespoons tomato ketchup
2 tablespoons sugar
2 tablespoons vinegar
2 teaspoons Chinese rice wine (shao-hsing)

Sprinkle the prawns with the salt and set aside for 10 minutes. Mix the eggs with the flour, add the prawns, and stir well. Heat the oil in a large wok and when almost smoking, add the prawns, with their coating of batter in several lots. Fry for 1 minute, drain on crumpled paper towels. Pour off all but 2 tablespoons of the oil. Reheat the oil and add the chillies, ginger, onion and garlic. Stir-fry for 1 minute then add the ketchup, sugar, vinegar and rice wine. Add the prawns and stir for 1 minute. Serve with steamed rice. Serves 4.

CRISP-SKIN SWEET-SOUR FISH ••

1 whole fish about 1.25 kg, scaled and gutted
1 teaspoon salt
1 egg white
2 tablespoons cornflour
oil, for deep-frying
2 tablespoons sugar
½ cup white vinegar
1 jar melon shreds
  (available from Chinese grocers)
½ cup melon liquor (from jar)
  or pineapple juice
2 teaspoons cornflour,
  blended with a little water

Clean and wash the fish, dry thoroughly and rub the salt all over. Score the fish in a diamond pattern on each side. Brush with the egg white, then dust with the cornflour. Shake off excess. Heat the oil in a wok or deep frying pan and deep-fry the fish. Baste with oil, while holding head or tail end against side of pan, until golden brown and the thickest part of the fish is cooked through, turning only once. Remove, drain on paper towels and lift onto a platter. Put the sugar, vinegar, melon shreds and liquor or pineapple juice in a saucepan. Bring to the boil, then add the blended cornflour and cook for 2 minutes to thicken the sauce. Pour over the fish and serve immediately. Serves 4.

CRAB WITH BLACK BEAN SAUCE ••

3 medium blue swimmer crabs
½ teaspoon freshly ground black pepper
1 tablespoon cornflour
oil, for deep-frying
1 tablespoon canned black soybeans
2 cloves garlic
6 spring onions, cut into 5 cm lengths
2 tablespoons Chinese rice wine (shao-hsing)
1 cup chicken stock
1 teaspoon light soy sauce
½ teaspoon sugar

Prepare the crabs (see p. 60), cutting into pieces with some of the shell. Dust the crab pieces with the pepper and cornflour. In a large wok, heat the oil and stir-fry the crab for 3 minutes. Remove and set aside. Wash the black beans under running cold water, drain and pound with the garlic to a paste. Sauté the paste in 2 tablespoons hot oil, put in with the crab pieces, and fry for 1 minute. Add the spring onions, wine, stock and soy sauce, and cook for 2 minutes. Sprinkle in sugar, stir, and serve immediately. Serves 4.

CRAB WITH BLACK BEAN SAUCE

BRAISED PRAWNS ••

750 g green (raw) prawns, shelled
  and deveined
1 tablespoon Chinese rice wine (shao-hsing)
1 teaspoon cornflour
2 teaspoons light soy sauce
125 g bamboo shoots, drained
1 Lebanese cucumber
6 tablespoons oil
½ teaspoon salt
½ teaspoon sugar

Devein the prawns and split their undersides, to prevent them from shrinking. Marinate with the wine, cornflour and half the soy sauce mixed together. Cut the bamboo shoots and cucumber into thin slices, about the same size as the prawns. Using a wok, heat 5 tablespoons oil and sauté the prawns over a high heat, until colour changes. Remove to a heated platter. Add the remaining oil and sauté the bamboo shoots and cucumber over a high heat for 2 minutes. Add the prawns, salt, sugar and remaining soy sauce. Toss until heated. Serve hot. Serves 4.

FRIED PRAWN BALLS ••

500 g green (raw) prawns, shelled,
  deveined and finely chopped
6 water chestnuts, chopped
1 teaspoon grated fresh ginger
1 egg white, unbeaten
1 teaspoon salt
2 teaspoons cornflour
1 teaspoon Chinese rice wine (shao-hsing)
oil, for deep-frying
4 spring onions, sliced

sauce:
1 teaspoon light soy sauce
1 teaspoon Chinese rice wine (shao-hsing)
½ teaspoon salt
2 tablespoons chicken stock or water

Mix the prawns, water chestnuts, ginger, egg white, salt, 1 teaspoon of the cornflour and wine in a bowl. Beat well with chopsticks or a spoon, until the mixture thickens slightly, for about 5 minutes. Roll teaspoonfuls into balls with wet hands. If necessary, roll in a little cornflour. Using a large wok, heat the oil and deep-fry the prawn balls in several lots for about 3 minutes. Drain on paper towels. In a small bowl combine the soy sauce, wine, remaining 1 teaspoon of cornflour and salt with the stock. Pour off all but 1 tablespoon of the oil. Add the spring onions and cook for 1 minute, return the prawn balls to the mixture, then add the soy and stock mixture. Cook for 1 minute, until very hot. Serve immediately. Serves 4.

VEGETABLES

The Chinese cook vegetables until they are tender, but still crisp. They are served both as a separate course and as parts of a meal with other dishes. Braising is the most typical method of cooking vegetables. The prepared vegetables are put into a pan with a small quantity of hot oil and stir-fried for a few minutes. Stock or water is added with seasonings and the vegetables are allowed to simmer for a further 2–3 minutes with the pan covered.

FRIED MIXED VEGETABLES •

2 varieties Chinese cabbage
6 dried mushrooms, soaked in hot water for 20 minutes
250 g fresh bean sprouts, or 125 g bamboo shoots
3 tablespoons oil
3 tablespoons chicken stock
1 teaspoon salt
1 teaspoon sugar
2 teaspoons light soy sauce

Wash the cabbage well and drain. Cut into short lengths. Remove the stems from the mushroom, and cut into strips. Remove the tails from the bean sprouts, or cut the bamboo shoots into strips.

Heat the oil and fry the cabbage first, then add the mushrooms and sprouts, and fry for 5 minutes. Add the stock, then the seasonings. Mix well. Do not cook for too long. The vegetables must be tender, but still crisp. Serve hot. Serves 2–4.

FRIED BEAN SPROUTS WITH CAPSICUM •

500 g fresh bean sprouts
2 green capsicum
3 tablespoons peanut or salad oil
1 tablespoon Chinese rice wine (shao-hsing)
1 teaspoon salt

Remove the tails of bean sprouts and soak in iced water, until ready to use. Drain before using. Wash and seed the green capsicum, and shred finely. Heat the oil and fry the sprouts and capsicum for 1 minute. Add the rice wine and salt, stir. Serve hot. Serves 2–4.

BRAISED MUSHROOMS •

This dish can be prepared successfully in advance. Serve hot with a meat or seafood dish. It also makes a lovely hors d'oeuvre served cold and thinly sliced.

125 g dried shiitake mushrooms
1 tablespoon sugar
1 tablespoon light soy sauce
2 teaspoons sesame oil
½ cup stock
3 tablespoons peanut or light olive oil

Soak the mushrooms in hot water for 20 minutes. Drain and cut off the stems. Mix together the sugar, soy, sesame oil and stock. Heat the oil and fry the mushrooms for several minutes. Add the stock mixture. Cover, and simmer for 25 minutes. Serve hot. Serves 2–4.

SUPERBLY SPICED AND AROMATIC CURRIES

A curry meal with all its accompaniments has many devotees. Curry can be an adventure in good eating but, contrary to general belief, curry dishes need not necessarily be hot. A dozen or more fragrant herbs and spices combine in the unforgettable flavour and, of these, only chilli is hot. Using more or less of this fiery ingredient can control the heat of any curry.

Rice, which accompanies curries, may be simply boiled or steamed, or it may be cooked in stock, flavoured with spices and saffron, and have nuts and sultanas added. It is served first and placed in a mound in the centre of the plate. Curries are then served and placed around the rice. There should be one or two meat curries, such as beef, lamb, pork, poultry or seafood. In addition, there should be at least one vegetable curry.

Almost any vegetable can be successfully curried, and the curry can be dry or made with gravy. Either way, the addition of curry spices and herbs adds a new dimension to vegetable cookery.

Accompaniments are then handed around. As these are usually in small dishes, they may be arranged on a tray for convenience. Guests help themselves to small portions and place them in separate piles around the rice. Curry should be eaten with a spoon and fork, not with a knife and fork. Each spoonful is mixed separately and should consist of rice, curry and a different accompaniment. This way, the contrasting tastes and textures are appreciated and it is possible to adjust the hotness of the curry by the amount of rice mixed with it.

PILAU RICE ••

60 g ghee (clarified butter) or butter
1 onion, finely sliced
1 pinch saffron threads
1 teaspoon turmeric
2 cups long-grain rice
8 peppercorns
2 cloves
4 cardamom pods, bruised
1 stick cinnamon
3½ cups chicken stock
2 teaspoons salt
½ cup sultanas
1 cup cooked peas
⅓ cup lightly fried almonds
6 hard-boiled eggs
salt and extra turmeric
oil, for frying

Heat the ghee in a saucepan and fry half the onion slices, until golden brown. Then add the saffron and turmeric, and stir well for a minute. Add the rice and fry for a few minutes, stirring until it is golden in colour. Add the spices, stock, salt and remaining onions, stir well, and bring to the boil. Reduce the heat to very low, cover with a tight-fitting lid and steam gently for 20–25 minutes. After 15 minutes, sprinkle the sultanas over rice, but do not stir.

When cooked, keep the pan covered, until ready to serve. A few minutes before serving, uncover the pan to allow the steam to escape. Fluff the rice up with a fork then lift onto a serving dish with a slotted metal spoon.

Garnish with the peas, almonds and the hard-boiled eggs, cut into quarters. The eggs may be rubbed over with salt and turmeric, pricked a few times with a toothpick, and fried until golden in a little oil. Serves 6.

CHICKEN CURRY ••

Prepare as for prawn curry, but use 1 kg chicken breasts or chicken pieces in place of prawns. Add to the curry sauce and simmer gently for 20 minutes, or until tender.

BEEF CURRY ••

Beef curry should be dark in colour. This is achieved by frying the curry powder and the other ingredients until brown, before adding the liquid and beef. It is given a piquant flavour with vinegar or tamarind.

1 kg blade bone or chuck steak
2 tablespoons oil or 30 g ghee
10 curry leaves (optional)
½ teaspoon fenugreek seeds (optional)
1 large onion, finely chopped
4 cloves garlic, crushed
2.5 cm piece fresh ginger, grated
3 tablespoons curry powder
1 teaspoon chilli powder (optional)
2 teaspoons salt or to taste
1 tablespoon vinegar
¼ cup instant tamarind, soaked in
  1 cup hot water
1 stick cinnamon
a strip of lemon rind
½ cup coconut milk

Cut the steak into bite-sized pieces. Heat the oil or ghee in a pan, add the curry leaves and fenugreek, and fry for 1 minute. Add the onion, garlic, ginger and fry for further 2 minutes. Add the curry powder and chilli powder and fry gently, stirring until brown, for about 3–5 minutes.

Add the salt and vinegar, then turn in the steak and cook over a high heat for 2–3 minutes, stirring to coat well with the curry mixture. Mix the tamarind pulp with the hot water and add the liquid to the pan. Add the cinnamon stick and lemon rind, bring to the boil, then reduce heat, cover and simmer until the meat is tender and gravy thickened. Add the coconut milk and cook, uncovered, for a further 15 minutes. Serves 4–6.

note: the tamarind extract may be substituted with 2 tablespoons malt vinegar and ½ cup water. Curry powder may be substituted with 1 teaspoon ground turmeric, 2 tablespoons ground coriander, 2 teaspoons ground cumin and ½ teaspoon ground cumin or aniseed.

PORK CURRY ••

Make as above, but substitute pork loin or trimmed shoulder for the beef.

MIXED VEGETABLE CURRY ••

Vegetables have an unusual but delicious flavour prepared in this way. They should be tender, but still crisp.

½ cup oil
½ teaspoon black mustard seeds
6–8 curry leaves
1 teaspoon turmeric
2 cloves garlic, crushed
3 cm piece fresh ginger, finely grated
a pinch of chilli powder (optional)
3 carrots, cut into 6 cm lengths
250 g green beans, cut into 6 cm strips
½ small cabbage, finely shredded
salt

Heat the oil, and fry the mustard seeds and curry leaves for a minute. Add the turmeric, garlic, ginger and chilli, and fry until golden. Add the carrots and beans, and fry over a moderate heat, stirring for 8–10 minutes, until vegetables are half-cooked and still crisp. Add the cabbage and fry for a further 5 minutes. Add the salt to taste, cover, and simmer for 2–3 minutes. Serve at once. Serves 4–6.

PRAWN CURRY ••

One of the most popular curries because prawns combine so well with curry spices. It is better made with raw prawns, though cooked ones may be used.

1 kg green (raw) prawns
30 g ghee (clarified butter) or butter
½ teaspoon fenugreek seeds (optional)
10 curry leaves
1 large onion, finely chopped
3 cloves garlic, crushed
3 cm piece fresh ginger, finely grated
2 tablespoons curry powder
½–1 teaspoon chilli powder (optional)
2 teaspoons paprika
1 cup coconut milk
1 teaspoon desiccated coconut
1 teaspoon ground rice, blended with a little coconut milk
8 cm stick cinnamon
juice of 1 lemon
salt

Shell and devein the prawns. Heat the ghee in a saucepan and gently fry the fenugreek seeds and curry leaves, until light brown. Add the onion, garlic and ginger and fry until golden, stirring to cook evenly. Add the curry powder, chilli powder and paprika and fry for 1 minute, then stir in the coconut milk, desiccated coconut, ground rice, cinnamon, lemon juice and salt, to taste. Cover and simmer gently for 15 minutes, adding extra coconut milk if necessary. Stir occasionally. Add the prawns, stir well, then cover and simmer again for 10 minutes. Serves 6.

DRY POTATO CURRY ••

This dry-fried potato curry is very popular and often featured as the main dish in vegetarian meals.

30 g ghee (clarified butter) or butter
½ teaspoon mustard seeds
1 medium onion, finely chopped
2 tablespoons chopped coriander or mint leaves
1 teaspoon turmeric
½ teaspoon chilli powder (optional)
1 teaspoon paprika
1½ teaspoons salt
4–6 potatoes, peeled and cubed
1 teaspoon garam masala
1 tablespoon lemon juice

Heat the ghee in a large saucepan and fry the mustard seed until it pops. Add the onion, fresh coriander, turmeric, chilli powder, paprika and salt. Mix well, and then stir in the potatoes. Stir for a few minutes, sprinkle with about ½ cup water, turn heat very low, cover and cook for 25–30 minutes, or until the potatoes are done, shaking the saucepan occasionally to prevent sticking. Add the garam masala and lemon juice about 10 minutes before the end of the cooking time. Serves 4–6.

PRAWN CURRY

SAMBALS AND OTHER ACCOMPANIMENTS

Accompaniments should be varied in flavour and texture, including cooked and fresh chutneys. Serve hot chutney or pickles and coconut sambal for extra bite, or cool the palate with sliced bananas, tomato and mint chutney, sweet fruit chutney, salads and cucumbers in sour cream. Crisp-fried pappadams are perfect for texture contrast.

TOMATO AND MINT CHUTNEY •

4 firm, ripe, medium tomatoes
2 tablespoons lemon juice
4 tablespoons chopped mint
a dash of Tabasco or hot chilli sauce (optional)
salt

Scald and peel the tomatoes *(see illustration)* and dice. Mix lightly with the lemon juice, mint and Tabasco, if using. Season with salt, to taste, and serve chilled.

COCONUT SAMBAL •

½ cup desiccated coconut
sufficient paprika to give a bright pink colour
1 tablespoon hot milk
1 tablespoon finely chopped onion
a pinch of chilli powder (optional)
lemon juice
salt
sliced chillies, to garnish (optional)

Place the coconut in a bowl, sprinkle with the paprika, milk, onions and, if desired, the chilli powder. Add the lemon juice and salt, to taste, and mix thoroughly. Taste and adjust the seasoning. Pile in a small bowl and garnish, if liked, with sliced chillies.

FRESH APPLE CHUTNEY •

2 red apples
1 tablespoon chopped onion
vinegar
salt
1 green chilli or chopped fresh coriander leaves

Cut the apples into shreds and mix with the onion in a bowl. Add enough vinegar to moisten and season with salt, to taste. Sprinkle with chopped chilli or coriander and serve immediately.

CUCUMBERS IN YOGHURT •

2 Lebanese cucumbers
salt
1 teaspoon finely grated fresh ginger
1 teaspoon finely chopped garlic
1 cup natural yoghurt
paprika, to sprinkle

Slice the cucumbers very thinly, place in a colander, sprinkle with salt and drain for 20–30 minutes. In a bowl, mix with the ginger and garlic then add yoghurt. Chill well. Sprinkle with paprika before serving.

BOMBAY DUCK •

This is actually fish, which is sold salted and dried. Fry in hot oil until crisp and golden, or grill until crisp. It is then crumbled into small pieces and sprinkled over curry dishes.

FRIED WHITEBAIT •

Dried salted whitebait, available at Chinese stores, is a favourite accompaniment to rice and curries. Fry in deep oil until crisp.

PAPPADAMS •

These spicy lentil wafers are fried in a little hot oil for only 3 or 4 seconds. They increase in size and become crisp and golden.

To peel tomatoes, place in a bowl and cover with boiling water.

Count to eight for riper tomatoes, 10 or more for less ripe, then transfer to a bowl of iced water.

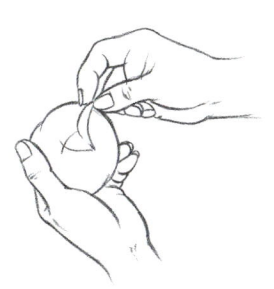

Make a tiny cross in the skin at the base and carefully peel the skin off.

COOKING WITH A SPANISH FLAVOUR

My enthusiasm for Spanish food may be somewhat prejudiced, but how could it be otherwise, for I spent some of the happiest days of my life in Spain.

The main ingredient in Spanish food is olive oil, or Spanish 'liquid gold' as it is called. Its advantages are known to experienced cooks. The flavour of pure olive oil gives distinction and finish to many dishes. Combined with butter it creates an excellent cooking medium, as the oil allows the butter to be brought to a high temperature, without burning, at the same time blending the two delicate flavours.

Another important ingredient is rice, which absorbs the aromas of garlic, capsicum, delicious seafoods and other riches of the world's harvest, including one of the costliest but most rewarding spices, Spanish saffron. Add the lovely wines, sherries and brandies which find their way into the food, as well as on to the table, and you have the flavour of Spain.

PAELLA VALENCIANA •••

½ teaspoon saffron threads
5 cups chicken stock
½ cup olive oil
4 half chicken breasts
2 onions, chopped
2 cloves garlic, chopped
1 red capsicum, seeded and cut into strips
2½ cups rice, washed and drained
2 tomatoes, peeled and cut into eights
1 cup shelled green peas
500 g seafood such as scallops, prawns, calamari or mussels *(optional)*

Bring the saffron and stock to the boil and set aside, until ready to use. Heat half the oil in a paella pan or frying pan (an electric frying pan is ideal). Sauté the chicken breasts until golden. Remove and cut each one into 3. Add the onion, garlic and capsicum strips, with more oil if necessary, and cook gently until soft. Remove the capsicum and set aside. Add the rice and fry gently for 3–4 minutes. Add the stock. When bubbling, reduce the heat and start the decoration of the paella. Add the chicken, capsicum, tomatoes and peas in a pattern, and the remaining foods around. If using seafood, add it for the last 10 minutes of the cooking time. Add more stock if necessary, cover with foil, and cook gently until the rice is cooked, for about 20–25 minutes. Serves 8.

SPICED ROAST PORK ···

2.5 kg loin of pork
3 cloves garlic, crushed
2 teaspoons salt
1 teaspoon freshly ground black pepper
½ teaspoon dried marjoram
½ teaspoon ground cumin
½ teaspoon saffron threads
1 tablespoon oil
½ cup boiling water
¼ cup grated onion
3 tablespoons finely chopped parsley
½ cup dry white wine
2 tablespoons wine vinegar
¼ teaspoon chilli powder

Pound the garlic, salt, pepper, marjoram, cumin and saffron to a paste with the olive oil. Rub into the pork. Wrap in foil and chill overnight.

Preheat the oven to 230°C. Put the pork in a shallow baking dish and roast oven for 25 minutes. Reduce the heat to 180°C, and continue to roast for 1½ hours. Transfer the pork to a serving platter.

Skim the fat from the baking dish and put the dish over a moderate heat. Add the water, onion, parsley, wine, vinegar and chilli powder and bring to the boil. Scrape the glaze from the bottom of the pan and simmer for a few minutes. Cut the pork into thick slices and serve with the sauce. Serves 6–8.

GAZPACHO ANDALUZ ···

750 g ripe tomatoes, peeled (see illustration p.275)
1 cup white wine
2 cups stock
1 large red onion
2 Lebanese cucumbers, peeled
1 small red capsicum
2 cloves garlic
1½ teaspoons salt
½ teaspoon ground cumin
½ teaspoon freshly ground black pepper
¾ cup dry breadcrumbs
⅓ cup olive oil
¼ cup wine vinegar
12–16 ice cubes

Cut half the tomatoes into quarters and cook with the wine and stock until tender, about 5 minutes. Puree in a blender and set aside. Dice the remaining tomatoes, onion, cucumbers and capsicum and set aside. Crush the garlic with the salt to a smooth paste. Place in a large bowl, add the cumin and pepper, mix in the breadcrumbs, and then very gradually stir in the oil. Add the vinegar a little at a time, then the cooked tomato puree. Combine with the diced vegetables, mix well, and chill for 2–3 hours before serving.

To serve, place 2–3 ice cubes in each bowl of gazpacho. Sometimes the chopped vegetables are served separately, with each guest helping themselves to desired quantities. Serves 6–8.

note: all stock may be used (3 cups) and the wine omitted, or use half and half. Canned tomato juice may be used as part of the liquid. The amount of liquid used is a matter of taste — it may be cut to 1 cup or increased to 4 cups.

GAZPACHO ANDALUZ

JAPAN

My early visits to Japan taught me many things. Japanese food is unique. The quiet appeal and natural beauty of each ingredient is highlighted with special seasonings, soy, miso, sake or mirin and the presentation of each dish is something that true cooks pays a great deal of attention to.

CHICKEN TERIYAKI ••

Although most westerners are familiar with teriyaki in various forms, this chicken teriyaki has a surprisingly different taste.

2 chicken breasts, boned
3 tablespoons oil
1 green capsicum, cut into strips or squares
a dash of salt and freshly ground pepper

marinade:
1 tablespoon sugar
1 tablespoon dry sherry
2 tablespoons light soy sauce

Pierce the skin of chicken with a fork, so it will absorb marinade. Plunge into boiling water for a few minutes. Dry with paper towel. Heat 2 tablespoons oil and sauté the chicken pieces over a high heat, until browned. Drain off the oil, pour in the marinade and cook, covered, for 7–8 minutes over a low heat. Remove the lid and cook, shaking pan over a moderate heat, until the marinade is almost evaporated.

Sauté the capsicum pieces in the remaining oil, sprinkle with salt and pepper. To serve, cool and slice the chicken, garnish with the capsicum. Serves 4.

SUKIYAKI ••

60 g beef suet, chopped
2 onions, thinly sliced
6 spring onions, cut into 4cm lengths
1 eggplant quatered lengthwise and sliced
125 g Chinese cabbage, cut into short lengths
6 dried shiitake mushrooms, soaked 20 minutes in hot water, and sliced
125 g bean sprouts
2 tablespoons sake (Japanese rice wine)
light soy sauce
sugar
1 cup beef stock
125 g bean curd, cut into cubes
60 g mung bean vermicelli soaked in warm water, drained and cut into short lengths
1 kg beef fillet, cut into paper-thin slices

Heat a large frying pan or electric frying pan. Rub with the suet, then fry the fat for 5 minutes, or until the pan is well greased. Remove any remaining pieces of suet. Sauté the onions and spring onions for 5 minutes. Add some of the vegetables with some of the sake. Add the soy sauce and sugar, to taste, and moisten with some of the stock. Add the bean curd and vermicelli, and cook over high heat for 5 minutes, stirring frequently. Push all the ingredients to one side of the frying pan, add some of the beef, and cook for 3 minutes. Each person helps themselves from the pan, to which more meat and vegetables are added for second helpings. Before cooking more, add more suet.

Add more soy sauce, sugar, sake and stock when necessary. If liked, dip the cooked food into lightly beaten raw egg or raw egg mixed with soy sauce. Serve with steamed rice. Serves 6–8.

note: the beef is easier to cut if semi-frozen first.

AGEDASHI TOFU ••

600 g silken firm tofu
cornflour, potato or rice flour, for dusting
oil, for frying
1 cup dashi broth (instant can be used)
2 tablespoons light soy sauce
3 tablespoons mirin
1 teaspoon sugar
1 spring onion, finely sliced
1 sheet of nori (dried seaweed)

Drain and rinse the tofu in water. Place on a rack on a plate, cover with paper towels and place a small weight on top. Allow to drain for about 30 minutes to remove excess liquid. Cut the tofu into 5 cm x 1.5 cm cubes. To make sauce, gently heat together dashi broth, soy sauce, mirin, sugar and simmer for a few minutes. Add sliced spring onion and set aside.

Dust the cubes of tofu carefully with cornflour to coat evenly. In a wok or heavy-based frying pan, add enough oil to coat the tofu and heat until hot but not smoking. Add the tofu cubes a few at a time and deep-fry, turning, until golden and crisp. Remove carefully with a slotted spoon and drain on paper towels.

Arrange fried tofu on serving plates and pour a little dashi sauce over reach. Alternatively, simply accompany the fried tofu with soy sauce for dipping. Serve immediately garnished with nori cut into thin strips using scissors. *Serves 4* as a starter.

PRAWN TEMPURA ••

This dish can be garnished with finely grated carrot or daikon (long white radish). The fresh raw vegetable makes a nice texture contrast to the fried prawns.

10 large green (raw) prawns
1 sheet dried seaweed (nori)
plain flour for coating
1 cup plain flour
1 cup iced water
1 egg yolk
oil, for deep-frying

Shell and devein the prawns. Slit the top section of each prawn and straighten out to open and flatten. Remove the dark vein from each. Cut the seaweed into 1cm-wide strips then cut each strip in half. Wrap a strip of seaweed around the base of each tail. Dust the prawns lightly with flour, leaving the seaweed and tail unfloured.

Combine the flour, water and egg yolk in a bowl. Heat the oil. Dip each prawn into the batter, again leaving the tail and seaweed uncoated. Slip one at a time, into the hot oil, cooking only 2 or 3 prawns at one time. Fry until golden, remove and drain thoroughly on paper towels. Repeat with remaining prawns. Arrange on rice paper or napkins and serve with soy or tempura sauce or with lemon and salt. *Serves 3–4* as a starter.

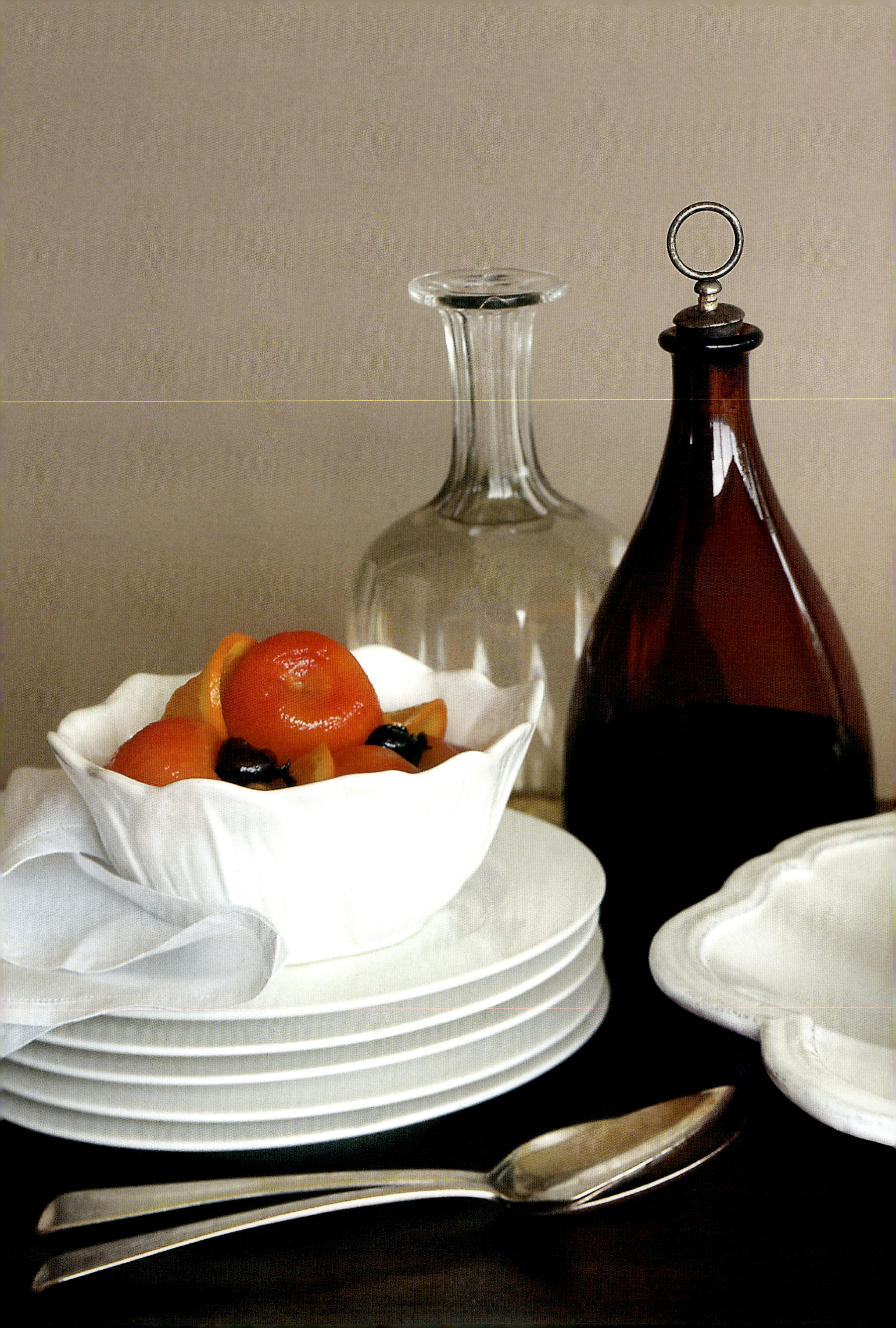

entertaining

BAKED GLAZED HAM AND SPICED FRUITS

PARTY FOOD AND DRINKS

For as long as I can remember, I have enjoyed the air of excitement that precedes a party. I have never outgrown this, and no matter how small or how grand the occasion, I get a lot of pleasure planning the food and entertainment for my guests.

A party should promise good fun, good company and good food. A light heart takes care of the fun, good friends take care of the company and a few good recipes take care of the food.

THE BUFFET PARTY

Buffet parties are an ideal way of entertaining informally, as more guests can be catered for than at a sit-down dinner.

BAKED GLAZED HAM ••

A baked glazed ham is a welcome sight on a buffet table, especially at Christmas. Stout, sugar and spices give a fabulous flavour to the ham, with the outside caramelised, so that each slice is a perfect mix of flavour.

1 x 5–6 kg leg of ham
whole cloves (optional)
1½ cups stout

glaze:
1 cup sugar
1 teaspoon ground cardamom
1 teaspoon ground ginger
extra 2–3 tablespoons stout

Preheat the oven to 160°C. Cut the skin around the thick end of the knuckle (can be made a scallop pattern) without cutting into the fat and flesh. Ease the skin from the fat by slipping the thumb of one hand under the skin, and firmly sliding it back and forth. Turn the ham over and ease away the rest of the skin, which should come off in one piece *(see illustration)*.

Place the ham, fat side uppermost, in a roasting pan containing the 1½ cups stout. Cover the ham with foil, making it as airtight as possible, and bake for 1½ hours. Lift the foil and baste the ham with the drippings several times during the cooking. Remove from the oven, take off the foil and pour off the liquid in the pan. Using a sharp knife, score the fat with 4 cm interval diagonal cuts, first one way, then the opposite way, to form a diamond pattern *(see illustration)*.

Spread half the glaze mixture over the ham and stud a clove in the corner of each diamond if liked. Increase the oven temperature to 200°C, and bake for a further 30–40 minutes, basting it every 10 minutes with the remaining glaze.

glaze: Mix the sugar and spices together with 1–2 tablespoons of the stout (enough to make a thick paste).

A NOTE ON COOKING TIMES

As the hams are already cooked, the cooking times for a baked glazed ham are not so critical. In general, a 3 kg ham should be baked for 1 hour before glazing while a 7 kg ham will need 2 hours before glazing.

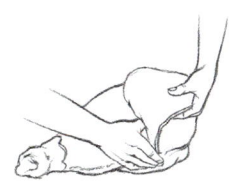

Cut the skin around the thick end of the knuckle, taking care not to cut into the fat and flesh. Firmly slid your thumb back and forth under the skin to ease it away from the fat.

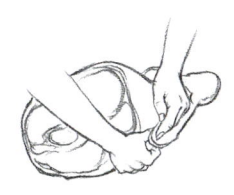

Turn the ham over and remove the rest of the skin, which should come off in one piece.

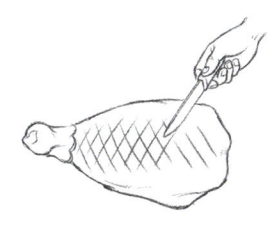

Using a sharp knife, score the fat in a diamond pattern.

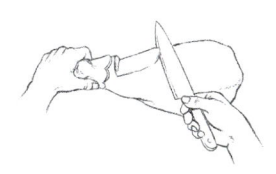

The easiest way to carve a ham is to cut a wedge two-thirds along the leg and use this as your starting point to carve on either side of the ham.

HOT OR COLD?

If serving hot, leave the baked glazed ham in the turned off oven for 30 minutes. If serving cold, cool and store in the refrigerator overnight. Place the ham on a stand, or a large serving platter, and garnish if liked with watercress or parsley.

CARVING

The essential requirement is a very sharp knife, preferably with a long thin blade. The easiest way to carve a ham is to cut a wedge out first, about two-thirds along the leg, and carve slices each side *(see illustration)*. This allows a good distribution of lean and fat, and makes manageable slices. Cold ham is cut in thin slices, but a hot ham may be cut into thicker slices. Before carving, wrap a sheet of foil around the knuckle. The carver may cover this with a clean napkin, and hold the ham without getting greasy.

HOW MANY PEOPLE WILL IT SERVE?

3 kg   serves 10–14
4 kg   serves 12–16
5 kg   serves 15–20
6 kg   serves 18–22
7 kg   serves 20–25

half hams: If a whole leg of ham is too big for your needs, look to the half hams. These are treated as for baked glazed ham, but reduce the baking time accordingly. A half ham will bake through in approximately 1 hour, basting several times, then for a further 30 minutes for glazing.

STORING LEFTOVER HAM

Cover with a clean tea towel or light cheesecloth bag which has been dipped in a solution of approximately 2 cups water with 1 tablespoon vinegar, and then squeezed out. Replace the tea towel about every 3 days with a fresh one to keep the ham moist and fresh.

ACCOMPANIMENTS

A large big bowl of boiled new potatoes, tossed in butter, with chopped parsley and a grinding of pepper, is always welcome. Serve the potatoes warm. Crusty bread, a large green salad and a choice of mustards and spiced fruits *(see following recipe)* are the main essentials.

SPICED FRUITS •

These spiced stone fruits are always a success at Christmas time when they are in season and can be prepared fresh. At other times of the year, drained canned fruits can be used instead. The flavour of the fruit will improve if made 4–5 days in advance and kept in the refrigerator.

½ cup sugar

1 cup water

¼ cup vinegar

1 stick cinnamon

½ teaspoon whole cloves

8 whole allspice

4 large peaches

4 apricots

4 large red plums

2 unpeeled oranges, sliced

Put the sugar, water, vinegar, cinnamon, cloves and allspice in a heavy-based saucepan and place over a gentle heat until the sugar dissolves. Bring to the boil and simmer for 5 minutes.

Pour enough boiling water over the peaches in a bowl to cover, leave to stand for 3 minutes. Drain and remove the skins. If the peaches are large, halve them and remove the stones. Carefully lower all the fruit into the syrup, return to the heat and cook gently for 10–12 minutes. Remove the plum skins, if desired. Spoon the fruit into a bowl and pour over the hot syrup. Leave to macerate for several hours before serving. Remove the spices if liked.

FILLET OF BEEF PROVENÇALE ••

2 kg fillet of beef (about 2), trimmed and tied

freshly ground pepper

30 g butter

2 tablespoons olive oil

3 tablespoons brandy

500 g green beans, trimmed

500 g zucchini, cut into short lengths

500 g patty pan squash, halved into rounds

1 kg medium tomatoes, quartered

1 cup black olives

2 tablespoons finely chopped fresh herbs such as parsley, basil, oregano or tarragon

green herb vinaigrette:

2 teaspoons Dijon mustard

2–3 tablespoons white wine vinegar

1 clove garlic, crushed

4 tablespoons chopped herbs such as chives, parsley, tarragon and basil

salt and freshly ground pepper

¾ cup extra virgin olive oil

Preheat the oven to 200°C. Season beef with pepper. Heat the butter and oil in a roasting pan over a moderate heat. Brown the beef on all sides. Warm the brandy in a saucepan, then set alight and pour over the beef. Shake pan until the flames subside, spooning juices over. Roast 15 minutes for rare and 20 minutes for medium-rare. Remove beef to a plate, cover and leave to cool. Cook the beans, zucchini and squash for 5 minutes in boiling, salted water. Drain and refresh under cold water. Carve the meat and arrange on a serving dish. Toss the vegetables, tomatoes and olives in green herb vinaigrette. Arrange the salad around the beef and sprinkle with herbs. Serves 12–16.

green herb vinaigrette: Combine the mustard, vinegar, garlic and chopped herbs. Season with salt and pepper, to taste, then whisk in the oil.

PASTITSO FOR A CROWD ••

Pastitso is an excellent plan-ahead party dish. The day before the party everything can be layered in oven dishes, ready to bake, and stored in the refrigerator.

90 g butter
3 tablespoons oil
4 medium onions, finely chopped
2 kg lean minced beef
500 g salami, finely chopped
1 x 440 g can peeled, chopped tomatoes
salt and freshly ground pepper
¼ cup tomato paste
2 cups grated cheese
1 kg instant lasagne noodles

white sauce:
3 tablespoons butter
5 tablespoons plain flour
4 cups milk
salt and freshly ground pepper
2 eggs, beaten
½ cup grated tasty cheese

Melt the butter and oil in a large frying pan. Sauté the onions, beef and salami for 2–3 minutes, stirring. Add the tomatoes, salt and pepper, to taste, and tomato paste. Cook gently until the meat is tender, about 40 minutes. Cover the pan if the mixture is too dry. Add the cheese. Preheat the oven to 180°C. Butter 2 ovenproof dishes, about 33 cm x 20 cm. Place a layer of lasagne in the base of each and cover with the meat mixture. Top with the remaining lasagne and top with the white sauce. Bake for 30 minutes or until browned. Serve hot.

white sauce: Melt the butter in a saucepan. Remove from heat, blend in flour, and stir in milk. Bring to the boil, stirring, and cook for 5 minutes, until thickened and creamy. Beat in the eggs and cheese and season. Serves 20.

BEEF STRIPS IN TOMATO CREAM SAUCE ••

This recipe can be made 2 days before the party and stored in the refrigerator. If making ahead, do not add the cream until almost ready to serve. The flavour resembles stroganoff.

2–3 kg round or blade steak
½ cup plain flour
1 teaspoon salt
freshly ground pepper
60 g butter
2 tablespoons oil
2 cups chopped onions
4 cloves garlic, crushed
2 cups diced green capsicum
500 g mushrooms, sliced
2 x 420 g cans peeled tomatoes
1 cup water
2 tablespoons Worcestershire sauce
3 cups sour cream

Cut the beef into thin strips. Coat with the flour seasoned with the salt and pepper. Heat half the butter and 1 tablespoon oil in a large frying pan, and sauté the meat in 3 or 4 lots, until brown. Add the remaining butter and oil when needed. Put the browned beef into a large saucepan. In the remaining fat in the pan, cook the onions, garlic and capsicum for a few minutes. Add to the beef. Add the mushrooms, tomatoes, water and Worcestershire sauce. Bring slowly to the boil and simmer gently for 1 hour.

Remove from the heat and just before serving stir in the sour cream. Place over a low heat, stirring until the mixture is hot. Do not allow mixture to boil. Taste and check for seasoning, adding salt and freshly ground pepper if needed. Serves 10–15.

FILET DE BOEUF EN CROÛTE ••
(BEEF WELLINGTON)

Advance preparation makes this an ideal dish for entertaining. Prepare the beef, wrap in the pastry, and cook when required.

1.5 kg eye of fillet beef
1 tin truffles, sliced thinly (*optional*)
90 g good pâté
salt and freshly ground pepper
60 g butter
⅓ cup brandy
375 g packet puff pastry
1 egg yolk beaten with 1 tablespoon water

sauce:
2 teaspoons plain flour
½ cup beef consommé or stock
madeira or dry sherry, to taste

Preheat the oven to 200°C. Strip all the fat from the beef. Make a tunnel with a knife from one end to the other. Push the truffle through the tunnel in the meat. Shape the pâté into a cylinder and push through the centre. Season the beef with salt and pepper. Heat the butter in a heavy-based frying pan, and brown the meat on a high heat for 2–3 minutes. Flame with brandy, remove from heat and cool.

Roll out the puff pastry large enough to encase the beef. Wrap the beef in the pastry, sealing edges well with water. if liked finish with leaves or flowers, cut from scraps of pastry. Glaze with the egg yolk. Bake for 40 minutes, until golden brown. Cut the beef and pastry across into 2 cm slices.

sauce: Add 1 teaspoon flour to the frying pan and stir over a moderate heat before adding another teaspoon. Blend in the beef consommé, and madeira or sherry. Stir in all the brown crustiness from the sides of the pan. Serves 8.

SALMON MOUSSE ••

1 tablespoon powdered gelatine
¼ cup water
2 teaspoons sugar
1 teaspoon salt
1 teaspoon dry mustard
¼ cup white wine vinegar
2 cups flaked red salmon
1 cup finely diced celery
2 teaspoons capers
½ cup whipped cream
a few sprigs of dill, to garnish

sour cream dressing:
½ cup sour cream
1 tablespoon grated onion
½ teaspoon salt
freshly ground pepper
1 teaspoon grated horseradish relish (*optional*)
2 teaspoons white wine vinegar
a pinch of paprika

Sprinkle the gelatine over the water in a small saucepan. Soak for 2 minutes. Add the sugar, salt, mustard and vinegar. Stir constantly over a low heat until the gelatine is dissolved. Remove from the heat and chill to the consistency of unbeaten egg whites. Fold in the salmon, celery and capers, mix well, then fold in the whipped cream. Turn into wetted 4 cup mould, or 8 individual moulds, and chill until firm. Unmould onto a serving plate and garnish with the sprigs of fresh dill. Serve with the sour cream dressing.

sour cream dressing: Combine all ingredients in a bowl. Serves 8.

THE COCKTAIL PARTY

Everyone loves the finger food and glamorous drinks at a cocktail party. It's a perfect way to entertain friends during the festive season. Take my advice though; decide on one cocktail and go with that. You'll be kept very busy if you have to mix up different kinds at once.

Try to introduce one or two other guests to the cocktail recipe so they can help out too. Have plenty of food to nibble on and several alternatives to drink, such as juice, mineral water, champagne and beer, for the non-cocktail drinkers.

APPETIZERS AND CANAPÉS

Canapés are small and in varying shapes, with toppings that have a good flavour and look pretty. Breads like pumpernickel and sliced baguette make good canapé bases, which must be firm enough to hold the topping. Soft white sandwich bread needs first to be cut into rounds or squares and fried or toasted to make bases for canapés (see next page).

Small crisp crackers may also be used as bases. Smoked salmon and trout, sliced roast beef, salami, seafood, and smoked chicken or ham make ideal toppings, and should be seasoned and garnished to make each canapé distinctive.

SIMPLE CANAPÉS

angels on horseback: Sprinkle oysters with lemon juice. Cut lean, rindless rashers of streaky bacon in halves, wrap each one around an oyster, fastening with a small toothpick. Grill, until lightly browned, and serve hot.

stuffed eggs: Hard-boil 4 eggs, cut in halves and remove yolks. Sieve yolks, and mix to a paste with a little cream or mayonnaise. Season with Dijon mustard, salt, pepper and lemon juice. Spoon or pipe the mixture into whites, and garnish the tops with strips of red capsicum or a little caviar.

avocado canapés: Mash avocado pulp, season with salt, pepper, lemon juice and a dash of Tabasco. Chill, covered, until ready to serve. Dollop on to canapé bases. Garnish with a strip of red capsicum or a little finely chopped fresh coriander.

salmon canapés: Arrange thinly sliced smoked salmon on canapé bases. Garnish with a dab of sour cream, capers and a tiny piece of lemon or snipped dill.

anchovy canapés: Mash 1 can of drained anchovy fillets. Stir in a little oil, a few drops of lemon juice and freshly ground black pepper, to taste. Spread on rounds of bread and heat under the griller.

... and a little more elaborate:

goat cheese, avocado and smoked salmon: Mash 1 small round of soft goat cheese in a bowl and lightly fold through 1 diced avocado, a few slices of diced smoked salmon, freshly ground pepper and a squeeze of lime or lemon juice. Slice a small baguette into 1 cm slices, and just before serving, pile a little of the goat cheese mixture on to each.

tapenade-stuffed tomatoes: You can buy a black olive spread or tapenade, but it is easy to make yourself *(see p. 308)*. Cut the tops off about 32 tiny tomatoes, leaving the stem end intact. Scoop out the pulp carefully and fill the tomatoes with the tapenade. Finish each with parsley, arrange on a serving platter.

sun-dried tomato: Place 1 red capsicum over a gas flame or under the grill to blister the skin. Peel and remove the seeds. Put the capsicum together with 8–10 sun-dried tomatoes, about 10 basil leaves and 1 tablespoon olive oil in a food processor. Season with salt and freshly ground black pepper then process. Spoon on fried bread canapé bases *(see following)* and top each with a small piece of anchovy fillet.

roast beef: Cut 1–2 small baguettes into 1 cm slices. Cut roasted rare beef fillet into thin slices. Spread each bread slice with a little butter or cooled béarnaise sauce *(see p. 304)*, and top with a few watercress or rocket leaves and a slice of beef fillet. Top each with a dab of béarnaise sauce, or horseradish mixed with mayonnaise or sour cream, and a good grinding of pepper. Arrange on a serving platter, sprinkle with snipped chives.

fried bread for canapé bases: Cut sliced bread into small square or round shapes. Heat enough oil, or a mixture of half butter and half oil, to cover the bottom of a frying pan, and fry the bread until delicately golden on one side. Turn to fry the other side. Drain on paper towels. Use immediately, or cool and store in an airtight container, until required. Reheat in a 180°C oven, until hot and crisp, before using. Some fillings are placed straight on to cooled canapé bases, while others require the base to be topped with mayonnaise or sour cream to help hold the topping.

CORN PANCAKES WITH SMOKED SALMON •

Cocktail-size corn and coconut pancakes, topped with a little sour cream and smoked salmon.

2 cobs sweet corn, kernels cut from the cobs or 250 g whole corn kernels
1 spring onion, finely sliced
1 tablespoon chopped fresh coriander
½ cup coconut cream
2 eggs
½ cup plain flour
½ teaspoon salt
vegetable oil, for frying

topping:
sour cream
200g smoked salmon or ocean trout, thinly sliced
1 tablespoon lime or lemon juice
1 tablespoon snipped chives

Put all the ingredients into a blender or food processor and blend until mixed. Heat a little oil in a heavy-based frying pan. Drop the corn batter, 1 tablespoon at a time, into the frying pan and fry until lightly browned on both sides, gently turning once. Cook 3 or 4 at a time, and repeat until all the batter is used, adding more oil when necessary. Add a little water to the batter if it becomes too thick.

topping: When ready to serve, top each pancake with a dollop of the sour cream mixed with lime or lemon juice, a thin strip of smoked salmon or ocean trout and a sprinkling of chives. Arrange on a serving platter.
Makes about 30.

CORN PANCAKES WITH SMOKED SALMON

PIROSHKI ••

These can be made, lightly baked, cooled and frozen then taken out when needed. It just wouldn't be a party or celebration at my house if these hot savoury yeast breads were not served.

3 cups plain flour
2 teaspoons salt
7 g dry yeast
1¼ cups milk
125 g butter
2 tablespoons sugar
1 egg yolk
beaten egg, to glaze

filling:
3 large onions
60 g butter
250 g speck
1 teaspoon freshly ground pepper

Sift the flour with the salt into a large mixing bowl. Stir in the dry yeast. Place the milk, butter and sugar in a saucepan. Heat gently until lukewarm and the butter has melted. Make a well in the centre of the flour and pour in the milk mixture and egg yolk. Stir, gradually incorporating the flour. Beat the dough with a wooden spoon, or your hand, for 3 minutes, until smooth and elastic. Sprinkle a little flour on top and cover with cling wrap, then a cloth. Leave in a warm place for about 1 hour, until the dough has doubled in bulk.

Meanwhile make the filling. Chop the onions and fry slowly in the butter until golden, cool. Chop the speck very finely and mix with the onion and pepper. Preheat the oven to 230°C.

Turn the dough out onto a floured board, knead lightly, and take a tablespoon-sized piece of dough. Flatten slightly into a thick disc and place a teaspoon of filling on top. Fold the edge over to enclose the filling and mould into a small ball. Place on a lightly greased baking tray. Repeat with remaining dough and filling and leave in a warm place to prove for 15 minutes. Brush with the beaten egg and bake for 10–15 minutes, until golden and cooked.

Makes 45–50 appetize-size piroshki. For picnics, barbecues or family eating, count on 30 larger ones.

to freeze: Pack in oven bags in serving-size lots. It is a simple matter to lift them out of the freezer and pop them straight into a moderate oven for about 10 minutes to reheat.

note: speck, a cured and smoked bacon, can be found at most good delicatessens. If unavailable, smoked streaky bacon is a good substitute.

TIROPETES ••

These savoury pastries from Greece and the Middle East are great for a party. The directions for folding tiropetes are usually on the filo pastry packet. Make small squares for a drinks party, larger fingers for fork food.

1 bunch English spinach
4 onions, finely chopped
60 g butter
5 eggs, beaten
1 cup finely chopped spring onions including a little green
250 g feta cheese, chopped
1 teaspoon ground nutmeg
1 cup chopped parsley
salt and freshly ground pepper
250 g filo pastry
150 g unsalted butter, melted

Wash the spinach thoroughly and steam for about 5 minutes until tender. Drain and squeeze to remove any excess moisture. Chop fairly finely. Fry the onions gently in the butter until golden brown. In a bowl, combine the eggs, spring onions, cheese, nutmeg and parsley. Add the onion and spinach and season with salt and pepper, to taste. Leave to cool.

Lay the filo flat on a dry tea towel and cover with a second dry tea towel. To stop the pastry from drying out, damp another tea towel and place on top. Preheat the oven to 190°C. Take out a sheet of filo, lay flat and brush with the melted butter. Place another sheet on top of the first. Cut the double sheet lengthwise into 8 cm-wide strips, or thereabouts, depending on the size of the sheets. Place a tablespoon of the filling on pastry strip at the end closest to you and fold the corner over it to make a triangle. Continue to fold the pastry strip up and over, in triangles, until you come to the top end of the pastry strip. Brush the top with more melted butter. Place on an ungreased baking tray and repeat with remaining pastry and filling. Bake for 45 minutes or until puffed and golden brown. Makes about 36.

note: tiropetes can be assembled in advance, frozen, and baked when required.

ROAST BEEF AND CAPERS ON PUMPERNICKEL •

Roast a well-trimmed piece of beef or, alternatively, buy rare roast beef from a delicatessen, in which case have them slice it very thin. Vary the bread, using sliced baguette, sour dough or squares of Turkish bread.

about 1 cup sour cream
2 tablespoons grated horseradish relish
1 packet pumpernickel rounds
250 g thinly sliced rare roast beef
baby capers
1 red onion, finely sliced
a few sprigs of dill, to garnish
freshly ground pepper
coarse sea salt

Season the sour cream with the horseradish so it has quite a bite to it. Arrange the pumpernickel rounds on a board and spoon a little sour cream on each. Top each with a small curl of roast beef. Garnish the rounds with the capers, a little slice of onion and a tiny dill sprig, giving each one a good grinding of pepper and a light sprinkling of sea salt. Makes about 40.

THAI CHICKEN BITES •

Cubes of tender chicken breast dipped in a delicious coconut sauce for nibbling with drinks.

3 tablespoons vegetable oil
2 tablespoons grated fresh ginger
½ stalk tender lemon grass, very finely chopped
2 red chillies, finely chopped
½ teaspoon ground coriander
1¾ cups coconut milk
1 tablespoon finely chopped coriander leaves
salt and freshly ground pepper
1 tablespoon fish sauce
1 tablespoon lime juice
450 g skinned and boned chicken breast

First make the sauce. Heat 1 tablespoon oil in a frying pan and fry the ginger, lemon grass and chillies. Add the ground coriander and gradually stir in the coconut milk, bring to the boil, then reduce the heat and simmer for 8 minutes. Stir in the coriander and season to taste with salt, pepper, fish sauce and lime juice. Reheat before serving.

Cut the chicken into 2.5 cm cubes. Heat the remaining oil in a large frying pan and sauté the chicken pieces, until lightly browned on all sides and cooked through. Set aside and keep warm. Place cocktail sticks or toothpicks in the pieces of chicken and arrange on a serving dish. Serve the sauce separately in a bowl for dipping. Makes about 30.

CRUNCHY PRAWN BALLS ••

These delectable morsels are great with drinks.

10 water chestnuts
4 spring onions, chopped
250 g shelled prawns, deveined
1½ tablespoons cornflour
½ teaspoon salt
1 egg white
1 tablespoon Chinese rice wine (shao-hsing)

Using a food processor with the metal blade in place, add the water chestnuts, spring onions, prawns, cornflour and salt to the bowl. Process, turning on and off rapidly, for 15 seconds. Add the egg white and wine and process until fairly smooth.

Shape into bite-size balls using 2 teaspoons, one to scoop from the other. Heat vegetable oil in a wok and fry the prawn balls, about 8–10 at a time, until brown and cooked through. Drain on paper towels and immediately sprinkle with additional salt. If liked, serve with hot mustard and Chinese plum sauce, or a chilli sauce. Remember to offer toothpicks and paper napkins. Makes about 20.

COCKTAILS AND SHORT DRINKS

PINA COLADA

Pina colada is the favourite cocktail of Hawaii, where pineapple and coconuts grow in abundance. The alcoholic version packs a real punch so there'll be some who may want to drop the rum. If you haven't a cocktail shaker, use a blender.

crushed ice
50 ml white rum
50 ml coconut cream
100 ml unsweetened pineapple juice
slice of fresh pineapple, or pineapple leaf, to decorate

Place 3 tablespoons of crushed ice in a cocktail shaker and add the rum, coconut cream and pineapple juice. Shake well until the drink is frothy. Pour into a tall glass and decorate with a slice of pineapple, or a tiny pineapple leaf. Makes 1 drink.

TEQUILA SUNRISE

A gorgeous-looking cocktail, glowing with the colours of a sunrise.

crushed ice
45 ml tequila
1 cup orange juice
20 ml grenadine
orange rind, to garnish

Fill two cocktail glasses with crushed ice. Pour in the tequila and top with orange juice. Slowly pour in the grenadine. Allow to settle, but stir once before drinking. Garnish with a strip of orange rind, twirled around a cocktail pick and, if liked, finish with a pretty flower from the garden. Makes 2 drinks.

BRANDY SOUR

Half-fill a cocktail shaker with ice and add 1 part sugar syrup or caster sugar, 2 parts lemon juice, and 8 parts brandy. Shake the mixture vigorously, strain into cocktail glasses and garnish with a cherry. Makes 1 drink.

BRANDY CRUSTA

Dip the rim of a glass in orange juice, then press into caster sugar. Put 3 parts brandy, 1 part Curaçao and 3 parts fresh orange juice into a shaker, top with ice, shake well, and strain into encrusted glass. Makes 1 drink.

PINK RUSSIAN

A long, pretty summer drink. The cranberry juice isn't the usual in a pink Russian, but it's a great addition.

1 cup cranberry juice
1 cup grapefruit juice
6 tablespoons vodka
6 tablespoons campari
orange rind, to garnish
soda water

Place everything together in a tall jug. Strain into 4 tall chilled glasses, garnish each with a twist of orange rind and fill with chilled soda water. Makes 4 long drinks.

SPRITZER

Put a wineglass of light wine, preferably white, in a tall glass with some ice. Top up with soda, and add a slice of lemon.

CHAMPAGNE

A 750 ml bottle of Champagne or sparkling wine pours 6–8 glasses. On this basis 8–12 bottles of dry Champagne will see you through the party for 25 guests. Serve Champagne well chilled. Lay flat in the refrigerator for 2–3 hours or, preferably, in tubs of ice for 1 hour.

PIZZA

Pizza is a great way of entertaining a young crowd. It's the one take-away food we all enjoy. Even though it started out centuries ago in Naples, as a rough, cheap peasant dish, it does meet a need for tasty, substantial food these days. Though few of us have a wood-fired brick oven we can make a great pizza at home with an ordinary household oven. Ripe red tomatoes are the best, and the canned Italian varieties are also good. The mozzarella or bocconcini should be the best you can get and only use olive oil. Once you have these basics right, the next most important thing is to try and stick to toppings that would get the nod from an Italian.

The following ideas should find Italian favour, but there's plenty more, and as you get into the spirit of it you will enjoy dreaming up your own combinations.

PIZZA CRUST ••

2 1/3 cups plain flour
1 teaspoon salt
1 teaspoon sugar
1 sachet dried yeast
3/4 cup lukewarm water
3 tablespoons olive oil
1 quantity tomato sauce *(see right)*

Sift the flour into a large bowl with the salt and stir in the sugar and yeast. Make a well in the centre and add the water and oil. Mix to a dough, then turn out on to a well-floured board. Knead lightly for 4–5 minutes, until smooth and elastic. Put the dough into a buttered bowl, turn it to coat with the butter and let it rise until doubled in bulk, in a warm place, for about 1 hour. Preheat the oven to 200°C.

Sprinkle 2 oiled Swiss roll tins about 35 cm x 25 cm or 2 x 30 cm diameter round pizza pans with a little cornmeal or flour. Now turn the dough out on to a floured board, halve and roll each half into a large rectangle or round to fit the prepared tins. Cover and leave to rise in a warm place for 15 minutes. Spread the tomato sauce over the bases leaving 1.5 cm free around the edge and top with filling. Bake for 20 to 30 minutes. Makes 2.

TOMATO SAUCE •

1 kg ripe tomatoes
6 tablespoons olive oil
10 basil leaves or sprigs of oregano
salt and freshly ground pepper

Peel the tomatoes and chop them roughly. Add to a pan in which the oil has been heated, with any juice from the tomatoes and the basil or oregano. Simmer for 10–15 minutes, stirring from time to time, until the sauce is thick. Remove the basil or oregano and season with the salt and pepper.

note: an excellent substitute is bottled Italian sauce (sugo) which is available from most supermarkets.

topping ideas:

- grated Parmesan or pecorino cheese
- prawns and black olives
- black olives and anchovy fillets
- salami with olives, anchovy fillets and strips of green or red capsicum
- prosciutto slices with olives and mushrooms
- prosciutto slices with rocket leaves, mozzarella cheese and bocconcini
- seafood such as mussels, prawns and squid
- slices of mozzarella cheese or bocconcini, oregano or basil leaves and sprinkling of grated Parmesan cheese
- sliced salami or ham with grated Parmesan cheese and sliced button mushrooms

PIZZA WITH PROSCIUTTO AND ROCKET

OTHER PARTY DRINKS

Don't forget the wine coolers and punches that give parties a special zing!

CITRUS SUMMER CUP •

An economical and refreshing drink that can be stored in bottles in the refrigerator, and diluted as needed.

8 cups sugar
1 litre water
rind of 2 oranges and 1 lemon
juice of 3 lemons
juice of 6 oranges
30 g citric acid
1 x 25 g packet Epsom salts
lemon slices, to decorate

In a large saucepan dissolve the sugar in the water and boil. Add the citrus rind and juice, citric acid and Epsom salts. Stir until dissolved, strain and bottle. Chill. Put 1–2 tablespoons syrup in each glass then fill with ice and water. Decorate with lemon slices. Makes about 20 drinks.

PERSIAN MINT CUP •

2 cups mint leaves
6 cups water
2 cups sugar
thin strips of lemon rind
$\frac{2}{3}$ cup lemon juice
a few sprigs of mint, to decorate

Wash the mint leaves, drain and put into a saucepan with 1 cup of the water, the sugar, lemon rind and juice. Stir over a gentle heat, until the sugar dissolves. Raise the heat and boil for 5 minutes. Add the remaining water and allow to cool. Strain and chill. Serve in a tall jug with ice cubes. Pour into tall glasses over ice cubes or crushed ice, and decorate each glass with a sprig of mint, if desired. Makes about 10 drinks.

SANGRIA •

1 cup water
½ cup sugar
1 stick cinnamon
2 oranges
2 lemons
1 x 750 ml bottle red wine
soda water

Combine the water, sugar and cinnamon in a saucepan over a gentle heat until the sugar dissolves. Increase heat and boil for 5 minutes. Cool the syrup. Slice the oranges and lemons and put in a bowl. Pour the syrup over the fruit and marinate for at least 4 hours. Fill a large glass jug with ice. Add the drained fruit, ½ cup syrup and red wine. Stir well and add chilled soda water, to taste. Serve in chilled wine glasses. Makes about 10 drinks.

BELLINI •

An adaptation of the legendary Bellini, from Harry's Bar in Venice. To be authentic it is made with a white peach purée, sometimes with a little sugar syrup added, and mixed with prosecco, an Italian version of Champagne. If you have access to peach sorbet, or any other fruit sorbet for that matter, such as strawberry or raspberry, try in place of the purée. It won't be the true Bellini, but it will be popular.

2 tablespoons puréed fresh peach
1 teaspoon peach schnapps (*optional*)
½ teaspoon lemon juice
chilled prosecco, Champagne or sparkling white wine

Place the peach purée, schnapps and lemon juice in a chilled, tall glass. Fill almost to the top with the chilled prosecco or Champagne and stir. Makes 1 drink.

BELLINI

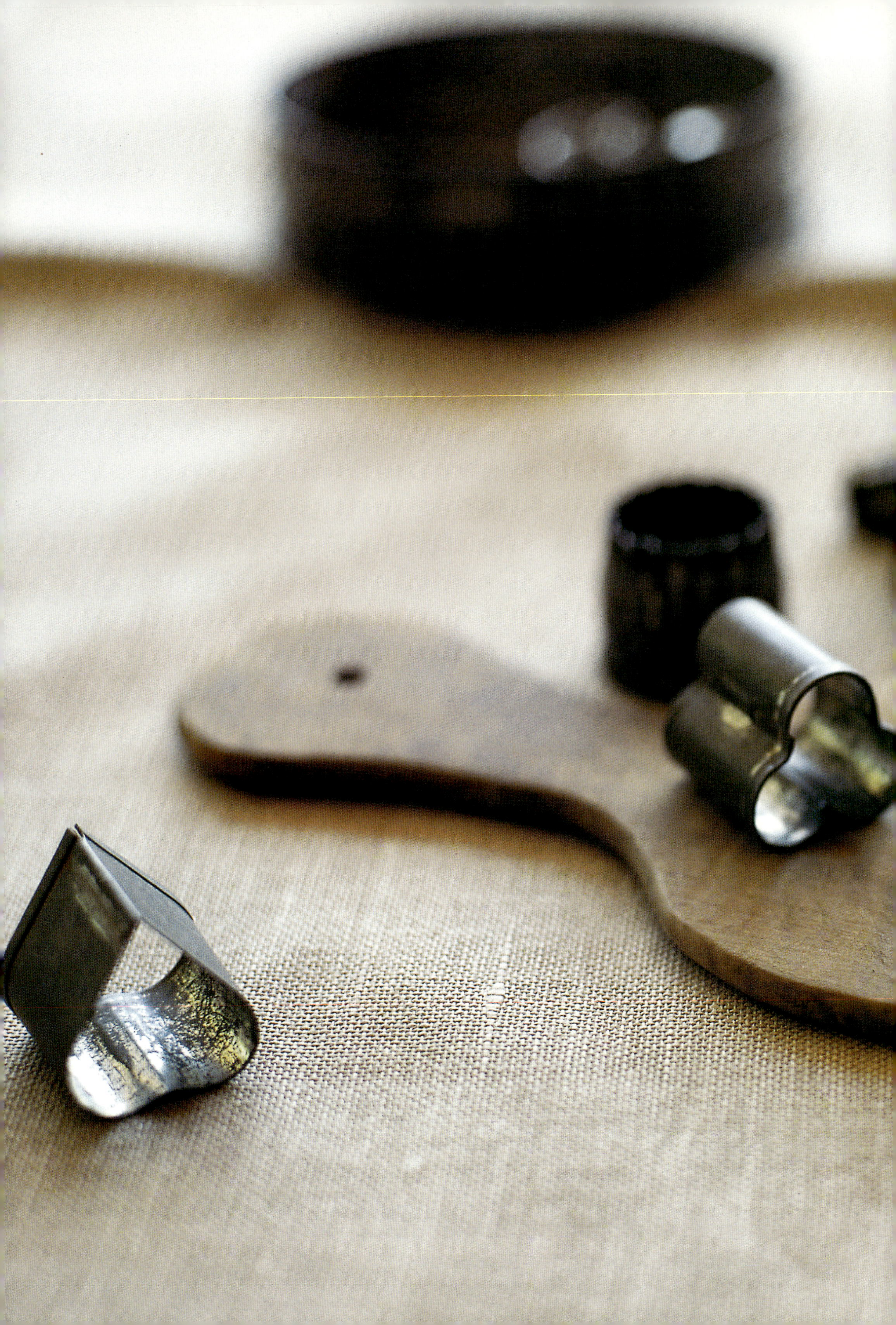

some of the basics

The art of cooking relies on a few techniques and a few good recipes.
Master two or three pastries, a béchamel sauce,
perhaps a béarnaise or hollandaise sauce and you're well on your way.
Learn to make a good home-made mayonnaise and some of
the other dressings that turn a salad into something special and
you'll never be short of ideas. These are the basics,
the recipes essential to a good cook's repertoire.

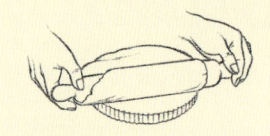

PASTRY

Quiches, savoury tartlets, profiteroles and glistening fruit tarts – the world of baking is open to you once you master the art of pastry.

SHORTCRUST FLAN CASE •

1 cup plain flour
a pinch of salt
60 g butter
1 egg yolk
2 tablespoons iced water
a good squeeze of lemon juice

Preheat the oven to 190°C. Sift the flour and salt into a bowl. Cut the butter into small pieces and rub lightly and evenly in the flour, until the mixture resembles breadcrumbs. Beat the egg yolk, 1 tablespoon water and the lemon juice together then sprinkle evenly over the flour, stirring with a spatula or knife to form a dough. Add a little extra water if necessary. Knead lightly on a floured board, wrap in cling wrap and chill for 1 hour, or until required.

Roll out on a lightly floured board to fit 20–23 cm fluted flan ring. Press pastry well into the fluted edge, being careful not to stretch it. Using a sharp knife, cut away the excess pastry so it is level with the top of the flan ring. Prick the base lightly with a fork. Line the pastry with a piece of greaseproof paper and half-fill with pie weights or dried beans. Chill for a further 15 minutes then bake for 10 minutes. Remove from the oven, remove the paper and beans and cool while preparing the filling. If not to be baked with filling, return to the oven for another 5–10 minutes until golden.

note: the flan case may be brushed with a little egg white before baking, if desired, as an extra precaution against the filling seeping through.

food processor alternative: Have the butter well-chilled, or even better, frozen. Fit the metal double-bladed knife. Sift the flour and salt into the food processor bowl. Cut the butter into small pieces and add to the flour. Process for 15–20 seconds, turning the motor on and off until the mixture resembles fine breadcrumbs.

Add the egg yolk and sprinkle over the water and lemon juice. Process for about 20 seconds or until the pastry clings together and forms a ball. Knead lightly to form a smooth dough. Chill and use as required. *(See above for rolling and baking.)*

Roll pastry out and use a rolling pin to transfer to the flan ring.

Press pastry well into fluted edge.

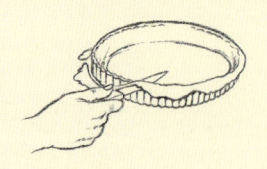

Using a sharp knife, cut away the excess pastry level with top of flan ring.

To bake blind, line pastry with baking paper and half-fill with pie weights or dried beans, then bake.

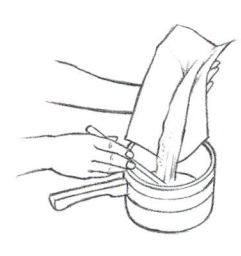

When making choux pastry, use greaseproof paper as a funnel to pour the flour into boiling mixture.

Using a wooden spoon, beat in the eggs gradually, until the paste is well combined, shiny and smooth.

To form puffs, use a pastry bag and plain tube or use two spoons to make well-shaped mounds of pastry on the tray.

SWEET FLAN PASTRY ••

60 g butter, cut into small pieces
1 cup plain flour
2 tablespoons sugar
½ teaspoon salt
1 teaspoon iced water
2 egg yolks
½ teaspoon vanilla essence

Rub the butter into the sifted flour, until the mixture resembles breadcrumbs. Combine the remaining ingredients, and blend them into the flour and butter with a spatula or knife. Turn onto a well-floured board. Knead lightly, wrap in cling wrap, and chill for at least 30 minutes. (*See shortcrust flan case for rolling and baking.*)

food processor alternative: As with the shortcrust flan case, adding the sugar to the flour and salt into the food processor bowl, and the vanilla essence with the iced water and egg yolks.

CHOUX PASTRY ••

Profiteroles, éclairs and gougères all use choux pastry in their making.

1 cup plain flour
1 cup water
125 g unsalted butter, cut into pieces
1 teaspoon sugar
½ teaspoon salt
4 eggs, beaten lightly

Sift the flour on to a square of greaseproof paper. Put the water, butter, sugar and salt into a saucepan. Bring to a rapid boil and, using the greaseproof paper as a funnel, pour the flour all at once into the boiling mixture. Over a gentle heat, incorporate quickly and thoroughly with a wooden spoon and beating until the mixture balls around the spoon and leaves the sides of the pan (a bit of muscle is needed here). This process dries the paste and cooks the flour.

Remove from the heat, transfer to a plate and cool to lukewarm. Put into a bowl and gradually beat in the eggs. If the paste is very stiff, beat an extra egg and add gradually, until a pliable consistency is obtained. Beat the paste until well combined, shiny and smooth. Use as required.

SAUCES

A good sauce is the secret of success to many dishes. The basic recipes are few and the ingredients simple, including fresh butter and eggs, milk, cream or a good stock. The variations and the uses of a good sauce are limitless.

BÉCHAMEL SAUCE •

This classic white sauce is the basis of many delicious sauces. Extra butter, cream and egg yolk can be added to enrich the basic sauce.

1¼ cups milk
1 bay leaf
1 onion, chopped
5 whole peppercorns
30 g butter
2 tablespoons plain flour
2 tablespoons cream (optional)
salt and white pepper

Slowly heat the milk with the bay leaf, onion and peppercorns over a low heat, to scalding point. Remove from the heat, cover, and infuse for 7–8 minutes. Melt the butter in a small, heavy-based saucepan, draw away from heat and stir in the flour. Return to the heat and cook for about 1 minute. Then add, all at once, the strained and slightly cooled milk. Stir constantly over a moderate heat until boiling. Simmer for 2–3 minutes. Add the cream, if using, add salt and pepper to taste.

variations:
To 1¼ cups béchamel sauce, add the following:

aurore sauce: Add 1 tablespoon tomato paste, adjusting the amount, if necessary, to give a good, pink colour and delicate flavour. Add ¼ cup cream. Serve with fish, meat, eggs or vegetables.

mornay sauce: Beat 2 tablespoons grated, tasty cheese into the hot béchamel sauce. Add ½ teaspoon Dijon mustard and extra salt and pepper, to taste. Add ¼ cup cream or milk. If the sauce has to be heated, do not boil. Use to coat fish, vegetables and eggs. If food is to be served 'au gratin', top with a little cheese and/or breadcrumbs, tossed in melted butter, and brown under the grill or in an oven.

onion sauce: Boil 2–4 finely chopped white onions in water to cover, until tender. Drain, then add to the béchamel sauce. Heat, stirring constantly. Serve with tripe, boiled beef, poached chicken and corned meats.

parsley sauce: Add 2 tablespoons finely chopped parsley to the béchamel sauce. Serve with corned meats, or fish.

caper sauce: Add 1 tablespoon capers and 1 teaspoon caper liquid to the béchamel sauce. Serve with boiled beef and corned meats.

curry sauce: Fry a finely chopped onion in 1 tablespoon butter. Add 1 tablespoon curry powder and fry for a few minutes. Add the hot béchamel sauce and simmer gently for 5–10 minutes. Serve with hard-boiled eggs or reheat with 1½ cups chopped diced chicken, turkey or lamb.

HOLLANDAISE SAUCE •••

A piquant sauce, creamy yellow in colour, and made of egg yolks, butter and lemon juice. It is served with vegetables, such as asparagus and broccoli, and with grilled or poached fish and poached eggs.

The main point to remember when making hollandaise sauce is to heat the egg yolks slowly and gradually. It is best to cook the egg yolk mixture in a basin over a saucepan of hot water, or in a double-boiler. Butter is added very gradually to the egg yolk mixture, rather in the way oil is added to mayonnaise, incorporating each small amount before adding the next. If added too quickly, the sauce will not thicken. Unsalted butter is the first choice for making these sauces, but you can also use salted butter.

125 g unsalted butter
1–2 teaspoons lemon juice, strained
3 egg yolks
2 teaspoons water
a pinch of salt
freshly ground white pepper

Have the butter at room temperature, and cut into small pieces, each equivalent to about a teaspoonful.

Put a piece of butter with the lemon juice, egg yolks and water in the top half of a double-boiler, or in a bowl. Beat well for 1 minute, until combined. Place over a saucepan of barely simmering water, mix in the salt and pepper, and beat until it thickens to a smooth cream.

If the sauce thickens too quickly, and becomes lumpy, immediately stand the bowl or pan in cold water, then return to the heat, and beat until thick and smooth. Turn off the heat, or remove from the stove, and add the butter one piece at a time, stirring briskly until each piece is well incorporated. For perfect smoothness, it is essential to keep beating without stopping between additions of butter. Taste and correct seasoning, if necessary.

Serve warm, not hot, as soon as possible. If sauce is to be kept, keep it no longer than 1 hour, put over a pan of lukewarm water and, just before serving, beat in 1 teaspoon of tepid water.

BLENDER HOLLANDAISE ••

This is a very easy, almost foolproof recipe. The finished sauce will not have quite the glossy appearance of a hollandaise sauce beaten by hand, but the natural flavours of butter, eggs and lemon juice will be the same.

3 egg yolks
2 teaspoons lemon juice
1 tablespoon water
¼ teaspoon salt
freshly ground white pepper
125 g unsalted butter

Put the egg yolks, lemon juice, water, salt and pepper in a blender. Cover and blend at a high speed for a few seconds. Melt the butter. While blending on high speed, add the hot melted butter very slowly to the egg yolk mixture and blend until creamy. Do not use the milky residue in the bottom of the pan. Taste and add more salt and pepper, if necessary.

MOUSSELINE SAUCE •••

This is hollandaise sauce, to which ½ cup whipped cream is added at the last moment.

BÉARNAISE SAUCE •••

250 g unsalted butter
3 sprigs of tarragon or ½ teaspoon dried tarragon
2 shallots, chopped
¼ cup tarragon vinegar
¼ cup white wine
3 egg yolks
1 tablespoon water
salt and a pinch of white pepper
1 tablespoons chopped parsley, chervil or tarragon

Have the butter at room temperature. In a saucepan, combine the tarragon, shallots, tarragon vinegar and white wine. Cook until the mixture reduces by two-thirds. Cool slightly then strain and pour into the top of a double-boiler or small bowl.

Place over hot but not boiling water, add the egg yolks and water, and stir briskly with a wire whisk, until the mixture is light and fluffy. Add about one-third of the butter and whisk constantly until the mixture thickens slightly. Add the remainder of the butter in small pieces, stirring briskly.

Allow the mixture to thicken after each addition. Season with the salt and pepper, to taste. Add the chopped herb. Serve with roast beef, chateaubriand or other steaks.

MINT SAUCE •

1 large handful of mint leaves
2 tablespoons sugar
3 tablespoons boiling water
3 tablespoons malt vinegar

Chop the mint finely and put in a bowl with the sugar. Add boiling water and stir until the sugar dissolves. Stir in the vinegar and leave for 1 hour before serving. Serve with roast lamb.

BREAD SAUCE •

1¼ cups milk
1 onion
1 bay leaf
6 black peppercorns
1 cup fresh breadcrumbs
salt
unsalted butter or cream

Gently simmer the milk, onion, bay leaf and peppercorns in a small saucepan for 15 minutes. Strain into a jug and return to the saucepan, add breadcrumbs and salt, to taste. Simmer until creamy. Stir in a little butter or cream. Serve with roast chicken.

APPLE SAUCE •

3 cooking apples such as Granny Smith
1–2 tablespoons water
2 tablespoons sugar
strip of lemon rind
strip of orange rind

Peel, core and slice apples thickly. Put into a saucepan with water, sugar and rinds. Cover and cook gently to a pulp, adding water if needed. Remove rinds and serve warm with roast pork.

PARSLEY BUTTER •

90 g unsalted butter
1 teaspoon grated lemon rind
1 teaspoon lemon juice
3 tablespoons finely chopped parsley
salt and freshly ground pepper

Cream the butter in a small bowl and beat in the lemon rind, then the juice, parsley and salt and pepper. Shape into a roll and wrap in a piece of foil. Chill until firm – this may take 1 hour and can be done well in advance.

SWEET SAUCES

These delicious sweet sauces are indispensable for enlivening meringues, ice-creams and steamed puddings.

RASPBERRY SAUCE •

2 cups fresh or frozen raspberries
juice of half lemon
¼ cup sugar
2 tablespoons Framboise liqueur or Grand Marnier (optional)

Blend the raspberries, lemon juice and sugar in a food processor. Just before serving, add the Framboise or Grand Marnier, if using, and mix well.

BUTTERSCOTCH RUM SAUCE •

1½ cups brown sugar
½ cup cream
90 g unsalted butter
¼ cup rum

Bring the sugar, cream and butter slowly to the boil. Cook vigorously for about 3 minutes. Remove from the heat, allow to cool for 5 minutes, and stir in the rum. Serve warm.

CUSTARD SAUCE •

1¼ cups milk
½ vanilla bean
1 teaspoon cornflour
2 large or 3 small egg yolks
45 g sugar

Heat ¾ cup milk with the vanilla in the top of a double-boiler. In a small bowl, blend the cornflour with the remaining cold milk. Add a little hot milk, then return to the saucepan and cook for 1 minute. Allow to cool. Beat the egg and sugar together then add to the mixture. Cook, stirring, until custard coats the back of a spoon.

HARD SAUCE •

90 g unsalted butter
1 cup icing sugar, sifted
2 teaspoons brandy or more, to taste
1 egg white, beaten (optional)

Cream the butter until soft. Add the icing sugar and beat until white and light. If liked, substitute ¼ cup ground almonds for ¼ cup of the icing sugar. Mix in the almonds, if using, and work the brandy into the mixture. Fold in the stiffly beaten egg white. Chill until ready to serve.

CUMBERLAND RUM BUTTER •

125 g unsalted butter
1¼ cups brown sugar
¼ cup rum

Cream the butter until light. Add the sugar gradually, and beat again until light and creamy. Add the rum gradually until well mixed. Pile high in a bowl and chill thoroughly before using. The mixture can also be spread in a shallow tin, chilled, and cut into slices when set.

BRANDY SAUCE •

45 g unsalted butter
2 tablespoons plain flour
3 tablespoons sugar
1 tablespoon golden syrup
½ cup cream
½ cup milk
¼ cup brandy

Melt the butter in a small saucepan and stir in the flour. Cook for a minute then add the sugar, golden syrup, cream and milk. Stir to blend and continue cooking over a gentle heat until thick and creamy. Stir in brandy and serve hot with Christmas pudding.

SALAD DRESSINGS

An essential to a good salad is a good dressing, and although the basic salad dressings are few in number, they work miracles in providing infinite variety. French dressing, or vinaigrette as it is called in France, and mayonnaise are the established leaders in the field, followed closely by sour cream, yoghurt and cooked salad dressings.

VINAIGRETTE (FRENCH DRESSING) •

2 tablespoons white vinegar
½ teaspoon salt
½ teaspoon freshly ground pepper
6 tablespoons olive oil

Combine the vinegar, salt and pepper in a bowl. Gradually whisk in the oil until thickened. Beat again if necessary before using.

variations:
To 1 quantity of vinaigrette, add the following:
mustard dressing: Beat ½ teaspoon sugar with the vinaigrette then add 1 teaspoon Dijon mustard.
anchovy dressing: 1 mashed anchovy fillet, 1 tablespoon finely chopped onion.
caper dressing: 1 tablespoon chopped capers.
garlic dressing: 1 clove crushed garlic.
tangy dressing: 1 teaspoon grated horseradish relish, 1 teaspoon Worcestershire sauce and a dash of Tabasco.
ravigote dressing: 1 teaspoon finely chopped green olives, 1 teaspoon finely chopped chives, 1 teaspoon finely chopped red capsicum and 1 finely chopped hard-boiled egg. Good with cold meats.

MAYONNAISE ••

The sumptuous dressing we all love. It has dozens of uses and can transform simple ingredients into an elegant dish. Delicious with poached fish or chicken salad, drizzled over steamed baby potatoes, shelled prawns or other seafood. Lemon mayonnaise is made the same way, using lemon juice in place of the vinegar.

2 egg yolks
½ teaspoon salt
freshly ground pepper
2 teaspoons Dijon mustard
2 teaspoons white vinegar or lemon juice
1 cup olive oil

Put the egg yolks, salt, pepper, mustard and 1 teaspoon vinegar into a bowl. Beat vigorously with a whisk and add the oil drop by drop, until a little more than half a cup has been added. As mixture thickens, add remaining oil in a thin stream, while beating continually. Stop now and then to check that the mixture is well blended. When all the oil has been added, stir in the remaining vinegar. Add 2 teaspoons boiling water to the mayonnaise that is to be kept briefly. Store in a cool place.

MAYONNAISE MADE IN A FOOD PROCESSOR •

Place the egg, seasonings and 1 teaspoon of the vinegar in the bowl of a blender or food processor and process for a few seconds. With the motor running, pour the oil in very gradually, ensuring that each addition has been absorbed before adding more. When all the oil has been incorporated, add the remaining vinegar.

variations:

To 1 quantity of mayonnaise, add the following:

curry mayonnaise: 1 teaspoon curry powder, 1 teaspoon lemon juice, 1 small clove crushed garlic and a pinch of salt.

green mayonnaise: 2 teaspoons finely snipped chives and 2 teaspoons finely chopped parsley.

roquefort mayonnaise: 1 tablespoon tomato ketchup and 2 tablespoons crumbled Roquefort cheese.

TARTARE SAUCE •

½ cup mayonnaise
salt and freshly ground pepper
1 teaspoon chopped capers
2 teaspoons chopped gherkins
1 teaspoon chopped herbs
white of one hard-boiled egg, chopped

Season the mayonnaise with salt and pepper then mix in the capers, gherkins, herbs and egg white. A little cream may be added, if desired. Serve with fried fish.

GREEN GODDESS DRESSING •

1 cup mayonnaise
½ cup sour cream
2 tablespoons anchovy essence
⅓ cup chopped parsley
2 teasspoons tarragon vinegar
2 tablespoons snipped chives
1 tablespoon lemon juice
salt and freshly ground pepper

Combine the mayonnaise and sour cream, add the remaining ingredients, and mix well. Add the salt and pepper, to taste. Serve with a green salad, prawns and other seafood, or spoon over a rice salad.

REMOULADE SAUCE •

½ cup mayonnaise
1 good teaspoon of Dijon mustard
1 tablespoon chopped gherkins
1 tablespoon chopped capers
1 tablespoon chopped herbs
1 teaspoon dried tarragon
a few drops of anchovy essence

Mix ingredients together then stir in a few drops of anchovy essence. Serve with egg salads, fish, prawns and pig's trotters.

COOKED SALAD DRESSING (SALAD CREAM) ••

1 tablespoon sugar
1½ tablespoons plain flour
2 teaspoons dry mustard
1 teaspoon salt
2 egg yolks
¼ cup melted butter
1½ cups milk
⅓ cup vinegar
a pinch of paprika *(optional)*

Combine the dry ingredients in the top of a double-boiler. Add the egg yolks, butter and milk, and blend well. Gradually add the vinegar. Cook, stirring constantly, until thick. Add a pinch of paprika, if desired. Use in the same way as you would mayonnaise and with the same variations.

ORIENTAL DRESSING •

¾ cup sunflower oil
4 tablespoons light soy sauce
2 tablespoons lemon juice
1 clove garlic, crushed
salt and freshly ground pepper

Put all the ingredients in a screw-topped jar, adding the salt and pepper, to taste. Seal the jar and shake well to blend.

TAPENADE •

Whether for a picnic, quick snack or a light lunch there is nothing nicer than a bowl of this delicious French paste of olives, anchovies, capers and canned tuna. Tapenade is all the better for being made a few days ahead and stored airtight in the refrigerator.

125 g pitted black olives
6 anchovy fillets, drained and rinsed
3 tablespoons capers, drained
100 g canned tuna in oil, drained
1 lemon
⅓ cup extra virgin olive oil

Crush olives in a mortar or chop in a food processor. Add the anchovies, capers, tuna and the juice of half a lemon. Pound or process until mixture has formed a fairly smooth paste.

With the motor still running, add the oil in a slow stream. Taste and add more lemon juice, if liked. Turn into a small serving bowl and serve with hard-boiled eggs, crusty bread and a few crisp vegetables. (See tapenade-stuffed tomatoes, p. 288.)

FROSTINGS AND ICINGS
CHOCOLATE FROSTING •

125 g butter, softened
1½ cups icing sugar mixture, sifted
60 g dark chocolate, melted

Cream the butter in a bowl using a wooden spoon or use an electric mixer. Gradually beat in half the icing sugar mixture. Beat in the chocolate then beat in the remaining icing sugar mixture.

note: melt the chocolate gently on a heatproof plate over hot water. Alternatively cocoa powder can be used by substituting ⅓ cup of the icing sugar mixture with the same amount of cocoa.

LEMON ICING •

60 g unsalted butter, softened
1 teaspoon grated lemon rind
1 teaspoon vanilla essence
1 tablespoon lemon juice
about 1 cup sifted icing sugar

Cream the butter with the rind, vanilla and lemon juice and gradually beat in the icing sugar until thick and smooth.

FUDGE FROSTING •

2 cups sugar
2 tablespoons light corn or golden syrup
⅔ cup milk
40 g unsweetened chocolate
¼ cup butter
1 teaspoon vanilla essence

Put the sugar, syrup, milk and chocolate in a large saucepan. Place over gentle heat, until the sugar is dissolved. Cook until a small amount forms a soft ball when dropped into cold water. Stir occasionally to prevent catching. remove from heat, add butter without stirring, and cool until lukewarm. Add vanilla and beat until creamy and barely holding shape. Spread quickly on cake.

GLACÉ ICING •

1 cup icing sugar
1 tablespoon water
flavouring and colouring

Sift the icing sugar and mix with the water, until the icing covers the back of a spoon smoothly and thickly. Warm over low heat. Add the flavouring and use as required.

INDEX

Page numbers in italics indicate photographs.

A

Aberdeen sausage	118
accompaniments for soup	31
agedashi tofu	279
almonds	
almond butter balls	240
almond cheese rounds	5
almond fingers	238
almond friandise	218
almond paste	227
chicken and almonds	264
American potato salad	150
anchovy dressing	306
anchovy canapés	287
angels on horseback	287
antipasto	4
Anzac biscuits	235
appetizers and canapés	4-5, 287–292
apples	
apple chutney	274
apple sauce	304
apple strudel	189
pork, apple and pistachio stuffing	82
tarte aux pommes (apple tart)	190, *191*
apricots	
apricot fingers	234
apricot glaze	190
apricot ice-cream	204
apricot jam	252, *253*
apricot soufflé omelette	183
pork chops with prunes, apricots and spinach	107
arroz con pollo	173
artichokes	**124**
to prepare	10
artichokes à la Grecque	10
artichokes in wine	124
globe artichokes	124
loin of lamb with artichokes and potatoes	104
asparagus	**125**
asparagus soldiers	35
cream of asparagus soup	22
pasta primaverde	162, *163*
steamed asparagus	125
avocado canapés	287
avocado soup	30
avocado with seafood	6

B

baby squid with garlic	65
bacon	
bacon and eggs	35
lamb's fry with bacon	113
baked cannelloni	166
baked eggs in ramekins	36
baked fish fillets with pine nut crust	57
baked glazed ham	282
baked pears in red wine	200
baked stuffed whole fish	58, *59*
banana cake	216
bananas with rum	202
barbecued pork	263
barbecued quail	86
basic butter cake	210
basic chicken sauté	74
basic hot sweet soufflés	182
basil butter	112
Basque chicken	78, *79*
beans	**125**
green beans with tomato, garlic and basil	126
hill of beans	125

broad beans	**128**
broad beans with mint and pancetta	128, *129*
rice with broad beans	172
béarnaise sauce	304
béchamel sauce	302
beef	**90–98**
Aberdeen sausage	118
basic steak and kidney	98
beef and vermicelli noodle salad	156, *157*
beef bouillon	16
beef bourguignonne	95
beef curry	271
beef pot roast	96, *97*
beef Provençale	95
beef steak	91
beef strips in tomato cream sauce	285
beef stock	16
beef stroganoff	92
cabbage rolls	115
carbonnade of beef	96
corned beef	119
fillet of beef en croûte (beef Wellington)	286
fillet of beef Provençale	284
grilled steak	91, *93*
hamburgers (and variations)	114
Malay beef satays	92
pan-fried steak	91
pastitso for a crowd	285
potted hough	119
roast beef and capers on pumpernickel	291
roast beef canapés	288
roast fillet of beef	94
roast sirloin of beef	94
rump roast	92
shredded beef with capsicum	262
spaghetti and meat balls	166
steak and kidney pie	98
steak and kidney pudding	98
steak and kidney sponge	98
steak au poivre	91
sukiyaki	278
Swedish meat balls	114
tournedos with béarnaise sauce	92
beetroot	**126**
beetroot and cucumber soup	31
beetroot and endive salad	126, *127*
beetroot chutney	247
hot buttered beetroot	126
Bellini	296, *297*
berries	
berry jam	252
berries with yoghurt cream	201
peach and berry compote	202, *203*
see also raspberries, strawberries	
biscuits	**234–243**
almond butter balls	240
almond cheese rounds	5
almond fingers	238
Anzac biscuits	235
apricot fingers	234
brandy snaps	242
burnt butter biscuits	236
cardamom cookies	234
cheese biscuits	5, *2*
coconut raspberry slice	241
date surprises	235
fudge brownies	240
ginger nuts	236
lemon melting moments	236, *237*
linzer biscuits	238, *239*
oatcakes	243
oatmeal raisin cookies	235

peanut chews	238
refrigerator biscuits	241
rosemary and cheese biscuits	243
shortbread	225
shortbread fingers	225
vanilla kippels	240
water biscuits	243
blender hollandaise	303
boiled rice	168
bouquet garni	16
brains in black butter sauce	113
braised broccoli romana	128
braised lamb shanks	105
braised mushrooms	269
braised prawns	268
braised red cabbage	130
brandy crusta	293
brandy sauce	305
brandy snaps	242
brandy sour	293
bread and butter zucchini pickles	250
bread sauce	304
broad beans with mint and pancetta	128, *129*
broccoli	128
brown stock	16
burghul	175
burnt butter biscuits	236
butter cakes	208
butterscotch rum sauce	305
butterfly cakes	211

C

cabbage	**130**
braised red cabbage	130
cabbage rolls	115
sour cream coleslaw	151
Caesar salad	146, *147*
cakes	**206–233**
almond friandise	218
banana cake	216
basic butter cake	210
butter cake variations	210
butter cakes, about	208–209
butterfly cakes	211
cardamom sour cream cake	218
cinnamon tea cake	217
coconut cake	211
cup cakes	211
Dundee cake	230
gingerbread	217
honey spiced sponge roll	216
iced coffee cakes	219
lamingtons	210
linzertorte	224
Madeira cake	216
madeleines	219
marble cake	212
nut loaf	220
orange cake	212, *213*
passionfruit cream sponge	215
pikelets	220
rich chocolate fudge cake	222, *207*
rich Christmas cake	226
rock cakes	221
seed cake	210
sour cream cheesecake	222, *223*
spice cake	210
spice crumb coffee cake	233
sponge cakes, about	214
sponge sandwich	214
strawberry sponge, glazed	215
Swiss roll	215
calamari *see squid*	
canapés	287

309

THE MARGARET FULTON COOKBOOK ••• INDEX

canary pudding	192
Cantonese roast duck	265
caper sauce	302
capsicum	**130**
fried bean sprouts with green capsicum	269
fried capsicum	130
Italian capsicum salad	148, *149*
roasted capsicum with couscous	179
shredded beef with capsicum	262
stuffed capsicum, Piedmont-style	131
zucchini and pepper frittata	41
caramel oranges	198, *199*
carbonnade of beef	96
cardamom cookies	234
cardamom sour cream cake	218
carrots vichy	131
cauliflower	131
cheese	
almond cheese rounds	5
cheese biscuits	5, *2*
cheese charlotte	49
cheese croûtes	31
cheese omelette soufflé	41
cheese pastry	5
cheese snacks	49
cheese soufflé	42, *43*
cheese soufflé (variations)	44
croque monsieur	49
goat cheese, spinach and tomato omelette	40
macaroni cheese	44, *45*
rosemary and cheese biscuits	243
winemaker's rarebit	49
chicken	**70–79**
arroz con pollo	173
basic chicken sauté	74
Basque chicken	78, *79*
chicken and almonds	264
chicken and sweet corn soup	23
chicken and vegetable broth	17
chicken chow mein	264
chicken curry	271
chicken liver pâté	12, *13*
chicken roasted in butter	72
chicken saute à la crème	74
chicken stock	17
chicken teriyaki	278
Chinese white chicken	76
Cobb salad	155
coq au vin	75
coriander chicken	76, *77*
devilled grilled chicken	78
easy chicken liver pâté	12
French roast chicken	71
fresh noodle soup with chicken	23
grilled chicken	76
Mediterranean chicken	72, *73*
oven-fried chicken	75
stuffing for chicken	72
Thai chicken bites	292
Chinese cooking	258–269
chocolate	
chocolate frosting	308
chocolate mousse	194
chocolate pudding	195
chocolate, rich fudge cake	222, *207*
chocolate roulade	184, *185*
chocolate sauce	194
chocolate sauce pudding	193
chocolate soufflé	182
choux pastry	301
chowder, fish	29
Christmas	
baked glazed ham	282, *280–281*
brandy sauce	305
Cumberland rum butter	305
fruit mince	228

little mince pies	230
rich Christmas cake	226
rich Christmas pudding	228, *229*
roast turkey for Christmas	80, *81*
spiced fruits	284, *280*
vegetables for Christmas dinner	83
chutneys *see pickles and chutneys*	
cinnamon pinwheels	233
cinnamon tea cake	217
citrus summer cup	296
clams	**66**
fresh clam chowder	66
spaghetti with clams	66, *67*
cobb salad	155
cocktail sauce	6
coconut cake	211
coconut raspberry slice	241
coleslaw, sour cream	151
combination fried rice	261
cookies *see biscuits*	
coq au vin	75
coriander chicken	76, *77*
coriander eggplant salad	153
corn pancakes with smoked salmon	288, *289*
corned beef	119
country terrine	116, *117*
country tomato relish	250
court bouillon	55
couscous	**176**
couscous with fruit compote	179
couscous with vegetables	176, *177*
grilled lamb with lemon couscous	178
roasted capsicum with couscous	179
spicy couscous with chickpeas	176
crab	**60**
crab cakes	60
crab quiche	46
crab with black bean sauce	266, *267*
crabmeat scrambled eggs	36
devilled crab	60
crayfish	**61**
crayfish (lobster) mayonnaise	61
crayfish (lobster) mornay	61
crayfish thermidor	61
cream of asparagus soup	22
cream of carrot soup	20
cream of mushroom soup	20
cream of oyster soup	28
creamy mashed potatoes	137
creamy rice pudding	193
crème anglaise	188
crème brûlée	188
crème caramel	187
crêpes suzette	197
crisp-roasted potatoes and parsnips	138
crisp-skin sweet-sour fish	266
croque monsieur	49
croutons	31
crumbed lamb cutlets	99
crunchy prawn balls	292
cucumbers	
beetroot and cucumber soup	31
cucumber and yoghurt salad	151
cucumber sauce	120
cucumbers in yoghurt	274
Danish cucumber salad	151
Cumberland rum butter	305
cup cakes	211
curries	**270–273**
beef curry	271
chicken curry	271
dry potato curry	272
mixed vegetable curry	271
pork curry	271
prawn curry	272, *273*
curry sauce	302

custards and creams	**187**
crème anglaise	188
crème brûlée	188
crème caramel	187
custard, English	188
custard sauce	305
plain baked custard	187
rice custard	188

D

Danish cucumber salad	151
Danish rum cream	198
date surprises	235
desserts	**180–205**
apple strudel	189
apple tart (tarte aux pommes)	190, *191*
bananas with rum	202
berries with yoghurt cream	201
canary pudding	192
caramel oranges	198, *199*
cheesecake, sour cream	222, *223*
chocolate mousse	194
chocolate, rich fudge cake	222, *207*
chocolate roulade	184, *185*
chocolate sauce pudding	193
chocolate soufflé, hot	182
Christmas pudding, rich	228
custard, plain baked	187
crème brûlée	188
crème caramel	187
crêpes Suzette	197
Danish rum cream	198
eggnog tart	196
figs with cinnamon and marsala	202
ginger, lime and melon compote	200
glazed strawberry tart	189
ice-cream, apricot	204
ice-cream, Italian coffee	205
ice-cream, old-fashioned vanilla	205
lemon delicious	193
lemon soufflé, cold	184
liqueur soufflé, cold	186
mango mousse	194
orange liqueur soufflé, hot	182
pancakes, with lemon	197
passionfruit flummery	201
passionfruit soufflé, hot	182
pavlova	196, *181*
peach and berry compote	202, *203*
peaches, Italian baked stuffed	201
pears, baked in red wine	200
profiteroles, with chocolate sauce	194, *195*
rhubarb and strawberry crumble	192
rhubarb and strawberry fool	204
rice custard	188
rice pudding, creamy	193
soufflé, basic hot sweet	182
soufflé, hot variations	182
soufflé omelette	183
soufflé omelette, variations	183
strawberries Romanoff	198
sultana pudding	192
sweet sherry soufflé, cold	186
vanilla soufflé, cold	186
zabaglione	197
devilled crab	60
devilled grilled chicken	78
devilled nuts	4
dolmades	174
dressings, salad	**306**
anchovy dressing	306
Caesar salad dressing	146
cooked salad dressing (salad cream)	307
garlic dressing	306
Oriental dressing	307
ravigote	306
sour cream dressing	286
tangy dressing	306

THE MARGARET FULTON COOKBOOK ••• INDEX

vinaigrette 58, 145, 155, 306
see also mayonnaise
drinks
  Bellini 296, *297*
  brandy crusta 293
  brandy sour 293
  Champagne 293
  citrus summer cup 296
  Persian mint cup 296
  pina colada 293
  pink Russian 293
  sangria 296
  spritzer 293
  tequila sunrise 293
dry potato curry 272
duck **84–85**
  Cantonese roast duck 265
  duck a l'orange 84
  grilled duck breast with
    mango salsa 85
Dundee cake 230

E
easy chicken liver pâté 12
egg flower soup 262
eggnog tart 196
eggplant **132**
  coriander eggplant salad 153
  eggplant and potato moussaka 115
  eggplant caviar 132
  eggplant parmigiana 134
  escalavida
    (Spanish-roasted vegetables) 132, *133*
  stuffed eggplant 132
eggs **30–48**
  asparagus soldiers 35
  bacon and eggs 35
  baked eggs in ramekins 36
  boiled 34
  crabmeat scrambled eggs 36
  eggs Benedict 37
  eggs tapenade 37
  eggs with spinach and
    hollandaise 36
  frying 35
  huevos rancheros 37
  omelettes 38
  poached 34
  scrambled 35
  stuffed eggs 287
see also custards, mousses, soufflés
escalavida
  (Spanish-roasted vegetables) 132, *133*

F
fennel and orange salad 148
figs with cinnamon and marsala 202
fillet of beef en croûte
  (beef Wellington) 286
fillet of beef Provençale 284
fillet of beef with béarnaise sauce 94
fish **50–67**
  baked fish fillets with
    pine nut crust 57
  baked stuffed whole fish 58, *59*
  baking 54
  batter 54
  crisp-skin sweet-sour fish 266
  deep-frying 52
  fish à la meuniere 55
  fish and French-fried potatoes 53
  fish chowder 29
  fish Florentine 56
  fish stock 16
  grilling 55
  Mediterranean fish soup 29
  pan-frying/searing 55
  poaching 54

steamed fish with coriander 57
see also salmon, tuna
fondant icing 227
French onion soup 24
French onion soup gratinée 24, *25*
French roast chicken 71
French roast lamb 101
French white bean salad 152
French-fried potatoes 139
fresh clam chowder 66
fresh noodle soup with chicken 23
fried bean sprouts with
  green capsicum 269
fried bread for canapés 288
fried capsicum 130
fried mixed vegetables 269
fried onion rings 136
fried prawn balls 268
fried prawns 64
fried scallops 64
fried zucchini salad with mint 146
frittata, zucchini and pepper 41
fritter batter 54
fruit
  couscous with fruit compote 179
  fruit mince 228
  spiced fruits 284, *280*
  see also specific fruit
fudge brownies 240
fudge frosting 308

G
garlic and oil sauce 161
gazpacho Andaluz 276, *277*
gem scones 221
ginger nuts 236
ginger, lime and melon compote 200
gingerbread 217
glacé icing 308
glazed strawberry sponge 215
glazed strawberry tart 189
goat cheese, avocado and
  smoked salmon canapés 287
goat cheese, spinach and tomato
  omelette 40
gougères 5
gravy 71, 83, 94, 101, 108
Greek lemon soup 22
Greek salad 152
Greek-style olives 4
green goddess dressing 307
green mayonnaise 306
gribiche sauce 121
grilled chicken 76
grilled duck breast with
  mango salsa 85
grilled lamb chops 99
grilled lamb with lemon couscous 178
grilled salmon with mango salad 56
grilled steak 91, 93
grilled tandoori lamb cutlets 100
grilled veal chops with basil butter 112

H
ham **282–283**
  baked glazed ham 282, *280–281*
  melon and ham 6
  pea and ham soup 26, *27*
  spinach and ham soufflé 44
hamburgers (and variations) 114
hard sauce 305
herbed olives 4
herbed potato salad 150
hollandaise sauce 303
honey spiced sponge roll 216
horseradish cream 120
hot and sour soup 262
hot cross buns 232

huevos rancheros 37
hummus with tahina 178
Hungarian goulash 110
hunter's mushroom pasta sauce 167

I
ice-cream
  apricot ice-cream 204
  Italian coffee ice-cream 205
  old-fashioned vanilla ice-cream 205
iced coffee cakes 219
icings and frostings
  almond paste 227
  chocolate frosting 308
  coffee glacé icing 219
  fondant icing 227
  fudge frosting 308
  glacé icing 211
  lemon filling 236
  lemon frosting 215
  lemon icing 308
  orange icing 233
  passionfruit icing 215
Indian ghee rice 173
Indonesian satays 8
Irish stew 104
Italian baked stuffed peaches 201
Italian capsicum salad 148, *149*
Italian coffee ice-cream 205

J
jams **246–255**
  apricot jam 252, *253*
  berry jam 252
  quick strawberry jam 254
  rhubarb and orange jam 254
  satsuma plum jam 252
  three-fruit marmalade 254

K
kichadi 175
kidneys in wine sauce 113

L
lamb **99–105**
  braised lamb shanks 105
  cabbage rolls 115
  crumbed lamb cutlets 99
  eggplant and potato moussaka 115
  French roast lamb 101
  grilled lamb chops 99
  grilled lamb with
    lemon couscous 178
  grilled tandoori lamb cutlets 100
  Irish stew 104
  lamb pilaf 104
  lamb's fry with bacon 113
  leg of lamb with haricot beans 102
  loin of lamb with artichokes
    and potatoes 104
  racks of lamb with cumin crust 102, *103*
  roast lamb coriander 101
  roast leg of lamb with vegetables 101
  roasting 100
  spiced lamb stew 105
lamingtons 210
leeks **134**
  how to prepare 30
  leek quiche 48
  leeks à la Grecque 10
  leeks Niçoise 134, *135*
  vichysoisse 30
lemons
  Greek lemon soup 22
  grilled lamb with
    lemon couscous 178
  lemon delicious 193
  lemon frosting 215

311

THE MARGARET FULTON COOKBOOK ••• INDEX

lemon icing	308
lemon melting moments	236, *237*
lemon soufflé	184
parsley and lemon stuffing	82
preserved lemons	249
preserved lemon olives	4
lettuce wedges with yoghurt dressing	150
linzer biscuits	238, *239*
linzertorte	224
lobster *see crayfish*	

M

macaroni cheese	44, *45*
Madeira cake	216
madeleines	219
mangoes	
mango chutney	248
mango mousse	194
Malay beef satays	92
mango salsa	85
marble cake	212
marinade	91
marmalade, three-fruit	254
mayonnaise	**306**
curry mayonnaise	307
green goddess dressing	307
green mayonnaise	307
remoulade sauce	307
roquefort mayonnaise	307
tartare sauce	307
meat	**88–121**
see also beef, lamb, offal, pork, veal	
meats, cold	116
meatballs, Swedish	114
Mediterranean chicken	72, *73*
Mediterranean fish soup	29
melba toast	31
melon and ham	6
meringues	242
meringue fingers	242
minced meat	114
mince pies, little	230
minestrone	24
mint sauce	304
mixed vegetable curry	271
mornay sauce	302
moussaka, eggplant and tomato	115
mousses	
chocolate mousse	194
Danish rum cream	197
mango mousse	194
mussels	**62**
mussels Pernod	62
mussels poulette	62, *63*
preparing mussels (illustration)	52
mushrooms	**136**
braised mushrooms	269
cream of mushroom soup	20
hunter's mushroom pasta sauce	167
mushrooms à la Grecque	10
mushroom quiche	48
mushroom salad	151
mushroom soufflé	44
mushrooms in cream	136

N

nasi goreng	170, *171*
noodles, how to cook	261
nut loaf	220

O

oatcakes	243
oatmeal raisin cookies	235
offal or variety meats	
brains in black butter sauce	113
kidneys in wine sauce	113
lamb's fry with bacon	113

ox tongue	120
pressed tongue	120
old-fashioned vanilla ice-cream	205
olives	
Greek-style olives	4
herbed olives	4
onion and olive tart	6, 7
preserved lemon olives	4
olla gitana	141
omelettes	**38–41**
basic omelette	38, *39*
cheese omelette soufflé	41
fillings	40
fluffy omelette	40
goat cheese, spinach and tomato omelette	40
omelette (variations)	38
soufflé omelettes	183
Spanish potato omelette	41
zucchini and pepper frittata	41
onions	**136**
French onion soup	24
French onion soup gratinée	24, *25*
fried onion rings	136
how to prepare	138
onion and olive tart	6, 7
onion sauce	302
onions à la Grecque	10
sweet and sour onions	136
oranges	
caramel oranges	198, *199*
duck a l'orange	84
fennel and orange salad	148
orange cake	212, *213*
orange icing	233
orange liqueur soufflé	182
orange rolls	233
rhubarb and orange jam	254
Oriental dressing	307
Oriental pork spare ribs	107
oven-fried chicken	75
oven-roasted potatoes	138
ox tongue	120
oysters	**62**
angels on horseback	287
cream of oyster soup	28
oysters au naturel	6
oysters catalina	62
oysters mornay	62

P

paella Valenciana	275, *256–257*
pancakes with lemon	197
pan-fried steak	91
pappadams	274
parsley and lemon stuffing	82
parsley butter	304
parsley sauce	302
passionfruit flummery	201
passionfruit cream sponge	217
passionfruit soufflé	182
pasta	**160**
baked cannelloni	166
lasagne	164, *165*
pasta primaverde	162, *163*
spaghetti alla carbonara	167
spaghetti and meat balls	166
spaghetti with clams	66, *67*
pasta sauces	**162**
bolognese sauce (ragu)	162
fresh tomato sauce	161
garlic and oil sauce	161
hunter's mushroom pasta sauce	167
pesto	164
pastitso for a crowd	285
pastry	
cheese pastry	5
choux pastry	301

shortcrust flan case	300
sweet flan pastry	301
pâté	
chicken liver pâté	12
country terrine	116
easy chicken liver pâté	12
shredded pork pâté	120
pavlova	196
peach and berry compote	202, *203*
peach and saffron chutney	248
peaches, Italian baked stuffed	201
peanut chews	238
peanut sauce	8
pears in red wine, baked	200
peas	
green peas	137
green peas, French-style	137
pasta primaverde	162, *163*
pea and ham soup	26, *27*
pea purée	87
peppers *see capsicum*	
Persian mint cup	294
pesto	164
pickles and chutneys	**246–250**
apple chutney	274
beetroot chutney	247
bread and butter zucchini pickles	250
country tomato relish	250
mango chutney	248
peach and saffron chutney	248
preserved lemons	249
red chilli jam	249
roasted tomato and chilli relish	247
spiced prunes	249
see also sambals	
pies and tarts	
apple strudel	189
eggnog tart	196
glazed strawberry tart	189
onion and olive tart	6, 7
rhubarb and strawberry crumble	192
tarte aux pommes (apple tart)	190, *191*
tiropetes	291
see also quiche	
pikelets	220
pilau rice	270
pina colada	293
pink Russian	293
piroshki	290
pizza	**294**
pizza crust	294
pizza toppings	294
pizza with prosciutto and rocket	294, *295*
plain baked custard	187
pork	**106–110**
barbecued pork	263
country terrine	116, *117*
Hungarian goulash	110
Indonesian satays	8
Oriental pork spare ribs	107
pork, apple and pistachio stuffing	82
pork chops with prunes, apricots and spinach	107
pork chops with sage	110
pork curry	271
pork involtini	106
pork rillettes	120
roast pork	108, *109*
roasted stuffed belly of pork	108
sang choy bow	263
spiced roast pork	276
Swedish meat balls	114
see also ham	
potatoes	**137**
American potato salad	150
creamy mashed potatoes	137
crisp-roasted potatoes and parsnips	138

312

dry potato curry	272	nasi goreng	170, *171*	salmon canapés	287
eggplant and potato moussaka	115	paella Valenciana	275, *256–257*	salmon mousse	286
French-fried potatoes	139	pilau rice	270	smoked salmon	6
herbed potato salad	150	rice custard	188	smoked salmon stack	11
loin of lamb with artichokes and potatoes	104	rice with broad beans	172	salt and pepper calamari	65
oven-roasted potatoes	138	risotto Milanese	169	saltimbocca	111
potatoes baked in their jackets	138	saffron rice	172	sang choy bow	263
salade Niçoise	154	Spanish rice salad	156	sangria	296
scalloped potatoes	139	steamed rice	169	satsuma plum jam	252
Spanish potato omelette	41	Thai fried rice	174	**sauces, savoury**	
potted hough	119	rich chocolate fudge cake	222, *207*	apple sauce	304
poultry	**68–80**	rich Christmas cake	226	aurore sauce	302
see also chicken, turkey, duck, quail		rich Christmas pudding	228, *229*	béarnaise sauce	304
prawns	**64**	rich sweet dough	233	béchamel sauce	302
braised prawns	268	risotto Milanese	169	black butter sauce	113
crunchy prawn balls	292	roast beef and capers on pumpernickel	291	blender hollandaise	303
fried prawn balls	268	roast beef canapés	288	bread sauce	304
fried prawns	64	roast fillet of beef	94	caper sauce	302
seafood cocktail	6	roast lamb coriander	101	cocktail sauce	6
prawn curry	272, *273*	roast leg of lamb with vegetables	101	cucumber sauce	120
prawn Sichuan	265	roast pork	108, *109*	curry sauce	302
prawn tempura	279	roast shoulder of veal	112	fresh tomato sauce	161
Thai sour spicy prawn soup	28	roast sirloin of beef	94	gribiche sauce	121
preserved lemons	249	roast turkey for Christmas	80, *81*	hollandaise sauce	303
preserved lemon olives	4	roasted capsicum with couscous	179	horseradish cream	120
pressed tongue	120	roasted stuffed belly of pork	108	mint sauce	304
profiteroles, tiny	31	roasted stuffed tomatoes	102	mornay sauce	302
profiteroles with chocolate sauce	194, *195*	roasted tomato and basil soup	22	mousseline sauce	303
puddings		roasted tomato and chilli relish	247	onion sauce	302
canary pudding	192	roasting lamb	100	orange sauce	84
chocolate pudding	195	rock cakes	221	parsley sauce	302
chocolate sauce pudding	193	rosemary and cheese biscuits	243	Roquefort mayonnaise	307
creamy rice pudding	193	Roquefort mayonnaise	307	sauce aurore	302
lemon delicious	193	rouille	29	sour cherry sauce	121
rich Christmas pudding	228, *229*	rum soufflé omelette	183	spiced mustard sauce	121
sultana pudding	192	rump roast	92	tartare sauce	307
pumpkin scones	221			tuna sauce	118
pumpkin soup	18, *19*	**S**		*see also pasta sauces, mayonnaise*	
		saffron rice	172	**sauces, sweet**	
Q		**salads**		brandy sauce	305
quail	**86**	salads, about	144	butterscotch rum sauce	305
barbecued quail	86	American potato salad	150	chocolate sauce	194, *195*
prosciutto-wrapped roasted quail	87	beef and vermicelli noodle salad	156, *157*	Cumberland rum butter	305
quail in vine leaves	86	beetroot and endive salad	126	custard sauce	305
quiche		Caesar salad	146, *147*	hard sauce	305
crab quiche	46	Cobb salad	155	raspberry sauce	305
leek quiche	48	coriander eggplant salad	153	sausage, Aberdeen	118
mushroom quiche	48	cucumber and yoghurt salad	151	scalloped potatoes	139
quiche lorraine	46, *47*	Danish cucumber salad	151	**scallops**	**64**
spinach quiche	46	fennel and orange salad	148	fried scallops	64
quick strawberry jam	254	French white bean salad	152	scallops mornay	61
		fried zucchini salad with mint	146	scallops Provençal	8
R		Greek salad	152	seared scallop salad	8, *9*
racks of lamb with cumin crust	102, *103*	herbed potato salad	150	**scones**	**221**
raddichio salad with shaved Parmesan	145	Italian capsicum salad	148, *149*	gem scones	221
rarebit, winemaker's	49	lettuce wedges with yoghurt dressing	150	pumpkin scones	221
raspberry sauce	305	mango salad	56	Scotch broth	26
raspberry vinegar	250, *251*	mushroom salad	151	seafood cocktail	6
ratatouille	141	raddichio salad with shaved Parmesan	145	seared scallop salad	8, *9*
ravigote	306	salade Niçoise	154	seared tuna salad	58
red chilli jam	249	seared scallop salad	8, *9*	seed cake	210
refrigerator biscuits	241	seared tuna salad	58	**shellfish**	**60**
remoulade sauce	307	sour cream coleslaw	151	skewered seafoods	64
rhubarb		Spanish rice salad	156	shellfish thermidor	64
rhubarb and orange jam	254	tabbouleh	175	*see also clams, crab, crayfish, mussels, oysters, prawns, scallops, squid*	
rhubarb and strawberry crumble	192	tomato and basil salad	145	shortbread	225
rhubarb and strawberry fool	204	tossed green salad	145	shortbread fingers	225
rice	**168**	Waldorf salad	153	shortcrust flan case	300
arroz con pollo	173	wilted salad	155	shredded beef with capsicum	262
boiled rice	168	**salmon**		shredded pork pâté	120
Chinese rice	261	corn pancakes with smoked salmon	288, *289*	simple hors d'oeuvre	4
cooking rice	168	goat cheese, avocado and smoked salmon canapés	287	skewered seafoods	64
combination fried rice	261	grilled salmon with mango salad	56	smoked salmon stack	11
creamy rice pudding	193			**soufflés, hot savoury**	**42**
dolmades	174			cheese soufflé	42, *43*
Indian ghee rice	173			herb soufflé	44
kichadi	175			mushroom soufflé	44

313

THE MARGARET FULTON COOKBOOK ••• INDEX

seafood soufflé	44
spinach and ham soufflé	44
soufflés, sweet	**182**
apricot soufflé omelette	183
basic hot sweet soufflés	182
chocolate roulade	184, *185*
chocolate soufflé	182
lemon soufflé	184
liqueur soufflé	186
omelette with peaches and brandy	183
orange liqueur	182
passionfruit soufflé	182
rum soufflé omelette	183
soufflé omelettes	183
sweet sherry soufflé	186
vanilla soufflé	186
soups	**14–31**
avocado soup	30
beetroot and cucumber soup	31
chicken and sweet corn soup	23
chicken and vegetable broth	17
cream of asparagus soup	22
cream of carrot soup	20
cream of mushroom soup	20
cream of oyster soup	28
egg flower soup	262
fish chowder	29
French onion soup	24
French onion soup gratinée	24, *25*
fresh clam chowder	66
fresh noodle soup with chicken	23
gazpacho Andaluz	276, *277*
Greek lemon soup	22
hot and sour soup	262
Mediterranean fish soup	29
minestrone	24
pea and ham soup	26, *27*
pumpkin soup	18, *19*
roasted tomato and basil soup	22
Scotch broth	26
soup chiffonade	20, *21*
Thai sour spicy prawn soup	28
tomato soup	18
vichysoisse	30
sour cherry sauce	121
sour cream cheesecake	222, *223*
sour cream coleslaw	151
sour cream dressing	286
spaghetti with clams	66, *67*
Spanish cooking	275
Spanish potato omelette	41
Spanish rice salad	156
spice cake	210
spice crumb coffee cake	233
spiced fruits	284, *280*
spiced lamb stew	105
spiced mustard sauce	121
spiced prunes	249
spiced roast pork	276
spicy couscous with chickpeas	176
spinach	**140**
pork chops with prunes, apricots and spinach	107
spinach and ham soufflé	44
spinach quiche	46
sponge cakes	215
sponge sandwich	216
spritzer	293
squid (calamari)	**65**
baby squid with garlic	65
salt and pepper calamari	65
steak and kidney pie	98
steak and kidney pudding	98
steak and kidney sponge	98
steak au poivre	91
steamed fish with coriander	57
steamed rice	169

stocks	**16–17**
beef stock	16
brown stock	16
chicken stock	17
fish stock	17
turkey stock	83
vegetable stock	17
strawberries	
glazed strawberry sponge	215
glazed strawberry tart	189
quick strawberry jam	254
rhubarb and strawberry crumble	192
rhubarb and strawberry fool	204
strawberries romanoff	198
stuffed capsicum, Piedmont-style	131
stuffed eggplant	132
stuffed eggs	287
stuffings	
parsley and lemon stuffing	82
pork, apple and pistachio stuffing	82
stuffing for chicken	72
stuffing for pork	108
sukiyaki	278
sultana cake	210
sultana pudding	192
sun-dried tomato canapés	288
Swedish meat balls	114
sweet and sour onions	136
sweet flan pastry	301
sweet potatoes	**140**
glazed sweet potatoes	140
sweet sherry soufflé	186
Swiss roll	216
T	
tabbouleh	175
tandoori mix	100
tangy dressing	306
tapenade	308
tapenade, eggs	37
tapenade-stuffed tomatoes	288
tarte aux pommes (apple tart)	190, *191*
terrine, country	116
tequila sunrise	293
Thai chicken bites	292
Thai fried rice	174
Thai sour spicy prawn soup	28
three-fruit marmalade	254
tiropetes	291
tofu, agedashi	279
tom yam goong	28
tomatoes	**140**
how to peel	275
country tomato relish	250
fresh tomato sauce	161
goat cheese, spinach and tomato omelette	40
green beans with tomato, garlic and basil	126
roasted tomato and basil soup	22
roasted tomato and chilli relish	247
roasted stuffed tomatoes	102
sun-dried tomato canapés	288
tapenade-stuffed tiny tomatoes	288
tomato and basil salad	145
tomato and mint chutney	274
tomato soup	18
tomatoes Provençale	140
tongue, ox	120
tongue, pressed	120
tossed green salad	145
tournedos with béarnaise sauce	92
tuna	
salade Niçoise	154
seared tuna salad	58
tuna and avocado tartare	11
tuna sauce	118

turkey	**80–83**
roast turkey for Christmas	80, *81*
stuffings	82
turkey gravy	83
V	
vanilla kippels	240
vanilla soufflé	186
veal	**110–112**
country terrine	116, *117*
grilled veal chops with basil butter	112
potted hough	119
roast shoulder of veal	112
saltimbocca	111
Swedish meat balls	114
veal cordon bleu	111
veal with mushroom sauce	111
vitello tonnato	118
Wiener schnitzel	111
vegetables	**122–141**
chicken and vegetable broth	17
couscous with vegetables	176, *177*
fried mixed vegetables	269
gazpacho Andaluz	276, *277*
mixed vegetable curry	271
pasta primaverde	162, *163*
vegetable stock	17
vegetables à la Grecque	10
vegetables for Christmas dinner	83
Spanish roasted vegetables	132
see also specific vegetables	
vichysoisse	30
vinaigrette	58, 145, 155, 306
vinaigrette, green herb	284
vine leaves, to prepare	87
vitello tonnato	118
W	
Waldorf salad	153
water biscuits	243
Wiener schnitzel	111
wilted salad	155
winemaker's rarebit	49
yeast breads	**231–233**
cinnamon pinwheels	233
hot cross buns	232
orange rolls	233
rich sweet dough	233
spice crumb coffee cake	233
yoghurt	
cucumber and yoghurt salad	151
cucumbers in yoghurt	274
lettuce wedges with yoghurt dressing	150
Yorkshire puffs	94
Z	
zabaglione	197
zucchini	**141**
bread and butter zucchini pickles	250
fried zucchini salad with mint	146
olla gitana	141
pasta primaverde	162, *163*
ratatouille	141
zucchini à la Grecque	10
zucchini and pepper frittata	41
zucchini, bean and tomato medley	141

314

WEIGHTS, MEASURES AND TEMPERATURES

The metric weights and liquid measures used in this book are those of the Standards Association of Australia.

To make these recipes you need a few inexpensive pieces of equipment obtainable at most supermarkets.
These are:
- A standard graduated 250 ml measuring jug for measuring liquids.
- A nest of 4 graduated metric measuring cups comprising:
  250 ml cup, ½, ⅓ and ¼ cup – used for measuring dry ingredients.
- A set of standard measuring spoons comprising:
  1 tablespoon (20 ml)   1 teaspoon (5 ml)   ½ teaspoon (2.5 ml)   ¼ teaspoon (1.25 ml)

How to measure correctly
dry ingredients: In measuring dry ingredients (flour, sugar, etc) heap the cup or spoon and level off the excess with a knife or spatula.
liquid ingredients: The metric measure cup shows 1 cup, ¾, ⅔, ½, ¼ and ⅛ cup measures and its metric equivalents. The litre jug has a similar breakdown from litre to ¼ litre and also shows graduations in millilitres (1000 ml – 4 cups – 1 litre). All cup and spoon measures are level.

- Many ingredients are given in rounded metric gram/kilogram weights. A small set of scales is a bonus therefore in the kitchen.
- The recipes in this book have been made with the 250 ml cup.
- 55 g–60 g eggs have been used unless otherwise specified.
- Can, pack and bottle sizes are given in metric. Some cans and packs may vary a little from exact sizes given according to the different brands available. It is best to use the nearest size.

Abbreviations used
gram g   kilogram kg   centimetre cm   millimetre mm   millilitre ml

Oven temperature guide
Oven temperatures are expressed in degrees Celsius (°C). Oven temperatures vary according to make; therefore, the table below gives only a general guide to temperatures of electric ovens. If using a gas oven, simply decrease the given temperature by 10°C (25°F). If using an older oven, see the chart below for conversion to Fahrenheit temperatures.

Oven

Celsius °C	Fahrenheit °F	Celsius °C	Fahrenheit °F
100	200	180	350
120	250	190	375
150	300	200	400
160	325	230	450